Salvation in the Flesh

# McMaster Divinity College Press
McMaster Theological Studies Series, Volume 7

Defining Issues in Pentecostalism (2008)

Pentecostalism and Globalization (2009)

You Mean I Don't Have to Tithe? (2009)

Baptism (2011)

Resurrection, Scripture, and Reformed Apologetics (2012)

The Globalization of Christianity (2014)

Salvation in the Flesh
Understanding How Embodiment Shapes Christian Faith

by
DAVID TREMENTOZZI

foreword by
AMOS YONG

☙PICKWICK *Publications* • Eugene, Oregon

SALVATION IN THE FLESH
Understanding How Embodiment Shapes Christian Faith

McMaster Theological Studies Series, Volume 7
McMaster Divinity College Press

Copyright © 2018 David Trementozzi. All rights reserved. Except for brief quotations in critical publications or reviews, no part of this book may be reproduced in any manner without prior written permission from the publisher. Write: Permissions, Wipf and Stock Publishers, 199 W. 8th Ave., Suite 3, Eugene, OR 97401.

Pickwick Publications
An Imprint of Wipf and Stock Publishers
199 W. 8th Ave., Suite 3
Eugene, OR 97401

McMaster Divinity College Press
1280 Main Street West
Hamilton, Ontario, Canada
L8S 4K1

www.wipfandstock.com

PAPERBACK ISBN: 978-1-5326-1786-7
HARDCOVER ISBN: 978-1-4982-4290-5
EBOOK ISBN: 978-1-4982-4289-9

Cataloguing-in-Publication data:

Names: Trementozzi, David, author.

Title: Salvation in the flesh : understanding how embodiment shapes Christian faith / David Trementozzi.

Description: Eugene, OR: Pickwick Publications, 2018 | McMaster Theological Studies Series 7 | Includes bibliographical references and index.

Identifiers: ISBN 978-1-5326-1786-7 (paperback) | ISBN 978-1-4982-4290-5 (hardcover) | ISBN 978-1-4982-4289-9 (ebook)

Subjects: LCSH: Salvation—Christianity | Edwards, Jonathan, 1703–1758 | Pentecostalism.

Classification: BT749 T75 2018 (paperback) | BT749 (ebook).

Manufactured in the U.S.A.   02/22/18

To Emily,
who daily shows me salvation in the flesh.

Contents

Foreword by Amos Yong / ix

Preface / xiii

Acknowledgments / xxi

Introduction / xxiii

Part One: Salvation and Embodiment

1 The Problem with Conservative Christian Soteriology / 3

2 Re-Imagining Soteriology through the Cognitive Sciences / 40

Part Two: Salvation and Orthodoxy

3 Jonathan Edwards and the Salvific Role of Orthodoxy / 65

4 Salvation in the Flesh through Edwards' Dispositional Orthodoxy / 91

Part Three: Salvation and Orthopraxy

5 Canonical Theism and the Salvific Role of Orthopraxy / 109

6 Salvation in the Flesh through Canonical Theism's Orthopraxy / 141

Part Four: Salvation and Orthopathy

7   Pentecostalism and the Salvific Role of Orthopathy / 157

8   Salvation in the Flesh through Pentecostal Orthopathy / 192

Part Five: Toward A Renewal Soteriology of Embodiment

9   Stating our Case / 209

10 Imagining Salvation in the Flesh / 229

Glossary / 255

Bibliography / 275

Names Index / 289

Subject Index / 293

Foreword

SALVATION! "WHAT MUST I do to inherit eternal life?" A "certain lawyer" and a "certain ruler" asked Jesus this question (Luke 10:25; 18:18). Interestingly, Jesus responded by telling the former a story about loving his neighbor and asking the latter to sell his things. In today's world, it is inappropriate for us to demand others to dispose of their private and personal belongings, even if s/he were affluent. And after the Reformation and its restoration of the teaching regarding justification by faith, Protestants are even more unlikely to encourage such assurance, if they were to receive a similar question about accessing eternal life, by urging a life of love.

St. Luke further records that on the Day of Pentecost, after hearing Peter's sermon, the crowd was "cut to the heart and said to Peter and to the other apostles, 'Brothers, what should we do?' Peter said to them, 'Repent, and be baptized every one of you in the name of Jesus Christ so that your sins may be forgiven; and you will receive the gift of the Holy Spirit'" (Acts 2:37–38). The same evangelical Protestants might be a bit suspicious about a text that sounds quite Roman Catholic since it suggests that our forgiveness of sins might be linked to our being baptized in water. Their worries also turn on what it means to receive the Holy Spirit: if this means to be regenerated by the Spirit (cf. Titus 3:5–6), fine; but if it means being filled with the Spirit and then speaking in tongues, etc. (earlier in Acts 2), then no deal! It would not help these Protestants that some pentecostals, particularly those of the Oneness and apostolic traditions including the United Pentecostal Church International (the largest Oneness body), point to this, in conjunction with John 3:5, as summarizing *the message* of salvation, tongues and all. The Protestant response might then be that yes, *repentance* is the *sine qua non* of our salvation because it reflects one has heard the call of the gospel and decided to put one's faith and trust in Jesus as savior, but

Foreword

the rest (baptism, forgiveness of sins, and reception of the Spirit) are added benefits one enjoys *after* our salvation that hinges on repentance.

Such evangelical Protestants are more likely to agree that the basic conditions are summarized later in Acts, for instance in the experience of the Philippian jailer. After the earthquake released the prisoners, he asked Paul and Silas: "Sirs, what must I do to be saved?' They answered, 'Believe on the Lord Jesus, and you will be saved, you and your household'" (Acts 16:30). Hah! That is all that God requires: believing on Jesus. Salvation requires belief in the truth of the gospel that is about Jesus, no more, no less. It's as simple as that and any one that says otherwise is mistaken. Underlying this belief is the notion that salvation consists in going to heaven when we die, and to do so, one needs a passport that is stamped with "believes in Jesus!" Once the latter is signed, sealed, and delivered, then leaving this life to be with Jesus in heaven is assured and guaranteed.

I am not sure how heaven actually works, but I have long thought about salvation in this way: "I was saved, I am being saved, and I will be saved." I was initially saved when I recognized my sinfulness and turned toward Jesus; I am being saved in my walk with Jesus, which is a life-long journey, lasting until whenever I take my last breath; and I will be saved in the transition from this life to whatever awaits us after death. As St. Paul himself—*the* theologian for most evangelical Protestants—writes: "you know what time it is, how it is now the moment for you to wake from sleep. *For salvation is nearer to us now than when we became believers*" (Rom 13:11, italics added). This means that there is some sense in which contemporary believers have been and are saved, but it also means that there are other senses in which they are being and will be saved. Thus: I was saved, I am being saved, and I will be saved.

David Trementozzi grew up, like me, among pentecostal churches influenced by these evangelical Protestant commitments but, also like me, has come to see that a more dynamic view of salvation is not only biblical but more theologically true. I now have his book to refer others to if I want to help them see the past-present-future tenses of salvation that constitutes Christian life. But beyond that, Trementozzi shows us three important truths: (1) that our journey of salvation is fully embodied, even *in the flesh*; this is consistent with the scriptural assertion that the Holy Spirit has been poured out not upon other spirits but upon human flesh (Acts 2:17a), itself an extension of the Spirit's conceiving and then descending upon the Word made flesh (John 1:14). (2) Salvation involves not only right beliefs but also

Foreword

right feeling and right behaviors: orthodoxy, orthopathy, and orthopraxy—these are all interwoven in God's saving of fallen human creatures. (3) Theological thinking is shaped by scripture and tradition, yes, but also can and ought to be informed by other sources, including the sciences; thus, recent neuroscientific perspectives are drawn upon rather than shunned for theological purposes.

David Trementozzi is among a new generation of pentecostal theologians and perhaps will galvanize evangelical theology itself in the coming years. I heartily recommend his book.

Amos Yong
Professor of Theology and Mission
Fuller Theological Seminary

Preface

SALVATION IN THE FLESH

Why would I title a book about soteriology, *Salvation in the Flesh*? Isn't this a contradiction of terms? Salvation is spiritual, flesh is physical. Salvation concerns a future after-life whereas flesh is locked into the present world of earthly existence. It is precisely on account of such questions and notions this book is written. It is *because* of our tendency to conceptualize salvation as a spiritual and intangible reality that we need to reflect on its more earthly and corporeal dimensions. Even more, until we learn to think about salvation in more concrete terms, the full implications of this fundamental Christian doctrine will remain beyond our reach and we will struggle to comprehend its contemporary relevance.

What is Salvation in the Flesh?

To make sense of "salvation in the flesh," we must first think about what salvation has to do with life this side of the grave. For many, this can be difficult because of the common assumption that salvation has everything to do with life *beyond* the grave. So, before too quickly offering future oriented answers—i.e., hope of heaven—let us pause and reflect on how this Christian belief directly impacts us today.

Without question, the believer's hope of heaven is, and should remain, a vital aspect of soteriological reflection. However, because this hope is so important for many Christians it is often understood as the primary purpose of salvation. Consequently, the rich treasure trove of this foundational

Preface

doctrine is not so often mined for its wealth of present earthly fortune. In this book, I show how the doctrine of salvation has much to say about life in the here and now not *in spite of* but *because of* our inescapably corporal, flesh and blood existence.

I have been on a life-long journey to know how salvation relates to everyday life. While I often find comfort and hope through trusting that my life in Christ extends beyond physical death, when it comes to the present challenges of now I have struggled to find a faith for today. Our soteriology must provide more than a spiritual tonic for our souls or abstract propositions on how we ought to think about God; it also needs to address the substantial and challenging realities of human life in our present-day world. To better fill out our phrase "salvation in the flesh" we next clarify some basic soteriological assumptions in this book.

Soteriological Clarifications

This section lays the groundwork for what we mean by salvation and why faith is factoring into this discussion. First, we recognize that salvation is a broad term and its biblical and theological usage covers a wide variety of topics.[1] Space does not allow us to consider all of these aspects, nor is such an examination necessary. However, despite its expansive use, it is enough to say that among conservative-traditional Christians "salvation"

---

1. For instance: salvation relates to the term *gospel* (i.e., good news), hence, salvation ensues from hearing and receiving the gospel (Luke 8:1–15; Matt 13:23; 28:19; Rom 1:16); the phrase *kingdom of God* was the good news (*gospel*) message Jesus preached and his ministry demonstrated that God's promised saving activity (as in OT prophetic books) upon the earth had already begun in him (Matt 10:7; 13:23; Luke 4:43; John 3:3; Acts 8:12; 14:22; Col 1:12–13; 1 Thess 2:12; 2 Pet 1:1; Rev 12:10); salvation is inextricably tied to Jesus' redemptive death on the cross and its validation by his resurrection. The NT writers thus relate salvation to the theological term *redemption*, wherein Christ has freed the believer from the power of sin and death by taking away their authority (Luke 1:77; Rom 8:1–4; 1 Cor 15:55; Eph 2:1–8; Col 1:13–14; 2:15); a closely related consequence of redemption is deliverance from the power of the devil, evil spirits, and sickness (Matt 6:13; 10:8; John 14:12; Heb 2:14); in the orthodox tradition, salvation is often described in terms of *theosis*—Christ imparting divine life to the believer (2 Pet 1:4); salvation is about the resurrection of our bodies and the promised new heavens and earth (Rom 8:18–27; 1 Cor 15:35–51; Rev 21–22). This is not an exhaustive list of soteriological topics; limited space prevents further discussion. For more on gospel and the kingdom, see Ladd, *The Gospel of the Kingdom*. For more on salvation, heaven, earth, and the kingdom of God, see Wright, *Surprised by Hope*, 189–206. For an overview of theological reflection on the doctrine of salvation through the ages see, Olson, *The Story*.

Preface

always (even if partially) has to do with the message Jesus preached, how he preached it (i.e., by the miraculous power of the Holy Spirit), and what he accomplished through his death and resurrection. So, when we speak of salvation we are referring to the ongoing divine work of God accomplished through the ministry, death, and resurrection of Jesus in the power of the Spirit. Second, salvation is inseparably related to a new quality of life Jesus brought to the world (often described as *eternal, abundant, life to the full*).[2] This life is so remarkable that it brings renewal not just to humans but all of heaven, earth, and the entire cosmos . . . inaugurated at Jesus' resurrection and to be completed at his return.[3] Third, to access this life, we affirm the Protestant emphasis of salvation by grace *through faith* bringing a person into relationship with God (Eph 2:8–9). So, herein we will be reflecting on how this *"salvation-life" of Jesus is actually received through faith by human beings*. Unfortunately, Christians are often hindered in grasping the present implications of this salvation life because of how they think about faith.

Thinking about Faith

In view of these clarifications, we need to think about how we think about faith because this salvation life is only accessible through faith. Specifically, we need to reflect on how faith is mediated to people and, likewise, how it is expressed through them. This kind of thinking requires an epistemological framework—a way of knowing how we know what we believe is actually true. Epistemology plays a critical role in this book because soteriology concerns the possibility of "salvific faith." How do we know if we really know God? When it comes to verifying truth claims, people typically accept that something is true based on one or more of the following "proofs"—they have the right knowledge, they respond-act a certain way, or they experience specific emotions and/or feelings. However, when it comes to the question of faith, the answer is not as straightforward as we might initially presume.

Is salvation *more* than "knowing the right things"? Is it more than having a proper understanding of God and Jesus? Of course it is. But what

---

2. See John 3:16; 4:14; 10:10.

3. Even though soteriology concerns more than just an individual's personal relationship with God (we could also speak of social, cosmic, biological, ecological, and artistic implications), this study limits it discussion to the notion of life Jesus brought to the human person.

Preface

exactly do we mean by "more"? Does it mean implementing certain *behaviors* or *actions* into our lives? "No!" cry certain sectors of Protestantism, "That would amount to works righteousness." Yet, those same Christians will not deny the importance of behavior . . . they just don't explain how or why it is important. Is one's *experience* of God, the "more"? Does a dynamic salvation consist in certain emotions and feelings blooming into a glorious life of faith? "Never!" cries another group of the faithful, "For that would amount to *emotionalism*." Yet, these same ones insist on the importance of a vibrant personal relationship with Christ transcending mere knowledge and behavior. In fact, almost any Christian would grant the importance of these three soteriological components and argue that salvation is more than simply *knowing the right information*. So then, in addition to right knowledge (orthodoxy), most Christians admit salvation to involve at least some degree of right behaviors (orthopraxy) and right affections (orthopathy). Interestingly though, many of these very people—especially conservative-traditional Christians—reveal a predominate tendency to treat salvation chiefly in intellectual-rational terms, even while they insist it is embodied[4] and that faith is more than rational function. I address this contradiction in chapter 1 and assert it is the result of specific epistemological presuppositions.

Throughout church history, various restoration movements have stressed one or more of these emphases to recover a more authentic New Testament faith. While these movements have been valuable, their impact has also resulted in more questions regarding the nature of faith and salvation. Does one movement have a better *understanding* of salvation and this is what makes the difference? Does another group have a superior set of *practices* which somehow makes their version of salvation better than others? Or does another simply have a more dynamic *experience* of faith whereby certain passions prove a richer salvation?

While such movements have been helpful, they've often been incomplete. In this book, I show how the way forward is integration and it is accomplished through an embodied soteriology, or, in other words—*salvation in the flesh*. Our underlying assertion is this—*the more faith is embodied, the more dynamic and transforming is our understanding and experience of salvation*. I develop this claim through the help of the cognitive sciences

---

4. Throughout, the terms *embodied, holistic,* and *embodiment* refer to a paradigm of cognition that is intimately engaged with intellect, behavior, and affectivity. Chapter 2 provides the scientific underpinnings for an embodied-holistic view of cognition, and the remaining chapters utilize this research to propose a renewal soteriology of embodiment.

Preface

(chapter 2) which illustrate how knowing-cognition is a holistic function mediated through the modalities of intellect, behaviors, and feelings-emotions. The general consensus among cognitive scientists is that cognition is most optimal (i.e., dynamic and transforming) when it is most embodied. We then relate this research to faith, as faith too is, at least, a cognitive function of knowing God.

Certainly, Christian faith is not limited to our cognitive capacities as we affirm there are other non-measurable and "spiritual" aspects that collectively influence our participation in this gracious gift of God. However, to not seriously and honestly recognize the cognitive nature of faith is to promote an inauthentic account of Christian salvation since we presently exist as embodied flesh and blood beings. Hence, it is on account of such cognitivity of faith and its relationship to the human body that this book is written.

Therefore, based on cognitive science research together with reflection on historical, theological, and biblical sources we stress that the more faith is embodied the more transforming it is. However, I do not just say that these modalities are merely *ways* faith is mediated but that *faith is most completely mediated when all three modalities are engaged*. Faith, as is cognition, is an intellectual (chapters 3–4), behavioral (chapters 5–6) and affective (chapters 7–8) reality all at the same time. Each chapter spells out the inseparability of faith from these three modalities all the while pointing towards an integrated soteriology of embodiment (chapters 9–10).

Why is this Book Important?

This study is important not because it argues that salvation is embodied but rather in its response to a lacking articulation of such embodied faith in conservative traditional Christianity. Appeals to a more embodied understanding and practice of Christian faith have already been made. For instance, Richard Foster in his book, *Streams of Living Water*, discusses the importance of an embodied faith through his emphasis on the "incarnate Christian tradition" as a means to a more dynamic Christian life.[5] Throughout, he emphasizes the reality of and need for a more Christ-formed life through integrating key ecclesial traditions in daily Christian living. Yet, though we both share similarities regarding the need for an embodied faith, I emphasize the need to identify and respond to a powerful culprit of such

5. Foster, *Streams of Living Water*, chapter 7.

Preface

vibrant Christianity—an intellectualist faith.[6] Additionally, our approaches are different. Foster focuses on ecclesiology by emphasizing various renewal traditions in church history while I employ epistemology to show how soteriology is profoundly impacted by the way we think about faith.

Another example is Dallas Willard's classic, *The Spirit of the Disciplines* which contends how central the body is for a dynamic and transforming life of faith.[7] As with me, he too draws from aspects of biology and psychology to undergird his appeal to an embodied understanding and practice of Christian life. Yet, despite these similarities our models still differ. His book focuses on the area of "practices" (which he refers to as the *disciplines*) and the seminal role they play in a renewed Christian life. This book, however employs a broader paradigm by emphasizing a more holistic understanding of salvation in which intellect, behavior-practices, and affections are inseparably integrated for the renewal of one's faith.

A final example of an embodied view of salvation comes from Gustavo Gutiérrez in his launching of "Liberation Theology" where he expounds acts of justice as central to Christian salvation.[8] As with our book, Gutiérrez also challenges an unembodied soteriological paradigm that prioritizes reflection and spirituality over action and behavior. Yet, again, his emphasis does not seek the same kind of holistic integration I propose; rather, his is an appeal mostly to acts-behaviors of justice as critical for a true expression of Christian faith.

So, in light of these examples, this book is important not because of its appeal to an embodied faith but because of its holistic accounting of faith (intellect, behavior, affections) and response to the lack of such embodied soteriological reflection in conservative-traditional Christianity. Even more, our method allows us to critique other salvation paradigms based upon how much the embodiment of faith plays into their theological epistemologies. Lastly, this book is important because it underscores the centrality of the Holy Spirit in the doctrine of salvation. Throughout, we expose soteriologies that tend to subordinate or truncate the Spirit from the Father and Son or treat his[9] work as virtually peripheral or post-salvific in the

---

6. An intellectualist faith paradigm emphasizes rationality and intellect over behavior and affections in the process of knowing God. A more thorough description of intellectualism is discussed in our next section, Introduction.

7. Willard, *The Spirit of the Disciplines*, especially chapter 3.

8. Gutiérrez, *A Theology of Liberation*, 83–104.

9. We associate the masculine pronoun (him and his) to the Holy Spirit solely as a way to speak consistently throughout this study; any gendered assumptions of the

Preface

soteriological process. Still more, we show how an unembodied awareness of faith necessarily leads to a minimized pneumatology. Therefore, we highlight the influential role that Pentecostal-Charismatic (hereafter PC) Christianity can play in a renewal soteriology of embodiment.[10] Now, having explained the meaning of our phrase "salvation in the flesh" and why this book is unique and important, I introduce our soteriological proposal and show how it will be accomplished. However, I first pause to acknowledge those who've played important roles in this book's completion.

---

godhead are not intended.

10. I use the term "renewal" to theologically identify with a pneumatological emphasis. Sociologically (in terms of religion), it refers to the global and interdenominational movement of pentecostal, charismatic, and Spirit-filled forms of Christianity.

Acknowledgments

EVERY BOOK IS A collaborative effort of numerous voices, contributions, and acts of kindness helping to transform abstract ideas into a concrete message. My book is no different. I am thankful for everyone who played a part; the book is better for it and so am I. Finally, as with any book, there are likely to be some errors and, for these, I take full responsibility.

I begin with Amos Yong, my PhD supervisor, whose critique of my chapters was invaluable. His extensive scholarship has influenced how I theologically reflect upon the Holy Spirit and his engagement with the physical world from a "renewal" perspective. I am also grateful for his generous foreword introducing this book. Special thanks also goes to Dale Coulter and Steven Studebaker who offered important feedback regarding my sections on canonical practices and the philosophical theology of Jonathan Edwards.

The cognitive sciences and patristic studies play a critical role in this research; for this reason I am indebted to Stan and Ruth Burgess. Ruth's research introduced me to the fascinating world of learning theory and the cognitive sciences. Stan's research in Patristic Theology and Eastern Orthodox Christianity inspired an enduring interest in early church spirituality and its relevance for renewal theology today. I am grateful for my colleague Steve Mills who helped me identify connections between soteriology, renewal, and cognitive science. I am also thankful for my sister and brother-in-law, Tina and Marc Santom. Their willingness to endure many long discussions about the meaning and implications of an embodied soteriology helped me organize my thoughts and keep my research on task.

Thank you to Wipf and Stock Publishers for accepting my book and for McMaster Divinity College Press including it in their Theological Studies Series. Thank you to the editorial board of MDC Press for their initial

Acknowledgments

and very helpful feedback. Finally, many thanks to Hughson Ong and David Fuller for their excellent editorial work, advice, and patience in helping to bring this book to print.

I cannot give enough praise and gratitude to my parents, Daniel and Stephanie Trementozzi, for being a constant source of encouragement and support in my life. They have always helped me see more clearly. Finally, my wife, Emily, has been my biggest supporter. Without her love, tireless strength, and numerous sacrifices I would have never completed this book. For many years she often bore the solitary role of caring for our three young children—Judah, Kaleb, and Halle—while I was buried in research either at home or away. Her patience, endurance, and faith daily remind me how blessed I am that God has placed her by my side and in my heart. It was therefore an easy and joyful decision to dedicate this book to her.

Introduction

Toward an Embodied Soteriology of Renewal

How we think about the nature of human life directly influences our understanding of salvation and what it concerns. If human beings are primarily spiritual then salvation is essentially a spiritual reality disconnected from the physicality of earthly life. If humans are chiefly spiritual beings then the body is only a means for salvation. If flesh and blood are only temporary necessities for the saving of an immaterial soul, then salvation never really concerns actual human experience and bears little relation to life in the here-and-now. Therefore, an embodied soteriology is inseparably linked to how we think about salvation.

Recognizing an Intellectualist Soteriology

Before discussing how we think about salvation, we first need to reflect on how we think about "knowing" or, more precisely, cognitive function. Therefore, we now return to the topic of epistemology. How do we think about what it means to know something? While a variety of views abound, one is extremely influential—intellectualism.

What is intellectualism? An awareness of cognition that depicts mind and emotion and/or mind and behavior as polar realities most commonly constitutes intellectualism. Dualisms of this type feature reason, intellect, and rationality over other cognitive duties like emotions and behavior. Hence, cognition is largely reduced to the intellectual tasks of comprehension and decision making. And while the behavioral and affective operations of cognition are not denied, they are subordinated and often ignored. Throughout this book, we reflect on how an intellectualist epistemology bears on our understanding of what it means to know God.

In view of all this, I refer to an intellectualist soteriology as a view of salvation that emphasizes intellectual access to knowledge of God and his saving actions in Christ over other cognitive functions like behaviors, affections, and emotions. For instance, this kind of soteriology tends to more frequently utilize a faith paradigm that favors static propositional understandings of Christ in Scripture over other more dynamic modalities of knowing (i.e., trust, persuasion, etc.). Therefore, because an intellectualist soteriology comprehends faith more in rational than behavioral or affective terms, specific assumptions have emerged which lead to correlative problems and inconsistencies in this soteriological paradigm (see chapter 1). These presuppositions nurture static rather than dynamic images of salvation that hinder concrete reflection on the transforming possibilities of divine grace and the countless ways the Holy Spirit is always at work in the ongoing soteriological process.

Throughout, I explain how intellectualist priorities can shape our thinking about what it means "to be saved." The greatest problem of such a soteriology is its tendency to foster abstract or "overly spiritual" impressions of salvation that do not address many of the material realities associated with human embodiment. Consequently, we need a soteriology that accurately accounts for the nature of human-being-in-the-world as a historically and physically constituted experience even as it affirms the spiritual quality of human life.

Introducing Intellectualism in Conservative Traditional Soteriology

This book maintains that large portions of conservative-traditional Christianity hold to an intellectualist epistemology (even if unknowingly) and, on account of this, often conceptualize soteriology chiefly as a rational activity, thus leading to a perception of faith that almost exclusively focuses on thinking or knowing. This critique is controversial because, at face value, it is rejected by those to whom it is addressed. For instance, when I began this project I was told by a prominent evangelical scholar that I came to the discussion too late. He insisted that my critique was already made and successfully defeated almost two generations ago. Yet, I remain convinced

Introduction

that my argument is relevant and not outdated. In fact, my contenders all admit that faith *is* more than rational and intellectual function; they even strongly *affirm* the importance of right behavior and affections (especially trust and assurance).

So how do you proceed with an argument that some say is irrelevant to begin with? You examine the epistemology undergirding the reasoning of your interlocutors. In the chapters that follow I explain it is not enough to merely assert, affirm, and reaffirm one's core convictions. Such beliefs must actually be consistent with one's *practices* and *epistemological priorities*. I return to this critique in chapter 1 when I challenge those who deny intellectualism exists in conservative Christian theology. There I argue that how one practices epistemology far more accurately reveals one's epistemological values than what one simply upholds as one's beliefs.

Nevertheless, despite such emphatic denials, my claim remains—conservative-traditional Christianity often fosters (even if unintentionally) an intellectual understanding and practice of salvation. Consequently, I believe that many of the epistemological presuppositions of this soteriology nurture images of a static salvation limiting its breadth, minimizing its tangible relevance, and therefore stifling its contemporary impact. I emphasize here and elsewhere that my critique generally addresses conservative evangelical soteriology focusing on tendencies rather than definitive statements and practices. Because of this, I have nuanced my interlocutor as "conservative Christianity"[1] since there are definite and clear exceptions within the evangelical movement—both historically and presently—that do not reflect the kind of intellectualist soteriology I am confronting. I do not focus on any specific denomination or aspect of this group but highlight

---

1. I prefer to use the term "conservative Christianity" because of the ambiguous and elusive realities associated with the term "evangelical" or "Evangelicalism." The boundary lines are not always clear for who or what is inside or outside of Evangelicalism. North American denominations or movements often considered within the movement have adherents that both identify and disassociate with the label "evangelical." Additionally, one could even say there are varying kinds of "evangelical theologies." Finally, "evangelical" and "Protestant" labels often mean different things in the United States and Canada than they do across Europe. Evangelical theologies and practices in Europe do not always correlate with evangelical theologies and practices in North America. For these and other reasons, even as broad as Evangelicalism is, for the purposes of this study, it makes more sense to broaden our focused category in terms of "conservative Christianity." Lastly, for our European readers, our phrase "conservative Protestantism" should be understood as synonymous with "conservative Christianity" despite whatever liberal connotations are often associated with the term "Protestant."

common tendencies and presuppositions spanning across the movement representing the majority of its constituency (even if in varying intensities).

In the next chapter we elaborate the problems associated with an intellectualist soteriology. Most specifically, we'll see that a soteriology which prioritizes intellect over behavior and affections usually minimizes the role of the body and dovetails with a neglect of pneumatology. Therefore, we propose a holistic soteriology (incorporating intellect, behavior, and emotions-feelings) that adequately accounts for the dynamic and transforming work of the Holy Spirit across the full spectrum of human life. Accordingly, our research draws from the cognitive sciences, psychology, philosophy, history, and theology. Altogether, these sources provide a critical perspective on rethinking conservative Christian soteriology. What exactly might this soteriology look like? To this we now turn.

A Renewal Soteriology of Orthodoxy, Orthopraxy, and Orthopathy

As already stated, this study challenges the dominant emphasis of intellect and reasoning for salvation throughout conservative Protestantism, including Pentecostalism.[2] As a response—in addition to the importance of right doctrine or right knowledge (orthodoxy)—we expound salvation as involving two other domains: right practices (orthopraxy) and right affections (orthopathy). So, within the context of this book, whenever we speak of "orthodoxy" we refer to that aspect of faith having to do with the theological knowledge, doctrine, and rational function of human cognition in the process of rightly knowing God. Similarly, when we speak of "orthopraxy" we refer to the element of faith that involves the roles of human behavior and practices in the cognitive process of knowing God. Finally, when we speak of "orthopathy" we are dealing with the aspect of faith that has to do with the functions of emotions, feeling, and affections in the cognitive process of rightly knowing God. Eventually, we will see that the synthesis of intellect, practices, and emotions-feelings (affections) facilitates a renewal soteriology of embodiment that better reflects the dynamic character of God's saving grace in and through human beings. I next highlight the need for our soteriology and conclude by laying out the purpose of this book.

---

2. This study will not capitalize *pentecostal* when used as an adjective (e.g., *pentecostal* theology) or when used as a noun, designating individuals (e.g., the *pentecostals*.) However, when used as the name of a movement (e.g., *Pentecostalism*), it is capitalized.

Introduction

The Need for a Renewal Soteriology of Embodiment

In view of the preceding, we recognize the need for a new vision of salvation that more clearly lays out the significance of human embodiment and the dynamic and transforming role of the Holy Spirit in God's salvific intentions. Such a soteriology must directly account for the body's full range of involvement in the cognitive process of faith (beyond just the brain). Therefore, we speak of an "embodied soteriology" because it accounts not only for intellect but behaviors and affections since these duties are attached to a broader range of human activities. Why is this soteriological vision so essential? *Without fully accounting for the body or the entire range of the Spirit's activity with human beings, salvation devolves into merely a static and abstract experience, inconsistent with its biblical portrayal in the Gospels and New Testament Epistles.*[3]

Towards this end, two disciplines are especially helpful. First, we draw from current research in the cognitive sciences to help structure our understanding of the embodied character of faith (chapter 2). Second, we employ the pneumatological sensibilities of pentecostal and charismatic theologians. Together, these research areas play a crucial role in our soteriological scheme. So, now that we have articulated the meaning of an intellectualist soteriology, how it is predominate in large segments of conservative traditional Christianity, and the need for a renewal soteriology of embodiment, let us next briefly summarize all that has been said into a concise statement to guide us on our way.

Summing Up and Looking Forward

This book is a response to the intellectualist soteriology often unintentionally practiced in conservative Christianity. Our proposal is warranted since faith is embodied and salvation is a dynamic and transformational process incompatible with the presuppositions of an intellectualist vision of salvation. How exactly will we facilitate this kind of soteriology?

---

3. The following are some scriptural references to the dynamic and transforming nature of faith and salvation: Matt 17:20; John 1:16; 7:38; 14:12; 15:7–8; Acts 1:8; Rom 8:10–11; 2 Cor 3:18; Gal 5:22–23; Eph 1:18–19; Col 1:2–6; 2:10; 3:9–10; 10:11; 2 Tim 1:7; and 2 Pet 1:3–4. Space does not permit more extensive biblical, cultural, and historical research on the meaning and implications of salvation as used in the New Testament. It is enough now to say that Scripture clearly identifies salvation in dynamic images and implications throughout the Gospels and Epistles.

Introduction

We will offer a new vision of salvation that integrates orthodoxy, orthopraxy, and orthopathy as inseparable components in a renewal soteriology of embodiment. Our approach transcends the intellectualist underpinnings embedded in conservative-traditional soteriology through holistically accounting for the intellectual, behavioral, and affective aspects of human cognition. This soteriology is transformational because it deliberately accounts for the dynamic role of the Spirit tangibly mediating faith across the wide spectrum of embodied human experience. Methodologically, embodiment is the *sine qua non* of our soteriological model. Without it, intellectualist impulses and pneumatological neglect has no tangible context against which to be critiqued. With it we have the means to truly offer a renewed vision of salvation able to overcome the obstacles and deficiencies of an intellectualist soteriology.

Hopefully, this book will encourage further research that will leave behind elusive and vague conceptions of salvation for more definite ones accounting for the myriad transformational possibilities of saving faith. At the end of the day, I consider this book a success not if I convince you of my claims about conservative Christian intellectualism but if we are motivated to discover salvation anew in the fullness of our bodily existence through the empowerment of the Holy Spirit—heads, hands, and hearts! Toward this end, chapter 1 unveils the problem of intellectualist soteriological trends in conservative-traditional theology, exposes specific presuppositions in its soteriology, and offers a solution for addressing these challenges to the doctrine of salvation.

PART ONE

Salvation and Embodiment

1

The Problem with Conservative Christian Soteriology

THANK GOD FOR PARADIGMS. They help organize our thoughts on a variety of topics, presuppose foundational concepts, and offer a frame of reference regarding basic beliefs and their associated practices. Paradigms provide a sense of intellectual grounding, behavioral consistency, and emotional security in a world of competing beliefs, practices, and values. But what happens when long-held paradigms are challenged?[1] We experience the discomfort of cognitive dissonance. Because of this we sometimes ignore the conflict even while still depending on inconsistent presuppositions. I believe this is especially true within conservative Christian theology regarding the doctrine of salvation. In this chapter we encourage honest interrogation of our soteriological assumptions. Toward this end, I challenge core presuppositions about the nature of faith and its relationship to salvation across certain segments of conservative-traditional Christianity. The chapter concludes with our proposed solution of a renewal soteriology of embodiment.

---

1. The American physicist and philosopher Thomas Kuhn (1922–1996) has written on the revolutionary force of paradigm shifts in the arena of science (*Structure of Scientific Revolutions*). Subsequently, the term has also been useful to describe major changes in fundamental models and concepts in other nonscientific arenas. While my expectations are more modest than a "Kuhnian paradigm shift," I do believe that the soteriological paradigm we suggest can offer a more dynamic and transformational way of thinking about the meaning and implications of salvation than typically envisioned in conservative Protestant Christianity.

Part One: Salvation and Embodiment

Intellectualism in Conservative Christian Theology

As previously stated, an underlying claim throughout this book is that conservative traditional soteriology generally imbibes an epistemology that fosters an overly dominant emphasis on proper thinking and knowledge in salvation. Such stress on intellect promotes a dualist paradigm of cognition that divides the mind from emotions and behavior and generates static notions of a once-for-all salvation in terms of adherence to right teaching. This kind of soteriology does not take embodiment seriously because it focuses on intellect (orthodoxy) over practices (orthopraxy) and affections (orthopathy). This view of salvation theologically subordinates the Holy Spirit to the Father and the Son, and relegates pneumatology to secondary status. Therefore a deliberate emphasis on the Holy Spirit will be vital to our proposal of a renewal soteriology of embodiment.

I advocate that one of the most problematic consequences of an intellectualist soteriology is a neglected pneumatology. We return more thoroughly to the negative consequences of a discounted pneumatology in chapters 5 and 6 through the work of various renewal theologians.[2] Now we begin to clarify our claim of an intellectualist soteriology through detailing important terms and concepts. Then we examine three predominant intellectualist presuppositions in conservative-traditional theology. But why is this important and what are its ramifications? These questions will help us move forward in crafting our soteriological program.

Clarifying the Claim

As with any conversation, clear communication is necessary if accurate understanding is to be gained. Such is especially important in our case since the audience addressed is large and the implications are far reaching. So, let us clarify what is meant and what is not meant regarding our claim of an intellectualist soteriology. To accomplish this we must first explain important terms and concepts and, second, clarify that the soteriology concerned is just one—even if the primary—among a variety of other faith paradigms within conservative Christianity.

---

2. These include Frank Macchia, Amos Yong, Lyle Dabney, Donald Gelpi, Steven Land, Daniel Castelo, Samuel Solivan, James Smith, Steven Studebaker, and others.

The Problem with Conservative Christian Soteriology

Key Terms and Concepts

This section explains key terms, cognitive models, and epistemological-theological paradigms central to our embodied paradigm of salvation.[3] First, based on current research in the cognitive neurosciences, I support an integrated model of human cognition and reject a faculty psychology that compartmentalizes cognitive function. As we will later see, an integrated model of cognition is intrinsically embodied and, therefore, will be fundamental in our soteriological paradigm of faith. This is important because an embodied view of salvation both challenges and informs our preconceived ideas about the nature of faith, particularly how it is expressed and mediated. Notwithstanding all of this, even though I envisage salvation as a fully embodied process involving three interrelated dimensions—orthodoxy, orthopraxy, and orthopathy—various cognitive capacities will be treated individually to help us most clearly delineate intellect, behavior, and affections as integral to human cognition. Eventually, chapters 9 and 10 will re-integrate these domains toward a renewal soteriology of embodiment.

Second, I identify *affections* as the emotional-perceptual inclinations that predispose people to respond in particular ways. Because the affections[4] are constituted only in part by emotions, the proposed soteriology is not an endorsement of emotionalism.[5] Thus, orthopathy has to do with instilling enduring emotional and habitual affections properly reflecting a dynamic construal of Christian salvation.

Third, *practices* refer to the behavioral-confessional actions that are integral to cognition. While often conceived as resulting from rational choices, contemporary research in the cognitive sciences attests that practices do not merely derive from intellectual deliberation but actually shape and inform discursive reasoning. Orthopraxy then has to do with being

---

3. For a more extensive list of key terms and concepts, refer to the glossary at the end of the book.

4. Throughout this study "affectivity" and "affections" are interchangeable terms when associated with orthopathy, except when I am specifically referring to Jonathan Edwards' use of affections in his dispositional ontology (chapters 3–4). Regardless, neither term refers solely to emotions or feelings, and thus, is not an endorsement of emotionalism.

5. In this book, emotionalism refers to a faith paradigm that is primarily informed by one's emotional experiences. In such a paradigm, emotions and feelings are often prioritized over Scripture in the process of discerning God's will. While the Scriptures are not dismissed, they are generally minimized if they contradict one's emotional state. Chapter 7 deals with this term when we address the charge of various theologians claiming that pentecostal spirituality necessarily endorses emotionalism.

Part One: Salvation and Embodiment

attentive to behavioral actions and patterns (i.e., practices) which are part of a dynamic soteriology.

Varieties of Conservative Christian Faith Paradigms

Conservative-traditional soteriology (which includes segments of conservative Evangelicalism) embraces a variety of faith paradigms. The differences lie largely in their emphases on the objective and subjective elements of human cognition as appropriated in the corresponding models of faith. This study focuses on the intellectualist paradigm that underscores various *propositions about Christ* (which center on the rational nature of intellect) rather than those that also highlight *trusting in the person of Christ* (which additionally accounts for the subjective and affective nature of intellect). It is the former understanding with which this study is mostly concerned.

For instance, within the American Reformed tradition, the theme of union with Christ has a history of oscillating between emphasizing either the forensic or transformative dimensions of salvation, thus bifurcating the objective and subjective aspects of redemption. Some have sought to hold these two poles together in an integrated fashion such as Jonathan Edwards (1703–1758), whom I address in chapters 3 and 4, and the Mercersburg Theology of John Nevin (1803–1886).[6] These theologians accounted for the affective nature of faith in addition to the intellectual task of comprehension. Among such theologians, terms like *trust, persuasion,* and *conviction* are vital for Christian salvation.

So, despite our focus on the prior paradigm, there are other sectors within conservative Protestantism that do not neatly fit within my general appraisal of its intellectualist view of faith. For sure, there are, and have been, evangelical and conservative streams that resist intellectualist assumptions of faith. My critique is not aimed at these groups. Their soteriological views are more dynamic than the otherwise intellectualist tendencies with which we are concerned. Nevertheless, while such exceptions (and others) exist,[7] I still contend that this notion of an intellectualist vision of faith, for the most part, reflects "conservative-traditional-Christianity" (hereafter, conservative Christianity or conservative Protestantism). Hence, I have focused my research on this constituency of Christianity.

---

6. Nevin, *Mystical Presence*, 200.
7. See also, Evans, *Imputation and Impartation*, chapters 3–5.

Next, we consider three dominant epistemological presuppositions about the doctrine of salvation. Taken altogether, these beliefs provide sufficient warrant for our claim of an intellectualist epistemology resident throughout conservative Christianity. This will provide the basis needed for our proposal of a renewal soteriology of embodiment as laid out at the end of the chapter.

INTELLECTUALIST PRESUPPOSITIONS IN CONSERVATIVE CHRISTIAN SOTERIOLOGY

This chapter maintains that aspects of conservative Christian theology have largely and uncritically adopted an intellectualist soteriology. While few conservative theologians and scholars would admit the charge of an intellectualist soteriology, the presuppositional underpinnings of their theology reveal such intellectualism. Some might argue that this assessment is belated, already taken up, and revised in the last generation or so. However, I submit that my charge remains timely since, first, intellectualism (though not stated as such) is still endorsed in the primary theology texts prevalent in conservative evangelical Bible institutes, colleges, universities, and seminaries, and second, the lay and ecclesial levels of conservative Christianity (and the PC movement) continue to reflect an intellectualist bias through their common practices of securing specific "decisions" and "choices" from individuals as initiation to salvation. So even if there is an emphatic denial of intellectualism in some theological sectors, an alternate soteriological paradigm has yet to be developed and implemented in those arenas.

I now delineate three intellectualist soteriological presuppositions, each of which lead to correlative problems in its soteriology. The first presupposition supposes *faith is mainly a rational and intellectual function of cognition*; the second presumes *justification is truncated from and prioritized over sanctification*; and the third assumes *salvation is mostly punctiliar and confessional*. This chapter's goal is to expose these presuppositions and explain how they sustain an intellectualist soteriology.

Part One: Salvation and Embodiment

Presupposition One: Faith is Primarily a Rational and Intellectual Function of Cognition

Presupposition One is reflected in the tendency to view faith as mainly a rational and intellectual activity of the human mind. The goal here is to establish that conservative Christianity favors an intellectualist soteriology when the language explicating saving faith predominately notes the rational and intellectual features of cognition. To this end, I challenge certain notions of faith that employ such categories over other more holistic ones that take affectivity and behavior seriously. The books critiqued in this section are used as standard texts[8] in prominent conservative Christian colleges, universities, and institutes of higher learning and, therefore, offer a good representation of this movement's soteriology.[9]

Charles Hodge (1797–1878) was an American Presbyterian and professor of Theology at Princeton Theological Seminary. He was a staunch defender of the fundamental beliefs of orthodox Christianity in opposition to the liberal theology of the early twentieth century. Hodge's classic theology textbook, *Systematic Theology* employed a "scientific" theological methodology (i.e., presuming great confidence in reason) that restated the classic Reformation theology of John Calvin. Hodge's textbook has since become a common text in many conservative evangelical schools.[10] In the introduction, Hodge held that theology is a science much like astronomy

---

8. The following theology textbooks will be evaluated in the sections related to Presuppositions One and Two: Hodge, *Systematic Theology*; Warfield, *Selected Shorter Writings*; Erickson, *Christian Theology*; Erickson, *Introducing Christian Doctrine*; Grudem, *Systematic Theology*; Williams, *Renewal Theology*; Duffield and Van Cleave, *Foundations of Pentecostal Theology*. The critique of the authors involved is limited to these specific textbooks because it is beyond the scope of this project to comprehensively evaluate their soteriology as per all of their publications.

9. The "conservative Christian" colleges were chosen based on their adherence to basic evangelical doctrines most commonly associated within conservative Christianity as found in the Statement of Faith at the National Association of Evangelicals website at http://www.nae.net/about-us/statement-of-faith. A list of textbooks was gathered based upon phone calls and/or emails to the designated list of colleges confirming the standard theology texts used in its introductory theological courses. Schools contacted were: Trinity International University, Dallas Theological Seminary, Fuller Theological Seminary, Wheaton University, Liberty University, Southeastern University, Regent University, Oral Roberts University, and Lee University.

10. Livingston, *Modern Christian Thought*, 305.

The Problem with Conservative Christian Soteriology

or chemistry that involves rational grasping of facts and evidences to arrive at divine truth.[11]

In this text, Hodge operates in line with Presupposition One when he discusses the essence of faith (chapter 6, "Faith"). Even though he tries not to associate faith with rationalism, he ultimately appeals to the intellectual functions of cognition as the prime modality for laying hold of faith. After introducing the central point of faith as trust,[12] Hodge explores the subject of biblical trust. Eventually, he adds that faith, as trust, is "a conviction of truth founded on testimony,"[13] but specifically, the testimony of God in the Bible.[14] He further reiterates that if faith does not rest on the testimony of the Bible, then there is nothing for it to rest upon.[15] At the end of his effort of arguing that faith is not merely rationalistic, he nevertheless concludes with a rationalist grounding of "the testimony of God" on an intellectual acceptance of God's word in the Scriptures: "Faith may, therefore, be defined to be the persuasion of the truth founded on testimony. The faith of the Christian is the persuasion of the truth of the facts and doctrines recorded in the scriptures on the testimony of God."[16] Throughout the lengthy discussion, Hodge upholds that faith is not grounded on feeling[17] but on the testimony of Scripture and the Spirit.[18] While faith is not explicitly communicated as "mental assent," he conveys it in a manner that accents the rational functions of human cognition, often utilizing words like *proof, evidence, reason,* and *knowledge*.

It is difficult to link Hodge to an intellectualist approach to faith and soteriology because of the numerous times he explicitly denies doing so. For instance, he distinctly rejects faith as mere intellectual assent when discussing the relationship between faith and feelings.[19] However, when he exposits the meaning of saving faith (as in chapter 15, "Regeneration"), he

---

11. Hodge, *Systematic Theology*, 1:1
12. Ibid., 1:43.
13. Ibid., 1:60.
14. He then goes on to provide three proofs that are used to convince the reader that his definition is unquestionably true (described as: proof from the general use of the word, proof from consciousness, and proof from Scripture [63–67]).
15. Ibid., 1:67.
16. Ibid.
17. Ibid., 1:57–60.
18. Ibid., 1:63, 69.
19. Ibid., 1:90.

favors an intellectualism that grounds the validity of faith in the attainment of a certain degree of knowledge. Here, Hodge portrays salvation as "new life":

> This new life, therefore, manifests itself in new views of God, of Christ, of sin, of holiness, of the world, of the gospel, and of the life to come; in short, of all those truths which God has revealed as necessary to salvation. This spiritual illumination is so important and so necessary and such an immediate effect of regeneration, that spiritual knowledge is not only represented in the Bible as the end of regeneration (Col 3:10; 1 Tim 2:4), but the whole of conversion (which is the effect of regeneration) is summed up in knowledge.[20]

Regardless of his many arguments that faith is more than a mental comprehension and acceptance of the truths of God's word, Hodge's final appeal to the meaning of faith falls predominately on intellectual ground. What is under-developed in Hodge's description of faith and salvation is a place for orthopraxy and orthopathy as integrated with orthodoxy to produce the assurance of the testimony of God in the life of a believer. There is hesitancy to venture beyond the intellect to describe faith.

The point here is that it is not enough for theologians to make statements that faith transcends intellectual assent. That conservative Christians repeat these assertions is evidence that they are trying to avoid over-intellectualizing their systems, but their failure is exhibited precisely in the emptiness of their claims. In the end, it is the entire fabric of their theological vision—rather than mere doctrinal affirmations or denials—that manifests their intellectualist commitments.

Similar intellectualism is also evident in Hodge's famous successor at Princeton, Benjamin B. Warfield (1851–1921). For over thirty years Warfield was the primary defender of orthodox Presbyterianism and the Princeton Theology which resisted the encroaching Modernist influence, especially European biblical criticism.[21] Warfield did not publish a substantial systematic theology text, since Hodge's *Systematic Theology* served as the definitive text for Princeton Theology. However, he did write many essays and articles that were influential in eventually establishing the doctrine

---

20. Ibid., 1:34.
21. Livingston, *Modern Christian Thought*, 316.

The Problem with Conservative Christian Soteriology

of inerrancy as a fixed belief in conservative Protestantism.[22] For this reason, Warfield's *Selected Shorter Writings* is used in this study.

In this text, Warfield displays Presupposition One as he consistently couples faith with attainment of certain knowledge. As with Hodge, despite that Warfield does not divorce knowledge from trust, the accent is still on right knowing. Warfield does not deny the importance of the subjective components of salvation; however, they are subordinated and isolated from the more rationally construed aspects of knowing God. In his chapter, "Christianity and Revelation," he says, "[I]t is only as God frames knowledge of himself in the human mind that man comes to know God at all."[23] Again, from the same text, he reiterates:

> Theology is itself a science, with its own proper object, method and content: it has its own certainties to contribute to the sum of ascertained truth; and it dare not do other than place these certainties, established by their own appropriate evidence, by the side of any other certainties which may exist, as equally entitled with the best attested of them all to the acceptance of men.[24]

Because Warfield often associates faith with comprehension of indubitable "facts" about salvation, the objective component of faith is not hard to notice:

> The great facts that constitute Christianity are just as "naked" as any other facts, and are just as meaningless to us as any other facts, until they are not only perceived but understood, that is, until not only they themselves but their doctrinal significance is made known to us. The whole Christianity of these facts resides in their meaning, in the ideas which are involved in them, but which are not independently gathered from them by each observer, but are attributed to them by those who interpret them to us—in a word, in the doctrines accompanying them.[25]

Then, after a long section contending the vital connection between facts and doctrine, Warfield concludes: "Christianity has thus from the beginning ever come to men as the rational religion, making its appeal primarily to the intellect."[26]

22. Ibid., 320, 323.
23. Warfield, *Selected Shorter Writings*, 1:27.
24. Ibid., 50.
25. Ibid., 237.
26. Ibid., 277.

Part One: Salvation and Embodiment

Since Warfield was an apologist, he was committed to rationally securing the truth of Christianity. Hence, he was often charged with denying or neglecting the subjective nature of faith. I am not stating that Warfield denied subjective expressions of salvation because trust is critical in his soteriology. However, for him, trust emerges from sure evidence that already provides warrant for an individual's complete dependence upon God. Because trust follows evidence in Warfield's soteriology, he epitomizes an intellectualist soteriology.[27] Almost a century later, the intellectualist epistemology of these (and other) Princeton theologians continues to influence the wider Christian world. Today, similar rationalist priorities can be seen in contemporary conservative theology, particularly the texts of M. J. Erickson.

Millard J. Erickson (b. 1932) is an ordained Baptist minister and prominent conservative theologian who is one of the most vocal opponents of the more liberal sectors of Evangelicalism. Erickson is currently Distinguished Professor of Theology at Western Seminary in Portland, Oregon. Because his widely received *Christian Theology* and *Introducing Christian Doctrine* books are used in many conservative Christian schools, they are included in this study.

In *Christian Theology*, Erickson's treatment of salvation unveils the propositionalism of Presupposition One, especially in his use of Scripture as basically the exclusive vehicle of knowledge needed to secure salvation. Erickson maintains that the Word of God is central for facilitating salvation. He defines the *Word of God*: "It is not the Bible alone, but the Word as applied by the Holy Spirit, that effects spiritual transformation."[28] He then contends that the Word of God is the means for beginning the Christian life.[29] Next, he directly joins the Word of God to salvation: "We have seen that the Word of God, whether read or preached, is God's means of presenting to us the salvation found in Christ; faith is our means of accepting that

---

27. For instance, Andrew Hoffecker defends Warfield against charges of rationalism by various evangelicals. While Hoffecker's defense of Warfield clearly identified many areas where the theologian stressed the importance of the subjective work of God, in doing so, the subjective ingredient always follows and is separate from the objective work of faith—i.e., trust is actually built upon the right facts and knowledge of God. Even while trust is emphasized it still follows the facts and evidence of the gospel (see, Hoffecker, *Piety*, chapter 3).

28. Erickson, *Christian Theology*, 1011–12. Drawing from Ramm, *The Pattern of Authority*, 28–37.

29. Erickson, *Christian Theology*, 1012.

The Problem with Conservative Christian Soteriology

salvation."[30] However, in spite of previously remarking that the Word of God is more than just the Bible, here he explicitly specifies that this "Word of God" is either "read or preached" (implying the Bible). By describing the means of salvation as exclusively involving the Bible, salvation is detailed in propositional terms (i.e., the words and truths of the Bible). The Holy Spirit is predominantly linked to mediating the Word of God via Scripture. By not elaborating additional vehicles by which the Spirit has historically mediated the Word of God for salvific ends (i.e., canonical practices), and by only or mostly emphasizing rational propositional knowledge (gained from studying the Bible) as the means for obtaining faith, intellectualist presuppositions are clear in Erickson's soteriology.

This is not an isolated example. In *Introducing Christian Doctrine*, Erickson again expounds the means of salvation occurring through the same type of rational process that appropriates such cognitive activities as accepting, deciding, believing, and choosing. He conceives faith as "acceptance of the promises and the work of Christ."[31] Later, defining faith in the New Testament, he also adds: "These and numerous other instances . . . establish that faith involves believing that something is true."[32] Salvation follows from believing certain information about God and then trusting God on the perceived veracity of that information. In bringing these two points together, Erickson advances: "The God in whom we are to trust reveals himself, at least in part, through communicating information about himself to which we are to assent."[33] As with Hodge and Warfield, Erickson also avers that salvation generally ensues from the mind assenting to certain truths. If (as Erickson previously put) God discloses himself "at least in part, through communicating information," then what other part is there? None is offered. Why, do these theologians insist that faith is more than mental assent yet continue to explicate faith within an epistemology that favors intellect over emotions and behaviors? I believe the reason is because *conservative Protestant theology has uncritically adopted an intellectualist epistemology.*

I do not deny the importance of a rational faith that enables a person to mentally apprehend information (i.e., biblical information) and then make a choice based upon that information. Erickson rightly draws out this

30. Ibid. Drawing from Carnell, *Case for Orthodox Theology*, 70.
31. Erickson, *Introducing Christian Doctrine*, 279.
32. Ibid., 310.
33. Ibid.

PART ONE: SALVATION AND EMBODIMENT

element of faith. However faith, as with any other cognitive modality, does not consist *only* of intellectual activity. While, few conservative Christians would assert that faith is purely intellectual, the consequence of failing to elaborate faith as involving other non-intellectual components suggests an uncritical rationalism persists.

Another influential conservative theologian who reinforces this mindset is Wayne Grudem (b. 1948). Grudem's text book *Systematic Theology: An Introduction to Biblical Doctrine* has become a widely used theology text that upholds general Reformed Calvinistic theology, yet is also endorsed by many in the PC movement because of his affirmation of spiritual gifts for the contemporary church. Grudem is currently Research Professor of Theology and Biblical Studies at Phoenix Seminary in Phoenix, Arizona.

In this text, Grudem illustrates Presupposition One when articulating the need for a conscious rational judgment based on a certain degree of knowledge for salvific faith (in chapter 35, "Conversion: Faith and Repentance").[34] In the final section, Grudem summarizes his thoughts: "In the case of saving faith in Christ, our knowledge of him comes by believing a reliable testimony about him. Here, the reliable testimony that we believe is the words of Scripture."[35] Overall, Grudem portrays the means of saving faith in propositional terms that stress knowledge gained from Scripture. An intellectualist epistemology frames his soteriology in a way that identifies faith mostly in terms of rational knowledge. Perhaps, most tellingly, Grudem denotes an intellectualist soteriology as follows.

> There must be some basic *knowledge* or *understanding* of the *facts* of the gospel. There must also be *approval* of, or *agreement* with, these *facts*. Such *agreement* includes a conviction that the *facts* spoken of the gospel are true . . . It also includes an *awareness* that I need to trust in Christ for salvation and that he is the only way to God, and the only means provided for my salvation. But all this still does not add up to true saving faith. That comes only when I *make a decision* of my will to depend on, or put my trust in, Christ as my savior.[36]

One can see throughout this passage the large number of references to logical, intellectual, and rational activities in the author's description of

---

34. Grudem, *Systematic Theology*, 709.
35. Ibid., 712.
36. Ibid. Emphasis added.

The Problem with Conservative Christian Soteriology

salvation. In addition, throughout the chapter, Grudem links a proper *comprehension* of justification with authentic Christian salvation.

> A right understanding of justification is absolutely crucial to the whole Christian faith . . . If we are to safeguard the truth of the gospel for future generations, we must understand the truth of justification. Even today, a true view of justification is the dividing line between the biblical gospel of salvation by faith alone and all false gospels of salvation based on good works.[37]

In other words, authentic Christian salvation requires a correct interpretation of justification. Grudem even infers that Martin Luther was not a true believer until he accurately grasped this truth.[38] I do not dispute the value of properly comprehending the doctrine of justification, but highlighting doctrinal knowledge as the chief prerequisite of justification overemphasizes the significance of right knowledge within the soteriological process. The point of this survey is to establish that if one does not endorse an intellectual idea of faith then a wider array of terms should be employed for a more dynamic, holistic, and embodied rendering of conversion that is not tied entirely to rational capacities.

Our last example is the late Reformed charismatic theologian J. Rodman Williams (1918–2008). Williams is important in this research because he manifests intellectualism within the PC segments of the church. Despite Williams' prominent pneumatology (influenced by his affiliation with the charismatic movement), intellectualism still prevails, most likely because of his Presbyterian background and long standing identification with conservative Reformed theology. He exhibits how a developed pneumatology is not enough to topple an intellectualist theology.

In *Renewal Theology*, vol. 2, *Salvation, the Holy Spirit, and Christian Living*, Williams hints at Presupposition One. He discusses faith in the first chapter (Calling) when he examines its relationship to salvation. For Williams, faith involves three prominent details—knowledge, assent, and trust.[39] Knowledge is apprehension of God's work of redemption in Christ; in other words, it specifically means *comprehending* the gospel message. Williams reiterates, "Nonetheless, knowledge is the beginning point of faith. For there must be a basic understanding of the gospel message for salvation

---

37. Ibid., 722.
38. Ibid.
39. Williams, *Renewal Theology*, 29.

to occur."[40] He then specifies "assent" as the rational function of cognition that moves beyond *understanding* to *acknowledgment* of the grace of God in Jesus Christ as seen in the gospel.[41] Williams rejects the judgment of faith as mere "mental assent" to certain doctrines but instead specifies that the locus of assent is the justifying work of God in Christ.[42] Regarding trust, Williams remarks, "Faith, lastly, is trust. Faith begins in knowledge, deepens in assent, and is completed in trust. It is the critical and final element in saving faith."[43] He pictures faith as more than simply believing in the gospel, but believing in the one who brings the gospel—namely, Jesus Christ.[44] Williams again recounts the singular association of faith with Jesus, "It is the conviction that He is totally trustworthy, that in Him and Him alone is to be found full salvation, and that one must surrender all to Him as Savior and Lord."[45] The remainder of the chapter maintains that faith climaxes in union with Christ. Finally, three christological lines further delineate faith: "In Christ"; "Christ in Us"; and "We in Christ and Christ in Us."[46]

As previously stated, I do not deny or minimize Christ in the order of salvation; I do, however, challenge the description of salvation as mostly a forensic, objective actuality centered principally on the justifying work of God in Christ. Williams denies a rationalist faith when he asserts that faith is more than "a matter of intellectual assent" or of "accepting as a fact that God has raised Jesus";[47] however, he does not fully elaborate on how these statements are true. As with the other theologians discussed, Williams enunciates the rational and intellectual dimensions of faith. For instance, when he talks about saving faith (in the section, "Inception of Faith"),[48] he clearly states that faith is not based on "human reasoning and attempted proof" and is "not a human effort to believe but the inward assurance and conviction that results from God's presence and action."[49] Yet, in the next section (the "Nature of Faith") he resorts to an almost exclusively intellectual

40. Ibid.
41. Ibid.
42. Ibid., 30.
43. Ibid.
44. Ibid.
45. Ibid., 31.
46. Ibid., 31, 32.
47. Ibid., 73.
48. Ibid., 28.
49. Ibid.

The Problem with Conservative Christian Soteriology

emphasis of faith as his groupings are: (1) Knowledge; (2) Assent; and (3) Trust.[50] In this last category his use of *trust* is most often associated with *proof* or *rational certitude* because such trust is based on knowledge of Christ as found in the Scriptures. For instance, he says, "Faith as trust is complete reliance on God's promise in the gospel. . ."[51] He later couples belief with faith and trust and says, "Faith, accordingly, is reception of God's truth. . . To believe the word means to trust in it and to depend on it as the way of salvation."[52] Then he concludes by saying that faith in Jesus is the most profound expression of trust.[53] It is significant to note how his use of faith as trust is consistently characterized as a type of assurance obtained from intellectual content—i.e., knowledge of Christ from Scripture.

While Williams surely intends to convey trust as derived by means other than a rational confidence in Scripture (such as the witness and ministry of the Spirit), he, nevertheless, underscores the source of such trust as the Bible. To be fair to Williams (in the section, "Christ in us" in the above category of "Trust"), he does briefly explain that Christ being in the believer is synonymous with the Holy Spirit being in the believer: "The indwelling of Christ in the believer is identical with the indwelling of the Spirit . . . Hence, Christ in us is not a bodily reality but a spiritual presence."[54] An affective element of faith is clearly identified; however, the space appropriated to this observation is overshadowed by numerous sections that do not make this connection. A careful reading of Williams indicates that he *does not* endorse faith as purely intellectual because he insinuates an affective impression of faith when he unites it with the Spirit. The problem is that the room given to rationalist conceptions of faith overwhelms the affective notions.[55]

50. Ibid., 29–30.
51. Ibid., 30.
52. Ibid.
53. Ibid.
54. Ibid., 32.
55. I searched the subject indexes of all three of Williams' volumes (*Renewal Theology*, 1–3) and it was only in volume 2 (in the sections just detailed) that he directly addressed the issue of saving faith. In chapter 13 ("The Incarnation") of volume 1, the role of the Spirit in awakening saving faith is addressed, but again is mostly presented as illuminating and vivifying knowledge of Christ already gained, rather than as a mediator of such "knowledge" through and through. The result is a sense of pneumatological subsequence following objective knowledge of Christ via Scripture when it comes to facilitating saving faith (see especially Section C: "Significance," [324–28] in which the affectivity of faith [via the Spirit] is mentioned but it still seems dependent [i.e., subsequent] on an

PART ONE: SALVATION AND EMBODIMENT

Nevertheless, I argue that Williams inadvertently *endorses* an intellectualist perception of faith due to the manner in which he unpacks the topic. My point in using Williams' text is that old paradigms continue to influence our epistemology unless we replace them with new models and ways of thinking. Although Williams truly rejects an intellectualist view of faith, his Reformed Presbyterian idea of faith still chiefly dictates the methodology by which he—an unashamedly charismatic theologian—crafts his soteriology. His pneumatological (affective) emphasis on faith remains obscured and his epistemology still resembles (if even faintly) the intellectualism he claims to reject. Why? Because he most frequently conveys the source of trust as originating from intellectual content gained from Scripture. His explication of the salvific function of faith as both rationally and subjectively derived would be stronger if he expanded the portions that focused on faith as pneumatological and incorporated them into his other sections that speak of faith issuing from knowledge of Christ via the Scriptures.

In summary of the above texts, I suggest that conservative Protestant theology largely expresses faith as a type of mental attainment and assent of specific knowledge about God. Regardless that the preceding theologians denied this view of faith, they nevertheless consistently explicated faith within an epistemological framework that mostly referenced the rational and deductive abilities of the human mind and neglected its corresponding affective and behavioral dimensions. Their method implies an intellectualist soteriology. *It is not what they said about faith but what they did not say that exposes their intellectualist presuppositions—faith is mostly presented in terms of human reasoning.* Vocabulary expounding faith should not confine itself solely to cognitive terms associated with rationality and intellect (like *evidence, certainty,* and *proof*) because other terms related with affections and behavior (like *assurance, conviction,* and *renewal*) can equally apply as well. The Holy Spirit breathes salvific faith into human hearts through both. An intellectualist soteriology mostly employs rational depictions of faith while neglecting the emotional and behavioral portions. The prioritization of the intellectual component of faith is problematic because human cognition is holistic and more comprehensive than mere intellect.

The preceding discussion identifies soteriological commitments in Christian theology reflecting an intellectualist epistemology. I propose that

---

intellectual understanding of Christ). I contend for a more thorough and robust pneumatology throughout the entire process of attaining saving faith (chapters 5–10 will address this more thoroughly).

The Problem with Conservative Christian Soteriology

an embodied soteriology appropriates faith as a holistic operation of cognition. For if faith is not such a cognitive process then it cannot be embodied, and if not embodied then there remains no way to meaningfully ground it to human experience (which is embodied). A purely spiritual or intellectual (i.e., unembodied) impression of faith should be rejected because human experience is neither abstract nor gnostic—it is embodied and experientially relevant. Chapter 2 will render human cognition as a dynamic interrelationship involving intellect, emotions-feelings-affectivity, and behavior. But if faith is cognitively holistic, there are soteriological implications. Chapter 10 lays out some of these consequences. The next section considers the prevalence and ramifications of Presupposition Two.

Presupposition Two: Justification is Truncated from and Prioritized over Sanctification

Presupposition Two is seen in the inclination to divide salvation into the objective and subjective categories of justification and sanctification while emphasizing the significance of the former. When justification becomes the favored soteriological descriptor, objective and rational terms tend to define the essence of salvation while inevitably obscuring the more subjective dimensions. The goal of this section is to show that valuing justification over sanctification fosters a subordination of pneumatology and leads to an intellectualist soteriology. It is to be granted that a separation of justification from sanctification in the order of salvation is not unique to the theologians being discussed (such a framework was standard in Reformation theology). However, it is the ramifications of such bifurcations that this section exposes, among which the most significant is an intellectualist soteriology. As previously, I begin with Charles Hodge's *Systematic Theology*.

In the table of contents, Hodge devotes chapter 17 to justification and 18 to sanctification. In each chapter, he separates and accents justification over sanctification. Beginning with chapter 17, Hodge conspicuously identifies justification apart from sanctification and binds it with objectivity. He upholds that "justification is . . . an act, and not, as sanctification, a continued and progressive work . . . It does not effect a change of character, making those good who were bad, those holy who were unholy. That is done in regeneration and sanctification."[56] He renders justification a forensic act: "What the Bible teaches of the justice of God, proves that justification is a

56. Hodge, *Systematic Theology*, 3:117.

Part One: Salvation and Embodiment

judicial declaration that justice is satisfied."[57] As will be repeatedly seen in this section, because justification is exclusively identified in forensic terms, salvation boils down to *knowing* that one has been pardoned by Christ. In addition to pardon, Hodge also asserts that justification must also include divine favor, so that one is in right standing with God. He reiterates that "[t]he righteousness of Christ is imputed to the believer for his justification."[58] He emphasizes such imputation as purely objective.

> Imputation never changes the inward, subjective state of the person to whom the imputation is made. When sin is imputed to a man he is not made sinful . . . So when righteousness is imputed to the believer, he does not thereby become subjectively righteous.[59]

Later (chapter 18, "Sanctification"), he again distinguishes justification in objective and sanctification in subjective terms.[60]

Throughout these chapters there is a clear distinction between justification (as an objective forensic act dealing with a person's guilt before God), and sanctification (as a subjective act of progressive growth into Christlikeness). As with Hodge's idea of faith, he also promotes a similar dualism between the objective (justifying) and subjective (sanctifying) work of God in the believer. In doing so, he essentially restricts pneumatology to issues of subjectivity and growth and thereby places it in a subordinate position to the ministry of Christ. Sanctification is viewed as a soteriological subcategory while justification specifically relates to salvation. Though such pneumatological subordination is not explicitly demonstrated within the individual discussions of justification and sanctification, when soteriology (as its own category) is taken up (as in chapter 16—Faith), such dualisms and subordinations are clearly exposed. For instance, in the following quote, Christ is highlighted as the immediate object of salvation while no mention of the Spirit is offered.

> It is, therefore, receiving Christ; receiving the record which God has given of his Son; believing that He is the Christ the Son of the living God, which is the specific act required of us in order to salvation. Christ, therefore, is the immediate object of those exercises of faith which secure salvation. And, therefore, faith is

---

57. Ibid., 3:126.
58. Ibid., 3:144.
59. Ibid., 3:145.
60. Ibid., 3:213.

expressed by looking to Christ; coming to Christ; committing the soul to Him, etc.[61]

Hodge advances that salvation largely requires a rationally framed understanding of Christological doctrine (because of the centrality of forensic justification) and that the believer can gain access to the empowering ministry of the Spirit only after Christ first secures her justification.

Benjamin Warfield's soteriology also illustrates Presupposition Two when he features justification over sanctification in the chapter, "Justification by Faith, out of Date?" He declares that if justification by faith is out of date then "the way of salvation was closed."[62] He discusses justification apart from sanctification; and, pneumatology is eclipsed by the ministry of Christ. Justification by faith is synonymous with salvation when he says: "Justification by Faith means, that is to say, that we look to Christ and to him alone for salvation . . ."[63]

Describing sanctification, Warfield acknowledges that "[i]n Protestant theology it [sanctification] is distinguished from justification and regeneration."[64] Both regeneration and justification are momentary acts, and acts of God in which the sinner is passive; sanctification, on the other hand, is a progressive work of God, in which the sinner cooperates.[65] Warfield teaches that sanctification follows regeneration (which includes justification). After justification, the human being "continues dependent upon the constant gracious operations of the Holy Spirit and is able to cooperate with the Spirit through sanctification."[66] In sanctification, "The Spirit gradually completes the work of moral purification commenced in regeneration [justification]."[67]

Even though Warfield attests that sanctification is inseparable from justification,[68] he unpacks justification as more directly joined to salvation while sanctification is merely its working out. As with Hodge, because of his emphasis on justification being fundamentally concerned with properly comprehending the salvific role of Christ, salvation is essentially an

---

61. Ibid., 3:97.
62. Warfield, *Selected Shorter Writings*, 1:283.
63. Ibid.
64. Warfield, *Selected Shorter Writings*, 2:325.
65. Ibid.
66. Ibid., 2:327.
67. Ibid.
68. Ibid., 2:325.

intellectual activity. Likewise, while he unites the Holy Spirit precisely to sanctification, the Spirit is virtually absent in relation to justification. Warfield defines sanctification as the supernatural work of God bringing forth increasing degrees of moral purity in cooperation with the believer, while depicting justification as wholly the act of God so as not to propose a "justification by our own works."[69] As already seen in Warfield's consideration of faith, so too does his shearing of justification from sanctification accent objective over subjective components of salvation, thereby further disclosing intellectualist tendencies. This dualism reflects the influence of intellectualism and conveys a static portrayal of salvation because the Spirit merely works out and applies the salvific benefits already wrought by Christ.

Millard Erickson demonstrates Presupposition Two when he polarizes salvation into objective and subjective modalities that yoke justification with objectivity. In chapter 34 (The Beginning of Salvation: Objective Aspects), justification comprises one of "three essential elements among the objective aspects of salvation."[70] Central to the chapter's objective depiction of justification, Erickson details its forensic quality: "Justification is a forensic act imputing the righteousness of Christ to the believer; it is not an actual infusing of holiness into the individual. It is a matter of declaring the person righteous, as a judge does in acquitting the accused."[71] Justification is essentially a forensic and christological event (i.e., static), distinctly removed from sanctification (i.e., dynamic); as such it is about *knowing* while sanctification is about being, doing, and growth.

In chapter 35 (The Continuation and Completion of Salvation), sanctification is mainly "moral goodness or spiritual worth."[72] Throughout the chapter, Erickson affirms a sharp dualism between sanctification and justification. He says, "In order to focus more sharply the nature of sanctification, it will be helpful to contrast it with justification. There are a number of significant differences."[73] And again, "Justification is an objective work affecting our standing before God, our relationship to him, while sanctification is a subjective work affecting our inner person."[74] In short, justification

---

69. Ibid., 2:283.

70. Erickson, *Introducing Christian Doctrine*, 314. The other two objective elements of salvation are *union with Christ* and *adoption*.

71. Ibid., 319 (quoting, Ziesler, *The Meaning of Righteousness*, 18).

72. Ibid., 325.

73. Ibid., 326.

74. Ibid.

The Problem with Conservative Christian Soteriology

and salvation involve our *knowing*, after which comes sanctification which is merely the post-salvific transformation of our lives.

Once again, this truncation leads to a prioritization and subordination between these two salvific modes. Such is clear, both in Erickson's chapter titles and in the way he develops these ideas—*justification is the primary work of God in the salvation of the individual and sanctification is secondary*. Even Erickson's description of sanctification bears out the favored role of justification: "The doctrine of sanctification continues God's work of justification by conforming us to the very image of Christ."[75]

Erickson delineates another significant difference between these two concepts. "There is a quantitative distinction as well. One is either justified or not, whereas one may be more or less sanctified. That is, there are degrees of sanctification but not of justification."[76] Thus, one can infer from Erickson's soteriology, that a person is only either saved or one is not, since salvation is elaborated mostly in terms of justification ("one is either justified or not . . ."). Additionally, since sanctification is construed as a post-salvific reality, and degrees are associated with it, then salvation is further reinforced as static rather than progressive. The first sentence of chapter 35 implies sanctification is less urgent in the order of salvation: "*After the miraculous work of salvation*, God continues the process of transforming the believer into the image of Christ. Sanctification is the process of turning from sin and toward holiness with the goal of leading a sinless life."[77] Note the secondary and subordinate status of sanctification as it follows the "work of salvation." A sense of indispensability describes justification (even as it is directly linked with salvation) while a mere auxiliary significance marks sanctification. Because there is less urgency insinuated with sanctification, the need for the dynamic and empowering presence of the Spirit (because it is commonly grouped with sanctification) remains underdeveloped in Erickson's soteriology. It thus logically follows that salvation is essentially objective and christological (i.e., justification) emphasizing one's ability *to know*. When Erickson places sanctification after the "work

---

75. Ibid., 336.

76. Ibid., 326.

77. Ibid., 324. Emphasis added. These sentences underscore the ministry of Christ and subordination of the Spirit in the order of salvation. Even in the sentence noted, sanctification is identified as christological in aim; and even though (on p. 326) it is viewed directly as the "work of the Holy Spirit" and as a "supernatural work of God," the manner in which it is explained appears little different than a general exhortation to mature and grow in one's walk with Christ.

of salvation" he severs sanctification from soteriology and suggests a decreased involvement of the Spirit in redemption. Throughout chapters 31 to 35 (dealing with soteriology) the number of references to Christ and his role in salvation far exceed references to the Spirit. The Spirit is largely limited to the discussion of sanctification and his place in sanctification is christological in aim. The soteriological presupposition of such dualism sensibly plays out in regards to pneumatology—*the Holy Spirit's ministry is subsequent to salvation rather than constitutive of the entire process.* Accordingly, the dualism of Erickson's soteriology resembles epistemological commitments of an intellectualist soteriology because it favors the rational and objective operations of cognition (via a prioritized justification) over its affective and behavioral constituents (via a subordinated sanctification).

Wayne Grudem indicates Presupposition Two on the first page of chapter 36 (Justification) when he defines justification as "an instantaneous legal act of God in which he (1) thinks of our sins as forgiven and Christ's righteousness as belonging to us, and (2) declares us to be righteous in his sight."[78] Throughout the chapter, justification as forensic and declarative acts of God is the dominating salvific theme.[79] Grudem explains justification in two parts—the first dealing with forgiveness of sins and the second as imputation of Christ's righteousness.[80] He proposes that forgiveness alone makes one "morally neutral" before God; he must also secure a "positive righteousness" in which he merits perfect righteousness to believers (i.e., imputation of Christ's righteousness).[81]

In the title for chapter 38 (Sanctification), Grudem unites sanctification with "growth in likeness to Christ"[82] and the Spirit's work is basically limited to sanctification. Grudem elaborates, "But it is specifically, God the Holy Spirit who works within us to change us and sanctify us, giving us greater holiness of life."[83] As expounded in chapter 36, once again Christ's mission directly relates to justification but is passive regarding sanctification. *Because* of Christ's work of justification believers are able to enjoy the

---

78. Grudem, *Systematic Theology*, 723.

79. The chapter's headings (in the same text) bear out the prominent emphasis on justification as forensic and declarative: "Justification Includes a Legal Declaration of God" (723), "God Declares Us to Be Just in His Sight" (724), and "God Can Declare us to Be Just Because He Imputes Christ's Righteousness to Us" (726).

80. Ibid., 725.

81. Ibid.

82. Ibid., 746.

83. Ibid., 754.

The Problem with Conservative Christian Soteriology

benefits of sanctification. Grudem states, "The role of God the Son, Jesus Christ, in sanctification is, first, that he *earned* our sanctification for us."[84] He considers sanctification consequent to justification; without the work of Christ in justification, Christians would not have the merit needed to partake in the blessings of sanctification. He construes sanctification in subjective terms and as an embodied experience involving intellect, emotion, will, and physical bodies (unlike justification, which he conveys in essentially unembodied—i.e., rational and intellectual—terms).[85] Although Grudem does not explicitly communicate that sanctification logically follows justification he, nevertheless, infers that it is peripheral and subsequent to the justifying work of God—thereby subordinating (because of his emphasis on justification) its soteriological import.

Grudem's development of justification, as with many conservative theologians, though biblical, is also incomplete when employed as the *sole* soteriological category. By spotlighting the objective theme of forensic justification (together with its emphasis on *understanding* Christ's role in such justification) while subordinating the emotional and behavioral constituents of sanctification, Grudem places high value on rationality and reason and, accordingly, presumes an intellectualist soteriology.

J. Rodman Williams discloses Presupposition Two in chapter 3 ("Justification") when he truncates justification from sanctification and, in doing so, displays a rationalist conception of faith. God justifies the person who "believes in Him" and does not depend on her own works.[86] Faith is "believing in" Christ as the one who redeems. Williams joins justification (apart from sanctification) to salvation via a rational faith when he summarizes: "From all that has been said it is apparent that faith *alone* is the instrument of justification . . . the singularity of faith is critical to a proper understanding of justification. Without such an understanding, salvation becomes precariously based."[87] Thus, faith is the instrument for justification and together they serve as the central descriptions of salvation.[88]

In chapter 4 (Sanctification), Williams clarifies: "Our concern will not only be with salvation in its initial occurrence but also with the wider area of Christian life. Accordingly, we will be viewing sanctification in all its

---

84. Ibid., 753.
85. Ibid., 756–57.
86. Williams, *Renewal Theology*, 73.
87. Ibid., 75.
88. Ibid., 71.

Part One: Salvation and Embodiment

dimensions."[89] Even though this statement rightly explicates sanctification as soteriological (i.e., Christian living), the remainder of the chapter illustrates sanctification as a description of the Christian life while not linking it back to salvation. The problem is not that he ignores sanctification in the Christian life, but that by no longer attaching salvation with Christian living, he envisions sanctification as a post-salvific actuality. This is particularly true whenever he discusses justification because he specifically fixes it to "salvation" (and not "Christian life"). The implication is clear—*salvation comes chiefly through justification* (as per divine pardon) *but spiritual growth and maturity through sanctification* (after one is already a Christian). Williams subordinates sanctification to justification by restricting it to "Christian living."[90] In doing so, he rightly communicates sanctification as a life-changing and embodied reality that speaks of the "renewal of the whole person according to the likeness of God."[91] However, this transformational claim to sanctification is framed as a post-salvific matter: "In salvation there has been a renewing of the spirit, an alteration of the heart, a purifying of the conscience. However, although this has occurred essentially (man has a new spirit/heart/conscience), there is the need for further sanctification."[92] Because Williams ties subsequence and subordination to sanctification, it cannot be constitutive of salvation, only additional.

Williams' disjunction of justification from sanctification suggests intellectualist underpinnings and hinders dynamic representations of salvation. While greater mention of the Holy Spirit occurs in the text (chapters 6–15), it is done outside of soteriology. He commonly identifies salvation with the redemptive, justifying work of God accomplished through Jesus Christ as propositionally communicated through Scripture. And while he expresses sanctification as robustly pneumatological he unfortunately still subordinates it to justification. As commonplace among other "pentecostal" theologians, he presumes the primary soteriological framework of conservative theology (i.e., truncating and prioritizing justification from sanctification). Finally, while Williams does give greater priority to the Spirit, pneumatology still relates to sanctification and Spirit baptism as post-salvific works.

89. Ibid., 83.

90. Elsewhere he also signifies sanctification as "the continuing life of the people of God" and "complete holiness" (Ibid., 88, 90).

91. Ibid., 93.

92. Ibid., 95.

The Problem with Conservative Christian Soteriology

Guy P. Duffield and N. M. Van Cleave were commissioned by Jack Hayford[93] when he was president of L. I. F. E. Bible College to write *Foundations of Pentecostal Theology* (1983).[94] The aim of the text was to expound theological motifs from a distinctively pneumatological and biblically rooted perspective. The authors, having served as pastors, missionaries, professors, and teachers wrote the book with the desire to help "ground and settle . . . our Pentecostal family throughout the world."[95] As a testament to their work, the text is used in many PC schools and institutes of higher learning and, as such, provides a helpful way of looking at pentecostal soteriology.[96]

While the authors do not clearly demonstrate Presupposition One (at least not enough to be included in the last section), they do exhibit Presupposition Two when they sever and feature justification from and over sanctification. In explaining the "method of justification" they say:

> Justification by faith does not impart Christ's Righteousness to the sinner nor infuse him with it so that it becomes part of his inner nature. That is the result of Sanctification, which we will consider later. Justification reckons to the sinner the Righteousness of Christ, so that God sees him through the perfect Righteousness of His Son.[97]

Hence, justification is disconnected from sanctification and bound exclusively with the work of Christ. Justification is objective (i.e., "reckoned to the sinner"), while sanctification is subjective (i.e., "impart[s] Christ's Righteousness"). Throughout the chapter, they unite justification with Christ and it is not until they approach the topic of sanctification that they introduce the soteriological significance of the Holy Spirit.

Justification is a forensic reality, conjoined with the work of Christ, and passively received.

> Justification is a legal term which pictures the sinner before the bar of God to receive condemnation for the sins he has committed. But instead of being condemned he is judicially pronounced as not guilty, being declared by God to be righteous. Justification has

---

93. Jack Hayford is a leading PC minister, author, and former president of the International Church of the Foursquare Gospel.

94. Duffield and Van Cleave, *Foundations of Pentecostal Theology*, x–xi.

95. Ibid., xv.

96. It is also one of the recommended theological resources for ministers on the Assemblies of God website (See, *Enrichment Journal*, "Pentecost—Resource List," item 12.).

97. Duffield and Van Cleave, *Foundations of Pentecostal Theology*, 224.

been defined as *that act of God whereby He declares righteous him who believes on Christ*.[98]

Likewise, they prefer justification in the order of salvation: "Justification by faith is the foundation truth of God's provision of salvation for guilty and lost sinners . . . Yet it must be understood if we are to grasp, and fully understand, the *so great salvation* (Heb 2:3) God has graciously and freely provided."[99] They intimate a favored preference of justification by relating salvation solely to the person and ministry of Christ (apart from the Spirit). The components of salvation are listed as: A.) The Death of Christ; B.) The Resurrection of Christ; and C.) The Ascension and Glorification of Jesus Christ.[100] However, they conceive of sanctification as a consequence of justification and signify it only in terms of "Christian living,"[101] whereas they consistently regard justification as central to salvation. They give the impression that sanctification is indirectly related to soteriology while justification directly deals with salvation proper. As with all the previous texts, Duffield and Van Cleave's bifurcation of justification from sanctification underscores the objective and intellectual qualities of forensic justification over the subjective and affective features of sanctification and construes the Spirit's ministry in post-salvific terms.

At this point it is necessary to provide a brief explanation of my methodological conclusion to discuss salvation in terms of justification and sanctification. Some may contest that because I support the integration of these categories, I discredit myself by treating them as individually distinct realities. My purpose for isolating them is to assess such a soteriology on its own terms (i.e., as an intellectualist soteriology). After the appraisal has been accomplished then a recasting of these parts will commence. Therefore, as the objective-justification and subjective-sanctification categories are elaborated, it is solely for exposing the intellectual underpinnings latent in its soteriology. I do not endorse polarizing salvation into objective and subjective categories nor does a renewal soteriology have to do so either. Furthermore, the point of concern regarding the lack of soteriological emphasis on subjectivity and pneumatology is not merely to call more attention to sanctification but to re-envision salvation within a framework that more accurately reveals the dynamic scope of God's saving work. The point

---

98. Ibid., 220.
99. Ibid.
100. Ibid., 180, 193, 203.
101. Ibid., 237.

The Problem with Conservative Christian Soteriology

is not to deny the existence of objective and subjective realities in salvation but to reject a soteriology that divides them.

An overview and reflection of the above observations indicate that conservative Protestantism often conveys salvation as a juridically-based divine event, thus spotlighting the doctrine of forensic justification and imputed righteousness. Within this soteriological scheme, trusting Christ commences in an eternal divine election where God declares the believer righteous and forgiven of all sins. Sanctification follows election and justification and is generally subordinated in theological significance. It represents the fruits of salvation and is sometimes not even considered in soteriological terms. This theological framework is amply revealed in the soteriology of the texts under consideration. Such a view was shown to be problematic because salvation is interpreted principally in christological terms (disconnected from the ministry of the Spirit) and predominately accompanied by the forensic doctrine of justification (which emphasizes the importance of *knowing* the details of these realities). Just as justification is severed from sanctification, so too is intellect sheared from emotions, affections, and behavior. These texts polarize salvation into objective (justification) and subjective (sanctification) categories that reinforce an intellectualist soteriology. Salvation as a subjective, holistic, and transformational process mediated by the Spirit remains subordinated to the more objective constituents of proper knowledge, forgiveness of sins, and acknowledgment of the imputed righteousness of Christ. The theological presupposition is that pneumatology follows and is dependent upon Christology in the order of salvation.[102]

In order to facilitate a non-intellectualist soteriology, conservative Christianity should recognize that the forensic model of justification is but one soteriological model among others. For instance, throughout church history other representations of justification have also been utilized, many of which emphasized the affective nature of salvation.[103] Why is it

---

102. Here I am merely providing further documentation for claims made elsewhere by Steven Studebaker on envisioning sanctification as consequent to justification. Studebaker deals with this subject in reference to common pentecostal tendencies in understanding sanctification and justification and how these tendencies directly flow from a common heritage with Fundamentalist theology (see, Studebaker, "Pentecostal Soteriology," 257).

103. For example, while Penal Substitution (a Reformation modification of Anselm's Satisfaction Theory) is the atonement theory generally associated with forensic justification, other atonement theories have also been utilized that underscore salvation's more subjective and affective impulses. Peter Abelard's (1079–1142) theory of the atonement

PART ONE: SALVATION AND EMBODIMENT

important to allow for other such representations? Because an embodied vision of salvation must account for both the objective and subjective realities of salvation. When an intellectualist epistemology drives the doctrine of salvation and employs objective vs. subjective dualism to the topic of justification, intellect is consistently prioritized. Hence, the subjective-pneumatological nature of salvation remains largely correlated with a post-salvific sanctification; consequently, the transformative, embodied, and progressive elements of salvation are muted. Other cognitive operations like emotions and behaviors (as mediated by the Spirit) are denied or insignificantly accounted for in the operation of faith. I argue that an important step toward a renewed doctrine of salvation requires additional representations of justification as a distinctly pneumatological event yet inseparable from the ministry of Christ. Hence, justification and sanctification will no longer be dualistically construed but portrayed as a dynamically integrated Trinitarian process.[104]

The numerous examples of Presupposition Two in the selected texts provide additional warrant that conservative Christian theology has embraced soteriological commitments reflecting an intellectualist soteriology. While the implications are many (as explored in chapter 8), the cumulative effect of these two soteriological presuppositions foreground proper teaching (orthodoxy) as the cardinal domain of salvation to the exclusion of right practices (orthopraxy) and right emotions and affections (orthopathy). Next, an appeal to common practice at the lay and ecclesial levels of many Protestant churches will substantiate the third presupposition of an intellectualist soteriology.

---

emphasized the power of God's love; the Ransom Theory (originating from the Early Church Fathers) highlights the need for radical deliverance from the oppressive power of the devil; and Irenaeus' (ca. 125–202) Recapitulation Theory points to Christ as the fountain head of divine life through which believers are transformed into the image of God. Each of these theories accents various affective realities of salvation that constituted prominent soteriological models throughout church history. Gustaf Aulén elaborates these different theories and argues that the theme of conflict and victory (i.e., Christ as Victor) was the original and dominant atonement motif of the church (see, Aulén, *Christus Victor*). Aulén brings attention to the fact that there are and have been orthodox ways to conceive justification and redemption in terms not dominated by objective and rational categories as is often the case with the forensic model. Some alternative models of justification can be seen in the works of: Macchia, *Justified in the Spirit*; Wright, *Justification*; and Martin, *Theological Issues*.

104. Chapter 9 revisits why soteriology needs to account for the doctrine of justification in more explicitly pneumatological terms.

The Problem with Conservative Christian Soteriology

Presupposition Three: Salvation is Primarily Punctiliar and Confessional

Presuppositions One and Two both underscore an intellectualist accent of conversion, therefore they tend to foster a corresponding set of practices which presume salvation to be a result of confessions (i.e., verbal articulations of specific propositions with intellectual content) made at a specific moment in time. Such a soteriology highlights past resolutions and moments (I was saved) while minimizing or neglecting the present and future promise of ongoing renewal (I am being saved; I will be saved). It is not surprising that an intellectualist soteriology will also reflect the same in its praxis.[105] For instance, many conservative denominations accent the moment-in-time and confessional aspects of salvation in the form of "decisions" or "choices" made for God as opposed to more dynamic markers highlighting "transformation" and "growth." David Finch relates how Evangelicalism's central soteriological emphasis of a "Decision for Christ" is now recognized as standard practice for authentic Christian conversion.[106] He contests (as do I) that the emphasis of a rational "choice" implies that salvation is more about knowing the right information than cultivating the image of Christ in one's life.[107] A brief look at influential conservative Christian churches and denominations will demonstrate the pervasiveness of the "decision" as constitutive of true Christian conversion.

---

105. Webster's dictionary defines praxis as "the application or use of knowledge or skills; practice, as distinguished from theory" (Random House, *Random House Webster's*, 1036).

106. Finch, *End of Evangelicalism*, 86.

107. Finch utilizes insights from the ideological theory of Slavoj Žižek to maintain that Evangelicalism has emerged as a social phenomenon defined by three beliefs/practices: "The Inerrant Bible"; "The Decision for Christ"; and "The Christian Nation." In regard to the purposes of this study, he contends that "The Decision for Christ" has become normative practice for validating authentic Christianity, however at the same time it also legitimizes duplicitous behavior because the "decision" is not intentionally linked to a particular type of lifestyle (i.e., it is unembodied). Elaborating on how the "Decision for Christ" does not lead to authentic embodied experience, Finch says: "The empty signifier allows us to believe without really believing. In this case, 'the decision' enables the formation of various kinds of churches that can appeal to various status-quo lifestyles, making little to no demands on changing one's life, all the while claiming allegiance to the gospel. It allows for Christianities to emerge that remain complicit with social systems of self-fulfillment, consumerism, or for that matter excessive sexual desire" (Finch, *End of Evangelicalism*, 85).

Part One: Salvation and Embodiment

At the Southern Baptist Convention website, under "How to Become a Christian," after the reader is told about her need for salvation, she is given a suggested prayer for salvation. Immediately after the prayer, the site identifies the act of praying the prayer with salvation when it says, "If you have trusted Jesus as your Lord and Savior, please let us know." Also, the terminology in explaining how to "accept" the gift of salvation (acknowledge, believe, confess, and receive) is driven by punctiliar and confessional soteriological assumptions.[108] At the Christian Missionary Alliance website, under its Statement of Faith, the section dealing with salvation again features decision making and while the significance of ongoing growth is mentioned, it is given in the section following salvation. The portion on salvation professes: "Salvation has been provided through Jesus Christ for all men; and those who repent and believe in Him are born again of the Holy Spirit, receive the gift of eternal life, and become the children of God."[109] At the Assemblies of God website, though not specifically stating the need for decision, the same seems to be implied in their statement on salvation: "Salvation is received through repentance toward God and faith toward the Lord Jesus Christ."[110] Here too, they include empowerment and growth, but just in sections outside the category of salvation (The Baptism of the Holy Spirit and Sanctification). The Church of the Nazarene website in their statement of faith describes salvation largely in the punctiliar and static terms of "repenting" and "believing" in Jesus Christ. Salvation is equated with the work of Christ as per the categories of justification and regeneration, and growth in holiness is envisioned as a post-salvific reality. For instance in their Statement of Belief it says of salvation, "*We believe* that the atonement through Jesus Christ is for the whole human race; and that whosoever repents and believes on the Lord Jesus Christ is justified and regenerated and saved from the dominion of sin."[111] Of sanctification it says, "*We believe* that believers are to be sanctified wholly, subsequent to regeneration, through faith in the Lord Jesus Christ."[112]

---

108. The Southern Baptist Convention, "How to Become a Christian," lines 31–34.
109. The Alliance, "The Alliance Stand," lines 21–22.
110. The Assemblies of God "The Salvation of Man," sect. 5.
111. The Church of the Nazarene, "Agreed Statement of Belief," lines 6–7. Emphasis original.
112. Ibid. Emphasis original. As with the other cited examples, the Holy Spirit is essentially limited to the work of sanctification.

The Problem with Conservative Christian Soteriology

My comments are not intended to deny the value of "prayers for salvation" or suggest anything wrong about "accepting" or "choosing" Jesus as one's savior. However, the point is clear that the vocabulary about Christian salvation predominately favors cognitive rationality within an objective framework stressing a specific moment in time and confessions correlated with a salvation procured "all-at-once," as it were. And while mention of renewal and growth is not missing, it is included in sections subsequent to the topic of salvation. As noted in the foregoing, once again, conservative Christianity tends to focus salvation on Christ while simultaneously regarding the ministry of the Spirit as mostly a post-salvific actuality.

Also, one can see why the practice of securing "decisions" of salvation is so common among such believers when one considers the numerous descriptions of justification occurring at a distinct moment, and the equally emphatic denials of it being progressive. The emphasis on rational and objective determinations reinforces the tendency of subordinating the ministry of the Spirit in the order of salvation. Hence, in practice, as in the textbooks, the subjective work of the Spirit follows the already completed work of justification (i.e., sanctified living *proceeds* from such "decisions"). For if the justifying work of God finalizes one's salvation in a moment through the means of a rational decision, then the sanctifying work of the Spirit is diminished, less urgent, and superfluous (at best) or dispensable (at worst).

It is problematic when ministers and theologians emphasize salvific decisions as the predominant markers for salvation because, in doing so, they often fail to discern the significance of history and the broad spectrum of human experience in the decision making process. The cognitive sciences suggest that conscious judgments are just one among many factors influencing human choices. This study stresses the perspective of *salvation as conversion* to affirm the progressive nature of salvation. When one interprets salvation solely in terms of specific events and choices, then past experiences or particular conceptualizations of God become the underlying foundation for faith. However, when salvation is understood as continual conversion then faith becomes a powerful phenomenon that anticipates experience and growth. Some theologians have realized the significance of history and human experience leading to a "conscious resolution" of surrender to Jesus Christ. They exposit salvation as continual renewal and transformation. When soteriology is expounded in terms of "conversion," then salvation as a past, present, and future sequence of events or experiences of the divine can be more plainly drawn out. Such an approach shifts one's attention from specific events and confessional resolutions to a progressive reality; salvation becomes multidimensional with a wide range of implications describing a life full of devotion to God.[113]

One cannot deny that there are punctiliar and confessional aspects of Christian salvation but when they become the primary means of depiction, they significantly hinder a dynamic soteriology. These emphases lead to a conception of *salvation that is developed more as a static decision than a transformational journey of ongoing growth and maturity*. Hence, I refer to such a vision of salvation as a "static soteriology" because it typically recounts redemption as rationally grounded, event-based, unembodied, and nonprogressive. In contrast to a more dynamic soteriology, a static soteriology highlights one's past history of "I was saved" over the other more dynamic expressions of "I am being saved" and "I will be saved."

Gordon T. Smith takes up the issue of language in dealing with salvation. He argues that the revivalist tradition influenced the language of conversion. Conversion, historically perceived as a dynamic term, came to be distinguished at a particular moment, as an event. The loss or minimization of *process* in salvation resulted from this shift. Smith contends that this change is not even "consistent with either the biblical witness or the actual experience of Christians."[114] Rather, the language of "conversion" stresses the powerful and unpredictable movement of coming to and growing in faith. Smith says that "what we urgently need is a language of conversion that accounts for the process—often an extended period—by which a person comes to faith."[115] He elaborates.

> Most, if not all, conversions are actually a series of events—often a complex development over time, perhaps even several years . . . Further, the proclivity toward thinking of conversion as singular and punctiliar has been matched by an assumption that the power of divine grace is evident precisely in the drama of the moment.[116]

Smith insists that a "theology of conversion" will delineate the experience of Christian conversion as a reality of ongoing growth. This book agrees with Smith that Christian salvation is an extended journey of conversion,

---

113. These theologians are discussed in chapters 7–10 regarding the possibility of a pneumatological approach toward a renewal soteriology of embodiment.

114. Smith, *Transforming Conversion*, 112.

115. Ibid., 7.

116. Ibid., 6.

but goes beyond him by elaborating on this "process" as a dynamic integration between orthodoxy, orthopraxy, and orthopathy. Next, we lay out how our soteriological proposal will be accomplished.

Solution: A Renewal Soteriology of Embodiment

We began this chapter by restating the claim of an intellectualist soteriology within segments of conservative Christianity. Our goal has been to show tendencies of how this movement relies on intellectualist notions of salvation and faith. With this end in mind, three intellectualist presuppositions were introduced—the first two through examining select theology texts of influential evangelical theologians and the third as common practice within the lay and ecclesial spheres of many Protestant churches. I do not contend that any one theology text proves an intellectualist soteriology; however, when collectively considered, they reflect a soteriology that favors an intellectualist epistemology, even if unwittingly. In our critique we recognized two interrelated soteriological consequences—the unembodiment of faith and a minimized pneumatology—and how they have fostered static, passive, and punctiliar images of salvation problematic and inconsistent with the more life-changing message of salvation depicted in Scripture. Thus, our solution is a renewal (pneumatological) soteriology of embodiment (involving the whole person).

Positioning the Cognitive Sciences for an Embodied Soteriology of Renewal

In the next chapter, we will see that even though neuroscience affirms cognition is dynamic and embodied, segments of the Christian world have yet to grapple with intellectualist presuppositions within their soteriology. As we have seen, such influences have led to static, abstract, and punctiliar notions regarding the meaning and practice of salvation. The implications of such intellectualism call for a new vision of faith's function to engender a more Spirit-empowered and embodied perception and experience of salvation.

Our research suggests that cognitive science can provide a framework to help us rethink the function of faith in salvation. Drawing from psychology, brain research, and learning theory, we contend that "cognition" ought

PART ONE: SALVATION AND EMBODIMENT

to be understood holistically as it is largely across the cognitive sciences.[117] Making use of prominent authorities in these fields we affirm a holistic model of cognition which then helps to structure our theological paradigm for an embodied conception of faith.

The driving purpose undergirding our use of the cognitive sciences is to emphasize how the embodied nature of cognitive function directly bears on the way we think about faith. To accomplish this we focus on Antonio Damasio, a world-renowned cognitive neuroscientist. Damasio convincingly reveals how cognitive function is a thoroughly integrated reality utilizing intellect, behavior, and emotions-feelings. In other words, he elaborates how the whole human body is inseparably involved in cognition. Damasio's research has profoundly influenced the understanding of how the brain processes information. This research has opposed the dualist paradigm of cognition that disconnects intellect from emotions and sentiment. Thus, Damasio calls for an embodied paradigm of cognition in which the whole body, not just the brain, is fundamentally involved in human knowing. For our purposes, this research lays the groundwork for the entire book because it helps us expound how faith (as, at least, a cognitive function), is more than just knowledge of who God is and the various theological doctrines one accepts. This is significant in regards to our earlier critique that it is not enough just to say *that* faith is more than an intellectual comprehending of knowledge about God but that we must go further by showing *how* such "more" practically plays out.

We also appropriate the research of Reuven Feuerstein, a pioneer in cognitive psychology, to draw attention to the transforming character of cognition. Feuerstein, like Damasio, also endorses an embodied paradigm of cognition. As a learning theorist, his work shows that knowing is more transforming to the degree it is most fully embodied. Throughout his career, Feuerstein demonstrated virtually "miraculous" results in his embodied learning methodology, especially among individuals with Downs Syndrome and autism. His Mediated Learning Experience program was so effective that it actually led to physical change in the brain structure

---

117. Not all cognitive scientists or neurobiologists necessarily share an embodied view of cognition, as some who are materialists believe that every aspect of the human mind or consciousness reduces to physical particles (see Dennett, *Consciousness Explained* and *Kinds of Minds*). These materialists generally consider emotions to be epiphenomenally dependent on brain states; hence, they separate reason from emotions. Nevertheless, an embodied view of cognition is prominent if not the consensus opinion among cognitive scientists.

of his students (neurogenesis). Feuerstein's work helps us to re-envision the central soteriological role that behaviors and emotions-feelings play in the reception and mediation of faith. Therefore, Damasio and Feuerstein's research helps us craft the kind of embodied epistemology needed to make our claim that saving faith literally involves the entire human body—not just the intellect.

In view of such research, we assert that just as cognition is understood as the embodied integration of rational thinking, behavior, and affectivity, so too should one's faith paradigm be similarly embodied. It is for this reason I recast salvation as not only concerned with knowing the right information but also as practicing certain behaviors and nurturing various dispositions and affections. Hence, our use of the cognitive sciences frames the embodied epistemology woven through each chapter of this book to both elaborate (chapters 3–8) and then assimilate (chapters 9–10) our soteriological components of orthodoxy, orthopraxy, and orthopathy. Ultimately, I integrate these three areas to construct our *embodied soteriology of renewal*. Now that we have explained our use of the cognitive sciences for our soteriological proposal, next we lay out our renewal methodology.

A Renewal Theological Method for the Doctrine of Salvation

As already stated, the intellectualist presuppositions in conservative Christianity have led to a minimized role of the Holy Spirit in how soteriology is envisioned. Consequently, without a strong pneumatology, the dynamic and transformational ramifications of salvation are stifled and stunted. How can we remain faithful to orthodox Protestant soteriology while also facilitating a more robust pneumatology to precisely reflect the work of the Spirit? We will look to specific theologians and scholars committed to a more prioritized place of the Spirit in theological and biblical reflection.

Towards this end, our book follows a *renewal* (pneumatological) *theological method*. Therefore, this study draws inspiration from but also extends the contemporary quest for a theology of the Third Article. In light of Lyle Dabney's work, I develop a soteriology of the Third Article. Dabney challenges the historic subordination of the Spirit to the Father and Son as illustrated in a theology of the First Article (emphasizing God the Father and his ministry of creation, i.e., Medieval Scholasticism), and in a theology of the Second Article (stressing God the Son and his ministry of redemption, i.e., Reformation Protestantism). Working toward a fully

Trinitarian theology, Dabney proposes a theology of the Third Article that joins the activity of the Spirit inseparably with the Father and the Son[118] and thereby highlights the vital ministry of the Spirit, especially in salvation.

Amos Yong takes up Dabney's emphasis of a pneumatological theology in his programmatic formulation of salvation via the metaphor of Spirit Baptism characterized in dynamic, holistic, and multidimensional terms. Expanding beyond the classical pentecostal construal of the Baptism of the Holy Spirit for power to witness, Yong submits that this metaphor can call "attention to the process of humans experiencing the saving graces of God along with the presence of crisis moments when such grace is palpably felt as radically transformative."[119] Yong then states that a pneumatological soteriology necessitates a theology of conversion that engages the full range of experience within which human beings can encounter the saving grace of God.[120] Building on Donald Gelpi's theology of conversion, Yong explains that the "dynamic, complex, and interactive series of conversion processes . . . in any domain serves as a gracious prompt for deeper conversion in other domains."[121] A renewal soteriology conceived in terms of ongoing conversion characterizes salvation in more diverse capacities.[122]

This book utilizes Dabney's work as expanded by Yong and then deploys and extends their pneumatological research. Hence, I engage contemporary studies in the cognitive sciences, the theology of Jonathan Edwards, William Abraham, patristic sources, and pentecostal and renewal theologians to draw attention to the following soteriological categories—orthodoxy, orthopraxy, and orthopathy. This approach invites a broad interaction between a variety of positions and voices and seeks a synthesis of the various dialogical sources from a renewal viewpoint.

---

118. Dabney, "Why Should the Last be First?" 240–61.

119. Yong, *Spirit Poured Out*, 108, 105.

120. Ibid., 106. Because conservative Christian theology associates conversion (understood statically) so closely with salvation, a dynamic soteriology requires a dynamic perspective of conversion.

121. Ibid., 108.

122. Additionally, such a soteriology is also more historically consistent with the canonical heritage of the church as practiced through the centuries.

The Remaining Chapters

Bearing in mind the challenge of an intellectualist soteriology, I now overview the forthcoming chapters in light of the methodology already put forth. Chapter 2 draws from contemporary studies in psychology, brain research, and learning theory to provide the scientific framework for our proposal of an embodied soteriology. In chapters 3–4, I expand the concept of orthodoxy by showing how Jonathan Edwards understood salvation as a thoroughly embodied process. This is accomplished through unpacking Edwards' philosophical theology of dispositions which articulates the dynamic character of faith as it relates to Christian conversion. This chapter is critical because it underscores how an esteemed evangelical theologian understood knowing God as an unmistakably embodied task. Chapters 5–6 elaborates the canonical theism of William Abraham to suggest a holistic appraisal of orthopraxy that draws deeply from the discursive practices of the early church. In this chapter, I establish how behavior and practices are central components of Christian salvation and serve to mediate transforming grace. These dialogue partners set up the heart of this project in chapters 7 and 8 to articulate how pentecostal spirituality illustrates the soteriological significance of orthopathy. Not only does pentecostal spirituality reveal the important role affectivity plays in an embodied soteriology but it also brings attention to how orthopathy can function as a linchpin between orthodoxy and orthopraxy so that no single sphere is highlighted more than the others. Finally, in chapters 9–10, I draw together the study's findings along with insights from select pentecostal, charismatic, and pneumatological theologians (Lyle Dabney, Amos Yong, Frank Macchia, James Smith, Samuel Solivan, Steven Studebaker, Steven Land, and Daniel Castelo). All of this together helps explicate a truly dynamic soteriology in terms that are embodied, progressive, and social. In so doing, a robust pneumatological soteriology of renewal is developed in response to an intellectualist soteriology. The study concludes with reflections on potential problems and possibilities of a renewal soteriology and offers suggestions for areas of future research.

In the next chapter we take an excursus into the cognitive sciences for a more holistic epistemology that already insists on an emotional brain and embodied reason. Ultimately, I will show how the contemporary cognitive sciences serve as a springboard for thinking about human cognition as it relates to an embodied view of salvation.

2

Re-Imagining Soteriology through the Cognitive Sciences

WE HAVE NOW COMPLETED our initial assessment of conservative Christian soteriology. Before launching forward, let us take a moment to briefly review our stated critique. Chapter 1 claims that conservative Protestant theology typically does *not* stress the importance of affections, emotions, and behaviors in salvation. I have suggested this is connected to the underlying intellectualist epistemology largely driving this movement's vision of salvation. I contend that the theological epistemology in question endorses a rationalist paradigm of cognition and, therefore, lacks the resources needed to develop an embodied soteriology of renewal. Embedded within such a soteriology are certain presuppositions and tendencies that disassociate subjectivity and embodiment from cognition. One of its most common assumptions is the belief that *knowing* is chiefly a rational enterprise dependent on the accumulation of objective information. Accordingly, emotions and behaviors are devalued in cognitive function.

FAITH AND THE COGNITIVE SCIENCES

In response to the kind of soteriology depicted in chapter 1, I now focus on resources gained from the cognitive sciences that enable a holistic judgment of cognition. George Lakoff and Mark Johnson explain how contemporary research provides a new way of thinking about human cognition:

> Cognitive science, the science of the mind and the brain, has in its brief existence been enormously fruitful. It has given us a way

Re-Imagining Soteriology through the Cognitive Sciences

to know ourselves better, to see how our physical being—flesh, blood, sinew, hormone, cell, and synapse—and all things we encounter daily in the world make us who we are.[1]

The cognitive sciences have helped set the stage for alternative construals of cognition that account for a holistic view of embodiment—the inseparability of intellect, emotions, and behavior.

This chapter shows how the contemporary cognitive neurosciences and cognitive psychology provide compelling reasons to envision faith's reception and expression through distinctly embodied means. Such an approach provides a foundation for the embodied soteriology this book proposes. Presently, I focus on two cognitive scientists—Antonio Damasio and Reuven Feuerstein—who see embodiment and affectivity as central components of cognitive function, without which "knowing" and "understanding" would be severely impaired. First, Damasio reveals how the neurobiology of feelings and emotions underscore the optimal functionality of human cognition. Here, emotions and feelings, together with rationality, are constitutive of reasoning. Second, Feuerstein's work in learning theory highlights the embodiment of cognition and the life-altering potential of behavior within the learning process. Finally, I incorporate this research into a holistic epistemology that includes rationality, emotions, affections, and behaviors as integral to our soteriological proposal.[2] Cognition, in this new perspective, is not just mental activity abstracted from life, community, culture, history, etc., but it is fully informed, constituted by, and emergent from these interrelated elements. Because this understanding of cognition does not separate the mental, emotional, and behavioral dimensions of experience, I call it *embodied cognition*. The proposition throughout is that an embodied paradigm of cognition provides dynamic and transformational implications for the doctrine of salvation.[3]

1. Lakoff and Johnson, *Philosophy in the Flesh*, 568.

2. My appropriation of Damasio and Feuerstein's research does not imply their endorsement of my research. Nevertheless, I contend that many of the key principles of their work relate to our soteriological topic—the cognitive nature of faith—and are, therefore, viable resources for this study.

3. Others have also utilized the cognitive sciences, in general, and Damasio's research, in particular, in ways related to this book. For instance, though addressing the relationship between morality and ethics, Amos Yong appropriates Damasio's research to highlight the implications of an embodied brain on moral reasoning. Yong's research helps pave the way for aspects of my methodology in utilizing the cognitive sciences via Damasio's work as a resource for theological reflection (see, Yong, "The Virtues," 191–208). More directly related to this book, Steve Mills interacts with Damasio's

PART ONE: SALVATION AND EMBODIMENT

Even though I am exploiting research in the cognitive sciences to strengthen my claim for an embodied cognitivism, my purpose is not to provide an exhaustive overview of the cognitive sciences or the various philosophical topics related to "mind," nor even the work of Damasio and Feuerstein. Rather, I focus on how contemporary studies in these fields recognize the influence of affectivity and embodiment in reasoning.[4] And this will be broadly accomplished through drawing attention to specific areas of our researchers' work. Yet, one important unanswered question still remains: What do the cognitive sciences have to do with faith?

Clarifying our Approach

Before delving into this chapter, let's first establish what we are and are not trying to accomplish. In doing so, we help to minimize misunderstanding the purposes and intentions of this book even as we further clarify the meaning of an embodied soteriology. The driving emphasis throughout is that human salvation involves bodies and to speak meaningfully and relevantly of God's salvific work for and in people is to affirm their embodied, flesh and blood existence. This focus does not deny the "spiritual" reality of salvation but rather, reinforces its very possibility. Just as God's plan of salvation required the body of his Son, so too does its reception by grace through faith require its working out in ours.

Interestingly, while many may agree with our statements about the importance of an embodied soteriology, such affirmers, nevertheless, often

---

research to contend that the Pauline exhortation to "renew our mind" involves more than mere attainment of new information. Like *Salvation in the Flesh*, Mills utilizes the cognitive sciences to elaborate an embodied or holistic soteriology (see, Mills, "Renewal of the Mind"). Curt Thompson integrates knowledge from the fields of neuroscience, psychology, and spirituality to elaborate a holistic-embodied view of how people grow in the transforming grace of Christ (see, Thompson, *Anatomy of the Soul*, chapter 10). Lastly, Mark Mann draws from the cognitive neurosciences, sociology of knowledge, and psychology to help renew the doctrine of holiness in the Christian tradition. Mann's project relates to mine at the points where I deal with the soteriological implications of orthopraxy and orthopathy (see, Mann, *Perfecting Grace*, chapter 2).

4. Damasio and Feuerstein are just some among many scientists that could have been utilized in this book. Examples of other researchers and their work include: Frank, *Passions within Reason*; Borod, *Neuropsychology*; Lane and Nadel, *Cognitive Neuroscience*; from more of a philosophical framework, see, Lakoff and Johnson, *Philosophy in the Flesh*; and from a sociological framework, see, Brothers, *Friday's Footprints*.

deal with the body in passive terms as though it were only a container for a solely spiritual work of God. Why is this? Intellectualist presuppositions run deep and are not always obvious. So, if salvation really is a holistic reality, let's begin to take embodiment seriously by fully accounting for all dimensions of our body's involvement in cognitive function. This is exactly the reason for our use of the cognitive sciences.

While we agree that faith is a gift of God, we also insist its reception is not passive—received apart from human interaction and intentional engagement with God. Because humans exist in and by means of their bodies then every choice, decision, and action of such engagement must really account for their bodies. If salvation requires human "choice" (regardless of the Calvinist and Arminian disagreements over the soteriological role of choice) to love and submit to God then such "choosing" and subsequent "knowing" (i.e., faith) depends on the brain. So, if salvation requires human participation, then how does the brain work in such an activity? It works in much the same way it does in any other act of "knowing" or "choosing." As previously mentioned, we are not saying that faith is solely reduced to the physio-chemical elements of human cognition. Nevertheless, while there will always be a mysterious quality to faith regarding its relationship with human biological systems, we can and we must speak of what we are capable—the cognitive process involved in knowing God.

So, in view of these clarifications, we must think of faith's reception in more critical terms than some sort of "divine download" bypassing human participation, otherwise rendering embodiment virtually unnecessary. Our use of the cognitive sciences does not minimize the wonder of salvation but helps us understand how our bodies and brains most effectively function in the activity of knowing God. Just as knowing and learning can be hindered and stifled in any area of study, so too can our faith. This is what we seek to avoid and, therefore, it is the reason for our appropriation of the cognitive sciences.

Methodological Limitations

We do not claim that our method introduces an exhaustive understanding of the nature of faith and salvation; nor do we intend to reduce faith to just a physically-driven formula. We are simply providing a tangible framework by which to reflect on and engage this unspeakably awesome gift of God—*salvation in the flesh*. Nevertheless, despite such clarifications here and elsewhere, our first and greatest limitation of utilizing the cognitive sciences will be presuppositional misunderstanding or confusion. The foundation of this book presumes the importance of human embodiment for soteriological reflection and practice. If this premise is rejected or misinterpreted, then our proposal will be misunderstood or misjudged as endorsing a message or theology contrary to our intended purpose. Our second greatest limitation—closely related to the first—is that those who already have a dubious and fearful view of the relationship between science and faith will find it difficult to accept our use of the cognitive sciences.

Regardless, such risks must be taken if critical theological-soteriological reflection is to ensue. We believe our presupposition is not only reasonable but scriptural and in accord with the historic orthodox Christian tradition. It is for this reason why we have been so committed to laying out, clarifying, and re-clarifying these foundational underpinnings of our embodied soteriological paradigm. Now it is time we turn our attention to the fascinating world of the cognitive neurosciences and, eventually, we'll see how incredibly relevant it is for our study.

Cognition and the Neurobiology of Feelings and Emotions

Contemporary findings in the neurosciences suggest that emotions and feelings are central to human cognition. Antonio Damasio (b. 1944) is the David Dornsife Professor of Neuroscience at the University of Southern California (USC), where he leads USC's Brain and Creativity Institute. As an internationally known neuroscientist, he writes extensively about the neurobiology of feelings, how they shape cognition, and how the brain is inseparable from embodiment.

Emotion and Cognition

Damasio is important for our purposes because he illustrates how emotions are central to the cognitive enterprise. He rejects the separation of emotion and reason and argues that emotions and feelings not only act upon cognition but are crucial components for its proper function. Damasio finds that brain-damaged patients with fully intact intellectual capacities but diminished or absent emotional responsiveness are severely affected in their abilities to function socially. They do not lack the intellectual content, but are incapable of processing their knowledge in a manner that allows for personal thriving or social interaction.[5]

> The process of learning and recalling emotionally competent events is different with conscious feelings from what it would be without feelings. Some feelings optimize learning and recall. Other feelings, extremely painful feelings in particular, perturb learning and protectively suppress recall.[6]

He therefore contends that reasoning does not function apart from emotions but actually depends on certain brain systems that manage feelings.[7]

Damasio explicitly rejects dualism between emotion and intellect in the introduction to his book, *Descartes' Error*. He recounts that he "never wished to set emotion against reason, but rather to see emotion as at least assisting reason and at best holding a dialogue with it . . . [and that he sees] emotion as delivering cognitive information, directly and via feelings."[8] Damasio upholds that emotion and feeling are necessary aspects of the mind.[9] In this book he opposes the legacy of dualism through which René Descartes, a seventeenth century French philosopher, initiated a wide collection of ideas in Western sciences and humanities presuming a separation between body, brain, mind, and emotion (Cartesian dualism).[10]

> This is Descartes' error: the abyssal separation between body and mind, between the sizable, dimensioned, mechanically operated, infinitely divisible body stuff, on the one hand, and the unsizable, undimensioned, un-pushpullable, nondivisible mind stuff; the suggestion that reasoning, and moral judgment, and the suffering that comes from physical pain or emotional upheaval might exist separately from the body. Specifically: the separation of the most refined operations of the mind from the structure and operation of a biological organism.[11]

Damasio addresses not only the notion of Cartesian dualism that divides the mind from the brain and the body, but also modern versions that admit

---

5. Damasio provides specific examples of this claim in his discussion of Phineas Gage and his modern counterpart "Elliott" in *Descartes' Error*, chapters 1, 3.
6. Damasio, *Looking for Spinoza*, 178 n. 25.
7. Damasio, *Descartes' Error*, 245.
8. Ibid., xiii.
9. Ibid., 86.
10. Ibid., 247.
11. Ibid., 249–50.

integration between the mind and *brain* but neglect the relationship between mind and *body*.¹² Emotions are entwined within cognition; he holds that they do not just act upon it but are constitutive of it.

> The action of biological drives, body states, and emotions may be an indispensable foundation for rationality. The lower levels in the neural edifice of reason are the same that regulate the processing of emotions and feelings, along with global functions of the body proper such that the organism can survive.¹³

As the body maintains homeostasis, it constantly uses such information on the body-proper's (that part of the body below the head) "neural edifice." Not only does Damasio insist that feelings emerge and coincide with certain body states of the organism but specific modes of thinking actually link with particular emotions derived from its corresponding body state.¹⁴ Even more directly, Damasio attests that "a feeling is the perception of a certain state of the body along with the perception of a certain mode of thinking and of thoughts with certain themes."¹⁵ So, even at a neurological level, one must reject the dualism between intellect and emotion. Reason and emotion are both neurologically emergent realities inextricably dependent on human embodiment.

Emotion and the Body

Another reason Damasio is significant for our study is because he depicts how emotions are not only constitutive of cognitive function but inseparable from the body. So, reason is dependent on emotions and feelings which themselves are dependent on the body. It is because of this relationship that Damasio so adamantly rejects the bifurcation of brain and body. In sum, were there no emotions and feelings there would be no mind and were there no body there would also be no mind since it is dependent on emotions and feelings.¹⁶ Therefore, in regard to the Cartesian separation be-

---

12. Ibid., 247–48.
13. Ibid., 200.
14. Damasio, *Looking for Spinoza*, 85.
15. Ibid., 86.
16. Damasio not only claims that the body is inseparable from cognitive function but also the person's sense of self. He explains that the body's ability to maintain homeostasis is not only functional for the physical survival of the organism but also is the very activity that provides the plans for what emerges as one's personality and sense of self

tween the mind and body, Damasio remarks: "It is not only the separation between mind and brain that is mythical: the separation between mind and body is probably just as fictional. The mind is embodied, in the full sense of the term, not just embrained."[17] Damasio argues that cognitive scientists must honestly admit the mind-body relationship for what it is.

> In the most popular and current of the modern views, the mind and brain go together, on one side, and the body (that is, the entire organism minus the brain) goes on the other side. Now the split separates brain and "body-proper" and the explanation of how mind and brain are related becomes more difficult when the brain-part of the body is divorced from the body-proper.[18]

Damasio explains that while marrying the brain with the mind is common practice in the cognitive sciences, this does not necessarily dismiss the charge of dualism—the "body" must refer to the entire body, not just the brain.

Drawing from his work with neurological patients, Damasio insists that cognition is inseparable from embodiment. His Somatic Marker Hypothesis alleges that the body is a "topographic map" upon which the limbic system spreads out and perceives various bodily sensations (body states) in conjunction with certain conditions and situations.[19] These states form the basic background feeling from which emotions develop.[20] Hence, the body-proper not only provides the physiological context from which emotions result but also from which reasoning arises.

> What I am suggesting is that the mind arises from activity in neural circuits . . . and that a normal mind will happen only if those circuits contain basic representations of the organism . . . I am not saying that the mind is in the body. I am saying that the body contributes more than life support and modulatory effects to the brain. It contributes a *content* that is part and parcel of the workings of the normal mind.[21]

(*The Feeling*, 144). In this study we limit our use of Damasio primarily to the role of the body and emotions on cognition because delving into the topics of consciousness and sense of self open up other areas of study that we do not have space or time to pursue in view of our more limited concerns.

17. Damasio, *Descartes' Error*, 118.
18. Damasio, *Looking for Spinoza*, 190.
19. Damasio, *Descartes' Error*, 173–75.
20. Ibid., 151–55.
21. Ibid., 226.

He attests that the mind, body, and brain are part of a single organism and that, even though these parts can be isolated under a microscope, in practice they are singularly intact in "normal operating circumstances."[22] In sum, Damasio de-constructs three dualisms which have contributed to modern intellectualism—the overarching mind-body dualism and the two related and subsidiary dualisms of emotion vs. mind and emotion vs. body.

Next I consider contemporary studies in cognitive psychology. New findings in this discipline provide further perspectives on the embodied scope of reasoning. In this section, I look to learning theorist, Reuven Feuerstein and his research in mediated learning.

Behavior and Embodied Cognition

The cognitive psychologist, Reuven Feuerstein, also accounts for the embodiment of human reasoning. Feuerstein (b. 1921–2014) specialized in the study of learning theory. He established and oversaw the International Center for the Enhancement of Learning Potential in Jerusalem, Israel. While much of Feuerstein's work was directed toward improving the cognitive abilities of children deprived of healthy reasoning abilities (whether from genetics or physical deprivation), his theories have been tested and proven across a wide range of populations. His research is just as relevant for the child struggling with Down syndrome as it is for the nontraditional sixty-five year-old retiree returning to school. With a focus on pedagogy, Feuerstein presumes the dynamic capacity of cognition—reasoning is interdependent with emotions and behaviors. Just as Damasio did not truncate intellect from affectivity and embodiment, so too does Feuerstein reject such dualism.

Embodied Cognition through Mediated Learning

Trained under the famed cognitive psychologist Jean Piaget (1896–1980), Feuerstein agreed with his mentor that individuals learn and progress through various learning stages. Piaget concluded that unless individuals successfully learn particular cognitive skills within certain age ranges, they will unlikely learn them later. Feuerstein however, went beyond Piaget by asserting the plasticity of cognitive abilities to be structurally modifiable

---

22. Damasio, *Looking for Spinoza*, 195.

through the intervention of human mediation in the learning process.[23] Ruth Burgess explains that Feuerstein rejected Piaget's notion of fixed stages because he insisted "that the order and timing of cognitive development is set, not by maturation, but by mediated social experiences."[24] Feuerstein contends that the brain can exhibit plasticity and physically modify itself, despite biological and cultural deprivations.

> When the brain is called upon to adapt, activities generated by the interaction between the organism and one's culture change the structure of the brain. This involves the neural networks, the relationships between parts of the cortical system, relay systems, blood flow, electrical activities of the brain—in short, the entire range of neuro-physiological functions of the brain and its related systems.[25]

As the brain exhibits plasticity, it has the ability to transcend deprivations sustained at earlier stages of cognitive development. As I will next indicate, Feuerstein's work directly flows from this awareness of brain plasticity through his practice of mediated learning.

Feuerstein's Mediated Learning Experience (hereafter, MLE) illustrates the dynamic interaction occurring between a learner and a teacher serving as the mediator. MLE is relevant for this study as it shows how cognition is an embodied and interpersonal-social phenomenon involving subjective realities. Since MLE presumes an embodied cognitive process, learning is facilitated through the interaction of a mediator who physically engages the learner, enabling him or her to increase comprehension of the learning task at hand. Furthermore, such learning incorporates intersubjective items like appreciation of culture, interests, likes, and dislikes in such a way that as curiosity is raised, so too is the motivation to learn and the ability to make sense of the subject matter. With MLE, learning is far more than an objectively dispassionate experience. The learner is physically and emotionally engaged through specific behaviors loaded with subjective meaning. How does MLE work?

MLE is concerned with two types of learning—direct learning and mediated learning. Feuerstein details the relationship between these types.

---

23. Burgess, "Reuven Feuerstein," 7.
24. Ibid.
25. Feuerstein et al., *Dynamic Assessment*, 73.

> MLE occurs when a person (mediator) who possesses knowledge, experience, and intentions mediates the world, makes it more understandable, and imparts meaning to it by adding to the direct stimuli . . . the more experience a person has had of exposure to mediated learning, the more he or she will derive benefit from direct exposure to the world.[26]

Hence, MLE facilitates successful learning. Direct learning includes unmediated contact between the learner and various environmental stimuli (objects, events, texts, pictures, etc.). Direct learning (such as traditional classroom instruction) usually involves a passive learner attempting to absorb intellectual content via an instructor or instructional stimuli. Such interaction typically flows one way—from instructor to learner. However, a human mediator can transform direct learning into mediated learning when she intervenes in the learning encounter and locates herself between the learner and the stimulus and between the learner and the response. The mediator selects, adjusts, amplifies, and interprets the stimuli that come to the learner and the learner's responses in terms that are culturally, ethnically, and intellectually discernible. The instructional flow in mediated learning is two way—moving from the instructor to the learner and from the learner to the instructor and back to the learner as many times as necessary for maximized comprehension. *When there is a deficiency in MLE, there tends to be an underdevelopment in an individual's cognitive functions and direct learning strategies.* However, when mediated learning is present, a person's cognitive deficiency may improve and the individual will eventually progress into an independent and self-regulating learner.

MLE: A Behavioral and Affective Cognitive Paradigm

Feuerstein's pedagogical approach follows from his vision of cognition that recognizes the vital role emotions and subjective features exert on cognition. Addressing early cognitive development in children, Feuerstein says, "It is undoubtedly true that, for MLE to occur, affection and emotional involvement of parents and siblings are important."[27] Therefore, Feuerstein places significant impact on the influence of affective-motivational causes impinging on the cognitive process. Where such motivation is missing,

---

26. Feuerstein et al., *Beyond Smarter*, 24.
27. Feuerstein, *Instrumental Enrichment*, 47.

cognitive function is hindered, and when it is present it is improved.[28] It is critical to note that while Feuerstein often speaks about the influence of behavior (in regard to MLE) it is never separated from the affective and emotional settings that either increase or decrease motivation for the particular behavior. The very practice of MLE presupposes an affective context for mediation to successfully ensue.

Feuerstein utilizes an embodied cognitive paradigm because his pedagogy is known for the prominent role that behaviors play on reasoning. The place of behavior is clearly seen in his MLE as both the mediator and student engage one another with distinct behaviors and practices that foster the reception of the targeted learning content. The types of behaviors that characterize Feuerstein's MLE exhibits at least four qualities. The significance of the forthcoming qualities is that they all require specific emotional attributes and unique pedagogical practices (behaviors) embodied in the mediator and learner. As the mediator transfers (i.e., mediates) these qualities to the learner and the learner internalizes them as part of his or her cognitive experience, learning becomes transformational. I next highlight the first four attributes of MLE to emphasize the critical role that embodiment plays in this remarkable instructional method.

First and second, *intentionality* and *reciprocity* depict mediated learning. They speak of commitment by the mediator and demonstration of learning by the one mediated. Feuerstein explains that mediated learning cannot be guaranteed to have occurred unless the mediator is certain the message (i.e., learning content) actually reached the intended learner.[29] Intentionality and reciprocity refer to the emotional state of the mediator and learner via a specific attitudinal mindset of motivation. Third, *transcendence* marks MLE. The mediator produces flexibility in the learner so that learning can transcend the immediate context in which it was received.[30] Transcendence is the ability to apply learning to new contexts through linking subjectively relevant content to the learning encounter. And fourth, MLE mediates *meaning* to the learner that transforms abstract or random learning into one that is relevant and meaningful to the learner. Feuerstein asserts that mediation of meaning requires subjectivity since it involves the "energetic, affective, and emotional power" needed to make the mediated

---

28. Ibid., 74–75.
29. Feuerstein et al., *Don't Accept*, 64.
30. Ibid., 65.

encounter overcome the normal resistance exerted by a learner and assures that the "stimuli mediated will indeed be experienced" by the learner.[31]

Therefore, a multidimensional and transformational belief about cognition undergirds Feuerstein's pedagogy. He insists that learning consists of much more than a rational grasping of facts. Through an embodied pedagogy, emotions and behaviors are just as crucial as intellectual ability.

> Mediated learning experience however goes beyond pure didactics and also represents a value system of paramount importance from an educational point of view, and a process that shapes and transforms the individual's personality. Mediation not only transmits but also transforms . . . Cognitive modifiability is brought about through this mediation.[32]

Education is more than the sole accumulation of knowledge or skills because it (via MLE) has the capacity to transform and modify an individual.[33] Feuerstein conceptualized his work under a unified theory (Structural Cognitive Modifiability) that accounts for the remarkable potential of human cognition to modify and be modified.

Cognitive Modifiability: The Transforming Power of an Embodied Mind

Feuerstein's Theory of Structural Cognitive Modifiability (hereafter, SCM) communicates his research and application of MLE. This theory contends that a person's cognitive potential is modifiable regardless of biological, social, psychological, and physical causes responsible for impairment.

---

31. Ibid., 66. Feuerstein actually describes eleven characteristics that distinguish MLE from other types of learning interaction. Due to space limitations, only the previous four were addressed as they are sufficient for the purposes of this study. However, all elements of MLE are marked by: (1) Intentionality and reciprocity; (2) Transcendence; (3) Mediation of meaning; (4) Mediation of feelings of competence; (5) Mediated regulation and control of behavior; (6) Mediated sharing behavior; (7) Mediation of individuation and psychological differentiation; (8) Mediation of goal seeking, goal setting, goal planning, and achieving behavior; (9) Mediation of challenge: The search for novelty and complexity; (10) Mediation of awareness of the human being as a changing entity; and (11) Mediation of an optimistic alternative (Ibid., 61). When these qualities are integrated in the learning encounter (via a mediator), a host of subjective items contribute to the cognitive process that not only allow learning to occur but also leads to transformation (i.e., modification) of the learner.

32. Feuerstein, *Biblical and Talmudic*, 59.

33. Feuerstein et al., *Beyond Smarter*, 140–41.

Re-Imagining Soteriology through the Cognitive Sciences

Likewise, the ability for a person to increase cognitive development depends on adequate exposure to mediated learning.[34] The impact of Feuerstein's SCM is powerfully seen as he applied his MLE to immigrant children seeking entrance into Israeli life from Russia and Ethiopia. Despite that many of these children lacked the necessary education and mediation needed for normal cognitive development, Feuerstein's MLE enabled these children to make massive strides in their intellectual growth.

A central presupposition of Feuerstein's SCM is that cognition is more adequately understood as *potential* than *accumulated knowledge*. Since human learning is dynamic and multidimensional, exposing individuals only to unmediated direct learning encounters limits them in the degree to which they can most fully actualize that encounter. Or, in other words, when embodiment and subjectivity are limited in cognition, learning suffers. For instance, Feuerstein holds that individuals deprived by lack of educational opportunities and physical or mental handicaps can rise above these obstacles and modify their intellectual capabilities. While many cognitive scientists hold that the human mind is locked in by genetic endowments and the ability to change is greatly limited, Feuerstein discovered a greater degree of cognitive modifiability in students experiencing significant deficiencies than many neuroscientists might be willing to grant.[35] Feuerstein challenges the static epistemology of modern intellectualism that envisions knowledge as accumulated facts and pieces of information; rather, he recommends a different construal of cognition more in terms of potential that associates knowledge with skills, intentionality, and practices.

Feuerstein also provides an alternative to the traditional static assessments in his Learning Propensity Assessment Device (LPAD). Rafi Feuerstein (Reuven's son) distinguishes the two: "Static assessments focus on the product of the assessment expressed in the cumulative score. LPAD is concerned with the thinking process, i.e., the quality of the process and the main difficulties (the deficient cognitive functions), experienced by the

---

34. Feuerstein, "Dynamic Cognitive," 158.

35. Consequently, Feuerstein eschews static IQ tests since they only measure how much a person has already learned rather than their potential to learn. He takes issue with the highly influential book, *Bell Curve*, by Herrnstein and Murray, from which the standard practice of IQ testing has largely derived. Feuerstein contests that these authors "present human beings as unmodifiable entities for whom the cognitive intellectual factor (as measured by IQ tests) is what determines their place in the world" (*Beyond Smarter*, 86).

examinee."[36] The LPAD's characteristic feature is that it evaluates the learning taking place in the examinees as opposed to just their current level of functioning.[37] Thus, the LPAD actually measures the existing level of cognitive development in an individual by evaluating the quality of learning that has occurred—i.e., the degree of embodiment and subjectivity in his or her pedagogical history.

In sum, brain plasticity is the underlying cognitive belief from which all of Feuerstein's research proceeds. MLE and the LPAD not only measure cognitive change but actually foster it. While Feuerstein illustrates cognitive modifiability at behavioral and intellectual levels, it is also indicated at an even more remarkable level—physiological. Feuerstein's paradigm of cognition not only appropriates the subjective factors of emotion and behavior (epitomized in MLE) as central to cognitive function, but he also shows how they actually produce *physical* change in the brain structure. Feuerstein declares that neuroscience can finally provide a physiological basis for SCM.

> Today, however, the neurosciences bring us evidence not only of the modifiability of the individual's mental functions, but also that the changes that can be produced are . . . changes in both the hardware and the software of the neural system. It is now no exaggeration to state that *the neural system is modified by the behavior, no less than the behavior is determined by the neural system.*[38]

Thus, sound neurological support now extends to the concepts of SCM and MLE. Therefore, Feuerstein's research not only demonstrates an embodied cognitivism by highlighting how affectivity and behaviors profoundly influence reasoning (i.e., mediated learning) but he reveals how a mediated pedagogy is transformational. For the purposes of our study, this assertion is important not only to explicate how emotions, affectivity, and behavior are central to cognitive function but how they can actually lead to physical change in the human brain.

This and the previous section have explored studies in the contemporary cognitive neurosciences and cognitive psychology that account for the

---

36. Feuerstein, "Dynamic Cognitive," 149–50.

37. Ibid., 149. The LPAD consists of three stages: The first examines the level of the examinees' cognitive function; the second intervenes to correct the deficient functions identified; and the third is a post-test that measures the level of modification that actually took place (Ibid.).

38. Feuerstein et al., *Beyond Smarter*, 134.

embodied and subjective aspects of human knowing. The embodied cognitivism of Antonio Damasio provides compelling reasons to take emotions and affectivity seriously in regard to human cognition. In Feuerstein's MLE, cognition is an embodied and subjective enterprise, holistically connected to and mediated by social interactions. Next, I explain how these findings address the problems posed by an intellectualist theological epistemology. I now show how the basic epistemological assumptions inherent in conservative Christian theology are inconsistent with the contemporary cognitive paradigms Damasio and Feuerstein represent.

Embodied Cognition and Faith in Conservative Christian Soteriology

The work of Antonio Damasio and Reuven Feuerstein represent developments in the cognitive neurosciences and psychology that invite a more holistic understanding of knowing as both embodied and affective. Yet, Christian theology has not often kept pace with this growing awareness of cognition, but continues to hold on to an intellectualist epistemology. How might contemporary research in the cognitive sciences open up new possibilities for Christian epistemology and, by extension, soteriology? Both Damasio and Feuerstein can be helpful for Christian theologians in reconsidering the nature of cognition as it relates to a renewal soteriology of embodiment. Next, I examine two common soteriological tendencies issuing from an intellectualist epistemology and how they hinder the kind of embodied soteriology we seek. Through the remaining chapters we will continue to address and respond to these leanings from a variety of perspectives.

Tendency One: Favoring an Unembodied Faith in Soteriological Reflection

Since intellectualism largely conceives cognitive function as a disembodied rational activity, the subjective components of human reasoning are often overlooked or ignored. This tendency can be seen in how faith is understood and appropriated in soteriological reflection. Most typically, an intellectualist faith paradigm does not account for the body and, therefore, salvation is mainly reduced to just an abstract or "spiritual" reality.

Part One: Salvation and Embodiment

Chapter 1 exposed this view with the consistent truncation of justification from sanctification and the prioritization of the former over the latter in conservative Protestant soteriology. Such is seen when faith is severed from behaviors and practices for fear of losing the gratuitousness of grace. Also, as was previously recognized, the extreme emphasis on the forensic doctrine of justification also reinforces a dualistic favoring of objective reasoning. Consequently, these presuppositions encourage a disembodied image of salvation emphasizing the need for correct knowledge over practices and behaviors while subordinating or ignoring the vital role of emotions and subjectivity. Lakoff and Johnson argue that in a disembodied picture of the mind, "[n]othing about the body, neither imagination nor emotion nor perception nor any detail of the biological nature of the body, need to be known in order to understand the nature of the mind."[39] Thus, reasoning has generally been identified with rationally knowing something to be true in which facts, evidence, and proof become the primary carriers of knowledge.

Today, however, contemporary research shows that reasoning is intertwined with embodiment in a natural and social world.[40] When embodiment is not taken seriously, salvation devolves into a speculative or intellectual enterprise. A soteriology that negates the role of the body dismisses the setting within which divine grace is made possible. Therefore, a disembodied epistemology leads to a disembodied faith that is inconsistent with the kind of dynamic and subjectively satisfying faith promoted and presumed within conservative Christianity.

Damasio's research opposes modern intellectualism—Christian or otherwise—and its dualisms (i.e., emotion vs. mind and emotion vs. body) that discount the somatic features of cognition. He alleges that any dualism minimizes the embodied foundation that makes cognition possible. Christian theology reveals such dualism when its view of faith privileges objective aspects of reasoning over subjective realities like feeling, emotions, affections, desires, and sociality. Damasio challenges such intellectualism by maintaining the necessity of emotions and embodiment in human cognition.

> [T]he comprehensive understanding of the human mind requires an organismic perspective; that not only must the mind move from a nonphysical cogitum to the realm of biological tissue, but

---

39. Lakoff and Johnson, *Philosophy in the Flesh*, 408.
40. Ibid., 4.

Re-Imagining Soteriology through the Cognitive Sciences

it must also be related to a whole organism possessed of integrated body proper and brain and fully interactive with a physical and social environment.[41]

So, without emotions cognition is deficient and without embodiment it is impossible.[42] Hence, an intellectualized-unembodied faith is incomplete in comparison to an embodied faith nurtured in the context of regular and strategic practices, subjective experiences, and social encounters.

Tendency Two: Equating Salvific Faith with "Right Knowledge"

Intellectualism identifies the primary function of cognition to acquire dependable knowledge and information. Though related to the first tendency, this inclination concerns the epistemological presupposition that salvation is basically about knowing the right information. This approach is evidenced in the early fundamentalist emphasis on the human ability to know God solely from an intellectual grasping of the "facts" of the Bible. Hodge's famous quote still represents the confidence of many Christians regarding the mind's ability to know God primarily on rational terms.

> The Bible is to the theologian what nature is to the man of science. It is his store-house of facts; and his method of ascertaining what the Bible teaches, is the same as that which the natural philosopher adopts to ascertain what nature teaches ... The duty of the Christian theologian is to ascertain, collect, and combine all the facts which God has revealed concerning himself and our relation to him. These facts are all in the Bible.[43]

Ascertaining facts, especially the "facts" of Scripture, most clearly illustrates this intellectualism. Mark Noll argues that Evangelicalism's commitment to objective truth and a unique "scientific" reading of the Scriptures are its most notable characteristics because they disconnect the objective from the

---

41. Damasio, *Descartes' Error*, 251.

42. For additional appropriation of Damasio on the profound role of feelings and behavior on reasoning, see Haidt, *Righteous Mind*, chapters 1–4. Haidt, a moral psychologist, cites Damasio extensively (in Part One: Intuitions Come First, Strategic Reasoning Second) to highlight the impact of emotions, behavior, and "gut feelings" on human reasoning.

43. Hodge, *Systematic Theology*, 1:10–11.

subjective functions of cognition.⁴⁴ As a respected authority, Noll's comment belies a tendency among conservative theologians to bifurcate reason from emotion or mind from body in the quest for theological knowledge and certainty. This epistemology, generally conceives emotions and behaviors independently from and subordinate to the mind.

Nonetheless, research today has discovered that much of human reasoning is unconscious and largely metaphorical and imaginative; there is no such thing as pure objective reasoning since cognition is influenced by far more than a person is ever aware.⁴⁵ Lakoff and Johnson explain.

> Reason is not disembodied . . . but arises from the nature of our brains, bodies, and bodily experience. This is not just the innocuous and obvious claim that we need a body to reason; rather, it is the striking claim that the very structure of reason itself comes from the details of our embodiment.⁴⁶

Human reasoning is accomplished, therefore, by means that involve not only what a person knows but the behavioral and affective aspects of an individual's life serve to influence his or her cognitive function. By the same measure, so too should Christians recognize—in addition to the role of objective knowledge—the inseparably vital roles of behaviors, practices, emotions, and social interactions in the mediation of saving faith. As this chapter comes to a close, let us briefly review the significance of our excursus into the cognitive sciences.

Summary: Cognitive Science, Damasio, Feuerstein, and Soteriology

In light of this research, I contend that Christian theologians should re-examine their paradigm of cognition and how the roles of emotions, practices, and behaviors apply to the divine-human encounter of salvation. Because an embodied model of cognition sees knowing as holistic (integrating subjective and objective factors), multidimensional (involving intellect, emotions, and behavior), and dynamic (expressing ongoing growth and transformation), then a broader awareness of what it means to know God should be sought. In doing so, we not only align with a more realistic

---

44. Noll, *Scandal*, 83.
45. Lakoff and Johnson, *Philosophy in the Flesh*, 4–5.
46. Ibid., 4.

understanding of how the human mind functions but we also better reflect the biblical notion of faith and its historic outworking in the church through the ages.

An Embodied Soteriology of Renewal is Dynamic and Transformational

When soteriology emphasizes attainment of indubitable knowledge, then salvation (as with cognitive function) is envisaged more as the static consequence of knowing the right information about God than as a dynamic and embodied process of ongoing transformation. Overemphasizing objective rationality minimizes the role of subjective components in salvation. Yet, such elements are essential for a healthy and life-altering realization of salvation.

Damasio's research is foundational to our soteriology because he provides convincing reasons to take the embodied nature of human cognition seriously. Though not a theologian or biblical scholar, he can help us rethink what it means for a person to know God. Just as he opposes a dualist view of the mind among various cognitive scientists, so too can he help us confront a similar dualism in an intellectualist soteriology regarding the nature of faith and the meaning of salvation. Just as Damasio shows how emotions, feelings, and the body are inseparable from cognitive function, so too can we re-consider the soteriological significance of behaviors-practices (chapters 5–6) and affections (chapters 7–8).

Feuerstein's pedagogical practices inform our understanding of how life-changing an embodied soteriology can be. Perhaps, Christian theologians, educators, and ministers can draw from Feuerstein's MLE to re-envision soteriology in a way that truly accounts for the normative influence of behavior and affectivity in the ongoing process of knowing God. Just as cognitive ability can be transformed (via MLE) so too can the quality and depth of one's faith be similarly strengthened through an embodied pedagogy. Furthermore, the theory of SCM rejects the modern intellectualist's exclusive attention on rational activity abstracted from performative relationships and behavior, and invites a more embodied and holistic pedagogy. Such pedagogical practice questions the tendency to emphasize salvation as having the right information about God's saving actions in Christ while discounting the profound influence of important subjective causes in facilitating and nurturing such salvation.

Feuerstein's research is also relevant because his articulation of cognition as transformational implies the need for a more dynamic expectation of faith in relation to salvation. For if, at a pedagogical level, affectivity and behavior can facilitate real change in learners (intellectually, emotionally, physically), then how much more should faith (also a cognitive function) be conceived in such terms? In other words, if it is misleading to speak of cognition solely in static (i.e., intellectual) terms, then it is also misguided to speak of faith with a similarly static vocabulary.

Harnessing the Soteriological Roles of Orthodoxy, Orthopraxy, and Orthopathy

I have now presented the need for an embodied soteriology in Christian theological reflection and corroborated this claim with research in contemporary cognitive science and psychology. As maintained in the beginning of chapter 1, uncritically adopting an intellectualist soteriology fosters a privileging of right thinking (orthodoxy) over right behaviors (orthopraxy), and right emotions and affections (orthopathy). Accordingly, I have argued for the rejection of such epistemological intellectualism in favor of an embodied and holistic epistemology. This will ultimately undergird our proposal of a renewal soteriology of embodiment. Therefore, if knowing God is not only an issue of obtaining and assenting to a particular set of doctrines and information about God *and* if a person's behaviors and practices together with emotions and affections are inseparable aspects of "knowing," then what might such faith actually look like?[47]

In view of all that has been presented, a soteriological paradigm is needed that integrates orthodoxy, orthopraxy, and orthopathy to effectively demonstrate the kind of embodied faith we have contended for in this chapter. The remaining chapters elaborate the meaning and implications of such a broadened and holistic conception of salvation. Chapters 3 and 4, based on epistemological presuppositions consistent with an embodied belief about cognition, will suggest an expanded notion of orthodoxy that faithfully accounts for embodiment in the process of knowing. Chapters 5 and 6 similarly expound orthopraxy and chapters 7 and 8 address orthopathy, each in a way that emphasizes an embodied and affective construal of cognition. Finally, chapters 9 and 10 pull together each chapter's

---

47. Faith is used here because of its central role in Protestant soteriology (i.e., *sola fide*).

contribution by showing how orthodoxy, orthopraxy, and orthopathy are inseparable and indispensable in the mediation of God's saving grace to and through human beings. Now, as we move forward, Part Two (Salvation and Orthodoxy) will help us rethink what it means to "rightly know God" and how such knowing relates to salvation—and this will be done in dialogue with the philosophy and theology of Jonathan Edwards.

PART TWO

Salvation and Orthodoxy

3

Jonathan Edwards and the Salvific Role of Orthodoxy

SO FAR WE HAVE exposed the tendency of practicing an intellectualist epistemology in large segments of Protestant theology and, accordingly, argued for a more embodied paradigm of saving faith that is in step with contemporary research in the cognitive neurosciences. While we have already claimed that conservative Christian soteriology has privileged the role of proper knowledge over behavior and feelings-emotions, we now recast this notion of orthodoxy in a way that resists such intellectualist impulses. To assist us, we look to a theologian of exceptional distinction who had much to say about the dynamic nature of religious knowledge—Jonathan Edwards.

Introducing Jonathan Edwards

The present chapter engages the philosophy and theology of Jonathan Edwards (1703–1758) because of his influence and renown within conservative Protestantism.[1] Edwards' elaboration of Reformed theology (*Freedom*

---

1. Jonathan Edwards was born October 5, 1703 to Rev. Timothy and Esther Stoddard Edwards. He studied languages (Latin, Greek, and Hebrew), philosophy, and natural sciences from an early age and gained his Bachelor's (1720) and Master's (1722) degrees from Connecticut's College (subsequently, Yale). Edwards served a long pastoral career, beginning in his father-in-law's church in Northampton from 1724–1750, and he was an influential leader in the Great Awakening (1734–1735). He was forced to leave his Northampton pastorate over a bitter controversy and later pastored a small frontier church in the town of Stockbridge and served as a missionary to the Native Americans of that region. In 1757 he was elected president of Princeton but died soon after from a

Part Two: Salvation and Orthodoxy

of the Will[2] and *Original Sin*), apology for evangelical revivalism (*A Faithful Narrative of the Surprising Work of God*),[3] and analysis of Christian spirituality (*Religious Affections*) were critical works that ensured his esteemed influence.[4] Today, many revere him as America's greatest religious thinker and the most significant American philosopher before the twentieth century.[5]

This chapter makes use of Edwards' theology through the lens of the cognitive sciences. While Edwards did not utilize the categories inherent in this milieu, the prominent role that "habits" and "affections" played in his theology maps well onto much of this research. This is most clearly seen in how Edwards understood *notional* and *sensible* knowledge as functioning inseparably in the human process of knowing.[6] I argue that this Edwardsean contribution is consistent with the existing neuroscientific view in which the objective and subjective functions of cognition are integrated in human reasoning.

At this point, I must clarify how "orthodoxy" is understood in our study. Recall that orthodoxy is typically envisioned by conservative Christians as an intellectual task primarily driven by rationality with minimal affective influence. I will establish that Edwards' orthodoxy is not as straight-forward as many may presume because his epistemology for "right knowing" is intimately connected with "right behavior" (orthopraxy) and "right emotions-affectivity" (orthopathy). This chapter maintains that Edwards' orthodoxy is more dynamic than normally recognized by his theological heirs. So when I speak of Edwards' *orthodoxy*, I refer not to a set of "orthodox" beliefs he embraced but to his theological epistemology regarding how humans come to know God.

In sum, the purpose of this chapter is to appropriate Edwards' theology to challenge the intellectualism of conservative Protestant theology. This will be accomplished by showing how he accounts for the saving work of the Holy Spirit in transforming human behavior and affections. In doing so, we help to recast the role of orthodoxy as part of a truly dynamic and embodied soteriological process consistent with present research in the cognitive neurosciences. The chapter concludes with discussing the

---

botched smallpox inoculation (Studebaker, *Jonathan Edwards' Social*, 1).

2. Edwards, *Freedom of the Will*.
3. Edwards, "Faithful Narrative."
4. Studebaker, *Jonathan Edwards' Social*, 1.
5. McDermott, "Introduction," 4–5.
6. These Edwardsean topics and categories are addressed later in this chapter.

promises and challenges of Edwards' ideas for a renewal soteriology of embodiment. However, before we begin, let us situate Edwards within the parameters of this study.

Edwards and Orthodoxy

There is an extremely large body of Edwardsean scholarship lying beyond the scope of our more limited concerns.[7] So, in order to get quickly to the issues at hand, I suggest our reading of Edwards is best guided by Sang Hyun Lee's Edwardsean dispositional ontology paradigm because he shows how Edwards' use of habit presumes and underwrites a dynamic epistemology and transformational soteriology. My use of Lee primarily draws from his landmark text, *The Philosophical Theology of Jonathan Edwards*.

Sang Hyun Lee's Edwardsean Dispositional Ontology

Sang Hyun Lee (b. 1938), an ordained Presbyterian minister, was the Kyung-Chik Han Professor of Systematic Theology at Princeton Theological Seminary.[8] In addition to systematic theology, Asian American theology, and theodicy, Jonathan Edwards occupies one of Lee's primary teaching and research interests. Lee is highly respected as an Edwards scholar, and his text has secured a prominent place in Edwardsean studies since its publication in 1988. One of the strengths of his dispositional approach is that it has provided a genuinely new perspective on Edwards' theology.[9] The purpose of Lee's text is to explicate Edwards' dynamic conception of God and creation through a dispositional ontology[10] within a Reformed

---

7. In regards to Edwards and philosophy, see Stephens, *The Philosophy*; Vetö, "Edwards and Philosophy," 151–70; and Leon, *Jonathan Edwards*. On Edwards and nature and/or beauty, see Zakai, *Jonathan Edwards's*; and Lee, *Philosophical Theology*. For Edwards on the Trinity, see Jenson, *America's Theologian*; Studebaker, *Jonathan Edwards' Social*; and Pauw, *Supreme Harmony*. On Edwards and original sin, see Storms, *Tragedy in Eden*; Wheeler, "Friends," 736–65; and Otto, "The Solidarity," 205–21. For Edwards and world religions, see McDermott, *Jonathan Edwards Confronts*. For Edwards and civil religion, see McDermott, *One Holy*. Finally, on Edwards and missions and/or revival, see Rooy, *Theology of Missions*; and Stout, "Edwards and Revival," 37–52.

8. Lee holds a Bachelor of Sacred Theology from Harvard Divinity School and a PhD from Harvard University.

9. Stein, "Philosophical Theology," 100–102.

10. Ontology is a sub-discipline of metaphysics (which is a branch of philosophy)

Protestant framework. In chapter 1, Lee overviews the term "habit"[11] and introduces Edwards' dynamic vision of reality as dispositional. Lee, in chapter 2, historically situates and distinguishes Edwards' notion of habit within the eighteenth-century context. Chapters 3 and 4 develop Edwards' dispositional ontology while chapters 5 and 6 clarify his epistemology and emphasize the ontological productivity of the imagination. Chapter 7 details Edwards' dispositional re-conception of the Trinity while focusing on the divine essence as both actual and becoming. Chapter 8 concludes with temporal and historical connotations of Edwards' dispositional ontology.

Lee maintains that habit or disposition functions as the most innovative element in Edwards' theology and by it he replaced the Western metaphysics of substance with a "dynamic network of dispositional forces and habits."[12] He claims that re-conceiving God has been a major challenge for modern theology as it has reacted against classical theism's prime emphasis on the changelessness of God while looking for more dynamic descriptors of the Godhead. Lee argues that Edwards' dispositional paradigm is capable of accounting for the dynamic character of God's being without "compromising God's prior potentiality" (i.e., changelessness).[13] Lee holds that such a dispositional ontology provides the interpretive key for ascertaining the logic of Edwards' theological reflections.[14]

In addition to presenting Lee's dispositional ontology, it is also necessary to justify his use of the word "disposition" since this term carries a variety of meanings in the modern setting. While dispositions are considered the typical moods or attitudes people exhibit in their lives, they carry other connotations in different academic disciplines. In virtue ethics, dispositions are defined as certain responses typical in certain situations. In Christian moral ethics, dispositions are the human orientations of love either to God or idols.[15] And in developmental psychology, dispositions are often

---

referring to the study of the nature of being, an entity's fundamental essence and its relationship to that essence. For a more detailed description of ontology and some of the challenges associated with this area of study, see the online Stanford Encyclopedia of Philosophy, under the section "3. Ontology" (http://plato.stanford.edu/entries/logic-ontology/). For our purposes, we are interested in Edwards' dispositional ontology which refers to his way of explaining the nature of human existence and how it relates to salvation.

11. Lee often exchanges "habit" for "disposition."
12. Lee, *Philosophical Theology*, 4.
13. Ibid., 6.
14. Ibid.
15. See, Yeager, "On Making," 105.

associated with motivations.[16] Dispositions or habits are even referenced in quantum mechanics research and chaos theory.[17] Some have developed actual theories of habits or dispositions based on such research.[18] Accordingly, the "laws of nature" as fairly exact determiners of events are becoming increasingly questioned as randomness, variation, and dynamism are now seen to better account for actions in the physical world. The idea of *habits, tendencies, powers,* or *capacities* are ways that physicists and philosophers of science are speaking of the laws of nature in ways that are not mechanistic or deterministic but as an open, dynamic, and varying system.[19] In light of this broad intellectual terrain, Lee provides his own interpretation of Edwards' concept of habit.

> Habit, therefore, is not the thoughtless way in which a sort of activity is mechanically carried out. The habit of mind, for Edwards, functions as the very possibility of rationality and moral action ... Through habit, knowing is connected with being and becoming.[20]

Far more than a well-rehearsed activity or automatic behavior, disposition is a reinforced way of being in the world that is mentally, behaviorally, and affectively integrated all at the same time. Consequently, Lee contends that Edwards envisions disposition as ontologically constitutive of the human person. He claims that habit or disposition, then, is a chief element in Edwards' epistemology. For Edwards, knowing is much more than merely acquiring information but is intricately linked to a dispositional ontology that conceives being and knowing in dynamic terms. Finally, while I recognize that Lee's dispositional framework is just one of numerous ways to comprehend Edwards' theology, it is, nevertheless, useful for revealing the dynamic and transformational implications of his theology of affections (which are fundamental to his soteriology). Nonetheless, let us consider

---

16. See, Perkins et al., "Beyond Abilities," 1–21.

17. See, Yong, "Natural Laws," 976–78.

18. For specific examples see: Cartwright, *How the Laws*; Molnar, *Powers*; and Mumford, *Dispositions* and *Laws in Nature*.

19. The American scientist and philosopher, Charles Sanders Pierce (1839–1914) employed the notion of "habit" as a general tendency arising from evolutionary development. He believed that habits are the basis from which the laws of nature eventually arise. For an introduction to Pierce's understanding of habits see, Rosenthal, "Meaning as Habit," 230–45.

20. Lee, *Philosophical Theology*, 8.

some of the primary arguments against Lee's interpretation of Edwards' metaphysics and then respond to these challenges.

Lee's Critics

One of the first significant critiques of Lee's dispositional ontology was by the English historical theologian, Stephen R. Holmes, who denied that Edwards ever embraced a dispositional ontology. Holmes argues that if Edwards did, then it would have required an unorthodox doctrine of God.[21]

> A "dispositional" account of God, inasmuch as it demands that there is unfulfilled potential in God's life, and so the possibility of God's "self-enlargement" or "increase," would have been unthinkable to Edwards. Jonathan Edwards did not use a dispositional ontology.[22]

Holmes reasons that a dispositional God is an "unfulfilled God." Yet, Lee does not speak of the divine triad as unfulfilled and *needing* "self-enlargement" but rather that God's self-enlargement has more to do with God's manifestation in a physical world of time and space, as opposed to the unlimited and infinite display of his being within the divine triad. Lee affirms that Edwards' dispositional ontology directly flows from his model of the divine triad.[23] Failure to understand this relationship will compromise foundational Reformed doctrine, something which Edwards was committed to upholding. Surely, Lee's doctrine of God (i.e., Trinity) would be unorthodox, if his dispositional ontology was presenting an "unfilled" God.

The British philosophical and historical theologian Oliver Crisp takes issue with Lee's assertion that Edwards *totally* rejected any form of substance, even regarding the nature of God. Crisp contends that in addition to a dispositional ontology, Edwards also held to an essentialist metaphysics,[24]

---

21. See Holmes, "Does Jonathan Edwards," 99–114.

22. Ibid., 108.

23. Lee, *Philosophical Theology*, 185–90. Lee directly addresses the issue of God's self-enlargement in chapter 7, "The Increasing Fullness of the Divine Being."

24. An essentialist metaphysics is a philosophical theory that ontologically allows for some sort of material substance, which in Edwards' case, Crisp argues would be an "immaterial substance."

Jonathan Edwards and the Salvific Role of Orthodoxy

mental phenomenalism,[25] and a doctrine of occasionalism[26] as he utilized various philosophical thoughts of his day.[27] Hence, Crisp does *not* deny that Edwards supposed all entities have dispositional properties but rather that *all* of those properties *must be* dispositional. So, for the purpose of this study, Crisp's allowance of dispositions in Edwards' ontology is a significant point because the issue at stake for Crisp is not that Edwards' employed a dispositional ontology but that his ontology was *only* dispositional. Therefore, Crisp's assessment of Lee does not challenge my appropriation of Lee because a dispositional ontology (even if only one ontology among others) necessarily presumes a dynamic—not static—operation of the mind. In other words, *knowing*—for Edwards—is embodied, dynamic, and transformational because intellect, emotion, and behavior are integrated elements of a dispositional ontology. On this account, Edwards' ontology (even if partially dispositional) requires the dynamic integration of multiple cognitive elements, not just intellect.

Another critique, by Crisp, against Lee's ontology is that Edwards actually used the word "substance" thereby, negating Lee's definition of disposition totally replacing substance.[28] However, Lee explains that when Edwards used "substance" he meant something wholly new. For instance, Edwards says, "The substance of bodies at last becomes either nothing, or nothing but the Deity acting in that particular manner in parts of space where he thinks fit. So that, speaking most strictly, there is no proper substance but God himself."[29] Lee clarifies that when the term "substance" is used by Edwards it refers to God's "dynamic activity of resisting" in which his power via the natural laws and habits causes the atoms of all substances to resist the separation of its parts.[30]

> Edwards sees God's activity as constituting the very being of the scientifically conceived atoms and their motions. Atoms as resistances are none other than God's own activity, and the laws of the

---

25. Mental phenomenalism is a philosophical theory in which all matter ultimately consists of ideas or as the sensory perceptions of mental operations.

26. Occasionalism is a philosophical theory stating that God creates the world *ex nihilo* in a series of ongoing repetitive moments, in order to secure that he is always the cause of all things.

27. Crisp, "Jonathan Edwards's Ontology," 1–20.

28. Ibid., 2, and endnotes 18, 33.

29. Edwards, "Of Atoms," 215.

30. Lee, *Philosophical Theology*, 52–54.

motions of those atoms are none other than "the stated methods of God's acting with respect to bodies."[31]

So, *substance* is another name for the dynamic power of God's activity via natural laws of creation he has set in place.[32]

James Hoopes contests Lee's dispositional ontology in stating that he was forcing metaphysical suppositions out of Edwards' theology rather than his metaphysics.[33] Lee though, makes clear that Edwards synthesized many of the philosophical notions of his day and that such thinking was reflected in his theology.

> He attempted to renew the original spirit of the trinitarian doctrine without ignoring the urgent philosophical issues of the Enlightenment. One aspect of Edwards' greatness as a theologian was that he did not merely study or oppose certain philosophical ideas and issues of his day but constructively offered possible solutions to them in philosophical and theological terms.[34]

Lee declares that Edwards' commitment was to Scripture, not philosophy, and all his philosophical assertions were made to help elucidate difficult concepts in the Bible, especially the Trinity.[35] Lee contends that Edwards' discussion of the Trinity is "a further manifestation of what divine truth the Word of God exhibits."[36] Hoopes also alleges that Lee is forcing a particular metaphysics on Edwards that even contradicts Edwards' own words.[37] I submit that Hoopes' evaluation is based on a "partial reading"[38] of Edwards'

---

31. Ibid., 54. Quoted is, Edwards, "Of Atoms," 216.

32. Lee, *Philosophical Theology*, 52–54. It is interesting to note how Edwards' dispositional metaphysics sounds similar in many respects to the language of quantum mechanics and chaos theory as referenced in contemporary views of "disposition" in the field of physics. McDermott comments, "He [Edwards] anticipated post-Newtonian physics, in which all matter is ultimately seen in terms of interacting fields of energy, with every part dependent on every other part, and the forces governing these rather mysterious. Physicists have been concluding for almost a century what Edwards declared two and a half centuries ago: there are no independent substances that can subsist on their own" (McDermott, "Introduction," 8).

33. Hoopes, "Philosophical Theology," 258.

34. Lee, "Christian Doctrine," 2–6.

35. Lee, "Edwards's Dispositional Conception," 9.

36. Ibid.

37. Hoopes, "Philosophical Theology," 258.

38. I later contend that such a partial reading (not only of Hoopes, but of others who try to interpret and utilize Edwards' theology) is probably the result of failing to

writings because Lee adequately addresses such "contradictions" in his explication of an Edwardsean dispositional ontology.[39]

In light of these critiques and the justifications provided, I propose that my utilization of Lee's dispositional ontology is warranted, especially since few of his critics would deny that Edwards endorsed some sort of dispositional ontology. The findings of this study are not compromised if Edwards' metaphysics was only partially dispositional because my epistemological and soteriological conclusions do not require wholesale endorsement of dispositions over substance. As stated earlier, even a partial dispositional ontology requires an epistemology that accounts for knowing in dispositional (and, thus, dynamic) terms. Nonetheless, I conclude that a partial reading of Edwards that fails to take seriously his dispositional ontology compromises the dynamic and transformational implications of his orthodoxy.[40] In order to further understand Edwards' theology, let's now situate him in the influential religious context (Deism) of his day.

Edwardsean "Orthodoxy" in Eighteenth-Century Deist Context

An accurate grasp of Edwards' orthodoxy requires awareness of eighteenth-century Deism. Edwards contradicted the Enlightenment mindset of his day as seen in Deism whereby knowledge of God came by the mind's access to universal common reason. Toward this end, rationality played the primary role and the affections were largely eschewed in this form of intellectualism.[41] Steven Studebaker holds that much of Edwards' theological efforts were spent combating the growing influence of Enlightenment Deism because of its overemphasis on human reason and rejection of written

---

thoroughly consider Edwards' understanding of the Trinity and the prominent role the Spirit plays in the *ad extra* communication of God's love and beauty.

39. See, Lee, *Philosophical Theology*, "The Idea of Habit," chapter 2, and "Being as Habit," chapter 3.

40. Despite that I have focused on critics of Lee's dispositional ontology in this section, there are many Edwardsean scholars who endorse Lee's dispositional paradigm. Among them are: McDermott, *One Holy*, chapter 3; Morimoto, *Jonathan Edwards*, passim; Studebaker, *Jonathan Edwards' Social*, 201 n. 229; Pauw, *Supreme Harmony*, 88–89; Daniel, *The Philosophy*; and Boyd, *Trinity and Process*.

41. Studebaker, *Jonathan Edwards' Social*, 210–11. Two influential Deist texts on the prominent role of reason are: Herbert of Cherbury, *De Veritate*, 289–307; and Toland, *Christianity not Mysterious*, 67–176.

revelation.⁴² The Deists affirmed that all human activity springs from either good or bad thinking but Edwards insisted that the motivation for such activity lies deeper than the mind. Rather, he offered that all human feeling, thinking, and acting are rooted in "dispositions."⁴³ Consequently, the Deist challenge led Edwards to articulate a paradigm of Christian orthodoxy that harmonized the intellectual, affective, and behavioral features of human knowing in a way that did not set the head against the heart. Gerald McDermott explains:

> On conversion, he avoids the dichotomy of head (beliefs as the best test of salvation) versus heart (it's a matter of how you feel about Jesus), saying that the heart of true spirituality is what he called the "affections," which are the basic inclinations of the soul, the root of everything we think, feel, and choose.⁴⁴

Hence, Edwards' utilization of orthodoxy flowed from a dispositional ontology in which the affections played a cardinal role.⁴⁵ With the preceding in mind, I refer to Edwards' theological epistemology as a "dispositional orthodoxy."

Finally, having established the parameters for my appropriation of Edwards, I can now develop how an Edwardsean dispositional orthodoxy can help expand the intellectualist rendering of orthodoxy commonly presumed within conservative Christianity. However, before launching forward, I first provide some background to Edwards' use of the term "habit" within his eighteenth-century context. Only then can we understand the critical role Edwards' ontology plays in relation to his epistemology and soteriology.

Edwards' Use of Habit-Disposition

Edwards borrowed "habit" from Aristotle (384–322 BC), who defined it as the deliberate or active tendency to a certain type of behavior.⁴⁶ Aris-

---

42. Studebaker, *Jonathan Edwards' Social*, 5.
43. McDermott, "Introduction," 6.
44. McDermott, "Conclusion," 203.
45. Studebaker refers to this as an intellectualist adaptation of Augustinian voluntarianism (though he uses the term "intellectualist" differently than I do in chapter 1) in Studebaker and Caldwell, *Trinitarian Theology*, 204. Also, see, Studebaker, *Jonathan Edwards' Social*, 142–67.
46. Aristotle, *Metaphysics*, 94.

totle (and Edwards) rejected the notion of habit as merely a custom.[47] Yet, Edwards went beyond Aristotle by concluding that God is the ultimate habit from which all others derive. Edwards also drew from Thomas Aquinas' (1225–1274) expansion of habit to include the supernatural perfection of human abilities through grace.[48] This Thomist extension enabled Edwards to reject both the Neoplatonic interpretation (postulated by the seventeenth-century Cambridge philosophers) that contrasted habit with eternal realities, and the empiricist approach that generally reduced habit to a mere custom.[49] In addition, the empiricism of Sir Isaac Newton's (1642–1727) universal physical laws (i.e., gravity) and John Locke's (1632–1704) explication of sense experience as paramount in the cognitive process both seem to have influenced Edwards' epistemology.[50] Edwards masterfully synthesized the theological and philosophical insights of his predecessors and contemporaries while adding his own contribution. Ultimately, his ontology of habit (hereafter, dispositional ontology) dynamically characterized human life and its potential for a transforming relationship with God. This dispositional ontology eventually took full bloom in Edwards' theology of the affections.

Lee posits Edwards' dispositional ontology as an improvement on classical theism's accent on the "unchangeability and self-sufficiency" of God and process theology's later focus on God's perpetual actualization. The former presents an overly static idea of God while the latter an overly dynamic one that compromises God's "perfect actuality."[51] In navigating a way beyond the confines of these theologies, Lee offers that Edwards redefines the Aristotelian and Scholastic worldviews by embracing much of the growing influence of both Newton and Locke in his own day while still adding to their contributions.[52] As we move forward, our guiding presupposition is that Edwards' dispositional ontology resists the reduction of orthodoxy to the present intellectualism of conservative Protestant theology.

---

47. Lee, *Philosophical Theology*, 17.

48. Aquinas, *Summa Theologica*, 20:7–8. See also, Lee, *Philosophical Theology*, 20–22.

49. Lee, *Philosophical Theology*, 22.

50. Cherry, *Theology of Jonathan Edwards*, 18.

51. Lee, *Philosophical Theology*, 4.

52. Ibid., 17.

PART TWO: SALVATION AND ORTHODOXY

EDWARDS' DISPOSITIONAL ORTHODOXY IN THEOLOGICAL PERSPECTIVE

We begin with an explication of Edwards' dispositional or habit-formed orthodoxy. Specifically, this requires a description of the three main components of his orthodoxy—dispositional ontology, dispositional epistemology, and a dispositional soteriology. Altogether, this lays the groundwork for the soteriological role of his religious affections. Though we have already referred to Edwards' dispositional ontology, we now clarify what exactly this is and how it relates to our purposes.

Edwards' Dispositional Ontology

In view of the previous exposition of Edwards' use of habit I now discuss his ontology as it influenced his orthodoxy. Therefore, to better grasp Edwards' ontology of dispositions, I distinguish two of its primary characteristics.

First, the actualization of being in Edwards' dispositional ontology occurs by means of radical relationality. This means that the essence of an entity's existence is not an immaterial substance but a nexus of law-like relationships. Lee elaborates the difference between an Aristotelian ontology and Edwards' dispositional ontology (of radical relationality).

> For Aristotle, an individual entity first exists and, in so existing, already is what it must be to be what it is—a human being, an animal, or a tree. Relations, in other words, are external to the being of entities. But in Edwards' ontology, relations are internal to being. Relations are elevated to the level of the substantial form. Being is being-in-relation. In short, habits and laws constitute *what* being is on its deepest level.[53]

Edwards diverges from classical Western ontology in that he contends the basis from which activities follow does not come from an individualized form or substance but from law-like relationships called dispositions.[54] Edwards writes, "For being, if we examine narrowly, is nothing else but proportion."[55] Dispositions are active laws and powers set in place by God to act in specific ways under certain conditions, "All habits [are] a law that

---

53. Ibid., 78.
54. Ibid., 42.
55. Edwards, "The Mind," 336.

God has fixed, that such actions upon such occasions *should* be exerted."[56] Lee explains that when Edwards speaks of an entity's structure as a law or habit,

> ... he is refusing to think of the what-ness of things in terms of individual, particulate forms. He is rather contending that the what-ness of entities can be conceived only in terms of their relations. *How* an entity is related with other entities is determinative of *what* that entity is.[57]

In other words, it is the content of laws of relations that determine the essence of a being's nature.[58]

In Edwards' dispositional ontology, not only is the nature of things realized as what they are through the actions derived from their dispositions but these things *only exist* through their dispositions. As previously mentioned, this assertion by Lee about Edwards' ontology was probably the most recurring challenge among Lee's critics. Yet, Edwards specifically proposed that the essence of *all* things are to be found in a complex interrelation of laws or dispositions. Such was addressed in a section of Edwards' notes called "Subjects to Be Handled in the Treatise on the Mind": "How *it is laws that constitute all permanent being in created things, both corporeal and spiritual.* In how many respects *the very being of created things depend on laws*, or stated methods fixed by God, of events following one another."[59] So, radical relationality, as the complex interplay between the myriad laws God has set in place, actualizes the essence of an entity's being.

When speaking about the soul, Edwards says the same again via the terminology of powers and habits, the "[soul's] essence consists in powers and habits."[60] For Edwards, the nature of an entity is bound up not in some type of metaphysical substance (i.e., an immaterial soul/spirit) but as a bundle of tendencies or dispositions (i.e., powers and habits) which both define the nature of an entity and direct its actions.[61] Again, Edwards deemed that dispositions are "something really abiding in the mind when there are no acts or exercises of them much in the same manner as there is a chair in

---

56. Edwards, "Regeneration," 358.
57. Lee, *Philosophical Theology*, 77–78. Emphasis original.
58. Ibid., 79.
59. Edwards, "Subjects to be Handled," 391–92. Emphasis added.
60. Edwards, "Regeneration," 358.
61. Lee, "Edwards and Beauty," 121.

this room when no mortal perceives it."[62] In other words, dispositions still exist even when they are not presently engaged because they are possibilities not yet acted upon. Yet, some will contend that such contradicts our statement about radical relationality as central to Edwards' ontology. For how can a disposition really exist as just "possibility" in which the relational circumstances are not present for their actuation? However, as we shall see, Edwards conceived God as the ultimate disposition from which all created entities derive their being (as dispositional). Such is spelled out in Edwards' notions of God's being and activity *ad intra* and *ad extra* wherein actuality and possibility coincide. Hence a disposition as possibility can still exist, even when isolated from physical circumstances because all dispositions (whether actual or potential) ultimately derive their existence from God, who is the divine disposition eternally existing as perfect relationality via the eternal Trinitarian Godhead. In this manner, dispositions play the role in Edwards' ontology that substance plays in Western thought and are able to explain the permanent nature of an entity's ongoing existence.[63] A dispositional ontology, then, accounts not only for the actuality of dispositions but also their potentiality.

Edwards' dispositional ontology flows from his theology—God is the divine disposition who communicates his goodness and beauty.[64] Edwards postulated that the "disposition in God . . . to [communicate] an emanation of his own infinite fullness, was what excited him to create the world."[65] Furthermore, all the laws of the universe are a unified system that stem from and are dependent on the communication of God. In this sense, an individual, as dispositionally constituted, only exists in relation to all other entities as one part of a unified whole. Edwards imagined that, "The world was made to have all the parts of it nicely hanging together and sweetly harmonious and corresponding."[66] God's inclination to communicate provides the ontological underpinning for all of creation. All created entities exist as an infinitely complex interplay of divinely sanctioned laws and systems of laws that subsist inter-relationally.[67]

62. Edwards, "The Mind," 385.
63. Lee, "Edwards's Dispositional Conception," 447.
64. Lee, "Edwards and Beauty," 116.
65. Edwards, "Concerning the End," 435.
66. Edwards, "Devotion," 189.
67. Studebaker holds that God's disposition to self-communicate his divine nature is probably the most indispensable conviction in Edwards' thought (Studebaker, *Jonathan*

Jonathan Edwards and the Salvific Role of Orthodoxy

Second, ongoing transformation marks the nature of being in Edwards' *dispositional ontology.* He conceptualizes being as both possibility and actuality; consequently, dispositions exist even prior to their actualization in time and space. However, as a Reformed theologian this presented an obstacle for Edwards. He needed to express how God (as the divine disposition) can be both possibility and actuality without compromising divine sovereignty as the "full . . . and final ground of all reality"; otherwise, God would be discredited by a principle of prior potentiality.[68] In other words, if God is envisaged in dispositional terms describing increasing degrees of actualization, then how can the Godhead not be conceived as less sovereign and supreme at a prior point in time than a later point? Such reasoning seems to contradict the absolute sovereignty of God. Or does it?

Edwards resolved this dilemma by offering that possibility and actuality coincide in God.[69] He maintained that God's nature as divine disposition *ad intra* (within the Trinity) is perfect actuality. Edwards stated that God is, "self-existent from eternity, absolutely perfect in himself, in the possession of infinite and independent good [and] above all need and all capacity of being added to and advanced, made better and happier in any respect."[70] Yet, since God's communication *ad extra* (outside the Trinity) concerning creation cannot convey perfect actuality due to the historical and temporal limitations of the physical world, it is realized as ongoing possibility. Thus, creation is "an inclination in God to cause his *internal* glory to flow out *ad extra.*"[71] Again, Edwards refers to these two modes of communication:

> These two ways of the divine good beaming forth are agreeable to the two ways of the divine essence flowing out or proceeding from eternity within the Godhead in the person of the Son and Holy Spirit: the one in an expression of his glory, in the idea or knowledge of it; the other the flowing out of the essence in love and joy. It is condecent that, correspondent to these proceedings of the divinity *ad intra*, God should also flow forth *ad extra.*[72]

Edwards' Social, 136).

68. Lee, "Edwards's Dispositional Conception," 448.

69. Ibid.

70. Edwards, "Concerning the End," 420.

71. Edwards, "End of the Creation," 496. Emphasis added.

72. Edwards, "End of the Creation," 153. For another example of Edwards' use of *ad intra* and *ad extra* divine communication see Edwards, "On the Equality," 146. Also, see Lee, *Philosophical Theology*, 196–201.

Because God, who is the divine disposition of perfect fullness, eternally communicates himself *ad extra*, this communication presumes the possibility of perpetual increase. The *ad extra* divine communication as an eternally progressing possibility is never equivalent to the *ad intra* communication but is always approaching perfect realization. In this way, possibility does not have to imply that there was a time in which God was not perfectly actualized because such remains an economic expression reflecting, but never exhausting, the immanent Trinity. Lee similarly states, "The consequence of Edwards' view is that being is incremental, and habit or disposition is the principle of ontological increase."[73] The very nature of God, as the divine disposition to communicate himself *ad extra*, requires infinite ontological growth for creation because this communication naturally aims for absolute actualization when existing in the physical world of time and space.[74] Hence, Edwards' dispositional ontology does not have to endorse an unorthodox doctrine of God, as some of his critics insist is inevitable. As will soon be shown, such ontological increase accounts for the ongoing transformational potential of divine grace in the believer through the religious affections.[75]

So far we have examined the basis of Edwards' dispositional ontology and how it ensues from his theology of the Trinity whereby God as the ultimate disposition is inclined to ever communicate his glory both *ad intra* within the Godhead and *ad extra* towards creation. Before addressing Edwards' soteriology we must first observe the dynamic character of his epistemology and see how his conception of orthodoxy often differs from that used in conservative Christianity.

Edwards' Dispositional Epistemology

Now, we look at the act of knowing or understanding within Edwards' dispositional orthodoxy and how it assists a broader perspective of orthodoxy. First, I reflect on Edwards' concept of the Trinity and how it allows for the possibility of knowing God as the Spirit mediates the *ad extra* communication to humanity. Then I examine how the sensory nature of knowledge within Edwards' epistemology presents knowing as both an integrated (rational and affective) and embodied (experiential) actuality. Together

---

73. Lee, *Philosophical Theology*, 108.
74. Lee, "Edwards's Dispositional Conception," 447.
75. See, Studebaker and Caldwell, *Trinitarian Theology*, 198–99.

Jonathan Edwards and the Salvific Role of Orthodoxy

these findings indicate a broadened meaning of orthodoxy beyond the constraints of an intellectualist theological epistemology.

Studebaker affirms that Edwards' perception of the Trinity undergirded his epistemology. While often presumed an offshoot of the Western psychological Trinitarian tradition, Studebaker contends that Edwards' Social Augustinian Mutual Love model is its own distinct tradition.[76] Within this scheme, one's understanding of the Trinity is grounded on the conviction that God communicates his divine goodness and beauty to creation by the Holy Spirit who is the mutual love of the Father and the Son. This *ad extra* communication of the Godhead mirrors its *ad intra* communication whereby the Holy Spirit in both modalities is the love of God between the Father and the Son.[77] Edwards says the same, "the emanation or communication (*ad extra*) is of the internal glory or fullness of God, *as it is*."[78] Therefore, just as the Spirit subsists within the Godhead as the mutual love of the Father and Son (*ad intra*), so too the Spirit exists (*ad extra*) to reveal the love of God to all of creation.[79] In such a manner, Edwards put forth that the *ad extra* communication was a "repetition" or "multiplication" of the *ad intra* communication.[80] It follows that in Edwards' epistemology, the *ad extra* communication of the Spirit fosters knowledge of God, which follows from awareness of his love and beauty.[81] Studebaker maintains that Edwards' epistemology unfolded from this Trinitarian representation: "The economic order reflects the immanent order of subsistence because the economic Trinity is the *ad extra* communication of divine goodness, which is the social love realized in the fellowship of the Trinitarian God."[82] So, all knowing ultimately flows from the Spirit expressing the love of God through countless expressions and means.

Edwards' Trinitarian beliefs also correlated with his psychology. Later we will see how these two areas critically shaped his epistemology. In Edwards' psychology, the human mind images the Father (who is the self-subsistent divine person) and the mind also mirrors the Trinity via

---

76. Studebaker, *Jonathan Edwards' Social*, 104.

77. Ibid., 200.

78. Edwards, "Concerning the End," 528. Emphasis added.

79. Studebaker, "Jonathan Edwards' Pneumatological Concept," 329. See also, Studebaker and Caldwell, *Trinitarian Theology*, 197–200.

80. Edwards, "Concerning the End," 433.

81. Edwards, "End of the Creation," 153.

82. Studebaker, *Jonathan Edwards' Social*, 200.

the modalities of *understanding* and *will*.⁸³ Edwards wrote, "yet our souls are made in the image of God: we have understanding and will, idea and love, as God hath, and the difference is only in the perfection of degree and manner."⁸⁴ Understanding identifies with the Son, who subsists as the "perfect idea of God," and will with the Spirit, who subsists as the mutual love of the Father and the Son.⁸⁵ Studebaker explains, "Edwards' teaching that the human soul is the image of the Trinity suggests a hermeneutical principle of reciprocity: as the soul reflects the Trinity, so the Trinity reflects the soul."⁸⁶ Such reciprocity shows how the human soul receives God's *ad extra* communication of the knowledge of the Son and divine love through the Spirit to both know and love God in return.⁸⁷ In other words, Edwards believed that all human knowledge is the direct result of God's ever-flowing communication of love by the Spirit. This is why we say Edwards' concept of the mind (his psychology) unfolds from his theology of the Godhead (the Trinity). All of this highlights the relevant point—for Edwards, there is a theological basis for all knowledge. We now explicate his view of the mind.

Just as the inner-Trinitarian persons of the Godhead are inseparable, so too does the mind or soul—Edwards regularly used the word "soul" and "mind" interchangeably—holistically consist of the understanding and will. For Edwards, *understanding* is capable of discerning, judging, and speculation, while the *will* is capable of being inclined toward or averse from that which it perceives.⁸⁸ Furthermore, just as the *ad intra* communication is an integrated divine disposition, the understanding and will should not be thought of as independent operations or functions but as fluid dispositional "powers" of the soul always operating in concert.⁸⁹ Additionally, Edwards associates even more dispositional qualities with the soul; he calls these affections and sees them arising as an operation of the will. He explains that the affections are "no other than the more vigorous and sensible exercises of the inclination and will of the soul."⁹⁰ Thus, the affections are *not* the

---

83. Ibid., 166–67.
84. Edwards, "Discourse on the Trinity," 113.
85. Studebaker, *Jonathan Edwards' Social*, 167.
86. Ibid., 166.
87. Studebaker, "Jonathan Edwards' Pneumatological Concept," 330 n. 36.
88. Edwards, "Religious Affections," 96.
89. Studebaker, *Jonathan Edwards' Social*, 160–61.
90. Edwards, "Religious Affections," 96.

fundamental disposition of the soul but arise as an operation of the exercise of the will. Because the mind mirrors the dispositional nature of God who communicates his love through the Spirit, the affections are the mind-soul's dispositional expression through which the Spirit can actualize the love of God. Edwards saw the human psyche as dispositionally grounded, from which all thinking, feeling, and acting derive.[91] For this reason, Edwards conceived the affections as not a separate faculty of the will but an articulation of its activity.

> [B]ut all the actings of the inclination and will, in our common actions of life, are not ordinarily called affections. Yet, what are commonly called affections are not essentially different from them, but only in the degree and manner of exercise.[92]

In Edwards' epistemology, the understanding (i.e., knowledge) and the will (i.e., motivation and behavior) serve together as a singular dispositional modality of the human mind. Because the affections are inseparable from the will—serving as a consistent expression of the will—they represent an important component in Edwards' epistemology. Since the Spirit's economic presence correlates with the affections (as part of the will) then the Spirit's ministry intimately relates to any activity involving the affections, which is the manifestation of dispositional transformation.

> The communication of the Spirit is prior to the knowledge of the Son because the Spirit must transform the dispositional orientation of the person before the person can apprehend the Son in faith. Edwards taught that a person's act of faith in Christ derives from the presence of the Spirit as divine love.[93]

Edwards conceived the Holy Spirit's role of communicating divine love as a consequence of dispositional transformation (and hence, reception of religious affections) to be the most vital aspect of God's salvific communication *ad extra* to the human soul. Edwards' soteriology, then, is incomprehensible without grasping his theology of the affections.

So far, I have discussed Edwards' dispositional epistemology as deriving from his Mutual Love Model of the Trinity and its correlation with his mind-understanding-will psychology for expounding the possibility of knowing God. The Spirit is central within this epistemological context,

---

91. McDermott, "Introduction," 6–7.
92. Edwards, "Religious Affections," 97.
93. Studebaker, "Jonathan Edwards' Pneumatological Concept," 330.

serving as the *ad extra* divine communication enabling dispositional transformation realized through the affections. Hence, I have established that a vibrant pneumatology undergirds Edwards' epistemology. This will become especially relevant later when I begin to exposit Edwards' dispositional soteriology. Nevertheless, it is now necessary to move from *how* Edwards justified the possibility of knowing God to his *description of* this knowledge.

Edwards alleged that God appeals to the sensory nature of human experience through the Spirit to impart knowledge of himself (which Edwards identifies with divine love and beauty). Consequently, he envisioned knowledge as two aspects of the body's perceiving and engaging the world—*notional* and *sensible* knowledge.[94] As we shall see, these two dimensions depend upon each other.

Notional knowledge is "merely the speculative faculty, or the understanding strictly so-called, or as spoken in distinction from the will or disposition of the soul."[95] Miklos Vetö describes the detached character of notional knowledge, "A notional understanding can determine objectively that an action or feeling is good or bad, it has no true 'sense' of what makes the bad bad or the good good; a true understanding of what constitutes the goodness of the good and the evilness of evil remains beyond its reach."[96] So, notional knowledge requires rational and logical reasoning.

Sensible knowledge, though, requires another form of reasoning. It has to do with the mind's ability to take pleasure in or dislike a particular thing. Sensible knowledge is distinct from notional knowledge because it is experientially based, not rationally defined.[97] Edwards compared sensible knowledge with notional knowledge through the analogy of tasting honey.

> There is a difference between having a rational judgment that honey is sweet, and having a sense of its sweetness. A man may have the former, that knows not how honey tastes; but a man can't have the latter, unless he has an idea of the taste of honey in his

---

94. The idea of notional and sensible knowledge does not seem unique to Edwards because John Calvin previously spoke of "speculative" and "spiritual" knowledge in regard to Scripture (Calvin, *Institutes*, 3.2.3). However, the way Edwards used "speculative" (notional) knowledge and spiritual knowledge as a consequence of the "new sense" and only being available to the regenerate via the Holy Spirit, appears to be his unique contribution (Nichols, *An Absolute Sort*, 57–58).

95. Edwards, "A Divine and Supernatural," 111.

96. Vetö, "Edwards and Philosophy," 160.

97. Studebaker, *Jonathan Edwards' Social*, 164.

mind . . . The former rests only in the head, speculation only is concerned in it; but the heart is concerned in the latter.[98]

Sensible knowledge facilitates a *first-hand-personal-experience* type of knowing that results in an individual feeling pleasure or displeasure over what has been learned. Yet, Edwards is clear that though these types of knowledge are different, they do not function separately but are related to a person's experience of God's beauty.[99] Nichols explains that Edwards embraced a covenantal view of knowledge. Though he distinguished notional and sensible knowledge, they are not two different kinds of knowledge but rather one's knowledge is influenced by one's relationship to the Spirit.[100]

In Edwards' epistemology, sensible knowledge has to do with the mind's ability to take simple (or sense) ideas (i.e., direct data via the five senses) and order them in a way that exists harmoniously with each other. Through repeated practice the mind attains a basic habit or disposition to automatically order these ideas.[101] Such ordering of sense ideas leads to an experientially oriented type of knowledge. Yet, because of original sin humans are blind to God's beauty in the world and do not have a natural disposition to order such beautiful ideas in a harmonious manner so as to actually experience divine beauty.[102] Before the Fall, humans had this disposition, but afterwards it was lost and could not be restored by human effort.[103] Edwards attested that without grace the mind is unable to order such ideas to identify the beauty of God and thereby gain saving faith.[104]

Edwards also distinguished two types of sensible knowledge—*physical* and *spiritual*. Physical knowledge follows from one's natural senses as the mind orders physical data from the natural world and makes it comprehensible. However, spiritual knowledge also requires the senses, but is of an entirely different nature. Spiritual knowledge comes directly from the Holy Spirit who enables one to know the true darkness of evil and the genuine loveliness of the good. Apart from spiritual knowledge sensible knowledge only deals with the natural physical senses and the pleasure or displeasure they bring to an individual. The spiritual knowledge that comes by the gift

---

98. Edwards, "A Divine and Supernatural," 111–12.
99. Edwards, "A Spiritual Understanding," 76.
100. Nichols, *An Absolute Sort*, 45.
101. Edwards, "Subjects to be Handled," 391–92.
102. Lee, "Edwards and Beauty," 119.
103. Edwards, "Part Four, Chapter Two," 380–88.
104. Edwards, "Spiritual Knowledge," 470.

of the Spirit is God's provision for humankind's inability (via original sin) to experience and know God's beauty and love on its own. Edwards affirmed that spiritual knowledge is "the experimental [experiential] knowledge of the saving operations of the Holy Spirit."[105] He compares the Holy Spirit's giving of spiritual knowledge in terms of receiving a new sense.

> There is not only a rational belief that God is holy, and that holiness is a good thing, but there is a sense of the loveliness of God's holiness. There is not only a speculatively judging that God is gracious, but a sense how amiable God is upon that account; or a sense of the beauty of this divine attribute.[106]

In Edwards' epistemology we can see that physical and spiritual knowledge are intimately connected via the senses—even more, accurate knowledge is incomplete without both.

The preceding suggests that Edwards' orthodoxy was more dynamic than the static intellectualist paradigm typically revealed in the conservative theology of his heirs. We saw this dynamism first in his Trinitarian theology as he correlated the integrated nature of the divine triad with the human mind (mind, understanding, and will), thereby advocating knowing as a dynamic rather than static process. We noted the same again in the paramount role he gave to the senses in knowing. In both cases cognition is a dynamic process constituted by many integrated aspects of human embodiment. Furthermore, the dynamic character of Edwards' epistemology also involved social factors because he deemed knowledge as covenantal and only those in relationship with the Spirit were privy to spiritual knowledge.[107] Next we see how Edwards' dispositional epistemology undergirded his transformational and pneumatological soteriology within the framework of his theology of affections. For now, it is enough to say that through Edwards' dispositional epistemology, the cognitive components of rationality, affectivity, and behavior exist as entwined elements of human embodiment.

---

105. Edwards, "A Spiritual Understanding," 80.
106. Edwards, "A Divine and Supernatural," 111.
107. Edwards, "Religious Affections," 306–307.

Jonathan Edwards and the Salvific Role of Orthodoxy

Edwards' Dispositional Soteriology via the Religious Affections

Based on the *ad intra* and *ad extra* divine self-communication, Edwards' beliefs about God as dispositional were not general but specific—*God is the divine disposition who communicates his beauty* (also love, goodness, and excellency). We now explore how this belief serves as the foundation for Edwards' dispositional soteriology. Lee advances that beauty and the perception of beauty are central in the philosophy and theology of Edwards. He explains, "The fundamental nature of anything that exists, for Edwards, is beauty, and the most distinctive characteristic of God is his divine beauty. To know and love God, therefore, is to know and love the beauty of God."[108] God's nature is the disposition to communicate his beauty. And he not only communicates to the created world but such communication comprises the very structure and existence of all created entities because all being is ontologically dispositional.[109] Thus, all things exist to communicate the love and beauty of God.

Since God's primary characteristic is divine beauty and this is perfectly communicated within the Trinitarian Godhead (*ad intra*), God's desire to communicate Himself outside of his being (*ad extra*) is what Edwards called "an increase, repetition, or multiplication"[110] of his flawless beauty in creation.[111] Edwards declared, "God is God, and distinguished from all other beings, and exalted above 'em, chiefly by his divine beauty, which is infinitely diverse from all other beauty."[112] Accordingly, Edwards claimed that the purpose of creation is to experience and reflect God's perfect beauty.[113] Similarly, Edwards' dispositional ontology elaborates how human beings inherently imitate the beauty of God, whether or not this disposition

---

108. Lee, "Edwards and Beauty," 113.
109. Lee, *Philosophical Theology*, 80.
110. Edwards, "Concerning the End," 433.
111. Lee, "Edwards and Beauty," 116.
112. Edwards, "Religious Affections," 298.
113. In this regard, Lee makes the interesting statement: "Now the physical universe, according to Edwards, is created to be so many images of God's beauty. But because the physical universe cannot know or love, how can its being truly be actualized? My reading of Edwards is that the true actuality of the physical universe is achieved through the converted person's perception of it as an image of God's beauty" ("Edwards and Beauty," 122). Such an interpretation suggests interesting implications for the Apostle Paul's words about the "groaning of creation" in Rom 8:19–21.

exists as actuality or possibility. When an individual recognizes how all things, including the very nature of their bodies, the vast complexity of the physical world, and all of life reflect the beauty of God, then this person most fully actualizes the dispositional capacity of his or her existence. The redemption of humanity is intrinsically connected to perceiving and experiencing God's beauty, love, and goodness. For this reason, the Christian does not "merely rationally believe that God is glorious, but he has a sense of the gloriousness of God in his heart."[114]

In light of God as the disposition to communicate beauty, Edwards made a distinction between two types of beauty—primary and secondary.[115] Primary beauty is grasped when one perceives the dispositional nature of creation to communicate the beauty and goodness of God. However, human beings are incapable of recognizing this beauty solely by human reason; it must come through enablement by the Holy Spirit, since this ability was lost at the Fall. Secondary beauty, though, is a reflection of primary beauty.[116] One can identify the beauty of nature without divine aid, because it naturally mirrors God's beauty. Secondary beauty is perceived regardless of whether or not one apprehends the divinely dispositional character of creation.

Edwards, as a Reformed theologian, was committed to the doctrine of original sin. He alleged that the Fall caused human beings to lose the dispositional capacity to know and love the divine beauty. Humanity has since been ruled by the inclination to only experience secondary beauty. Edwards referred to these dispositional capacities as "principles" and attested that since the Fall the inferior principles became the "absolute masters of the heart."[117] Consequently, secondary beauty was elevated to a "superior"[118] status and primary beauty demoted as "inferior"[119] so that human beings live only for those things which satisfy their carnal desires. Sinful "man did immediately set up himself, and the objects of his private affections and appetites, as supreme; and so they took the place of God."[120] The corruption of humanity is a corruption of dispositions. This is why

---

114. Edwards, "A Divine and Supernatural," 111.
115. Edwards, "Nature of True Virtue," 564–65.
116. Lee, "Edwards and Beauty," 115, 121, 125.
117. Edwards, "Part Four, Chapter Two," 382.
118. Ibid., 381–82.
119. Ibid., 382.
120. Ibid.

Jonathan Edwards and the Salvific Role of Orthodoxy

Edwards rejected any rationally driven ideas of revelation; he postulated that human reason alone, unaided by God, cannot perceive or respond to the beauty of God. Humanity does not have the capability or an object of reference by which to conceive God as absolute beauty and love. Edwards then affirmed that God as the divine disposition perfectly communicates Himself through Jesus Christ. McDermott explains, "Edwards taught that our eyes are opened when we are captivated by the beautiful love and glory of God in Christ, when we see this love most powerfully demonstrated in Christ's sacrificial love for the undeserving."[121] Edwards supposed, because of sin, that awareness of Christ (i.e., the beauty, glory, and love of God) can only be apprehended through the Holy Spirit. Hence, knowledge of God is far more than rationally comprehending the person and work of Christ.

It is at this point where Edwards' theology of affections becomes a vital component of his soteriology. As a minister in the time of the Great Awakening, Edwards was well aware of spiritual experiences that fell short of authentic Christian living. Out of his concern to discern the truly converted soul, Edwards depicted conversion as receiving a new "indwelling principle" through dispositional transformation realized as the religious affections. He, thus, spoke of the need for the Spirit to impart a new "principle of life . . . springing up into spiritual and everlasting life."[122] He contends that it is solely through the Spirit that Christ is manifested to the believer who is then enabled to experience the beauty of God.[123] So, when an individual experiences the beauty and glory of God in Christ, she does so because the Spirit has imparted spiritual knowledge that enables such knowing.[124] This transformation is the result of gaining more than an intellectual understanding about God (i.e., notional knowledge), but involves an affective dimension (i.e., spiritual knowledge) as the person comes into a covenantal relationship with God.

Accordingly, Edwards combined the understanding (rational attribute of the mind) and will (the judging or perceptive facet of the mind), so that knowledge of God literally issues from the very depths of one's soul in the manifestation of religious affections.[125] Envisioned as a spring of motivation and behavior, deeper than reason, the affections are foundational

---

121. McDermott, "Introduction," 7.
122. Edwards, "Religious Affections," 200.
123. Ibid., 129.
124. Edwards, "Treatise on Grace," 196–97.
125. Nichols, *An Absolute Sort*, 53.

for Edwards' dispositional soteriology. They are the underlying force and expression of the will (whether regenerate or not) and represent the heart of true religion and the aim of Christian conversion.[126] Conversion, then, is transformation, and it is none other than the reorientation of the affections to more accurately engage God as the chief religious object.

In sum, since Edwards declared that the cardinal human problem is corrupted dispositions then salvation is necessarily a dynamic process of dispositional transformation. Transformation occurs after the Spirit enables an individual to comprehend the divine disposition of beauty perfectly imaged in Christ. Edwards' soteriology is pneumatological from start to finish, for God unveils his beauty to humankind by the Spirit through displaying the image of the Son, and then gives the Son to humankind through the impartation of the Spirit. In doing so, the Spirit removes the carnal disposition to live for and pursue secondary beauty and enlivens the previously dormant disposition to exist in a way capable of perceiving and reflecting the beauty of God according to the divine nature of the Son.[127] When this disposition is restored, it no longer exists as only a *possibility* but becomes *actuality*. It is for this reason that in Edwards' dispositional soteriology, the true Christian proves the authenticity of her faith through the vibrant display of religious affections.[128] Having provided a theological foundation for Edwards' soteriological reflection, we next show how his dispositional orthodoxy provides the resources needed for our soteriological proposal.

126. Ibid., 7.

127. Lee, *Philosophical Theology*, 168.

128. Edwards elaborates twelve distinguishing signs that mark the truly converted ("Religious Affections," 120–347).

4

Salvation in the Flesh through Edwards' Dispositional Orthodoxy

JONATHAN EDWARDS' THEOLOGY OF religious affections brilliantly models the dynamic and transforming capacity of religious knowledge (i.e., orthodoxy). Here we'll see how his dispositional framework (in dialogue with the cognitive sciences) exemplifies the embodied nature of salvation. The chapter closes with specific implications regarding a partial reading of Edwards' theology as it relates to our proposal for a renewal soteriology of embodiment.

EDWARDS' DISPOSITIONAL ORTHODOXY FOR A RENEWAL SOTERIOLOGY

This section illustrates the dynamic nature of Edwards' dispositional orthodoxy and how it challenges intellectualist presumptions of orthodoxy in conservative Christianity. We'll see how the principal themes characterizing "right knowing" in Edwards' orthodoxy (affectivity, embodiment, and transformation) can be related to findings in the contemporary cognitive sciences because they both use similar categories to describe cognition. It is our goal to align Edwards' dispositional orthodoxy with the cognitive sciences so we can provide sound reasons to embrace a dynamic and embodied view of orthodoxy.

Part Two: Salvation and Orthodoxy

Edwards' Epistemology Corroborated by the Cognitive Sciences

As a thread running through Edwards' epistemology, pneumatology plays a substantial role. However, before taking up these matters, I constructively link Edwards's epistemology with two categories in the cognitive sciences used in describing human reasoning—*objective* and *subjective* knowledge.

Though Edwards does not explicitly define notional knowledge as "objective" or sensible knowledge as "subjective," he did utilize their equivalents. Just as Edwards identified notional knowledge as rational and sensible knowledge as experiential,[1] his epistemology correlates with the cognitive sciences affirming that human knowing incorporates both objective and subjective aspects of reasoning.[2] In addition to Edwards asserting that human reasoning requires "objective" (notional) and "subjective" (sensible) knowledge, he also maintained that these types of knowing depend upon each other for human cognition to operate most effectively. Such an integrated paradigm of cognition will be compared with findings in the cognitive sciences later in this chapter. Edwards accomplished this through a covenantal portrayal of knowledge. He does not describe two types of knowledge as much as two types of relationships an individual can have in relation to God. Only the regenerate can have spiritual knowledge because they, unlike the unregenerate, are in relation with the Spirit who alone imparts spiritual knowledge.[3] Edwards reasoned that the heart and mind both have prejudices against Christian truth because of corrupted dispositions.[4] The natural mind is at enmity with the things of God, being "full of prejudices against the truth of divine things."[5] So, there is not merely an objective knowledge of God and another subjective form of divine knowledge. Rather, when a person comes into a right relationship with God, the Spirit gives spiritual understanding and the prejudices are removed as the person begins to sense the beauty, sweetness, excellency, and love of God.[6] For Edwards, spiritual knowledge comes through a direct (subjective) en-

---

1. Edwards, "A Divine and Supernatural," 111–12.
2. Damasio, *Descartes' Error*, 245. See also, Lakoff and Johnson, *Philosophy in the Flesh*, 408.
3. Edwards, "Religious Affections," 201.
4. Edwards, "A Divine and Supernatural," 112.
5. Ibid.
6. Ibid., 113.

Salvation in the Flesh through Edwards' Dispositional Orthodoxy

counter with the beauty and love of God in Christ through the Spirit. Yet, it still operates in relationship with notional (objective) knowledge, and in this manner implies the holistic capacity of objective and subjective reasoning in human cognition. Based on such a correlation between Edwards' epistemology and cognitive studies, I advance that the objective and subjective qualities of reasoning in Edwards' epistemology can facilitate a broader orthodoxy than generally presumed in conservative Christianity. Towards this end we will show that Edwards' orthodoxy actually aligns more closely with the dynamic awareness of knowing in the cognitive sciences than the intellectualism of conservative Christianity.

An Affective Orthodoxy

Edwards' dispositional orthodoxy supplements the conservative theological emphasis on objective rationality in cognition by providing an affective dimension to "right thinking." It is precisely such objective intellectualism that Edwards was writing against in his own time, namely the problem of a rationally driven impression of cognition as seen in Enlightenment Deism. I next identify and discuss three elements of Edwards' orthodoxy that emphasize the importance of affectivity.

First, subjective and objective features of cognition are not polar opposites but integrated characteristics of the same task—knowing. An affective orthodoxy is complementary with objective reasoning. Edwards maintained a picture of orthodoxy in which sensible-subjective knowledge builds upon and completes notional-objective knowledge. In describing the religious affections, Edwards concluded that they arise from notional knowledge but lead to sensible knowledge. He even eschewed the enthusiasts who only stressed spiritual knowledge. Edwards declared that "holy affections are not heat without light."[7] So, the experience of God's beauty via sensible knowledge (i.e., "heat") depends upon a certain degree of information via notional knowledge (i.e., "light") about the nature of God.[8] Hence, objective and subjective elements of cognition are both inseparable and indispensable in Edwards' view of religious knowledge.

Second, Edwards' orthodoxy is more than just a proper balance between objective and subjective knowing; it depends on acquiring the holy affections. Right knowing for Edwards consisted of the objective content of Scripture,

---

7. Edwards, "Religious Affections," 266.
8. Nichols, *An Absolute Sort*, 61.

the subjective encounter of God's love and beauty, and its transforming effect upon the human person altogether dispositionally bound up as the religious affections. This is why Edwards strongly reacted against those theologies that overemphasized the rational and objective dimensions of cognition while minimizing its more affective features informed by personal experience.

Third, soteriology begins and ends with pneumatology. Note how this is in contradiction to the way conservative theology often limits affectivity in its soteriology by relegating the Spirit mostly to sanctification as a post-salvific reality. Studebaker proposes that Edwards' soteriology stretched the boundaries of Reformed orthodoxy regarding redemption. Because pneumatology played a central role in Edwards' theology he was able to both challenge and modify the common Reformed perspective on redemption as primarily focused on the work of Christ objectively securing salvation and the Spirit as just applying the more subjective benefits. Instead, Edwards asserted, "What Christ purchased for us, was that we might have communion with God in his good, which consists in partaking of or having communion of the Holy Ghost."[9] Accordingly, one can see the necessity of pneumatology for Edwards' soteriology.

Additionally, the value of Jonathan Edwards' contribution for a broadened meaning of orthodoxy is also corroborated by the cognitive sciences. Insofar as Edwards recognized that notional knowledge of God is incomplete without spiritual understanding, he anticipated Antonio Damasio's research on cognition involving both objective and subjective dimensions. Both individuals attest that cognition is deficient when objective rationality is bifurcated from subjective experience. Edwards upheld the dependency of notional knowledge on sensible knowledge and Damasio advances that the limitation of emotion from intellect hinders one from cognitively thriving and socially flourishing.[10] I draw from Edwards and Damasio to offer that "right thinking" is incomplete without "right emotions" and that human transformation requires both rationality and affectivity.

---

9. Edwards, "Discourse on the Trinity," 136. Studebaker claims that Edwards contends "the Spirit does not merely apply the benefits of redemption procured by Christ, but rather that the Spirit is the benefit of redemption" (*Jonathan Edwards' Social*, 98).

10. Damasio, *Looking for Spinoza*, 178 n. 25.

Salvation in the Flesh through Edwards' Dispositional Orthodoxy

An Embodied Orthodoxy

Edwards' dispositional orthodoxy can correct conservative Christianity's largely unembodied treatment of orthodoxy. Because such an approach typically envisions faith (i.e., religious knowledge) mostly in terms of how one thinks, salvation often devolves into "mental" or overly intellectual connotations, unrelated to the rest of the body. However, aspects of this conservativism can also place *too much accent* on the emotions, thereby disregarding a more fully embodied soteriology. In Edwards' day, this tendency was seen in the "enthusiasts" who placed too much stress on subjective-emotional characteristics of conversion. Gerald McDermott explains,

> After the Great Awakening's excesses, Edwards became uncomfortable with declaring that someone was regenerate because of an emotional experience, and he decided that only the test of time, proven by Christian practice, was a reliable sign of true religion.[11]

Such subjectivity didn't deny the body but severely restricted its relevance. Edwards' embodied orthodoxy provides a corrective to such emotionalism in at least three ways.

First, an embodied orthodoxy means that "right knowing" is not divorced from the practical realities of Christian community. Amy Plantinga Pauw elaborates.

> His [Edwards'] observations of Christian susceptibility to religious self-deception drove him to deny the primacy of the individual as the locus of spiritual insight and to reemphasize the role of the community in discerning the Spirit's presence.[12]

The true saint is one marked not by a particular experience or knowledge of God but a specific lifestyle—love for God and others. Therefore, an embodied orthodoxy is needed to faithfully fulfill the Christian mandate of love. Scripture teaches that Christian profession of belief is not enough; it must also be lived out in love and compassion to others (1 John 4:20).

Second, properly knowing God necessitates embodiment because spiritual-sensible knowledge must ultimately express itself through transformed affections and behaviors. Salvation as transformed affections involves embodiment because spiritual knowledge is concerned not only with how one thinks (orthodoxy) but with how one behaves (orthopraxy) and how one

---

11. McDermott, "Conclusion," 203.
12. Pauw, *Supreme Harmony*, 166.

feels (orthopathy). Edwards insisted a person cannot truly taste the sweetness of God's beauty and not be compelled to act in a beautiful manner.[13] Such knowledge of God's beauty, after all, would be miserably incomplete unless compelled to action.

Third, an embodied orthodoxy flows from the centrality of the Spirit. A dynamic experience of God is vital in Edwards' soteriology and would be impossible without human embodiment because salvation as ontological increase necessarily results from the *ad extra* communication of God through the Spirit. After the Spirit changes a person's affections, her thinking also changes in a way that compels her to live according to the beauty and love of God.[14] The embodied subjective realities of new behavior and affective experience follow from the *ad extra* communication of the Spirit historically mediated to a human body in time and space.

Just as Edwards believed that knowing God is not possible until one's corrupted dispositions are transformed into embodied affections,[15] he made a similar assertion as Reuven Feuerstein that behavior has the potential to transform cognition.[16] Both individuals insist that praxis plays a profound influence on cognition. Feuerstein (via his Mediated Learning Experience) alleges that mediation enables a learner to grasp certain levels of knowledge previously unattainable. Edwards similarly upheld that behavior (i.e., actualizing of affections) can enable the regenerate to experience knowledge of the beauty of God in a way transcending previous levels of natural knowing. How? He supposed that the transforming encounter of God's love and beauty follows from the embodied synthesis of notional and sensible knowledge. Based on these insights, I draw from Edwards and Feuerstein to advocate that "right thinking" is incomplete without "right practice," and that both rationality and behavior are necessary components of embodiment for authentic Christian transformation.

---

13. Edwards, "A Divine and Supernatural," 124.

14. McDermott, "Introduction," 7. Such ontological increase facilitated by the *ad extra* communication of the Spirit relates to 2 Cor 3:18: "But we all, with unveiled faces beholding as in a mirror the glory of the Lord, are transformed into the same image *from glory to glory*, even as from the Lord the Spirit." Emphasis added.

15. Edwards, "Part Four, Chapter Two," 380–88.

16. Feuerstein et al., *Beyond Smarter*, 134, 140–41.

Salvation in the Flesh through Edwards' Dispositional Orthodoxy

A Transformational Orthodoxy

Edwards concluded that when an individual truly knows God, he or she will be transformed because such knowledge changes the dispositional core of a person. I advance that Edwards' dispositional orthodoxy can expand the intellectualist rendering of orthodoxy through its stress on the transformational potential of knowledge. I now reiterate three aspects of Edwards' orthodoxy as dispositional transformation.

First, his soteriology is grounded on the proposition that human beings are dispositionally inclined for ontological increase. Humans, as ontologically composed by God's *ad extra* communication, exist as a dynamic expression ever approaching God's perfectly actualized *ad intra* communication. So, ontological growth is an integral characteristic of human nature. Rightly knowing God for Edwards is marked by perpetual development into the likeness of Christ.

Second, a dispositional orthodoxy leads to transformation because Edwards' concept of disposition paradoxically conveys both dynamism and permanence. Not only does the saint begin to experience and reflect the beauty and love of God, but this change is not fleeting, it is permanent.

> Conversion (if we may give any credit to the Scripture) is a great and universal change of the man, turning him from sin to God. A man may be restrained from sin, before he is converted; but when he is converted, he is not only restrained from sin, his very heart . . . is turned from it, unto holiness: so that thenceforward he becomes a holy person, and an enemy to sin.[17]

A dispositional soteriology fitly speaks of salvation as ongoing conversion. The one who rightly knows God is distinguished not merely by short-term change but enduring transformation.

Third, as with an affective and embodied orthodoxy, so does a transformational orthodoxy follow from a robust pneumatology. In Edwards' soteriology, conversion is nothing less than the Holy Spirit transforming corrupted human dispositions into wholly new ones ruled by the power of God's love and beauty. Because Edwards denied that any amount of knowledge can transform human nature, he described transformation in dispositional terms . . . as the reception of a "principle" or "spiritual sense" from which the saint henceforth lives.[18] Not only is dispositional transformation

---

17. Edwards, "Religious Affections," 341.
18. Ibid., 114, 205–6.

the work of the Spirit, but such is also the new principle enabling one to "taste" the sweetness of God's beauty and love.[19] Therefore, rightly knowing God requires a right relationship with the Spirit, after which comes dispositional transformation realized as the religious affections.

In chapter 2, just as Damasio exposed the transforming power of emotions and feelings in neuro-biological studies and Feuerstein illustrated the profound impact of behavior and emotions on brain physiology and learning outcomes, so too did Edwards similarly contend for the soteriological significance of emotions and behavior through his theology of affections. Just as research in the cognitive sciences recognizes that the more cognition incorporates embodiment and subjective experience the more transforming it is, so too will a soteriology that accounts for these factors be more transformational than one that doesn't. On that account, I draw from Edwards, Damasio, and Feuerstein that truly *knowing* God requires obedient Christian *behavior* and authentic *experience* of God because the most profound kind of knowing comes when all three components are integrated—head, behavior, and heart!

I have now shown that Jonathan Edwards' dispositional orthodoxy resists intellectualism because his view of "knowing God" is affective, embodied, and transformational—the same criteria brain science argues is needed for the maximum potential of human cognition. In doing so, we've shown the significance of Edwards' orthodoxy for our proposal of a renewal soteriology of embodiment. Finally, to conclude this section, we have one more topic to address—Edwards' contemporary relevance. Can we really appropriate a theologian whose cognitive models and philosophical theories may not match the present paradigms in play? After all, in Edwards' day, cognitive neuroscience and cognitive psychology hadn't yet even emerged and the field of philosophy would undergo major shifts and new developments in the centuries ahead.

Is Edwards Relevant Today?

Does one have to embrace Edwards' dispositional ontology of God as the ultimate disposition communicating his glory *ad intra* and *ad extra* to be convinced of the need for an embodied orthodoxy? Does someone have to accept Edwards' psychological models—either of God or the human mind—to be persuaded of the need for a more embodied and subjective

---

19. Ibid, 209, 220.

Salvation in the Flesh through Edwards' Dispositional Orthodoxy

rendering of "right thinking"? Must one assent to Edwards' theology of affections and its uniquely robust pneumatological outworking to appreciate the need for a renewal soteriology of embodiment? These questions are vital because it does us no good to successfully argue a case (the need to reject an intellectualist orthodoxy) at one level (Edwardsean philosophical theology) yet lose it at another level—present day relevance. Interestingly, these are not infrequently expressed concerns because one needs only look at the massive number of books and articles still being written on this profoundly important scholar, philosopher, theologian, and pastor. People are not only asking the question, but answering in a resounding, "Yes, Edwards is still relevant!" Why is this so?

Edwards' continuing influence and relevance are not found so much in the theories, models, and philosophies he so soundly articulated but rather in his incredibly creative, biblically reflective, and experientially acute— perhaps even "prophetic"—ability to communicate timeless truths in fresh new ways adaptable to different times and diverse eras. Though modern psychology and cognitive science explain the human psyche, the brain's ability to perceive sensory stimuli, and their cognitive roles in different ways than Edwards, his insight somehow transcends the theoretical boundaries in which they were introduced. As already mentioned, his dispositional ontology presumed aspects of quantum theory not even developed until over two hundred years later. Likewise, his theology of affections—also an outgrowth of his dispositional ontology—provided critical insight regarding the renewing work of the Holy Spirit that was just as relevant in his day as it has been for every generation since. And though we may not think of cognition in exactly the same way he did, his awareness of its dynamic and embodied nature is corroborated by contemporary cognitive science.

So, for our purpose of challenging the intellectualism of conservative Christian theology, Jonathan Edwards is, indeed, relevant. He definitely helps us think creatively and imaginatively—in light of Scripture and the historic Christian tradition—when we approach important Christian topics (ex., the Trinity, Christian spirituality, and beauty). Yet, he also helps us think clearly and specifically about those topics that do not shift with the changing tides of philosophical paradigms, scientific models, and technological breakthroughs.[20] There is a reason why he is considered one of

---

20. For instance, some common topics are: knowing Christ, mentoring new believers, prayer, missions, original sin, government, world religions, and more. See the bibliography for relevant sources.

PART TWO: SALVATION AND ORTHODOXY

America's greatest theologians and, for our purposes, it is significant why this title is so often claimed among conservative Protestant Christians.

Now, having made our case for the relevance of Edwards' dispositional soteriology for a renewal soteriology of embodiment we must now turn a critical eye to possible problems overlooked. Despite Edwards' profound contributions, is there still a need for caution? If so, why? Our final section concerns this question.

The Challenge of an Edwardsean Soteriology: A Partial Reading of Edwards' Theology?

In spite of Edwards' dependence on the Spirit and the challenge his dispositional ontology posed to the theological rationalism of his day, I suggest that his reception is limited by a partial reading of his theology. Because Edwards' dispositional ontology is philosophically complex, a partial reading follows when his use of disposition is ignored or misunderstood. Just as I claimed that the arguments of Sang Hyun Lee's critics were largely fueled from such a partial reading, so too is there a similar effect among a more popular audience. Because such a readership will likely be unfamiliar with Edwards' dispositional ontology, they will often fail to appreciate the dynamic character of his theology. Therefore, I now cautiously propose that certain theological emphases may have been encouraged by such a partial reading of Edwards.[21] This final section suggests two tendencies that he maintained, which when extracted from their dispositional context, could have ultimately bolstered the very mindset (i.e., intellectualism) he was opposing.

Isolating Justification from Sanctification in the Order of Salvation

To miss the dispositional framework of Edwards' theology of affections is to fail to see how conversion is necessarily holistic. Even more, Edwards'

---

21. Perhaps, it may be more appropriate to term my thoughts in this section as a "hunch," since, as I have already explained in the introduction to this chapter, my research is specifically focused on Edwards' dispositional paradigm via Lee. Nevertheless, I still contend that Edwards' dispositional model is a vital hermeneutical tool for interpreting Edwards and without it his innovative theological contribution cannot be fully appreciated.

Salvation in the Flesh through Edwards' Dispositional Orthodoxy

theology of the affections is paradigmatic for his dispositional soteriology. Without this dispositional context, his reference to the affections sounds little different than a post-salvific rendering of sanctification.

The objective vs. subjective bifurcation is central to an intellectualistic epistemology and is not like Edwards' description of notional and sensible knowledge. However, even though Edwards' epistemology clearly brought together the objective and subjective aspects of knowing, he still retained the objective-justification vs. subjective-sanctification categories of Reformed Protestant soteriology. We now reflect on the soteriological implications of these categories vis-à-vis Edwards.

Though he himself did not embrace the isolation and subordination of sanctification to justification, Edwards' employment of these categories has not prevented his heirs from embracing the same kind of intellectualism he resisted. Without proper insight into the dispositional soteriology undergirding Edwards' use of "justification" and "sanctification," his innovative interpretation of "right thinking" as affective, embodied, and transformational is lost and, by extension, vulnerable to misinterpretation. I offer that the separation rather than integration of these terms is precisely the kind of misinterpretation that followed. Thereupon, the theological rationalism he opposed in the church of his day has continued to exert its intellectualist influence through the legacy of his heirs.[22]

An example of such a misconstrual of Edwards can be seen in the Princeton school of thought within only a few generations of his death in the writings of Charles Hodge (1797–1878) and Benjamin Warfield (1851–1921). Chapter 1 already addressed this same issue in regards to Hodge and Warfield's treatment of justification and sanctification as integral to their soteriology. While neither of these theologians specifically said that Edwards taught such a separation of these terms, they were heavily indebted to him and considered themselves faithful stewards of his theological tradition.[23] Of Edwards' tremendous influence, McDermott says, "Nineteenth-

---

22. The New Divinity movement, however, did consciously attempt to apply Edwards' program, especially via Samuel Hopkins (1721–1803) and his influential New Divinity textbook, *The System of Doctrines*. Hence there was a degree of variety in how Edwards' heirs appropriated his theology. Nevertheless, my point remains that conservative theological streams following Edwards were largely unable to stem the growing tide of intellectualism as I have already elaborated, despite whatever influence the New Divinity may have had on such intellectualism. Further elaboration falls beyond the limits of this study.

23. This is not to say that Hodge embraced all of Edwards' ideas. For instance, Michael McClymond says, "Presbyterian stalwart Charles Hodge wrote that Edwards' theology

century American theologians at Andover, Princeton, and Yale nearly universally claimed his mantle."[24] Yet, as I already presented in chapter 1, these theologians clearly embraced an intellectualist epistemology; this is something Edwards would have unequivocally rejected. Once again, a prime reason for such treatment of justification and sanctification follows from the acceptance and use of an intellectualist soteriology (whether of Hodge, Warfield, Erickson, or Grudem). Could it be that if the early Princeton theologians had more than a "partial reading" of Edwards, they would have understood his integrated epistemology, appreciated his dispositional orthodoxy, and been less likely to treat justification and sanctification in the dichotomized manner they did?[25]

Perhaps, if Edwards had identified the practices of the church as indispensable in the formation of religious affections he could have linked the beliefs of the church with the practices of the church and revealed how right thinking is inseparable from right behavior and right emotions.[26] Had he done so, Edwards would have taken his epistemological

---

'in its consequences is essentially pantheistic'" ("Salvation as Divinization," 139). Here Hodge is referring to some of Edwards' comments about the believers' relation to God. Such a statement further reinforces my claim that Hodge and the early Princeton school did not understand Edwards' dispositional ontology that emphasizes the close relationship between the Spirit and creation as the conveyor of God's *ad extra* communication. Admittedly, in the nineteenth century some of Edwards' writings were not yet published or heavily edited in order to eliminate what were perceived to be problematic in relation to Reformed theology. Without such a dispositional context, readings of Edwards' statements about the believers' relation to God would naturally sound pantheistic. However, as a committed Calvinist, Edwards' would not make fundamental statements about the nature of God contradictory to such Reformed positions as the Creator/creature distinction. The likely reason is that interpreters of Edwards had not recognized the import of a dispositional ontology undergirding his theology.

24. McDermott, "Introduction," 6.

25. Studebaker and Caldwell (*Trinitarian Theology*, 172–86) explain that while Edwards clearly aligned himself in the Reformation tradition of forensic justification, he conceived of the Holy Spirit as the grace of Christ. In doing so, Edwards envisioned the Spirit as central in the work of redemption. Edwards' predecessors often portrayed the Spirit as imparting Christ's *blessings of redemption*; however, Edwards understood the Spirit as *the gift of redemption*. Though Edwards upheld the redemption terminology of *justification* and *sanctification*, he did not endorse a subordination of the latter to the former, and by association a subordinated influence of the Holy Spirit. Accordingly, Edwards' theology of affections is inconceivable without a truly robust pneumatology. Without understanding the prominent role of the Holy Spirit for dispositional transformation, Edwards' theology of affections can appear little more than an elaborate rendering of sanctification and thereby miss the transformational foundation of his soteriology.

26. Here I refer to the "practices" of the church as the wide array of ecclesial traditions

Salvation in the Flesh through Edwards' Dispositional Orthodoxy

assumptions one step further by disclosing how the affective, embodied, and transformational qualities of "right knowing" are incompatible with a salvation that truncates an objective-justification from a subjective-sanctification. For if godly behavior is part of the process of knowing God, wouldn't it be natural to presume that the practices of the church and the beliefs of the church are inseparable components? By not articulating such an epistemology as fundamental to a transformational soteriology, even Edwards' dynamic theology of the affections could still be misunderstood in terms of a post-salvific sanctification subordinated to an intellectually received justification.

Positing Scripture as the Sole Epistemological Criterion

This final portion considers the implications of how Edwards' dispositional ontology undergirds his epistemology in regards to the use of Scripture. Within Edwards' dispositional soteriology, the human person actualizes her existence when she comprehends the dispositional nature of her life—to communicate and experience the beauty of God. Thence, for Edwards, the objective of Scripture is to display the beauty and perfection of God in all of life to the believer, not merely treating it as the sole means for securing truth.

Knowledge of God is covenantal in Edwards' epistemology; only those in relationship with the Spirit are able to receive not just notional but also spiritual understanding. These ones gain the "new sense" needed for tasting the sweetness of God's beauty and goodness in the world. Because Edwards was committed to the doctrine of original sin, he asserted that dispositional transformation of corrupted dispositions (i.e., religious affections) was unlikely without the revelation of Scripture imparted by the Spirit. For Edwards, the principal purpose of Scripture was to facilitate dispositional transformation of the person through its objective content by the Spirit who then imparts the new nature to the believer. While Edwards did not envision "knowledge of God" as just a rational task, unfortunately, with only a partial reading of his theology (i.e., nondispositional), it can appear that he comes close to positing Scripture as the sole epistemological grounding for such knowledge.

---

that have been a part of the canonical heritage of the church. In the next chapter, I focus on such practices when I discuss William Abraham's canonical theism.

Part Two: Salvation and Orthodoxy

Perhaps, Edwards' stress on the importance of Scripture in salvation was due in part to the early and mid-eighteenth century New England discussions about revival and free-will.[27] His Arminian opponents advocated that individuals could freely choose to believe rather than Edwards' conviction of the absolute sovereignty of God. Nevertheless, Edwards needed to raise up the necessity of Scripture for salvation as opposed to one's choice. Yet, in doing so, he presumed the prominent role of the Spirit acting upon the mind to lay hold of God's divine revelation. Without his dispositional context, Scripture can appear as its sole epistemological foundation.

As a specific example, Edwards emphasized the critical role Scripture plays in providing the "subject matter" for notional knowledge and thereby grounding spiritual knowledge.

> The Word of God is only made use of to convey to the mind the subject matter of this saving instruction: and this indeed it doth convey to us by natural force or influence. It conveys to our minds these and those doctrines; it is the cause of the notion of them in our heads . . . but that due sense of the heart, wherein this light formally consists, is immediately by the Spirit of God.[28]

Edwards posited that spiritual understanding is normally contingent upon Scripture and the Spirit together at work within a person. The new sense is linked with the opening of one's eyes and the removal of darkness inherited through original sin.[29] For ongoing dispositional transformation, Scripture is the most essential means for spiritual growth.[30] Without Edwards' dispositional context and pneumatological assumptions, it can appear that he treated Scripture as the sole objective epistemological foundation merely disclosing necessary truths for the salvation of one's soul. In other words, he appears to endorse the very intellectualism we rejected in chapter 1. How can this be so?

I wonder if in attempting to right the perceived abuse of the Arminian enthusiasts relying on spiritual experience to the neglect of the Bible as well as in his ongoing battle with the Deists' minimization of Scripture, Edwards may have unwittingly reinforced an intellectualist epistemology in those who followed after him. By combating such viewpoints, perhaps Edwards felt the need to reiterate the importance of objective-rational knowledge

---

27. Studebaker, *Jonathan Edwards' Social*, 145.
28. Edwards, "A Divine and Supernatural," 115.
29. Edwards, "Religious Affections," 206.
30. Sweeney, "Edwards and the Bible," 68.

of Scripture and, in doing so, weakened the very thing he intended to strengthen—a nonintellectualist soteriology.

Also, since Edwards linked the purpose of Scripture so closely with the Spirit, it can seem as though the "new sense" cannot be received without the objective content of Scripture. Without a dispositional context, Scripture's value (of providing objective content) can appear to be on equal footing with the Spirit. Could this be another form of, or precursor to, the subordination of subjectivity and pneumatology prevalent in an intellectualist soteriology? Once again, without a clear grasp of Edwards' dispositional ontology and the role of the Spirit as the *ad extra* divine communication, his approach to Scripture can reinforce an intellectually-driven view of salvation and hinder the dynamic and embodied soteriological beliefs he fought so hard to communicate.[31]

Here also, I wonder if Edwards had coupled the use of Scripture with the practices of the Church that he might have minimized the intellectualist impulses he may have unknowingly passed on to his heirs. For when Scripture is utilized together with the practices of the Church then additional mediums become available for the Spirit to convey divine revelation to the individual. Ecclesial practices like communion, prayer, baptism, worship, and the teachings of the Fathers are some among the varied means that have historically communicated the revelation of God to the church. When this is done, the intellectualism associated with locating God's revelation exclusively in Scripture is safeguarded against, and the appreciation of Scripture as one, even if the primary, epistemological norm among many is preserved.

Ultimately, this book challenges the dominant *intellectualist* paradigm at play in conservative Christian soteriology by suggesting that a renewal soteriology of embodiment better accounts for the embodied nature of faith and the expansive role of the Holy Spirit in its mediation. The point of these past two chapters is that we actually hinder "right knowing" when we insist salvation must prioritize the intellectual domain of faith over its more behavioral and affective expressions. So, when we speak of a "renewal soteriology of embodiment," we contend for an orthodoxy that does not pit the head against the heart or the mind against behaviors. We simply bear witness to the embodied nature of faith and more accurately account for

---

31. This is especially true when one does not recognize how epistemology and ontology are related in Edwards' soteriology. Epistemological certainty is only possible because of an "underlying ontological certainty" by virtue of the *ad extra* function of the Spirit (Nichols, *An Absolute Sort*, 45).

the dynamic ministry of the Holy Spirit ever at work towards and within the whole human person—intellectually, behaviorally, and affectively. Towards this end, I contend that Jonathan Edwards' dispositional orthodoxy can challenge an intellectualist theological epistemology through re-envisioning the meaning of "right thinking" in terms that are affective (vs. objective), embodied (vs. unembodied), and transformational (vs. static) for the kind of soteriology we propose. As we move into Part Three (Salvation and Orthopraxy), we'll see how Jonathan Edwards' dispositional soteriology segues into canonical theism's emphasis on the established canonical practices of the church as soteriologically significant means of grace for Christian transformation. Hence, intellectualism will be further discredited even as the vital role of praxis is reinforced for a renewal soteriology of embodiment.

PART THREE

Salvation and Orthopraxy

5

Canonical Theism and the Salvific Role of Orthopraxy

WHAT IS THE RELATIONSHIP between praxis and salvation?[1] What does human behavior have to do with faith? These questions launch us beyond the theological, scientific, and epistemological foundations we have already established. Our proposal is based upon and reinforced by three interdependent soteriological categories. Jonathan Edwards helped us introduce and expand the first—orthodoxy. Now, we present the second pillar of *orthopraxy*. Finally, chapter 7 will introduce orthopathy. However, before moving forward, it is important that the ground we have covered in the first four chapters is logically clear and comprehensible. So, let's briefly review the predominant soteriological and cognitive observations already presented.

A QUICK SUMMARY

Chapter 1 affirmed the fundamental Protestant confession that salvation comes through faith. We also showed that—despite objections to the contrary—conservative Christian theology and practice typically reveal an intellectualist soteriology in regard to its treatment of faith. Chapter 2 introduced research in the neuro-sciences and cognitive psychology disclosing the dynamic nature of knowing. We saw that learning is mediated not only through objective accumulation of knowledge but also by means

---

1. In this book, behavior, practices, and praxis are used interchangeably *when referring to orthopraxy* or *orthopraxis*.

of behavior and emotion. Yet, despite the cognitive sciences establishing the embodied nature of knowing, Christian soteriology often continues to favor an intellectualist epistemology that privileges the rational dimension of cognition.

A dynamic view of faith then understands the integrated nature of intellect, behavior, and affectivity in much the same way that the cognitive sciences understand the embodied nature of reasoning. Therefore, a core theological affirmation of our study is that salvation is an embodied reality, inconsistent with the presuppositions of an intellectualist epistemology. One's beliefs about God (orthodoxy) are but one part of a threefold strand together with behavior (orthopraxy) and affections (orthopathy) by which God mediates saving faith.

Chapters 3–4 expounded Jonathan Edwards' embodied awareness of religious knowledge through the grid of his dispositional soteriology. We saw how Edwards' theological epistemology expanded the idea of orthodoxy beyond the boundaries of intellectualism. He did this by showing how knowledge of God was not just an objective reality (obtaining correct knowledge) but also affective, embodied, and transforming all at the same time. In doing so, Edwards mirrored similar assertions in the cognitive sciences regarding the affective, embodied, and transforming nature of the human mind. Edwards helped us theologically articulate "knowing God" as a dynamic reality situating orthodoxy as one soteriological component in need of two others (orthopraxy and orthopathy).

Our appropriation of Edwards illustrates how our proposal of a renewal soteriology of embodiment, while not identical to his dispositional soteriology, shares similar soteriological and cognitive assumptions. Above all, we both affirm that "orthodoxy" alone is incomplete in the process of knowing God because salvation is a wholly embodied reality. Hence, despite the prominent intellectualism in conservative Protestant soteriology, we can nevertheless claim significant theological and epistemological similarity with one of its most esteemed theological heroes.

In this chapter, just as I previously looked to the dispositional ontology of Jonathan Edwards to expand the soteriological category of orthodoxy, I now employ canonical theism to do the same for orthopraxis. Toward this end, William J. Abraham serves as our primary springboard into canonical theism's vision of canonical practices as soteriologically significant.[2] Yet, such begs the question, "What is canonical theism?" To this we now turn.

---

2. Other advocates of canonical theism from whom we draw are: Frederick D.

Canonical Theism and the Salvific Role of Orthopraxy

Canonical Theism and Orthopraxy

In order to set forth canonical theism as a new theological movement, we must recognize its connection with William Abraham because of his influence as founder and primary spokesman. While this chapter draws from a variety of canonical theism advocates, our main interest is in Abraham's explication of the movement as it bears on canonical practices.[3] In this section I first introduce canonical theism by situating it as a theological movement arising in the early twenty-first century, primarily through Abraham's research. Next, I note the key criticisms of this movement to justify our use of Abraham's work. Then, I appraise the use of orthopraxis within contemporary Christianity and, finally, conclude by showing how soteriological transformation was an important theme of the canonical tradition.

Situating Canonical Theism—Historically and Theologically

I now highlight canonical theism as a relatively new theological movement and then overview its genesis through the influence of Abraham as its founder. Canonical theism evolved within the first decade of the twentieth century as a collaborative team of scholars responded to Abraham's research on the canonical practices of the Church in his magnum opus, *Canon and Criterion: From the Fathers to Feminism*. These scholars gathered to discuss Abraham's research and reflect on how the canonical heritage of the church could offer innovative perspectives on old problems and formulate "new ways of thinking about perennial theological issues."[4] The initial emergence of canonical theism's core features largely derived from a series of meetings over three years at Perkins School of Theology at Southern Methodist University in Dallas, Texas. The research deriving from these meetings was later synthesized in *Canonical Theism: A Proposal for Theology and the Church*.[5] Coming from a variety of disciplines and backgrounds, all who

---

Aquino, Paul L. Gavrilyuk, Charles Gutenson, Douglas M. Koskela, Natalie B. Van Kirk, and Jason E. Vickers.

3. Our primary text explicating canonical theism as a new field of historico-theological study is Abraham et al., *Canonical Theism: A Proposal*. For an overview of canonical theism, see Abraham's chapter (from same text), "Canonical Theism: Thirty Theses," 1–7.

4. Abraham, "Introduction," xviii.

5. Charles Gutenson explains that Abraham's *Canon and Criterion* is the "programmatic work that lies behind this collection of essays" ("Canonical Heritage," 244).

attended were passionate about contributing to the health of their ecclesial communities; yet, they agreed that the standard ways conservative and liberal Protestants have traditionally addressed such "theological issues" have been ineffective.[6] Abraham explains,

> [W]e have come to accept fresh ways of thinking and speaking about old topics that are usually housed in discussions about the church, scripture, tradition, reason, experience, and the like. More controversially, we have reworked the idea of canon so that it has connotations and intellectual aspirations that are radically different from its standard usage.[7]

A central element of canonical theism is its new perspective on "canon" as freed from the epistemological priorities with which it has been historically associated. Similarly, Abraham upholds that canonical theism is not merely one more "speculative effort in systematic theology; it is an attempt to find an expression of the faith that nourishes the soul and provides shape and motivation for lively involvement in the life and ministry of the church."[8] Canonical theism arose as a theological project hoping to lay hold of a vibrant form of theism exhibited and experienced in the church's canonical tradition.[9] As true to the vision of the initial research team, canonical theism exists to spur the kind of theological reflection that cultivates ecclesial renewal and growth.

Here I pause to clarify how canonical theism relates to orthopraxis and soteriology. Accordingly, I now shift to Abraham's personal journey of faith leading to the movement's fundamental assertion that canonical practices are soteriologically transformative. William Abraham (b. 1947) was born in Belfast, Ireland and studied at Queen's University in Belfast and Asbury Theological Seminary in Asbury, Kentucky before earning his PhD in Philosophy at Oxford University. Abraham is the Albert Cook Outler Professor of Theology and Wesley Studies at Perkins School of Theology, Southern Methodist University where he teaches as a philosophical and systematic theologian. Abraham is also an ordained elder in the United Methodist Church and is well respected in the evangelical community as a gifted scholar and theologian with a wide breadth of intellectual interests

---

6. Ibid.
7. Ibid.
8. Abraham, "Emergence," 141.
9. Abraham "Canonical Theism: Thirty Theses," 1.

and expertise.[10] While Abraham's research has had its critics, few contest his passion for the renewal of the church.[11] As a philosopher of religion, Abraham has written extensively on the epistemology of theology, with a focus on inspiration and revelation and their relationship to Scripture.[12] As a historian of religion with an interest in evangelism, Abraham's research on the evangelistic practices and beliefs of the early church led him to explore the impact of canonical practices on Christian formation.[13] Ultimately, Abraham's greatest interest in ecclesial renewal led him to investigate how effectively the church's canonical heritage passed on a vibrant and dynamic faith to each new generation of believers.[14]

Abraham traces the origins of canonical theism as coinciding with his own personal journey of faith when he became aware of the dynamic relationship between canonical practices and salvation.[15] His religious transition from intellectually understanding faith to personally experiencing ongoing renewal motivates much of his scholarly and ecclesial work. In his own tradition, Abraham recognized that enduring renewal requires both *intellect* and *behavior*.

> While the Methodist tradition is very much alive and its renewal is much further along than its critics acknowledge, it has enormous difficulty securing a sufficiency of content and *practice* to nourish one's spiritual life over time.[16]

Thus, the integration of intellect with behavior would become an underlying characteristic of canonical theism. Eventually, Abraham's quest for renewal in the church led him to see that the Church's understanding of the canonical tradition (both Wesleyan and corporately) was flawed in that it had wrongly comprehended that tradition to be chiefly epistemological

---

10. Jason Vickers describes Abraham's wide range of study covering, "analytic philosophy, philosophy of religion, epistemology, systematic theology, history of Christianity, patristics, evangelism, mission, biblical studies, Wesley studies, politics, and, more recently, international terrorism" (Gavrilyuk et al., *Immersed*, viii).

11. Two books bear this out as a collection of essays in honor of Abraham's scholarship, in general, and research in canonical theism, in particular (both books were released in 2008). See, Abraham et al., *Canonical Theism: A Proposal*; and Gavrilyuk et al., *Immersed*.

12. See, Abraham, *Crossing*.

13. See, Abraham, *Logic of Evangelism*.

14. See, Abraham, *Logic of Renewal*.

15. For a full account see, Abraham, "Emergence," 141–55.

16. Ibid., 147. Emphasis added.

PART THREE: SALVATION AND ORTHOPRAXY

rather than soteriological. Consequently, he researched evangelism in the early church and discovered that the central aim of the catechetical schools was the formation of Christians in the early and patristic periods of the church.[17]

The term *catechetical* comes from the word *catechesis* which is the task of receiving instruction from a teacher. The early church designated clear-cut means for the evangelization and training of new converts (i.e., catechumens) through establishing "catechetical schools." Usually, such schools centered on the teachings of a revered leader (often a bishop) in the church.[18] Subsequently, Abraham noticed the wide range of canonical practices within the catechetical process and the soteriological context within which they existed. For instance, the catechetical lectures of St. Cyril of Jerusalem concern the soteriological value of practices—particularly the sacraments of Eucharist and baptism, and the prayerful study of Scripture—to strengthen believers' faith and facilitate growth. St. Cyril's seventeen lectures constituted the teaching material in his catechetical school and he emphasized the fullness of the Spirit by canonical means for salvific transformation.[19] Space does not permit a more in-depth study of ancient Christian catechesis and its wide use of the canonical tradition, however, it is sufficient to say that the soteriological aims of the catechetical schools and the canonical tradition worked hand in hand—both were committed to the spiritual renovation of new believers and growth of the faithful.

Abraham recounts how this research opened his eyes to the dynamic and vibrant faith these schools instilled in the believing community:

> Where before I was reading ancient texts professionally and following the institutional developments sociologically or merely historically, the whole life of the church came alive as a place where folk were brought to faith, nourished in holiness, helped in the battle against evil, motivated to persevere, and energized to plumb the full depths of gospel conviction . . . The creeds of the

---

17. Ibid., 150.

18. For instance, Clement (150–215 AD), a revered teacher from Alexandria, was elected to lead the catechetical school in Alexandria; St. Cyril (313–386 AD) was the Bishop of Jerusalem in 350 AD and was the leader of the catechetical school there in Jerusalem; and later, St. Didymus the Blind (313–398 AD), a famous teacher of the church in Alexandria, led the catechetical school of that city (Burgess, *Holy Spirit: Ancient*, 70–72, 105–12, 113–16).

19. For a more thorough study, see McCauley and Stephenson (translators), *The Works of St. Cyril of Jerusalem*, vols. 1 and 2.

Canonical Theism and the Salvific Role of Orthopraxy

church ceased to be mere summaries of scripture; they took on a life of their own in the formation and preservation of authentic discipleship.[20]

This awareness implicitly conveys a rich sense of orthopraxy, as the "life of the church" through canonical practices in one way or another led to the "preservation of authentic discipleship."[21] Ultimately then, it was his research in the catechetical tradition that exposed the relevance of practices in the early church for cultivating a dynamic experience of salvation. Abraham details such practices as singularly fixed on one outcome—salvation. For this end, the early church canonized sure rituals, sacraments, and behaviors commonly believed to mediate the salvific grace of God for a richer participation into the divine life. Abraham lays out six common pieces of this canonical heritage:

> First, there are *practices*, experiences, and rites intimately related to baptism and the Eucharist. Second, there are *liturgical traditions* concerning the general conduct of worship. Third, there is a sophisticated *iconographic tradition*. Fourth, there are *ecclesiastical regulations* or canons concerning the internal regulation of the life of the Church and its members. Fifth, over time certain leaders and teachers are designated as *Fathers, saints, and teachers* . . . The sixth and final canonical tradition [*episcopate*] . . . relates to the internal structures and ordering of the community . . . as a way of securing the internal supervision of the Church as a whole.[22]

Together these six elements comprised the general scope of the canonical tradition and, in various ways, utilized certain practices for soteriological ends. For the aims of this chapter, "canonical practices" specifically refer to baptism, the Eucharist, and reading of Scripture. Later I elaborate the meaning of each practice and its relationship to soteriology.

Taking into account the foregoing, even though canonical theism more frequently speaks of the "practices of the church" as opposed to the "church's orthopraxy" or a "canonical orthopraxy," our terminology refers to the same thing—ecclesial practices that mediate salvific grace. Both canonical theism and this study speak of the soteriological import of practices. Abraham elucidates that the canonical practices, each in their

---

20. Abraham, "Emergence," 150–51.
21. Ibid.
22. Abraham, *Canon and Criterion*, 37–39. Emphases added.

own way "function in the healing and restoration of the human soul."[23] In short, canonical theism reveals the importance of "canonical practices" for soteriological ends and this study uses the term "orthopraxis" to refer to practices that can mediate saving grace.[24] Ergo, I coin the phrase "canonical orthopraxy" as shorthand to note canonical theism's emphasis on the soteriological relevance of praxis in the canonical tradition. In this, we share the same concept despite the use of different terms. As will be seen, "orthopraxis" is used within conservative theology in diverse capacities and each with different emphases on the value of praxis.

Finally, in view of the transforming potential of behavior, I contend that the early church understood salvation as not only grounded in "right knowledge" but also in "right behaviors and practices." We will soon see that when "right practices" are associated with ecclesial canons, it becomes evident how intimately orthopraxis and orthodoxy soteriologically relate. For now it is enough to say that retrieving the canonical practices of the church can bring to light the foundational work of orthopraxy for a renewal soteriology of embodiment. For this reason, canonical theism exemplifies the soteriological significance of orthopraxy because it discloses how ecclesial practices and behaviors are salvifically central to the church's canonical tradition. Yet, despite its positive contributions, canonical theism still has its critics; though they have mostly been focused on Abraham's research. We next attend to the main challenges raised about Abraham's canonical theism.

Abraham's Critics

Canon and Criterion became the catalyst text from which canonical theism emerged. Therefore, it serves as the vehicle from which I now address Abraham's critics. Generally, the reviews were positive; however, even among those who were most critical, the arguments basically dealt with two issues. The first issue concerned Abraham's understanding of what constituted the "canonical tradition" and the second was Abraham's chastened approach

23. Abraham, "Canonical Theism: Thirty Theses," 3.

24. A brief note on my use of the terms: *faith*, *grace*, and *salvation*. Throughout this chapter I stress the significance of the canonical tradition for "mediating grace" and then enunciate such grace as salvifically effective. Yet, chapter 1 closely identified salvation with "salvific *faith*" for the end of *rightly knowing God*. Therefore, when I speak of salvific *grace* I do so with the assumption that salvific *faith* is involved, whether or not such is explicitly stated.

Canonical Theism and the Salvific Role of Orthopraxy

toward epistemology in Western theology. I discuss the second matter in greater detail later in this chapter.

First, some critics press that Abraham's use of the word "canon" presumes a clearer acceptance and more common understanding of the term in the early church than may have actually been the case. The consequence of this, some hold, is that a false dichotomy is set up between soteriology and epistemology.[25] Canonical theism advocate, Daniel J. Treier acknowledges it is clear that,

> [T]he early church did situate Scripture within a network of, materials, persons, and practices, without some of the problematic epistemological fixations introduced by the Enlightenment. It is not clear, however, that all the elements of this network were deemed "canonical," or labeled as such without any distinctions in how the terminology pertained.[26]

Similarly Maurice Wiles alleges that Abraham does not thoroughly consider the disparate historical realities at play on the church's perception of canon and thereby, again, creates a false dichotomy between soteriology and epistemology.[27]

I agree with Treier and Wiles that greater clarification should be sought in how the first-century church used the word "canon" and if there were distinctions among the canonical materials. However, such concerns do not nullify Abraham's thesis that the church's canonical tradition operated as "means of grace" rather than "epistemic criterion." The false dichotomy critique misses the point of Abraham's canonical theism; he is not introducing two constituents but simply arguing that the Western church has placed too much weight on the epistemological capacity of canon to the neglect of its transformational (soteriological) benefit. In other words, few would contest that epistemology and soteriology work together (even Abraham grants this); the issue is how much emphasis should be placed on epistemology within soteriology. Abraham upholds that epistemology has gained too much authority in Western soteriology. I maintain now, even as I did in chapter 1, that conservative Christianity has overemphasized the intellectual aspect of salvation thereby creating a soteriological paradigm driven by epistemological concerns. This too is what canonical theism advances.[28]

25. Treier, "'A Looser Canon?'" 101–16.
26. Ibid., 106.
27. Wiles, *Review of Canon and Criterion*, 828–30.
28. While Abraham does not use the phrase "intellectualist soteriology" he does

PART THREE: SALVATION AND ORTHOPRAXY

Second, others are opposed to how Abraham minimizes epistemology in the canonical tradition and Scripture, in particular. For instance, Kenneth J. Stewart remarks that Abraham's claim of the church misinterpreting Scripture as criterion over canon is not supported by enough evidence.[29] He further charges that the early church did utilize Scripture for epistemological ends and that such was fully justified. Interestingly, Abraham agrees with this assertion and he too grants that such was appropriate; the point is that Abraham does not hold to the epistemological purpose of Scripture as strongly as Stewart.[30] Nevertheless, Stewart does not deal with the early church's awareness of the soteriological service of canon as means of grace. Even if it is admitted that the early church frequently read Scripture epistemologically, such does not bear on my appropriation of Abraham's canonical theism because Stewart's critique does not touch on Abraham's use of practices (orthopraxis) as soteriologically meaningful.

In sum, the most relevant criticisms have to do with Abraham's unapologetic indictment of Western Christianity's epistemizing of the canonical tradition.[31] While the issues raised in the preceding examples are important, none speak to the deeper problem that the Western church has come to view salvation in increasingly intellectualist terms, as evidenced by the soteriological weight placed on epistemology within the canonical tradition. I do not deny that epistemology is essential in soteriological reflection; otherwise, what one believes is inconsequential. However, when salvation centers more on believing the "right information" than being transformed into the fuller life of God, then such an understanding fails to reflect the pneumatological dynamism resident in the early church's soteriology.[32] It follows that the only major objection to Abraham's project bearing on this chapter regards his lack of priority on epistemology in the

---

contest the overly rationalist use of epistemology in soteriology. We are both basically referring to an intellectualist soteriology as I have enunciated in chapter 1.

29. Stewart, "William J. Abraham's Canon," 13–28.

30. For Abraham's explanation of the epistemological use of Scripture by the early Church, see: Abraham, *Canon and Criterion*, 469–70.

31. For instance, Stanley J. Grenz (in, "Deconstructing" 37–45) suggests that the practical implications of how to not confuse canon with criterion are not clearly and practically laid out. Others such as Kenneth Stewart and George Lindbeck, (in, Stewart, "William J. Abraham's Canon," 25; and Lindbeck, "Canon and Criterion," 68) argue against an unfair portrayal of Aquinas and the early Reformers, especially Martin Luther and John Calvin in their alleged epistemizing of canon.

32. Abraham does not deny that the canonical heritage has epistemic features, but he says they should not be conceived as the paramount end of that heritage.

Canonical Theism and the Salvific Role of Orthopraxy

canonical tradition, especially the canon of Scripture. This very objection further exposes the intellectualism I contend is so imbedded in Western soteriology.

Overall, Abraham's plea for the church to not confuse its canons as epistemic criteria but envisage them as soteriological means of grace has been well received. Abraham's exposition of canonical theism illuminates orthopraxy as an indispensable ingredient of a dynamic soteriology. I next explore two examples of orthopraxis in Protestantism and how each relates to soteriology. First, I consider the organization, Evangelicals for Social Action and second, George Lindbeck's postliberal theology. Finally, I compare and contrast each with how canonical theism renders the canonical practices for soteriological ends.

Orthopraxy in Contemporary Protestantism

The term orthopraxy is used in varying purviews of theological discussion and carries a variety of meanings in soteriology. The soteriological paradigm associated with each domain determines what behaviors and practices are important based upon how they contribute to its soteriology. This is markedly true of its use in Evangelicals for Social Action and George Lindbeck's postliberal integration of religious beliefs and practices. While there are other examples of orthopraxy, I have chosen these two because they represent influential strands of orthopraxis in present-day Protestantism.[33] We now briefly survey each movement and reflect on why orthopraxy is so important to its mission.

Evangelicals for Social Action and Orthopraxy

Evangelicals for Social Action (ESA) is a conservative evangelical organization that emphasizes the importance of Christian behavior and practices for the mission of the church. In 1973, ESA was launched following the completion of the Chicago Declaration of Evangelical Social Concern.[34]

---

33. Other contemporary theological examples of orthopraxy can be found in feminist theology (see Chopp and Davaney, *Horizons*), green theology (see Deane-Drummond, *Gaia*), and post-colonial theologies (see Keller et al., *Postcolonial Theologies*).

34. The Chicago Declaration of Evangelical Social Concern (http://www.evangelicalsforsocialaction.org/about/history/chicago-declaration-of-evangelical-social-concern/) was a document signed by a diverse gathering of evangelical leaders at a

Part Three: Salvation and Orthopraxy

Through this document, numerous evangelical leaders collectively affirmed the need for increased social engagement of faith within conservative Christianity. Even though ESA does not highlight the word "orthopraxis" or "orthopraxy" it does believe in the power of actions and behaviors directed toward social transformation. The words they use instead are "social action" and "holistic ministry." To best understand their emphasis on Christian practices, I begin with a brief introduction of its founder, Ron Sider and his theological appropriation of behavior.

Ronald J. Sider (b. 1939) is professor of Theology, Holistic Ministry, and Public Policy at Palmer Theological Seminary and author of numerous books and articles concerning a variety of social justice concerns.[35] Sider is the founder and President of Evangelicals for Social Action. ESA's mission is to develop and communicate a Christian approach to social justice. Sider articulates his views about the theological significance of behavior in his most popular book, *Rich Christians in an Age of Hunger*. This book was a rally call for Christians to conscientiously limit their spending, live simpler lives, and choose to act in ways that empower the poor and reduce poverty worldwide.[36] Sider sees such behavior as not merely an option but essential to the Christian gospel of salvation. Such emphasis on the power of choice to effect moral change in society reflects awareness of the soteriological significance of praxis. In a 1976 article in *Christian Century*, Sider repudiates what he calls the "evangelical heresy that orthodoxy is more important than orthopraxis" and later he contends that "orthodoxy is as important as orthopraxis."[37] He, thus, rejects dualism between behavior and belief. Next we see how Sider's opinions are similarly reflected in ESA.[38]

Evangelicals for Social Action argues that the Christian should be responsibly engaged not only in evangelistic preaching but activities and

---

Thanksgiving workshop at Calvin College in 1973. The gathering was focused on improving Christian awareness of pressing social concerns. The document emerged as these leaders corporately confessed failure as a movement to confront injustice, racism, and discrimination against women, while pledging to do a better job in the future. Much of the radical shift in Evangelicalism becoming more socially aware and active in the public sphere followed this historic gathering of delegates.

35. Sider has written extensively on the need for a holistic understanding of Christian ministry and mission. See bibliography for some of his most popular books (*Completely Pro-Life*; *Evangelism*; *Good News*; *Just Generosity*; *The Scandal*).

36. Sider, *Rich Christians*, 189–208.

37. Sider, "Call for Evangelical Nonviolence," 753–57.

38. Hereafter, when I refer to the praxis of Evangelicals for Social Action, or their beliefs about practice, I presume Sider's views and praxis.

Canonical Theism and the Salvific Role of Orthopraxy

behaviors focused on social justice and compassion. They depict such praxis as *holistic* ministry,

> Holistic ministry addresses the full range of human needs, from material deprivation to spiritual alienation. All people are both spiritual and material beings. To minister effectively, churches must work through both evangelism and social action—addressing the needs of both body and spirit.[39]

Holistic ministry implies the need for an orthopraxis of compassion, justice, and social action.

This book identifies the mission of ESA as orthopraxically driven because its understanding of Christian mission is holistic. Orthopraxy is implied in the following statement.

> Jesus' ministry was both proclaiming and demonstrating the Good News of the kingdom, and ESA believes that followers of Jesus should therefore do the same. As long as poverty, injustice, and oppression exist, God's people must continue to address material and spiritual issues in their ministries.[40]

In other words, an orthopraxis of compassion and justice is necessary if Christians are to faithfully follow the example of Christ.

In view of the preceding, ESA affirms the necessity of orthopraxy because a holistic mission requires acts of compassion and justice for the marginalized poor of the earth. However, ESA regards Christian praxis mostly in post-salvific terms as seen in the number of references imploring Christians to embrace the kinds of sacrificial, compassionate, and just practices already mentioned. For instance, in *Rich Christians in an Age of Hunger*, even when Sider mentions such practices in the context of repentance and salvation they are subsequent to salvation (i.e., acceptance of evangelistic offer) rather than integral channels for mediating faith. Again, in *One-Sided Christianity?* when Sider responds to whether evangelism and social action should be seen as distinct, he says they should because only evangelism provides knowledge of Jesus whereas social action improves living conditions.[41] The point, for our purposes, is that when Sider relates social praxis with salvation, orthopraxis seems to function separately rather than conjointly with orthodoxy. Regardless that Sider affirms equality between or-

---

39. See, ESA, "Holistic Ministry Defined."
40. ESA, "Shouldn't we be Focused on Evangelism?"
41. Sider, *One-Sided Christianity*, 159–73.

PART THREE: SALVATION AND ORTHOPRAXY

thodoxy and orthopraxis, "right behavior" is identified with a post-salvific social action whereas knowledge about Christ is identified with salvation. This represents the same kind of dualism (justification vs. sanctification) we argued against in chapter 1. Next, we look at George Lindbeck's treatment of practices in postliberal theology.

George Lindbeck and Orthopraxy

George Lindbeck (b. 1923) is a Lutheran ecumenical theologian who has engaged both inter-religious and extra-religious research and dialogue. He was a faculty member at Yale Divinity School (1952–1993) until he retired. For most of his career, Lindbeck was involved in ecumenical efforts, including his appointment as a "delegate observer" at the Second Vatican Council (1962–1965) and, subsequently, was a member of the Joint Commission between the Vatican and Lutheran World Federation (1968–1983).

Lindbeck's theological contribution arose out of his dissatisfaction with how the classical tradition and modern liberalism both conceived doctrine; consequently, he crafted an alternative model. The former had come to understand doctrine largely from an intellectualistic perspective where it was understood chiefly as propositional statements whereas the latter viewed doctrine on essentially subjective and existentialist terms.[42] Lindbeck asserts that doctrine functions in a regulative or rule enforcing capacity. Its task is to exclude certain ranges of meanings rather than definitively nail down an unequivocal definition.[43] Doctrine serves a regulative rather than an explicative role in regard to religious truth. Lindbeck also recognized that there is a similarity between how religious doctrines and the practices of its tradition relate and how grammar influences language.[44] For instance, Lindbeck states, "There are numberless thoughts we cannot think, sentiments we cannot have, and realities we cannot perceive unless we learn to use the appropriate symbol systems [i.e., languages]."[45] Consequently, he proposed a cultural-linguistic theory delineating how doctrines are both informed by and informing of Christian traditions and the practices associated with them. For this reason, his proposal has been termed "postliberal" theology and as such, has opened up fresh new ways

42. Yong, *Hospitality*, 50.
43. Lindbeck, *Nature of Doctrine*, 18–19.
44. Ibid., 32–41.
45. Ibid., 34.

Canonical Theism and the Salvific Role of Orthopraxy

of thinking about the relationship between practices and beliefs in religious thought.[46] Lindbeck's theory has been so influential it has launched a "postliberal" theological movement taking orthopraxis more seriously in the formation of doctrine.[47]

Here, I am not interested in unfolding the philosophical and historical details of Lindbeck's postliberalism but to note how his methodology accounts for the integration of orthodoxy and orthopraxis in theological reflection. Lindbeck's application of orthopraxis was motivated by ecumenical concerns to help overcome divergent doctrinal beliefs in intra and inter-religious discussion.[48] A postliberal endorsement of practices affirms the capacity of orthopraxis to both influence and be influenced by orthodoxy. Rather than religion evolving from an *a priori* cognitive-propositionalist awareness (i.e., traditional view) or an experiential-expressive approach (i.e., liberal view), it actually is the source of such truths and experiences. Lindbeck explains, "Rather, to become religious—no less than to become culturally or linguistically competent—is to interiorize a set of skills by practice and training."[49] So with a focus not on the disparity of varying truth claims but on intra-religious practices, rituals, and behaviors, divergent beliefs evolve in response to the specific conditions which occasioned them.[50] The undergirding presupposition is that religious belief is shaped more by the practices one learns in a religion than the reverse. Hence, Lindbeck attests that religious knowledge evolves more out of reflection on the practices one has adopted as part of a religious community than merely the contemplation of various scriptural and theological assertions. Far from a peripheral influence on the acquisition of theological knowledge, religious practices (as embedded in a cultural-linguistic milieu called "religion") are instrumental in shaping what one believes.

Specifically, postliberal theology relates to soteriology because it resists the static estimation of salvation based on intellectualist models of orthodoxy highlighting rationality over behavior and affectivity. Lindbeck

---

46. Other than Lindbeck's *Nature of Doctrine*, for more on postliberal theology see Lindbeck, *Church in a Postliberal Age*.

47. See, Vidu, *Postliberal Theological Method*, and to see a dialogue between evangelical and postliberal theologians see, Phillips and Okholm, *The Nature of Confession*.

48. Lindbeck, *Nature of Doctrine*, chapter 5.

49. Ibid., 35.

50. Lindbeck illustrates how divergent views can be accommodated through applying his cultural-linguistic approach to the Nicean-Chalcedonian creeds, Marian dogma, and papal and scriptural infallibility doctrines (see *Nature of Doctrine*, 92–104).

Part Three: Salvation and Orthopraxy

claims that religious doctrines do not *describe* salvation as much as it affirms salvation *is a process* whereby one is continually formed by doctrine and the practices associated with it.[51] However, Lindbeck's use of "salvation" has more to do with the church being a "faithfully witnessing people" to the God who saves.[52] The salvific mandate of the church to remain faithful to God and "a sign of the promised redemption" seems to stress salvation more in terms of consistent faithfulness than as a dynamic reality of ongoing growth.[53]

As we have considered orthopraxy in ESA and George Lindbeck's postliberal theology, the former reveals an appropriation of praxis as a post-salvific response of holistic ministry, while the latter endorses praxis as inseparable from doctrine to form lifestyles that reflect the church's mission to testify of God's saving grace. While both endorse orthopraxis as vital for healthy and effective Christian mission and faith formation, neither emphasize its relevance in mediating grace for soteriological transformation. Of the two movements, Lindbeck's most fully grasps the potential of praxis to influence orthodoxy. However, his application was generally more limited to the specifics of *understanding* doctrine than to our more general sense of "knowing God" in regard to salvific faith.

Taking into account the preceding, one can see how orthopraxy is a prime feature in ESA and George Lindbeck's postliberal theology. Nevertheless, there are distinctions between how the canonical tradition and these two movements appreciate orthopraxy in respect to salvation. While both endorse the importance of orthopraxis, neither exploits praxis for the soteriological mediation of grace. Once again, the canonical tradition identifies Christian praxis with the historical canons of the church as mediators of salvific grace for ongoing transformation into the image of God. In ESA, orthopraxis is chiefly a post-salvific actuality whereby the believer engages in practices of social justice and compassion as part of the gospel call to holistic ministry. In Lindbeck's postliberal theology, praxis is critical because it is necessary for fully grasping the import of Christian doctrine. While such "orthopraxic knowledge" may indeed allow for a more robust rendering of doctrine, Lindbeck does not specifically link behavior to soteriological growth into the fullness of God. Next, we quickly review what we have covered and how it serves the overall purpose of this chapter.

---

51. Ibid., chapter 3.
52. Lindbeck, *Church in a Postliberal Age*, 159.
53. Ibid.

Canonical Theism and the Salvific Role of Orthopraxy

Clarifying Canonical Practices

In keeping with the aims of this section, I have situated canonical theism, with the help of William Abraham, as a new theological movement in the twenty-first century. Then I addressed key critiques against aspects of this movement as articulated in Abraham's text, *Canon and Criterion*. Next, I contextualized orthopraxis in conservative Protestantism as engaged within Evangelicals for Social Action and George Lindbeck's postliberal theology. Finally, I compared both examples with the orthopraxis of canonical theism. All that remains now is to lay out how canonical theism can move us forward in our soteriological proposal. However, such a road map will be more meaningful if we can move from a general awareness of canonical practices to one that is specific. Heretofore, I have referred to "the practices of the church" or "canonical practices" without paying special attention to any in particular. Now, I identify three major practices of the early and patristic church (baptism, the Eucharist, and reading of Scripture) and elaborate how each served the soteriological mandate of the canonical tradition.

I begin with a discussion of baptism as the "rite of entrance" into the church, typically implemented by immersion to Christians following an initial period of instruction.[54] In the early church there was flexibility in how one was baptized, likely accounting for the varying settings in which baptism occurred. It did not matter if the water was running or still or where one was baptized and even though the norm was immersion, baptism could still be accomplished in different ways.[55] In the catechetical tradition, baptism often concluded after many months (sometimes years) of instruction for initiation into the Christian faith. Baptism was both an *act of repentance* and a *confession of faith*.[56] As repentance, it symbolized one's identification with the death and resurrection of Christ and the washing away of sins.[57] As confession, baptism was a two-fold pledge of commitment to Christ and the Church as well as renunciation of Satan and his works.[58] In the early church, baptism was immediately followed by the anointing of oil (chrismation) for the infilling of the Spirit.[59]

---

54. Ferguson, "Baptism," 131.
55. See Roberts and Donaldson, "Teaching of the Twelve," 377–82.
56. Ferguson, "Baptism," 134.
57. McKinion, *Life and Practice*, 6.
58. Ibid.
59. Ibid.

Part Three: Salvation and Orthopraxy

In light of the foregoing, baptism was an initiatory practice (rite) that officially welcomed the participant into the community of faith and divine life in Christ. Canonical theism emphasizes the sacramental quality of the water in this rite to mediate the presence of God to literally wash away sins and impart a new nature.[60] As such, baptism was soteriological because of the grace it mediated for transformation. Its impact was singularly definitive in the life of the believer. We now consider the Eucharist.

The Eucharist is the consecrating of bread and wine in the sacramental practice of Christ's death and resurrection in the Church's liturgy.[61] Also known as the *Lord's Supper*, *Holy Communion*, and *Communion*, the Eucharist was a canonical practice reserved only for those who had already been baptized. In this practice, believers regularly gathered to drink a portion of wine and eat an allocation of bread. Justin Martyr (100–165 AD) describes baptism:

> And on the day called Sunday, all who live in cities or in the country gather together to one place, and the memoirs of the apostles or the writings of the prophets are read, as long as time permits... Then we all rise together and pray, and, as we before said, when our prayer is ended, bread and wine and water are brought... and there is a distribution to each, and a participation of that over which thanks have been given.[62]

This passage signifies weekly eucharistic participation (i.e., on Sunday). After this manner, just as Christ commanded his disciples, "Do this in remembrance of me" (1 Cor 11:24, 25), the faithful repeatedly met for this sacred rite. The gathering of believers at this "meal" ever reinforced their pledge of faith to Christ and each other.[63] While other themes have been associated with the Eucharist (eschatological hope, fellowship, compassion for the poor, healing, forgiveness of sins, etc.), I focus on this practice as a recurring means of grace for nourishment of faith, strengthening of community, and growth into the *imago Dei* as believers gathered in remembrance of Christ.

Through the materiality of bread and wine, God nourishes the soul of his saints by the Spirit for gradual formation into the divine nature.[64] Ca-

---

60. Van Kirk, "Christ Present," 86.
61. Ferguson, "Eucharist," 320.
62. Justin Martyr, "The First Apology," 186.
63. Bradshaw, *Early Christian*, 40.
64. Ibid., 91.

nonical theist Natalie Van Kirk explains that, "The fathers were convinced that Christians did indeed become what they ate . . . Consumption of the elements of the eucharist made body and soul more like Christ, transforming Christians into the little christs that Paul called them to become."[65] In this manner, through the frequent practice of eucharistic participation the believer nurtured ongoing reception of transforming grace in his or her life. Next we consider the reading of Scripture as our third canonical practice.

Scripture played a formational role in the lives of believers in the early and patristic church and was frequently utilized in a variety of contexts. Scriptures were read in conjunction with worship to emphasize the beauty of God's attributes and they were read for meditation and prayer to facilitate communion with God, as seen in the practice of *Lectio Divina* (divine reading).[66] For more pragmatic ends, Scripture was read for liturgical (church order), instructional (catechetical), leadership (episcopal oversight), theological (preaching), and apologetic (defense of the faith) purposes. Canonical theism contends that Scripture was not read in isolation of the canonical heritage but in unison and so mediated salvific grace for healing, restoration, and renewal. As incorporated with such practices, Scripture enabled ongoing renewal in the life of the church. Along similar lines, Abraham argues that the practice of Scripture was not primarily as an epistemological criterion to justify truth claims but as a soteriological means of grace. While this will be further developed, it is enough to say that reading Scripture was one canonical practice, even if primary, within a broad canonical heritage.

Let's now pull all of this together. By illustrating how the early church's practices—or, a canonical orthopraxy—were soteriological means of grace, we show how orthopraxy plays an important role in crafting a renewal soteriology of embodiment. Toward this end, I employ canonical theism to unveil the value of orthopraxy in the early church's soteriology. Next, we look at how transformation is a central theme in the canonical tradition and how this relates to our soteriological purpose of orthopraxy.

---

65. Van Kirk, "Christ Present," 88.
66. For more on *Lectio Divina* see, Masini, *Lectio Divina*.

PART THREE: SALVATION AND ORTHOPRAXY

CANONICAL THEISM'S ORTHOPRAXY IN THEOLOGICAL PERSPECTIVE

In this section, we examine transformation as the overall aim of the canonical heritage and how the practices of this heritage are largely marked by communal, ritual, and sacramental attributes. Then we explore how the meaning of canon has shifted from being a means of grace to an epistemological criterion. Finally, we will see that because the canonical tradition was focused more on soteriological growth than epistemology, the shift had significant soteriological ramifications.

As we proceed, two points bear repeating. First, when I speak of "canonical practices" I limit our discussion to baptism, the Eucharist, and reading of Scripture. Even though the canonical practices are not reduced to these, the soteriological implications I draw from them will be applicable to the others. Second, my references to the practices and theology of the early church are based on Abraham's interpretation of the same and whether there were more or less canonical practices than he contends or whether epistemology played as little of a role for the early Christians as he insists is not important. What is vital for our present purposes is Abraham's assertion that canonical practices were ultimately soteriological and, as such, means of grace for the believer.

Transformational Practices

Canonical theism highlights the transformational potential of behaviors and practices in the early church. Abraham states the singular focus of the canonical tradition was always to mediate grace for the renewing work of God in the believer.

> In attempting to give a tacit account which would fit with the writings and practices available, my favoured category [of the canonical tradition] is that of means of grace. Thus the sacraments, the Scriptures, the Creed, the canon of Fathers, and the like . . . were construed as materials and practices . . . which mediated the life of God . . . to bring about participation in the life of God.[67]

---

67. Abraham, *Canon and Criterion*, 112. Charles Gutenson defines *means of grace*: "By calling these sacraments 'means of grace,' the church has affirmed that in some mysterious way, by participating in these means of grace, individual believers and the church as a whole are changed through an inner working of God's Spirit" ("Canonical Heritage," 248).

Canonical Theism and the Salvific Role of Orthopraxy

Describing the canonical practices as "means of grace" indicates it is effective for healing and transforming the believer through the ministry of the Holy Spirit.[68] Canonical theist, Jason Vickers envisions the canonical heritage as a medicine chest and the various canons as divine medicine.

> Canonical theists conceive of the canonical heritage of the church as a grand medicine chest full of prescriptions that have the power to cure all that ails human persons spiritually, intellectually, emotionally, physically, and morally. The medicines are, as we have seen, the materials, persons, and practices that make up the canonical heritage, including scripture, images, sacraments, episcopacy, teachers and saints, liturgy, doctrine, and so on.[69]

The canons existed as receptacles of grace for furthering formation into the likeness of God. They initiated "new believers into the life of God, returning them to the original intention of their creation. They were to mediate salvation . . . and bring about profound transformation."[70] The telos of such transformation was *theosis* or *deification*, which literally means to be made like God or to be conformed into the *imago Dei* (i.e., image of God).[71] Deification was rooted in the conviction that Christ came not only to take away the sins of the world but to enable humans, by grace, to participate in the life of God. On that account, *theosis* suggests the kind of soteriological transformation the early church expected of its canonical heritage. Canonical theist, Charles Gutenson explains,

> [O]ne looks not to the canonical heritage merely to receive satisfaction of one's inquisitiveness; rather one consults the canonical

---

68. Abraham, *Canon and Criterion*, 1; and Vickers, "Medicine," 11–26.

69. Vickers, "Medicine," 19.

70. Abraham, *Canon and Criterion*, 467.

71. *Theosis* is a common doctrine in Eastern Christianity. Since the inception of the first-century church, Western Christian theology illustrated distinctly different emphases than Eastern Christian theology; such was particularly evident after the two halves of the Church officially divided in 1054 AD. These differences can be detected in the respective Churches' doctrines of salvation. Western Christianity generally emphasized the problem of sin and its solution via proper knowledge of God while Eastern Christianity principally focused its soteriology on the problem of a corrupted human nature and the solution of a transformed nature into the *imago Dei* via grace (these shifts are broadly traced later in this chapter). However, prior to the schism, *theosis* was a common theological belief in the majority of Christendom. It is within this soteriological aim of transformation that the canonical traditions of the church existed. For a more thorough understanding of the doctrine of *theosis*, see: Lossky, *Mystical Theology*, esp. chapters 4, 6, and 10; Christensen and Wittung, *Partakers*; and Ware, *Orthodox Way*, 22, 74, 109, 124.

heritage of the church in order to have sanctifying grace mediated to one in such a way that one is actually sanctified ... One does not read, pray, reflect, and act upon the canons of the church so as to know what it means to be conformed to the image of Christ; one does these things so as to be conformed to the image of Christ.[72]

The canonical tradition facilitates the soteriological call of believers to become "partakers of the divine nature" (2 Pet 1:4) as implied in the doctrine of *theosis*.

Certainly, any tradition as complex and diverse as the canonical heritage defies simplistic characterization. Nevertheless, my intent is not to exhaustively detail every aspect of that heritage but to focus on some of those components that were participatory—i.e., baptism, the Eucharist, and Scripture reading. I next speculate how the communal, ritual, and sacramental character of the canonical practices influenced its transformative capacity.

Transformation through Communal Practices

The canonical practices are transformational because they are communal. That such practices existed within an ecclesial domain means that the canonical practices are social. The canonical tradition was birthed out of a shared sense of common life together in which many of the canons required communal participation. For instance, baptism and the Eucharist involved communal participation and Scripture was to be read in corporate worship. Robert Louis Wilken (scholar of early Christian thought and practice) states that, "in the early church baptism was not a private affair but a communal celebration of the entire community. Everyone had a role, the bishop and other clergy, neighbors, friends, and family."[73] Of the Eucharist, he notes, "the preacher sought not only to explain the words but also invited the congregation to enter into the reality itself, the mystery of Christ, by the use of words."[74] Similarly, Douglas Koskela (a canonical theism advocate) remarks, "Thus one who reads Scripture from outside the practicing community of faith will inevitably experience something very different than one immersed in the full range and riches of the canonical heritage."[75]

72. Gutenson, "Canonical Heritage," 253.
73. Wilken, *Spirit*, 39.
74. Ibid., 44.
75. Koskela, "Authority of Scripture," 220.

Canonical Theism and the Salvific Role of Orthopraxy

The ecclesial community, then, provided a critical backdrop within which the canonical practices existed. The social arena of these practices provided ample opportunities for the kinds of encouragement, accountability, motivation, and instruction needed for continued formation.[76]

Transformation through Ritual Practices

The ritualistic nature of canonical practices encourage transformation. Ritual activities refer to "any practice or pattern of behavior regularly performed in a set manner."[77] Such a definition accurately reflects many features of the canonical tradition. Canonical theist, Frederick Aquino attests that *The Philokalia*[78] often references elements of the canonical tradition when it mentions the ritual practices of prayer, fasting, contemplation (on Scripture and/or teachings of the Fathers), baptism, and the Eucharist.[79]

The canonical tradition sanctioned certain ritual behaviors because they mediated grace to the believers in a way that was consistently transforming. For this reason, these practices became normative for the community of faith. For instance, Eastern Orthodox theologian Vladimir Lossky notes the value of ritual activities for formation, "As for fasts, vigils, prayers, alms and other good works done in the name of Christ—these are the means whereby we acquire the Holy Spirit."[80] As ritualistic, the canonical practices provided a fixed structure of proven practices (whether engaged daily, weekly, monthly, etc.) that offered an ordered approach toward *theosis*.[81] The regularity of canonical practices, especially the weekly Eucha-

---

76. Lindbeck expresses the power of the Christian community to transform and impact members through their shared sense of embodied experience of the gospel message. He says, "The proclamation of the gospel, as a Christian would put it, may be first of all the telling of the story, but this gains power and meaning insofar as it is embodied in the total gestalt of community life and action" (*Nature of Doctrine*, 36).

77. Random House, *Random House Webster's*, 1137.

78. The *Philokalia* is a compilation of writings spanning the fourth to fifteenth centuries and used as a guide to implement long-term practices to sustain godly habits for continued growth into the life of God (Aquino, "Epistemic Virtues," 184).

79. Palmer et al., *The Philokalia*. Though not comprehensive, for prayer, see 15, 17, 20, 25, 35, 54, 106, 307, 311, 317, 320, 367, 377, 387; for fasting, see 25, 42, 45, 57, 61, 308, 319, 321, 327, 344; for contemplation, see 64, 128, 141, 163, 179, 186, 201, 203, 208, 219, 238, 255; for baptism, see 14, 39, 45, 109, 133, 152, 274; and for the Eucharist, see 351, 356, 363, 372.

80. Lossky, *Mystical Theology*, 196.

81. For more on ritual and *theosis*, see Ibid., chapter 10.

rist and numerous opportunities for reading and meditating on Scripture, nurture a lifestyle of discipline and prayerful attentiveness that sensitize the believer to the work of the Spirit. Finally, the transforming power of ritual can be seen in its ability to keep the believer focused on God and his purposes rather than the worries and distractions of daily life. Natalie Van Kirk succinctly echoes, "The mysteries are, at one level, ways in which the church remembers its future."[82] Jason Vickers similarly attests that whether the believer engages in canons of confessional statements or creeds, canons of Scripture for study, devotion, or worship, canons of liturgy for the practice of worship, or canons of revered teachers for study, most contain ritualistic attributes that facilitate the church's growth in divine grace.[83] Thence, ritual practices can serve as effective means of grace to cultivate progressive degrees of holiness.

Transformation through Sacramental Practices

Canonical practices are transformational because they are sacramental. While "the sacraments" usually refer to the canonical practices of baptism, the Eucharist, and Chrismation, the term is used here more broadly. Because canonical practices are sacramental, they are soteriologically transforming. Furthermore, to say that canonical practices are sacramental is to say that they mediate the grace of God in a way that is not abstract or intangible but physically and materially embodied. Wilken describes how God mediates salvation through the materiality of human existence.

> Christianity is an affair of things. At the center of Christian worship is a material, palpable thing, the consecrated bread and wine, through water one is joined to the church, and through things, the Holy Cross, the rock of Calvary, the sacred tomb, God accomplished the salvation of the world.[84]

As sacramental, the canonical practices link transcendent grace to the physicality of earthly life so that human beings can actually encounter divine grace.

Van Kirk unfolds how the sacraments prove that the material world is important to God because, "without the presence of the Trinity in the

---

82. Van Kirk, "Christ Present," 77.
83. Vickers, "Medicine," 26.
84. Wilken, *Spirit*, 261.

Canonical Theism and the Salvific Role of Orthopraxy

materiality of the sacraments, there can be no union of God and humankind in the person of Christ."[85] The physicality of sacramental practice anchors the believer's experience of God in the present moment and keeps it from becoming just a vague mystical experience. In other words, embodied human life requires a tangible experience of God if it is to be authentically transformed. Note how the early and patristic Fathers linked sacramental practice with concrete religious experience. St. Mark the Ascetic (fifth century) said, "Everyone baptized in the orthodox manner has received mystically the fullness of grace; but he becomes conscious of this grace only to the extent that he *actively observes* the commandments."[86] St. Theodoros the Great Ascetic (ninth century) speaks of the sacrament of baptism to purify the saint.[87] And finally, the catechetical and mystagogical[88] lectures of St. Cyril of Jerusalem are filled with teachings on the sacramental power of baptism and the Eucharist.[89]

To say that canonical practices are transformational in that they are communal, ritualistic, and sacramental is to say that God discloses himself to humans as embodied beings. It was not through an abstract mental assent or a mysteriously transcendental state by which the early believers encountered God but through practices that tangibly mediated the divine presence. For this reason the early Church made sure that set practices were embedded in its canonical tradition so that through faithful engagement believers could slowly progress into the fullness of God.

Now that I have enunciated the soteriological relevance of practices in the early church's canonical tradition, why do we not see similar emphases in Christianity today? Abraham contends that the loss of practices as soteriologically relevant is tied to the church confusing *canon* with *criterion*. So, the canonical heritage was increasingly construed as an epistemological criterion rather than soteriological means of grace. Next, I clarify what is meant by canon and criterion, the heart of this confusion, and how it bears on the soteriological presuppositions of conservative Christian theology in respect to Scripture.

---

85. Van Kirk, "Christ Present," 78.
86. Palmer et al., *The Philokalia*, 133. Emphasis added.
87. Ibid., 45.
88. *Mystagogical* refers to initiation into the "mysteries" (i.e., sacred rites of the initiated believer); hence, these lectures are those following the catechumen's baptism after which he or she is prepared for the remaining sacraments in the canonical tradition.
89. McCauley and Stephenson, *Fathers of the Church*, vols. 1 and 2.

PART THREE: SALVATION AND ORTHOPRAXY

Shifting of Canonical Tradition: Means of Grace to Epistemological Certainty

This section suggests that the canonical items were originally practiced as means of grace but over time became epistemological centers for warranting belief. Specifically, I will expose the prevalence of this shift within the Protestant understanding of Scripture. I conclude with the implications of an epistemologically-driven practice of reading Scripture.

The early and patristic church commonly understood that canonical items uniformly functioned for the believer's growth into the likeness of God. Though the canons varied in use, all served the goal of transformation. Abraham explains how the canonical tradition works.

> The canonical heritage of the church . . . operates as a complex means of grace that restores the image of God in human beings and brings them into communion with God and with each other in the church. Each component is primarily an instrument to be used in spiritual direction and formation.[90]

Utilized in such a harmonious fashion, the canonical heritage displayed a reliable method of initiation and formation throughout the believer's life. Every aspect of the canonical tradition has its own unique purpose; Scripture was not canonized for the same ends as the creeds, nor were the creeds to fulfill the duty of the episcopate any more than the episcopate was to replace baptism.[91]

Canonical theism draws attention to a crucial shift in the church's expectations of these canonical materials (particularly, Scripture) and, consequently, its soteriology. Abraham associates this deviation with a confusion of the term *canon* with *criterion*.[92] He defines canon as, "a means of grace: that is, materials, persons, and practices intended to initiate one into the divine life."[93] Over a span of many centuries, ecclesial canons were reconceived in epistemological terms.[94] "Epistemic criteria," says Abraham, "belong to a very different arena [than canon] . . . Historically they have arisen out of intellectual curiosity and out of conflict concerning what to believe as

---

90. Abraham, "Canonical Theism: Thirty Theses," 3.

91. Ibid.

92. Abraham's seminal text, *Canon and Criterion*, serves as our primary text in evaluating this shift.

93. Abraham, *Canon and Criterion*, 27.

94. Ibid., 2.

Canonical Theism and the Salvific Role of Orthopraxy

true."[95] The confusion of these terms is not insignificant, but signals a whole new paradigm regarding the function of the canonical heritage. One of the driving theses of canonical theism is that epistemological certainty was never the principle of any canon, much less, Scripture. Abraham contends, "[I]n the early days of the Church, canons were not epistemic norms. They were means of grace given by the Holy Spirit to bring order to the life of the Church and to mediate salvation to those who would use them in a way appropriate to their nature."[96] In the canonical tradition, epistemology served soteriology. Nevertheless, epistemological matters were not absent, they were simply not dominant. While the church did not ignore the need to determine what was or was not theologically orthodox, epistemological issues were situated amidst the practices of the church, not in isolation of them.[97] Orthodoxy and orthopraxis worked conjointly within the canonical tradition. As mediators of salvific grace, the practices of the church provided opportunities for believers to encounter God within their ecclesial context. The canonical heritage pertained to more than just ensuring accurate reception of divine revelation; it was a response to that revelation.[98]

The confusion of these terms follows from epistemological expectations that most keenly evolved in the church since the official separation of its Eastern and Western halves in 1054 AD. According to Abraham, the church in the West (both Roman Catholic and later Protestant) underwent a radical transition in how it grasped the purpose of its canons. The canon of Scripture and the tradition of the Church were thereby interpreted as divinely dictated, and the office of the papacy was believed to have, under the right circumstances, a kind of epistemological access to the mind and will of God that was not commonly held in the early and patristic periods of the church.[99] The canonical heritage was essentially reduced to the episcopate (i.e., Tradition) and Scripture as they were increasingly used for epistemo-

---

95. Ibid., 1–2.

96. Ibid., 81–82.

97. The value of orthodoxy is manifest in the numerous battles the early Church faced (especially up to the Second General Council at Constantinople in 381 AD). However, such emphasis on sound orthodoxy arose out of the church's common practice of the canonical tradition. The canonical practices (orthopraxy) informed orthodoxy and as such, the two were inseparable. The subsequent trend of conceiving the canonical tradition as an epistemological vehicle ensuring proper belief was a confusion of the original principle of the Church's canons.

98. Abraham, *Canon and Criterion*, 468.

99. Ibid., 471.

logical ends. While soteriological concerns were not absent, the canonical tradition was largely framed in epistemological terms. Abraham explains.

> This [epistemological] reading of the canonical tradition began to overshadow any soteriological vision of the canonical heritage, even though soteriological considerations were never abandoned... Within the Church in the West, how one knew that one knew the truth about God overshadowed knowing God.[100]

So, what was previously a manifold array of canonical means of grace eventually became epistemological criteria leading to the creation of additional canons. Such is starkly seen in how the epistemizing of the episcopate led to the canonization of the doctrine of papal infallibility (in Western Catholicism), and the same of the Bible led to the canonization of the doctrine of the inerrancy of Scripture (in many segments of Protestant faith).[101] In both cases, specific canonical items were reinterpreted as epistemological criteria to validate specific appeals to absolute truth. Accordingly, the material content and duty of the canonical heritage was radically transformed.

Now we reflect on how this shift has impacted our understanding and practice of Scripture reading. Scripture was greatly impacted by the epistemizing of the canonical tradition. From the inception of the church, the main rationale for canonizing Scripture was to provide an authorized compilation of books for use in worship.[102] The overarching purpose of Scripture was more about providing spiritual sustenance than finding epistemic criteria for securing theological truths. Abraham reiterates,

> [T]he church that evangelized the Roman Empire needed more than a canon of scripture to get the job done; minimally, it also needed a canon of doctrine. The whole canonical enterprise,

---

100. Ibid.

101. Space does not permit more discussion about the epistemizing of the episcopate into the papacy and the eventual canonization of the doctrine of papal infallibility. Abraham helpfully summarizes this shift: "[T]he deployment of papal infallibility transformed what was originally a tacit claim about divine guidance in the Church as a whole into an explicitly formulated canon of divine revelation which gave precedence to the Pope in resolving crucial disputes about the very content and meaning of divine revelation itself. Thus two canonical changes were really taking place at once. A complex practice was transformed into a norm of truth, which was constructed by making what was originally one part of a tacit vision of divine revelation into an explicit and canonical theory of special revelation. This complex development represented a radical re-conception of the canonical heritage of the Church. It constituted a deep epistemizing of the canons of the Church" (*Canon and Criterion*, 116).

102. Ibid., 140.

Canonical Theism and the Salvific Role of Orthopraxy

including the adoption of a canon of doctrine, was driven by soteriological and theological concerns; the place of epistemology was relative and secondary.[103]

Even more, the most capable and revered theologians of the patristic period knew that their theological systems involved more than just Scripture.[104]

Abraham advances that when one separates Scripture from the matrix of canonical items and uses it for epistemic means, one fails to recognize that mediation of grace had always been its highest end.[105] The "Rule of Faith," as a part of the canonical tradition, was a compilation of core theological beliefs to which the early church referred and against which Scripture was read to aid in interpretation. So, the common practice of reading Scripture as a solitary exercise apart from the fellowship of Christians without engaging other canonical practices diverges from the early church's practice. Rather, Abraham claims, "Scriptures found a home alongside and within a whole series of canonical materials and practices . . . It needed to be read and pondered in the context of worship, sacramental practice, creedal summary, pedagogical expertise, devout commentary, and iconographic display."[106] The canon of Scripture then was consolidated within the widely diverse array of canonical practices and materials of the church. Koskela explains how the Reformation led to changes in the practice of Scripture reading.

> [O]ne significant consequence of the Protestant Reformation was the detachment of the Bible from the ecclesiastical practices that were intended to facilitate healthy interpretation. Embracing mottos such as *sola scriptura*, heirs of the Reformation espoused a notion of an authoritative Bible that stood alone, free from the entanglements and distortions of church tradition.[107]

Hence, the perception of an autonomous Scripture removed from the milieu of canonical materials and practices was contrary to the early practice

---

103. Abraham, "Emergence," 149.

104. For instance Abraham comments that "Gregory of Nazianzus, [was] well aware that [his] theological proposals went well beyond the text of the Scriptures. [His] proposals involved an appeal to nonscriptural axioms, to various empirical considerations, to human insight, to developments of biblical ideas, and to the mystical experience of believers" (*Canon and Criterion*, 140).

105. Ibid., 7.

106. Ibid., 141–42.

107. Koskela, "Authority of Scripture," 210.

of the church. Early Christians did not look to Scripture as a source for absolute truth on all things concerning Christian living; instead, Scripture was one source of truth among many in the discernment of God's will. Scripture was integrated within the canonical tradition so that all components played vital roles in a way that did not pit the mind against the heart or intellect against behavior.

However, in conservative Protestantism, the canonical tradition became largely identified with the Bible and with the epistemological presuppositions associated with an inerrant Scripture.[108] Accordingly, the driving priority of soteriology was to rationally secure proper knowledge of God. Furthermore, with the Reformation, the canon of Scripture became the primary canon and, again, was designated as such through the Protestant cry of *sola scriptura*. The switch from canon to criterion resulted in a massive reconceptualization of soteriology. Thereafter, salvation was associated with knowledge or information more than the reception of divine grace. No longer pictured as just a medium of grace unto salvation, Scripture became the source of such grace. Abraham attests that when Scripture becomes the foundation or norm for Christian epistemology, it is forced to be something never intended.

> Neither the gospel nor the deep intellectual content of the Christian faith are a theory of knowledge . . . It is surely a radical mistake to think that this depends on any particular philosophical theory designed to resolve long-standing questions about rationality, justification, and knowledge.[109]

In short, epistemology was never the leading concern of the canonical tradition.

As can be seen, within conservative Protestant theology, the epistemizing of the canonical tradition is uniquely revealed through various attitudes toward and practice of Scripture. Such epistemizing highlights not only a shift in the early church's canonical grasp of Scripture but it also exposes a shaving down of the canonical heritage essentially to the canon of Scripture. Yet not only has the church lost sight of the relevance and variety of the early canonical tradition but also of its soteriological goal. The church

---

108. There are exceptions within conservative Christianity as some theologians have moved from an emphasis on *Scripture as inerrant* to *Scripture as a soteriological means of grace*. For instance see, Dorrien, *Remaking*, chapter 5; Dayton, "Pietist Theological Critique," 76–89; and Webster, *Holy Scripture*.

109. Abraham, *Crossing*, 39.

Canonical Shifting and Soteriological Ramifications

began to envisage its canons, especially Scripture, more for epistemological warrant than mediation of grace. Abraham concludes that when this happened, Christian theology in general and soteriology in particular were placed at the mercy of epistemology. I conclude this section by discussing how this canonical shift led to enduring soteriological implications.

Canonical Shifting and Soteriological Ramifications

The canonical tradition is inextricably linked with its soteriology. From the beginnings of the church, the goal of the canonical tradition had always been soteriological; however, that began to change with the confusion of canon with criterion. The canonical tradition drove the church's mission, for it emerged in the actualization of that mission. Therefore, it was no small thing when the common understanding of canon changed because within this new mindset were the seeds of a different soteriological paradigm. While the shift did not deny the church's mandate as soteriological, it did alter the fundamental orientation of its soteriology. The accent on *salvation as transformation* through the canonical mediation of grace became *salvation as epistemological certainty* through the canons of Scripture and Tradition. For the early church, salvation had far less to do with certitude of one's theology than with immersion into the fuller life of God.

Prior to the schism, the church commonly understood the practices of its canonical tradition as soteriologically focused. Afterwards, epistemological certainty began to overshadow the transformational temper of the canonical practices. While the value of orthopraxy was never denied in the later Western canonical tradition, it was subordinated to orthodoxy and a rational approach to faith. Such was further exacerbated by the vigorous stand the Reformers took against pious works in comparison to the preeminence of faith (i.e., *sola fide*) in the order of salvation. This attitude reinforced intellectualist tendencies already implicit in their soteriology.

Why does such an epistemological reinterpretation of the canonical tradition matter? The soteriology of the church gradually had less to do with engaging the canons as means of grace for transformation and more with securing correct theological knowledge through various methods of reading Scripture. Canonical theism uncovers how such an intellectualist soteriology is out of sync with the canonical heritage of the Church. While justifying truth claims was not unimportant, the early Church did not focus on such efforts as much as a life led by the Spirit and immersed in the grace of God.

For the sake of clarification, I reiterate what was said earlier in response to Abraham's critics. While their concerns were legitimate about how much emphasis the church placed on epistemology in its canonical tradition, such does not alter Abraham's driving assertion of canonical theism. The underlying thesis in *Canon and Criterion* and the theme of *Canonical Theism* is that the purpose of that tradition was soteriological transformation. Perfect accuracy in the minutiae of such historical details does not negate the soteriological aims of the canonical practices because I am building from the commonly accepted practices of this history (i.e., baptism, the Eucharist, Scripture reading). In the next chapter, we progress from Abraham's declaration *that* the canonical tradition is soteriological to my application of his research indicating *why* it is soteriological.

6

Salvation in the Flesh through Canonical Theism's Orthopraxy

Now we build on the previous exposition of canonical theism to unfold how behavior and practices "qualify" as mediators of salvific faith. Once again we draw from our findings in chapter 2 that cognition requires behavior, emotions, and feelings. Here we explain how the canonical practices (orthopraxy) can be considered cognitively productive (for faith formation) because of their unmistakably embodied nature. In looking ahead, chapter 8 repeats the same methodology (for the final time) to clarify how orthopathy plays an equally essential task as orthodoxy and orthopraxy in our soteriological proposal.

Canonical Orthopraxy for a Renewal Soteriology

For our present purposes, just as chapter 3 laid out how the affective, embodied, and transformational characteristics of "right beliefs" enable it to mediate salvific faith, I now contend that because these same qualities are found in "right practices" then they too can mediate salvation (i.e., orthopraxic soteriology). As before, our theological affirmations are coupled with similar claims in the cognitive sciences.[1] With this in mind, I now

1. Even though some of the cognitive scientific research in this section has been previously stated (chapters 2 and 3), I employ it once again to ensure a clear connection between research in the cognitive sciences regarding the influence of behavior on learning and the corresponding theological assertions I make in this chapter (i.e., the influence of behavior on faith).

attend to the soteriological role of canonical practices in terms of an affective orthopraxy.

An Affective Orthopraxy

So far, I have established that canonical practices mediate salvation to the believer as continuing growth in God as per our understanding of salvation in chapter 1 (i.e., dynamic, progressive, and transforming). Here, I characterize such salvific growth as affective transformation (e.g. emotional healing, lifestyles of Spirit-filled living, and the like).[2] Since I have already stated that affectivity is a crucial feature of cognition, I can now affirm that because the canonical practices foster affectivity they contribute to the mediation of faith for the goal of knowing God. I begin by describing how the canonical practices engender affectivity and then link such observations with cognitive scientific findings about the relationship between emotions and behavior with cognition.

The early and patristic church's articulation of salvation as *theosis* rather than *theological certainty* fitly appertains to the affective texture of canonical practices.[3] Abraham maintains, "The church in the New Testament and patristic period was first and foremost a school and haven of salvation rather than a seminar in religious epistemology."[4] The early church surely understood the pedagogical value of integrating "knowing" and "doing" for encouraging affective transformation, as evidenced in how the catechetical schools linked orthodoxy and orthopraxy in the canonical tradition. The practices of baptism, the Eucharist, and reading Scripture within these schools clearly illustrate how behavior was integral to its teaching method. The fruits of such praxis reveal profound affective transformation in the lives of these early catechumens despite the oppression, persecution, and martyrdom they often faced. Testimonies of these believers disclosed such

---

2. Eph 5:22–24 (NRSV).

3. My linking canonical theism's articulation of soteriology to the early church's belief in *theosis* is solely heuristic. I am not pressing that canonical theism proposes a theological plan distinctly endorsing *theosis*. However, the way that CT lays out the transformational aim of the canonical practices resembles many of the same descriptions used in the doctrine of *theosis* (i.e., salvation as perpetual growth into the likeness of God, purity, holiness, and sanctification). I am not committed to the term "theosis" but I am committed to the soteriological descriptions it employs for a transformational image of salvation.

4. Abraham, "Emergence," 153.

Salvation in the Flesh through Canonical Theism's Orthopraxy

affective qualities as overflowing love, joy, peace, and self-control to such an extent that wherever the gospel was preached it was well received and the faith of the church flourished.[5] Historical testimony of such vital faith is recorded by the second-century Church Father Tertullian (160–230 AD) in his memorable phrase: *The blood of the martyrs is the seed of the Church.*[6] The witness of these martyrs envisages the profound impact of affective transformation through their lives upon those in the non-Christian community. Tertullian even compares the greater number of Christian disciples won by the church than those of Cicero's disciples. He remarks that the reason is that Christians "teach by deeds." This is a clear example of orthopraxy in early church soteriology and how praxis was a powerful part of the church's pedagogical method used for initiation and formation.[7]

Throughout *Canon and Criterion* and *Canonical Theism*, one can find abundant references to the canonical tradition mediating grace for transformation into the image of Christ. I argue that such transformation (as often associated with deification, divinization, or *theosis*) involves, among other things, affective renewal.[8] Charles Gutenson relates how the canonical tradition promoted affectively transformed lifestyles as believers turned from sinful behavior to holy living.[9] Through the Eucharist, Van Kirk says, "The community is made into one body that participates in the body of Christ by virtue of its partaking of one loaf together. This is not just a symbolic act. It is an ontological change."[10] Most notably, such "ontological change" was evinced in the remarkable quality of love these believers modeled toward God and others.

For as we have seen how canonical practices were inextricably tied to affective transformation, so too does research in the cognitive sciences establish how behavior is inseparable from affectivity and how emotions play an evident role in learning. Antonio Damasio's research shows that when emotional content is abstracted from cognition, learning is hindered. He alleges that "some feelings optimize learning and recall"[11] and

---

5. See, Forbush, *Fox's Book of Martyrs*.

6. Tertullian, "Apology," 227.

7. Ibid.

8. See, Abraham et al., *Canonical Theism: A Proposal*, 23, 123–25, 173, 181, 183, 187, 192–94.

9. Gutenson, "Canonical Heritage," 250.

10. Van Kirk, "Christ Present," 88.

11. Damasio, *Looking for Spinoza*, 178 n. 25.

that emotions can actually help to deliver cognitive information by way of feelings.[12] Accordingly, behaviors that generate such emotions can be instrumental in the learning process. Perhaps the transformation of the early catechumens included the kinds of emotions and "feelings that optimize learning" because their pedagogy proved so effective (as seen in the faith of the martyrs). Reuven Feuerstein echoes that when MLE (Mediated Learning Experience) is exploited, affectivity is engaged because the mediator emotionally identifies with the learner; thus, learning is more effective than otherwise. He similarly indicates that affectivity is crucial in learning and is mediated by the necessary behaviors required for shared interaction.[13] Could it be that the communal nature of baptism, the Eucharist, and Scripture reading validate Feuerstein's research about the impact of "shared interaction"? As with Feuerstein's MLE, the canonical tradition utilized certain practices to make use of specific emotions for particular ends. For instance, baptism was practiced for freedom from the guilt of sin, Scripture was read for nurturing awareness of God's glory and appreciation of his beauty and goodness, and the Eucharist was practiced for cultivating gratitude, peace, and joy for Christ's redemption.

In view of all this, what can we say about the significance of an affective orthopraxy for faith formation? We have to reiterate what we have already established—*cognition is significantly mediated through affective experiences*. In showing that the canonical practices encouraged affective transformation, we can affirm that a canonical orthopraxy is cognitively productive for faith formation. Hence, canonical orthopraxy unveils the vital component of an affective praxis for mediating a renewal soteriology of embodiment. Next, I consider the implication of embodiment in the canonical practices.

An Embodied Orthopraxy

When orthopraxy is dismissed or minimized in soteriological reflection, faith typically defaults into abstract or other-worldly notions. Orthopraxy, in a sense, puts "feet and hands" to salvific experience; or, stated differently, embodied orthopraxy is the vehicle by which transcendent grace becomes immanently accessible through faith. Just as I previously highlighted how the canonical practices contribute to cognitive formation (faith) because

---

12. Ibid., xiii.
13. Feuerstein et al., *Beyond Smarter*, 134.

Salvation in the Flesh through Canonical Theism's Orthopraxy

of their affective impact upon its practitioners, here, I expound how the embodied nature of such practices is cognitively significant. As before, I first depict how the canonical practices are embodied and second, link such observations with cognitive scientific assertions about the relationship between embodied behavior and cognition.

The early church modeled embodied praxis in its canonical tradition in general and, catechesis, in particular. The church understood that to maintain a relevant and active witness its soteriological pedagogy had to be embodied. Thusly, it was more concerned with initiating believers into a fuller life of God than just securing intellectual confidence for assurance of heaven. The soteriological end of the canonical tradition was to provide, "a means whereby we are enabled to love God and neighbor, whereby we are renewed in the image and likeness of God, whereby we become by grace what Christ was by nature."[14] As already advanced, the canonical tradition accomplished this through a broad network of canonized materials and practices that necessitated bodily participation of believers.

Yet not only did such embodiment result in a more deeply experienced faith, but it also facilitated a greater degree of sustained transformation. This is why a central belief of *The Philokalia* is that "long-term practices sustain knowledge of God."[15] St. Peter of Damaskos (twelfth century) similarly echoes that the initiated believer "should cultivate and practice what is good, so that it becomes an established habit operating automatically and effortlessly when required."[16] For these reasons, canonical practices were embodied because of their ability to practically accomplish soteriological transformation. So, whether the behavior is baptism, Holy Communion, Scripture reading, or any other canonical practice, all require embodied participation for growth in faith. Such was and is the benefit of a canonical orthopraxy.

Therefore, to discount the soteriological implications of an embodied orthopraxy is to ignore the embodied constitution of human knowing and the sustained impact of such learning. Current research in the contemporary cognitive sciences bears this out as well. Damasio attests that because brain function is embodied, then intellect, behavior, and emotions are holistically integrated. To ignore embodiment is to stifle learning. It seems that the early church had similar insight when it proclaimed, *Lex orandi, lex*

14. Abraham, *Canon and Criterion*, 54.
15. Aquino, "Epistemic Virtues," 184.
16. Damaskos, "Treasury of Divine Knowledge," 87.

credendi (the law of prayer is the law of belief). In other words, one's beliefs about God emerge out of one's practice of worship and prayer (particularly in the Eucharist). So the *raison d'être* of theology in the early and patristic church was not so much to articulate novel ideas as much as to reflect on and put words to the common embodied experience of God shared by believers through the canonical tradition. Interestingly, centuries of conciliar debates culminating in orthodox belief on the nature of God was a product of theological reflection on the embodied practice of baptism and the Trinitarian confessions associated with it. Perhaps the early church intuitively understood, over two thousand years ago, what cognitive scientists empirically understand today—*reasoning is entwined with embodiment*.[17]

Damasio's book, *Descartes' Error* systematically dismantles dualistic images of cognition that isolate the mind from the body. In a similar way, I too reject such dualism because it leads to abstract and overly "spiritualized" ideas of salvation that do not take the physically and relationally embodied aspects of human life seriously. Subsequently, a disembodied assessment of cognition leads to an intellectualized faith that is inconsistent with the transforming vision of salvation we regularly see throughout Scripture.[18] Damasio defends that the mind cannot exist without all the physiological realities constituting embodiment. The mind literally needs the body, not just the brain. For instance, through the Eucharist believers celebrate Christ's incarnation as a physical and historical reality rather than a metaphysical or "spiritual" state and thereby affirm the significance of embodiment in knowing God. Just as "the mind needs the body" so too does our growth in faith come through the materiality of human experience. Salvation occurs amidst the actualities of embodiment, not in spite of it.

Once again, we highlight what chapter 2 already established—the greater the degree of embodiment in cognition the more optimal its functionality. Therefore, we can say that because cognition is embodied and since the canonical practices are embodied, canonical orthopraxy is cognitively productive in faith formation. Canonical orthopraxy, then, illustrates the critical role of an embodied praxis for our soteriological proposal. Next, I discuss the canonical practices as transformational because they are affective and embodied.

---

17. Lakoff and Johnson, *Philosophy in the Flesh*, 568.
18. Chapter 6 elaborates on the scriptural foundation of an embodied soteriology.

Salvation in the Flesh through Canonical Theism's Orthopraxy

A Transformational Orthopraxy

So far I have detailed the soteriological importance of affectivity and embodiment within canonical theism. I now contend that because orthopraxis is affective and embodied, it encourages soteriological transformation. Canonical practices are transformational because they derive from a tradition that consistently mediated salvation to believers in a trustworthy manner proving itself in the purity and holiness of life modeled in its participants.

Though already mentioned, the testimonies of the martyrs so profoundly displays such transformation, it warrants repeating once more. The second-century philosopher, teacher, and scientist, Galen (129–200 AD) highlights such uncommon affections of these early Christians manifested in specific behaviors:

> For their contempt of death [and of its sequel] is patent to us every day, and likewise their restraint in cohabitation. For they include not only men but also women who refrain from cohabiting all through their lives; and they also number individuals who, in self-discipline and self-control in matters of food and drink, and in their keen pursuit of justice, have attained a pitch not inferior to that of genuine philosophers.[19]

The transforming power of God was unmistakable in these martyrs because such honor and beauty of character were so uncommon among the populace. Even more, these Christians were often uneducated (unlike the philosophers). This further reinforced the power of God's saving grace since such virtue was unheard of among the unschooled.

The transformational quality of canonical practices is again seen in canonical theism's association of salvation with *theosis*. Abraham repeatedly distinguishes that, "[c]anonical theism gives intellectual primacy to ontology over epistemology."[20] Baptism illustrates the power of praxis as this canonical act not only symbolized the acquisition of a new nature but led to its realization. Van Kirk comments on the transformational power of baptism:

> Baptism is a union of the believer with Christ Jesus in his death and resurrection. The newness of life conferred upon Christians in baptism involves a *freedom from the ordinary human condition*

---

19. Walzer, *Galen on Jews*, 15.

20. Abraham, "Canonical Theism: Thirty Theses," 5. Elsewhere, in the same text, similar statements are found on 22, 88, 156–57, and 172–74.

of enslavement to sin . . . It is a whole *new sort of existence* which begins in the mystery of our conformity to the death and resurrection of Christ in baptism.[21]

The early church understood that the end of salvation is not about securing theological certainty but about acquiring a new nature—no longer ruled by carnal pleasures and self-interest.[22]

Salvation, as *theosis*, is transformational precisely because of the affective and behavioral changes witnessed in such saints. Nothing less than the Holy Spirit's empowering presence can bring about such a radical change; this is why the early church's canonical tradition was more concerned with disseminating grace than securing epistemological certainty.[23] Since only God can change human nature, the early church envisaged the transforming power of the Spirit at work in and through the canonical practices.

Reuven Feuerstein's research in learning theory underscores the extraordinary transformation that can occur in children with severely impaired brain function through the praxis of mediated learning. He remarks that such transformation (which can only be mediated via behavior) is possible because of brain plasticity and its ability to modify itself, despite physiological or cultural limitations.[24] Feuerstein upholds that behavior, as mediation, is so pivotal in learning that when it is absent, learning suffers. Correspondingly, his research validates our point that a person's ability to know God is made possible because of the affective and embodied nature of orthopraxis. As Feuerstein's scientifically derived pedagogy has often produced amazing results among his students, so too have the canonical practices of the church led to such degrees of transformation that even the greatest skeptics and those most hostile to the faith have paused to acknowledge God's involvement.

What is our take-away about orthopraxy and transformation? We can assert that because the canonical practices are transforming they are cognitively effective in mediating and nurturing faith. Because of this, we can claim that canonical orthopraxy illustrates the soteriological significance of praxis.

---

21. Van Kirk, "Christ Present," 83. Emphasis added.

22. Such a description resembles Jonathan Edwards' association of salvation with attainment of religious affections.

23. Abraham, *Canon and Criterion*, 54.

24. Feuerstein et al., *Dynamic Assessment*, 73.

Salvation in the Flesh through Canonical Theism's Orthopraxy

Herein, I have shown that orthopraxis resembles some of the chief characteristics of cognition in that both are affective, embodied, and transformational. As I developed in chapter 2, when these same characteristics are soundly evident in cognitive function then human reasoning exists as a dynamic (rather than static) and transforming (rather than abstract) force. Because I have indicated that canonical orthopraxy cultivates faith in a way that is affective, embodied, and transformational then I now submit that canonical orthopraxy exemplifies a renewal soteriology of embodiment. Such an orthopraxic soteriology is dynamic and transformational because practices are central rather than subordinate in its vision of salvation. Behavior is no longer relegated to post-salvific fruits (i.e., sanctification) as commonly depicted in some soteriologies. Yet, despite such endorsement and the soteriological benefits that can be gleaned from the church's canonical tradition, is there still something missing? Considering this question, we now approach the final section of this chapter.

The Challenges of a Canonical Soteriology: Minimized Soteriology and Pneumatology?[25]

In chapter 3, I concluded that had Jonathan Edwards more prominently incorporated the canonical practices of the church within his soteriology, he might have advanced a greater appreciation for the salvific capacity of behavior and stemmed the trend of intellectualizing soteriology. In this chapter I asserted that canonical theism uncovers the soteriological significance of behavior and, thereby, reflects findings in the cognitive sciences that the embodied and affective features of behavior can positively transform mental function. Yet, despite such contribution, I now suggest that the dominant ecclesial framework for canonical practices might inadvertently lead some to wrongly interpret canonical theism as endorsing a minimized soteriology.

To begin, I need to reiterate that my critique is not against any particular portrayal of a canonical orthopraxy as explicated by canonical theism, but rather a *possible interpretation of such an orthopraxy by conservative Christians* in light of their often static soteriology enunciated in chapter 1. Could the soteriological presuppositions within such a readership hinder a fuller appreciation of the soteriological potential of canonical practices? For

---

25. By "canonical soteriology" I refer to canonical theism's impression of the canonical heritage of the church whereby its practices mediate salvation.

PART THREE: SALVATION AND ORTHOPRAXY

these readers, I wonder if the prevailing ecclesial domain for soteriology in canonical theism might eclipse other more global and cosmic conceptions of salvation in at least two ways. First, such an audience could confuse the transformational emphasis in a canonical soteriology as an endorsement of an overly personalized soteriology. Second, a canonical soteriology might unintentionally restrict pneumatology largely to the canonical tradition and fail to affirm the dynamic ministry of the Spirit in non-ecclesial arenas. Let us now elaborate on each possibility.

Presuming a Personalized Soteriology

Here, I simply wonder if canonical theism might be inadvertently endorsing a personalized soteriology among conservative Christians. How could canonical theism's association of salvation with *theosis* and progressive transformation engender a personalized soteriology? Truly, one of the strengths of canonical theism is its dynamic soteriological backdrop that links practices with vibrant life in God. Awareness of the many canonical practices that can mediate grace for continuing growth is relevant in a time when many Christians feel powerless to overcome personal vices or the static sense of a nominalized faith. However, as important as personal formation is, one must understand that the canonical heritage was not only concerned with personal empowerment or growth of individual believers. In chapter 1, I assessed conservative Christianity regarding its emphasis on faith as a personal decision occurring at a moment, while neglecting the dynamic and ongoing nature of faith conversion. Hence, if one approaches the canonical tradition from such a setting, while simultaneously failing to understand the social nature of the early and patristic church, one could mistakenly interpret the canonical tradition as proposing a soteriology of personal interests and self-improvement. For just as chapter 1 introduced salvation as conversion and constant process, a dynamic soteriology of embodiment extends beyond the transformation of individual lives to families, communities, nations, and, ultimately, the cosmos. All these aspects of conversion affirm the multidimensionality of salvation.[26]

Nevertheless, could it be possible that some Christians could draw from canonical theism only a more individualistically oriented soteriology that does not take the social heart of salvation seriously because it primarily

---

26. In chapter 1, I discussed how Amos Yong references these levels of conversion in terms of a multidimensional soteriology. For more, see Yong, *Spirit Poured Out*, 105, 108.

Salvation in the Flesh through Canonical Theism's Orthopraxy

locates grace within the canonical traditions of the church? For instance, recall that, in chapter 2, I discussed how learning theory indicates that knowledge is mediated through a variety of historically contingent actualities (culture, geography, economics, educational opportunity, relationships, health, etc.). Yet, while canonical theism rightly accounts for the social disposition of embodiment by elaborating how the canonical tradition mediates salvation through the particularities of one's *ecclesial* situation, I wonder if it went far enough. Because human knowing is so deeply shaped by historical realities, might faith also require a more holistic rendering of historical contingencies than just the ecclesial framework?[27] Might a more expansive orthopraxic soteriology better depict the Spirit's mediation of grace to believers for continuing growth as well as for conversion of nonbelievers? It is toward this concern that I take up a second challenge posed by canonical theism—a limited pneumatology.

Fostering an Ecclesial Pneumatology

Here I examine how canonical theism's accent on the pneumatological mediation of grace through the canonical practices may inadvertently suggest a pneumatology that denies the life-changing ministry of the Spirit in non-ecclesial contexts. A truly dynamic soteriology must admit the renewing activity of the Spirit in and through the socially multifarious make up of human existence. Since the Spirit has been "poured out on all flesh" to testify of God's glory, goodness, and love, then "all" indicates that faith is mediated both within and outside ecclesial domains. Just as Feuerstein already explicated that learning is conveyed through the affective and embodied behavior of a human mediator, so too I assert that the Holy Spirit unceasingly mediates knowledge of God to human beings through the broad spectrum of affective and embodied realities (excepting explicitly sinful ones) by virtue of their social nature. Likewise, as Damasio has shown that the physiological constitution of human embodiment produces essential neurological data that is cognitively productive, so too ought behavior in

---

27. George Lindbeck's cultural-linguistic approach to religion accounts for such historical factors. Though it remains to be seen if his approach undercuts the dynamic experiential current of personal (inner) experience of Christ by the Spirit, especially in pentecostal and charismatic theologies. See Lindbeck, *Nature of Doctrine*, chapters 5 and 6.

nonecclesial settings produce similar data that is cognitively productive in the potential formation of faith.

However, foremost to such a proposition is the unbounded dynamic ministry of the Spirit renewing, healing, and transforming a broken creation through ceaselessly mediating divine grace. Unfortunately, even when Abraham applies the findings of canonical theism to the contemporary life and practice of the church, he still chiefly locates the Spirit within the canonical structures of the church. He concludes that canonical theism is not so much a program to be applied as much as an effort to liberate the power of the Spirit *within the existing contexts of the church*. He explains, "Canonical theism is an enrichment of what is already in place rather than an abstraction that has somehow to be applied from scratch."[28] While canonical theism does not deny the ministry of the Spirit outside ecclesial dimensions, it focuses on the Spirit's ministry within and through the church.[29] Nevertheless, such pneumatological restriction may unintentionally suggest the Spirit's activity to chiefly reside within ecclesial spheres. Consequently, one might fail to account for the Spirit's ministry in such extra-ecclesial fields as politics, education, finance, arts, science, environment, recreation, and the like.

It is understandable that Abraham wants to spotlight pneumatology as soteriologically intrinsic to the canonical tradition, for a major aim of canonical theism is to underscore the purpose of ecclesial canons for mediating grace. However, could canonical theism not be strengthened by a broader pneumatology implicitly testifying of God's grace outside the church even as the Spirit explicitly provides divine revelation through the canonical tradition within the church? Interestingly, Abraham has recently published such a proposal, though in relation to John Wesley and his Aldersgate experience.[30] Toward elaborating Wesley's ideas on obtaining knowledge of God, Abraham develops Wesley's theology of prevenient grace through personal experience in the physical world. Despite that Wesley strongly believed in the problem of spiritual blindness and the urgency

---

28. Abraham, "Canonical Theism," 313. To more comprehensively deal with application, see full chapter (303–315).

29. See, Vickers, "Medicine," 12–13.

30. Abraham, *Aldersgate and Athens*. The Aldersgate experience refers to Wesley's profound experience of divine presence on May 24, 1738 at a meeting on Aldersgate Street in London in which he described his heart to be "strangely warmed" by the presence of Christ. For more on Wesley's description see: Ward and Heitzenrater, *Works of John Wesley*, xviii, 249–50.

of the unregenerate to gain "spiritual vision" through the Spirit, he still included such nonecclesial revelation as an aspect of his theological epistemology. Though Wesley did not give much credit to natural revelation in and of itself, he did not dismiss this aspect of the Spirit's ministry but, rather, validated it. Abraham argues that Wesley treated natural revelation as one more item in the vast epistemological network of grace God makes available to human beings.[31] Alone and apart from special revelation, the grace of natural revelation is soteriologically incomplete but when partnered together (especially via canonical practices), the believer or committed seeker can find great assurance of God's love and sound reasons to trust his grace. Applying Wesley's theology, Abraham expounds,

> [I]n prevenient grace God irresistibly and universally restores in us the initial capacity to perceive the truth. This grace is manifest, for example, in conscience and in the initial desire to seek after God as something good and attractive. This action of God simply provides the preparatory work for what we really need, namely, the more direct action of God by the Holy Spirit to enable us to become aware of and see for ourselves what God has done for us in Jesus Christ.[32]

In Wesley's theology, God is ever at work in the world. Through the Spirit, he leads individuals to respond to his revelation already available, notwithstanding their place. While the preaching of the gospel or access to other canonical means of grace is the normative way by which individuals are initiated into saving faith, such preparatory acts of the Spirit in prevenient grace remains a critical aspect of Wesley's theological epistemology.

Perhaps if Abraham had incorporated some of Wesley's prevenient grace theology with the canonical practices as mediators of salvific grace, he might have more explicitly recognized the Spirit's gracious presence throughout the world as a contemporary application of canonical theism. For does salvific transformation (whether affective, intellectual, or behavioral) come to the believer as though descending from above and down solely through the canonical tradition? Is it not dynamically mediated through the collective historical experiences of one's social life because of human embodiment? For if people are intrinsically social, would salvation not potentially involve *all* social realities within all possible spheres of human existence? In other words, if a renewal soteriology involves more than

---

31. Abraham, *Aldersgate and Athens*, chapter 2.
32. Ibid., 26.

personal transformation, then what might communal, social, institutional, environmental, global, or cosmic manifestations look like? In chapters 9–10, I return to these questions as I elaborate on the meaning and scope of an embodied soteriology of renewal. Nevertheless, canonical theism plays an important role in illustrating how orthopraxis is a vital component in a dynamic soteriology because of its ability to mediate grace for ongoing growth into the *imago Dei*.

In view of the preceding, when we speak about the significance of orthopraxy for a renewal soteriology of embodiment we insist that behavioral transformation is not independent of intellectual or affective transformation. Orthopraxis has a way of protecting orthodoxy from devolving into irrelevant religious knowledge and steering orthopathy away from becoming too inwardly focused on personal experience or emotions. The Holy Spirit is able to use orthopraxy to help foster a living faith in Christians by putting "hands and feet" to the knowledge of God mediated to our heads and the love of Christ mediated to our hearts.

Finally, in consideration of the two potential challenges of a canonical soteriology, Part Four (Salvation and Orthopathy) examines how pentecostal spirituality provides additional soteriological perspectives on the transforming power of the Spirit in the world. I will identify how affective transformation (orthopathy) of the believer informs behavior (orthopraxy) and expands knowledge of God (orthodoxy) in a way that facilitates greater growth into the *imago Dei*. Then I will have presented the final component of our soteriological paradigm articulating how "knowing God" is necessarily an intellectual, behavioral, and affective reality—always holistically integrated and ever dynamically transforming.

PART FOUR

Salvation and Orthopathy

7

Pentecostalism and the Salvific Role of Orthopathy

WE HAVE NOW COME to the "heart" of this book—the impact of human affections on faith. Throughout, we've contended at length for a faith paradigm that transcends intellectualist boundaries. We are not proposing an untethering from objective and rational faith but neither are we willing to be limited by the same. Yes, there are dangers in arguing for a faith of more emotion—and we will address such concerns—but to avoid these dangers altogether is to do violence to the biblical notion of faith. Without the heat and tears of holy passion and without the intimacy of personal encounter, Christian faith is profoundly stripped of its full soteriological import. This is not new ground. In this chapter we offer historical and contemporary legacies of such fiery faith.

We now introduce the third and final category of our proposal as we expound the meaning and soteriological significance of pentecostal orthopathy.[1] Just as *orthodoxy* had to do with the salvific feature of proper knowledge and *orthopraxy* with the soteriological capacity of specific practices and behaviors, I presently explicate *orthopathy* to show the salvific relevance of affectivity. For this end, I present pentecostal spirituality to illustrate how its treatment of emotions, sentiment, and experience plays a key role for a renewal soteriology of embodiment.

---

1. Herein, our use of orthopathy corresponds with emotions, feelings, sentiment, affections, and personal experience. For an excellent survey of how pentecostal experience is variously understood across the spectrum of leading pentecostal theologians, see Neumann, *Pentecostal Experience*. With a robustly pneumatological approach, Neumann elaborates on the triad of pentecostal experience of the Spirit through the Word (chapter 3), Tradition (chapter 4), and Reason (chapter 5).

PART FOUR: SALVATION AND ORTHOPATHY

Pentecostalism and Orthopathy

I begin by introducing Pentecostalism as an orthopathic spirituality in the lineage of Pietism, Wesleyanism, and the American Holiness movement.[2] Then, I respond to four critics of pentecostal orthopathy and, finally, situate the pentecostal orthopathic orientation amidst wider contemporary developments. These three tasks clear the way to elaborate the significance of the chapter.

Situating Pentecostal Orthopathy

Pentecostal orthopathy is a form of Pietism mediated through John Wesley's (1703–1791) Methodism, the Wesleyan-Holiness stress on sanctification, and the pentecostal experience of Spirit baptism, and other practices.[3] Throughout this religious trajectory, Pietistic impulses in search of a "religion of the heart" helped secure personal assurance and authenticity of faith. Emotions, affectivity, and subjective experience, while not the sole constituents of such faith are, nevertheless, unapologetically embraced.

Philip Jakob Spener (1635–1705) was a founding leader of German Pietism, a renewal movement within seventeenth century Lutheranism.[4] Wesley's soteriology, coupling justification and sanctification, with an accent on "inward religion" and practical Christianity likely derived from Spener, even if indirectly.[5] The Pietist mark on Wesley esteemed affectivity and emotions in Christian living. Such Pietism stressed the importance of penitential struggle and genuine repentance for an enduring conversion and a vibrant personal salvation.[6] Pietism was a major source of experiential spirituality emerging in Protestantism at that time.[7] Pietism highlights

---

2. Pentecostalism is actually a more diverse movement than what I present in this chapter. Due to space constraints I have limited my scope of treatment. Consequently, this book focuses on North American Trinitarian Pentecostalism.

3. Dayton, *Theological Roots*, chapters 2–4.

4. "Pietism" is a broad term not easily defined. The temporal and geographical boundaries are difficult to delineate. Even though there is no direct evidence that Wesley read Spener, it is clear that he was motivated by his thought, probably through Johann Arndt (1555–1621) and August Hermann Franck (1663–1727), because Spener and Wesley shared common theological elements (Oh, *John Wesley's Ecclesiology*, 90–93).

5. Ibid., 93.

6. Ibid., 101.

7. Stoeffler, *Rise*, 7.

Pentecostalism and the Salvific Role of Orthopathy

orthopathic intuitions in its formation of small groups (conventicles) for people who were "earnest about their soul's salvation" to privately meet for mutual edification.[8] Wesley was indebted to the existential tenor of Pietism which understood "the value of an inner, vital, living faith to be held personally and shared corporately."[9] Hence, Wesley's legacy is largely remembered for its focus on personal religious experience.

In Wesley, the holiness and purity inclinations of Pietism translated into his soteriological paradigm of justification and sanctification, whereby the latter is ongoing maturity into the image of God.[10] The affective temper of sanctification is seen in his radical view of salvation as a present reality of "limitless grace and limitless love."[11] For Wesley, forensic pardon led to a journey of ongoing sanctification. In other words, salvation was transformational and, as such, recognized as an embodied actuality *emotionally experienced*.[12] The famous Wesley scholar, Albert Outler (1908–1989) depicts Wesley's soteriology in orthopathic terms such as "God's love, immanent and active in human life."[13] Wesley's belief in an experiential sanctification culminated in his doctrine of Christian perfection by which love for God and others becomes the defining characteristic. Following Wesley's deeply personal "Aldersgate experience" on May 24, 1738 where he described his "strangely warmed" heart, emotions have since played a chief role in his theological legacy.[14] There is little wonder why his heirs emphasized the importance of "heart religion."[15] This orthopathic theology significantly influenced the later evolution of pentecostal spirituality.

Wesley's preaching of sanctification as a second definite work of grace led to an eruption of revivals through his ministry and again in the Wesleyan-Holiness movement of his successors. The latter, conjointly with Reformed streams issuing from Puritan influences through Jonathan Edwards (1703–1758), Charles Finney (1792–1875), and the First (1735–1742) and

8. Oh, *John Wesley's Ecclesiology*, 96–97.
9. Stein, *Philipp Jakob Spener*, 255.
10. Wesley, *Nature of Salvation*, 59.
11. Turner, *John Wesley*, 75.
12. Outler, *John Wesley*, 33.
13. Ibid.
14. For more on Wesley's "Aldersgate experience" see: Maddox, *Aldersgate Reconsidered*; Abraham, *Aldersgate and Athens*; Knight III, *From Aldersgate*; Dabney, "What Has Aldersgate," 47–50; and Collins, "Twentieth-Century," 18–31.
15. For example see, Mack, *Heart Religion*; Clapper, *Renewal of the Heart*; or Wood, *Burning Heart*.

Part Four: Salvation and Orthopathy

Second (approx. 1800–1835) Great Awakenings, precipitated the beginning of American Revivalism. Within this religious landscape, salvation was construed as more than pardon from sin; it was also an *experience* of heart-wrenching remorse over sin and genuine celebration for forgiveness. The "mourner's bench" practice evolved in the late eighteenth and early nineteenth century American revivalist customs. Repentant individuals earnestly prayed to God for forgiveness, repentance, or against whatever obstacle was preventing their attainment of a fuller righteousness.[16]

Such emotional spirituality was also manifest at the famous Cane Ridge Revival of Kentucky (1800–1801) bringing together an estimated 10,000 to 25,000 people. Bernard Weisberger remarks that at these meetings "godly hysteria" was seen through such behavior as falling, jerking, barking as dogs, falling into trances, the holy laugh, and "such wild dances as David performed before the Ark of the Lord."[17] Vinson Synan adds, "From Kentucky the revivalistic flame spread over the entire South reaching into Tennessee, North and South Carolina, West Virginia, and Georgia. In most places the same phenomena were repeated."[18] Orthopathic expressions continued in the American revivalist ministry of Charles Finney. His sermons were filled with emotional petitions for people to receive a fresh outpouring of the Spirit as he frequently preached on the doctrine of Christian perfection.[19] Following the "mourners bench" convention, the "altar theology" of Holiness minister Phoebe Palmer evolved out of her "Tuesday Meetings."[20] There she taught that "[b]y placing 'all on the altar,' . . . one could be instantly sanctified through the Baptism of the Holy Ghost."[21] These orthopathic practices were incorporated into the evolving Wesleyan-Holiness and American revivalist movements.

---

16. For more on the "mourner's bench" see, Lovelace, "Invitation," 231.

17. Weisberger, *They Gathered*, 20–21.

18. Synan, *Holiness-Pentecostal Tradition*, 13.

19. Ibid., 14–15. Entire sanctification derived from Wesley's views on an experiential sanctification that can ultimately remove the compulsion to sin so that an individual can choose not to sin. For more on entire sanctification see, Wesley, *Plain Account*; and Grider, *Entire Sanctification*.

20. Initially called "Tuesday Meetings for the Promotion of Holiness" and held by Mrs. Palmer's sister, Mrs. Sarah Lankford, these interdenominational "Tuesday Meetings" were eventually headed by Phoebe Palmer and became a sort of beachhead that helped launch the 1857–1858 Revival.

21. Synan, *Holiness-Pentecostal Tradition*, 17–18.

Pentecostalism and the Salvific Role of Orthopathy

Finally, perhaps one of the most noteworthy orthopathic religious sources leading up to Pentecostalism was African slave religion as primarily mediated through the ministry of William Joseph Seymour (1870–1922) at the Azusa Street Revival (1906–1909). As a son of former slaves, Seymour's ministry nurtured an affective spirituality springing from the deluge of passionate worship and prayer so indelibly marking the famous Azusa Revival.

> The roots of Seymour's spirituality lay in his past. He affirmed his black heritage by introducing Negro spirituals and Negro music into his liturgy at a time when this music was considered inferior and unfit for Christian worship.[22]

Estrelda Alexander reflects how music, as central to African spirituality, prominently surfaced within African American Pentecostalism in its regular connection with song, dance, worship, and prayer.[23] Contemporary social scientists, historians, and theologians increasingly recognize the emotional and affective quality of African spirituality on the expansion of American Pentecostalism.[24]

Phenomenologically, contemporary American Pentecostalism continues to cherish its orthopathic roots inherited from its forebears. Above all, pentecostal *church services* exemplify orthopathy as their worship services typically incorporate lively music with impassioned singing. Affective themes like gratitude for God's love, celebration of intimacy with Christ, joy over one's godly inheritance, and renewed pleas for evangelization of the lost fill such meetings. Pentecostal pneumatology usually fosters an atmosphere of anticipation for God to answer prayers and meet needs as oral testimony reminds its believers to remain steadfast and faithful. Finally, times of prayer are often emotional as believers bring their burdens to God and find renewed joy and hope.

Pentecostal *revival services* also display orthopathy. Such services—even more than church services—employ emotional worship. It is not unusual to see individuals basking in God's presence with arms raised up as tears flow down. These events exude a tangible sense of solidarity as people in unison pray over corporate needs. Pentecostal revival services often employ emotional preaching styles as ministers urgently exclaim the need for personal salvation and freedom from the power of sin and the devil.

---

22. Hollenweger, "After Twenty," 5.
23. Alexander, *Black Fire*, 35.
24. Ibid., 44–45.

Among other aims, revival services also encourage passionate anticipation for Christ's return and hope for heaven. Finally, in these services, the charismatic gifts of healing, prophecy, and words of knowledge are often accompanied with emotions like anticipation, joy, peace, encouragement, and thanksgiving.

The preceding illuminates how Pentecostalism participates in a long and rich heritage consistently affirming the religiously affective impulse. Emotions and feelings were often the distinguishing marks of the Pietist "religion of the heart" offering people assurance of God's love and acceptance. The pentecostal stress on personal encounter with God via spiritual gifts, empowered ministry, and Spirit-baptism similarly indicates an orthopathic sensibility. Yet, notwithstanding the positive impact of pentecostal orthopathy, critics have registered caution.

Critics of Pentecostal Orthopathy

In the above orthopathic legacies there have been, and continue to be, individuals and groups who place excessive attention on emotions and feelings. As with any religious tradition that values affectivity, emotionalism is likely to surface from time to time. Nevertheless, despite the dangers of subjectivity, orthopathy remains an essential element of a renewal soteriology of embodiment.

As we consider the following critiques, each essentially characterizes pentecostal and Charismatic Christianity as endorsing emotionalism. However, these generalizations misrepresent PC Christianity in practice and theological emphasis. Today most of this movement's theologians provide a more embodied and balanced use of intellect and emotion. Later we will engage three of these theologians.

We now turn to four critics of pentecostal spirituality. None directly address *pentecostal orthopathy*; however, their concerns focus on the subjective and emotional aspects of pentecostal spirituality and experience. So, this study identifies criticisms of pentecostal *experience* to include an emphasis on emotion, feelings, sentiment, and affectivity—precisely what I refer to as *pentecostal orthopathy*. I will show, however, that common to each appraisal is an uninterrogated intellectualist epistemology that minimizes affectivity in the same way I laid out in chapter 1.

Benjamin B. Warfield (1851–1921) was longtime professor of theology at Princeton Seminary (1887–1921). Warfield vigorously resisted

Pentecostalism and the Salvific Role of Orthopathy

the rising tide of liberalism which he believed threatened the authority of Scripture. Among his concerns with liberalism was an excessive subjectivism that eschewed any form of external authority.[25] As developed in chapter 1, while Warfield did not deny the subjective quality of faith, he often subordinated it to rational knowledge and objective evidences.[26] Firmly rooted within Scottish common-sense realism, Warfield's epistemology favored objective rationality over subjective affectivity.

For our purposes, since for many evangelicals, Warfield provides the definitive statement on biblical revelation and the cessation of modern-day miracles, his evaluation of pentecostal religious experience is very influential.[27] Hence, this is why his text, *Counterfeit Miracles* (1918), has become a familiar apologetic for cessationism among many American evangelicals.[28] One of his central theological assertions is that the purpose of a miracle is *evidential,* validating the bearers of divine revelation. He defends that miracles "belong to revelation periods, and appear only when God is speaking to His people through accredited messengers."[29] Warfield asserted his evidentialist view of miracle by concluding that with the Bible complete, miracles were no longer needed and, therefore, ceased to exist.[30] He judged that any religious group appealing to miraculous or supernatural religious experiences were influenced by "an infusion of heathen modes of thought."[31] He sought, accordingly, to discredit those who embraced any form of post-Apostolic charismatic religious experience. Warfield charged that they are blinded by excitement,[32] while inflamed by enthusiasm,[33] and led astray by hysteria,[34] among other indictments.[35] He maintained that

---

25. Warfield, "Recent Reconstructions," vol. 2.
26. Jon Ruthven makes a similar argument in his, *On the Cessation*, 190.
27. Ibid., 22. For instance see: Barr, *Fundamentalism*, 262; Kelsey, *Uses of Scripture*, 16; and Noll, "Benjamin B. Warfield," 1156.
28. Warfield, *Counterfeit Miracles*.
29. Ibid., 26.
30. Ibid., 27–28.
31. Ibid., 61.
32. Ibid., 13.
33. Ibid., 48, 129.
34. Ibid., 111, 153.
35. Ibid., 199–207.

whenever Protestants have appealed to the miraculous it was merely a result of "religious excitement."[36]

> Individuals have constantly arisen so filled with the sense of God in their own souls, and so overwhelmed by the wonders of grace which they have witnessed, that they see the immediate hand of God in every occurrence which strikes them as remarkable, and walk through the world clothed in a nimbus of miracle.[37]

Warfield was wary of Pentecostalism because it accepted the supernatural and miraculous as part of its spirituality. He concluded that individuals who believed in contemporary miracles are subjectively influenced by superstitious worldviews, pathology, and hysteria.[38] Unfortunately, Warfield's prejudice against subjectivity and his rejection of the supernatural has alienated future generations from recognizing the worth of pentecostal orthopathy.

Given that modern Pentecostalism basically emerged during the final two decades of Warfield's life, he likely saw, or heard about, extreme examples of "enthusiasm" in the movement. Nevertheless, Warfield's cessationist polemic, by and large, reveals rationalist priorities suspicious of experiential and subjective spirituality. While he does not directly condemn pentecostal orthopathy he does subordinate the affective elements of such spiritualities to his more rational and objective Princeton orthodoxy. Such implicitly discounts the orthopathic dimensions of Christian life as a viable and significant theological resource.

Frederick Dale Bruner (b. 1932), former Professor of Religion at Whitworth University in Spokane, Washington, is an evangelical biblical scholar. Bruner was motivated to study Pentecostalism's doctrine of the Spirit because of its increasing mark upon the church by virtue of its sheer growth. In *A Theology of the Holy Spirit*,[39] Bruner applies the historical-critical hermeneutic to assess pentecostal "doctrine and experience of the Spirit" in light of Scripture.[40]

---

36. Ibid., 127.

37. Ibid.

38. Ibid., 75. In the same text, Warfield also applies the pathological and hysterical categories to Catholics (73–124), Irvingites-Methodists (127–53), and Faith Healers (157–96).

39. Bruner, *Theology*.

40. Ibid., 34.

Pentecostalism and the Salvific Role of Orthopathy

After a detailed study of the Holy Spirit in the Book of Acts and select New Testament books, Bruner concludes that the pentecostal emphasis on emotion and subjectivity, as a second experience subsequent to justification, denotes a path to abundant life that is not dependent on Christ.[41]

> On receiving Christ there should be no thirsting after "deeper" spiritual experiences as though the water faith receives from Christ were not entirely satisfying or empowering. The sighing and thirsting of Pentecostal candidates for "more" is placed in question.[42]

Bruner identifies "more" with the pentecostal quest for Spirit baptism. He retorts that such pursuits imply that faith in Christ is insufficient for full salvation. Bruner rejects the pentecostal desire for a fuller experience of God through Spirit baptism and spiritual gifts—especially tongues—because he believes it presumes lack of trust in Christ.[43]

Underlying Bruner's criticism is a similar rationalist epistemology already seen in Warfield whereby suspicion is placed upon those with a subjective-experiential desire for a fuller experience of God. Bruner states:

> Positively, Paul sees the characteristic, perhaps the classic work of the Holy Spirit in the intelligible and simple confession that Jesus is Lord. The man who confesses "Lord Jesus" has experienced the deep work of the Spirit. The Spirit does not exhibit himself supremely in sublimating the ego, in emptying it, removing it, overpowering it, or in ecstasy extinguishing or thrilling it, but in intelligently, intelligibly, christocentrically using it.[44]

The thrust of Bruner's argument is that because pentecostal spirituality favors experience in its ongoing quest for a fuller life, it is not content with what has already been objectively given in Christ. For instance, Bruner disputes that, "[T]he Pentecostal quest for 'more' through a second 'way' should be transformed into evangelical thanksgiving for the 'all' of the one way—the way who is Christ."[45] While he does not explicitly say so, Bruner clearly prefers the rational and objective over the subjective and affective aspects of cognition in his theological epistemology.

41. Ibid., 318.
42. Ibid., 254–55.
43. Ibid., 255, 284, 319.
44. Ibid., 287.
45. Ibid., 255.

Regardless the validity of Bruner's concerns about the dangers of experientialism, his critique presupposes that the pentecostal experience of the Spirit is insufficiently focused on Christ precisely because of its quest for a fuller life in the Spirit.[46] As such, Reformed Protestant christocentric-orthodoxy is elevated over a pentecostal pneumatological-orthopathy. Unfortunately, Bruner's assessment of the pentecostal doctrine of Spirit baptism insinuates that such believers ought to discard their orthopathic sensibilities. However, to do so would be contrary to the most original instincts of pentecostal spirituality.

We now turn to the prominent pastor, author, and radio broadcaster, John F. MacArthur (b. 1939).[47] MacArthur is well known for his internationally-syndicated radio program, Grace to You, the *MacArthur Study Bible*, and many other books and articles. While he does not specifically deny the importance of affectivity in knowing God, he regularly spotlights the centrality of biblical knowledge while warning the dangers of charismatic emotionalism. In his book *The Charismatics*, MacArthur spends numerous pages describing extreme charismatic and pentecostal practices that he feels subordinate Scripture to spiritual experiences.[48] He declares, "The Charismatic emphasis on experience relegates Scripture to a secondary status of authority."[49] He alleges that, "Instead of checking someone's experience against the Bible for validity, the Charismatic tries to get the Bible to fit the experience or, failing that, he just ignores the Bible."[50] Again, "The teaching of a postsalvation experience of the baptism of the Spirit opens the floodgates for believing that vital Christianity is one 'experience' after another."[51] In these examples, MacArthur reveals his concern that pentecostal spirituality necessarily prioritizes experience over Scripture.

As with Warfield and Bruner, MacArthur also discloses an intellectualist epistemology as he regularly favors objective propositional knowledge over subjective emotional experience. For instance, throughout *Speaking in Tongues*, whenever MacArthur broaches the topic of knowledge he draws on rational and intellectual practices such as Bible study, preaching,

---

46. Ibid., 319.

47. MacArthur is the Lead Pastor-Teacher at Grace Community Church in Sun Valley, California, a non-denominational conservative Christian church.

48. MacArthur, *Charismatics*, chapters 1–3.

49. Ibid., 199.

50. Ibid., 58–59.

51. Ibid., 59.

Pentecostalism and the Salvific Role of Orthopathy

and teaching rather than affective practices such as worship and prayer, as means to grow in knowing God.[52] In *Charismatic Chaos*, MacArthur contends, "Charismatics err because they tend to build their teachings on experience, rather than understanding that authentic experience happens in *response* to truth."[53] In *Speaking in Tongues*, MacArthur rebuffs Charismatics for seeking "the emotional experience [of tongues] rather than an intellectual understanding."[54] Again, in referring to lessons learned from his exposition of 1 Corinthians 14, he insists that the believer should "[n]ever seek an emotional experience" but to instead pursue knowledge.[55]

In these examples, MacArthur registers valid concerns about emotionalism however; he characterizes all pentecostals and charismatics as experientialists. His critique minimizes affective knowledge by subordinating it to objective knowledge, which he associates with Scripture. While he does not explicitly dismiss *pentecostal orthopathy*, when he refers to the affectivity of pentecostal spirituality he basically conceives the adherents as mindless, unintelligible, and irrational.[56] These examples portray a pattern of subordinating experience to rational knowledge in MacArthur's theological epistemology.

So far, in the works I examined, Warfield, Bruner, and MacArthur have overlooked the affective and emotional components of knowing. They reinforce the intellectualist tendency to construe salvation as mostly a matter of "knowing the right information" while minimizing the role of emotions in human cognition. And even though only some pentecostal and charismatic spiritualties have led to excessive emotionalism, both Bruner and MacArthur largely characterize all orthopathic traditions as subjectively dangerous. Unfortunately, they fail to recognize that nearly all pentecostal and charismatic teachers vigorously defend that Christian experience must not contradict biblical teaching.[57] Altogether, Warfield, Bruner, and

---

52. See examples in, MacArthur, *Speaking*, 60, 62–63, 73.
53. MacArthur, *Charismatic Chaos*, 24.
54. MacArthur, *Speaking*, 117.
55. Ibid.
56. MacArthur, *Charismatic Chaos*, 53.
57. For instance, the Assemblies of God website says, "Miraculous manifestations are never the test of a true revival. Fidelity to God's Word is the test" (Assemblies of God, "Statement on Revival," p. 3). And quoting William Seymour it says, "We are measuring everything by the Word, every experience must measure up with the Bible (*Apostolic Faith*, Sept. 1907). The Church of God (Cleveland, Tennessee) website says, "The Church of God was founded in 1886 on the principles of Christ as have been revealed in the

PART FOUR: SALVATION AND ORTHOPATHY

MacArthur's suspicions about experience reinforce the orthodoxy-driven soteriology of contemporary conservative Christianity.

Our final critic is the Reformed scholar, Mark Noll (b. 1946), who is currently the Francis A. McAnaney Professor of History at the University of Notre Dame. Noll's critique is most clearly spelled out in his *The Scandal of the Evangelical Mind*. He upholds that out of the fundamentalist-modernist controversies of the early twentieth century, evangelicals developed intellectually disastrous habits of the mind that have limited their witness. Consequently, the Christian cause suffered as theological liberalism and secularism rapidly spread across North American culture.[58]

Noll's critique mostly concerns Fundamentalism but he clearly implicates pentecostal and Holiness spiritualties as well.[59] He broadly blames much of the scandal on "innovative fundamentalists doctrines in the line of dispensational, Holiness, and pentecostal theologies."[60] He charges that these spiritualties encouraged intellectual habits such as "Bible reading as puzzle solving" and social isolation that failed to interact with the broader cultural, institutional, and theological issues.[61] Instead, such believers "fled from the problems of the wider world into fascination with inner spirituality or the details of end-times prophesy."[62] Noll laments that this isolationism led to tragic intellectual consequences. He maintains that evangelicals "gave birth to virtually no insights into how, under God, the natural world proceeded, how human societies worked, why human nature acted the way it did, or what constituted the blessings and perils of culture."[63] Noll assesses the intellectual worth of these groups by their ability to rationally

---

Bible, the Word of God. His faith and practice, and the experience of its members are grounded in Scripture" (Church of God, "Church of God," lines 1–3). Finally, the Church of God in Christ's website clearly endorses biblical authority when it affirms the absolute authority of Scripture in all matters of life (Church of God in Christ, "What We Believe," lines 1–2; and Church of God in Christ, "Statement of Faith," line 1). These three organizations are the largest representations of contemporary American Pentecostalism and each affirms the authority of Scripture over all matters of life, which in our case, includes personal experience.

58. Noll, *Scandal*, 107.
59. This is most directly seen in, Ibid., chapter 5.
60. Ibid., 24.
61. Ibid., 137, 142.
62. Ibid., 107.
63. Ibid., 137.

Pentecostalism and the Salvific Role of Orthopathy

provide biblically innovative and cross-disciplinary insights on how God interacts with the world.

Noll indirectly refers to the orthopathic sensibilities of pentecostals in his section "Theological Innovations" where he groups them together with Holiness and fundamentalist evangelicals.[64] He faults Holiness (Keswick and higher-life movements) theologies of sanctification for their *experiential* accent on a closer and deeper walk of faith.[65] Then he scrutinized the pentecostal doctrine of Spirit Baptism for stressing a verbal and physical *experience* of the Spirit.[66] He lastly chides Dispensationalism because its *anticipatory* concern of the immanent return of Christ through a secret rapture fostered intellectual habits of disengagement from society.[67] He further contends that Pentecostalism cultivated anti-intellectual habits when it required its adherents to turn away from the world in order to encounter the goodness of God.[68]

Whereas Noll rightly notes many of the negative consequences of such isolationism,[69] he fails to recognize the intellectually significant orthopathic contributions of certain evangelical groups. While admitting its power as a religious force, Noll nevertheless asserts that the "affectional character of the revival weakened its intellectual power."[70] Later, he similarly echoes,

> In my case, as one who does not believe that the distinctive teachings of dispensationalism, the holiness movement, or Pentecostalism are essential to Christian faith, it is not surprising that I find the intellectual consequences of these theologies damaging.[71]

---

64. Ibid., 115–20.
65. Ibid., 115–16.
66. Ibid., 116–17.
67. Ibid., 117, 120, 123. Briefly, Dispensationalism asserts that God is presently transitioning the church from the present dispensation, the Age of the Church, to its removal (doctrine of secret rapture) which initiates a period of seven years of massive global suffering known as the Great Tribulation. At the end of the Tribulation, Christ returns with the Church to judge the world and begin one thousand years of physical rein on the earth (See, Yong, *In the Days*, 318–20).
68. Noll, *Scandal*, 123.
69. Ibid., chapter 5.
70. Ibid., 24.
71. Ibid., 142.

Part Four: Salvation and Orthopathy

In short, Noll implies that for evangelicals to overcome the scandal they need to shed their affective and experiential conventions in favor of more orthodox (which he means as Calvinistic and Lutheran) theologies.[72] So, even though the *Scandal's* purpose was not to evaluate the cognitive value of emotions and feelings, it does reveal specific epistemological priorities. Such are portrayed in the way Noll underestimates the cognitive potential of experiential spiritualties by consistently subordinating behavior and emotion to intellect.[73]

Interestingly, my charge that Noll's critique embraces an intellectualist epistemology that limits its ability to appreciate the cognitive significance of orthopathic spiritualities is similarly noted by pentecostal theologians James K. A. Smith and Cheryl Bridges Johns in their previously mentioned articles (Smith "Scandalizing Theology" and Johns "Partners in Scandal"). For the sake of space, let's look at Smith's review of Noll's *Scandal*. He argues that Noll misunderstands pentecostal affectivity as causing social isolation and being harmful to the life of the mind. Smith, rather, defends that Pentecostalism is intimately engaged in society *because* of its affective yearning for the kingdom and as such has a "long history of critical scholarship."[74] Smith challenges Noll's Reformed understanding of faith as overly intellectual, not accounting for praxis or affectivity. Admitting that pentecostal communities sometimes exhibit anti-intellectual attitudes, Smith explains this is more likely traced to its dispensationalist connections than with original pentecostal spirituality. This alliance has engendered in many pentecostals the same distrust of secular education and isolation from "worldly institutions" as seen in Fundamentalism.[75] However, early pentecostal spirituality as linked to its Wesleyan ties was different. Smith remarks, "Pentecostals, following a Wesleyan paradigm, do not consider theoretical theological formulations as indicators of faith; rather, faith is expressed in 'works of love,' in praxis."[76] He claims that at its heart, Pentecostalism is "anti-intellectual" in that it views faith as *more* than a mental task. For our purposes, Smith concludes that Noll's critique against Pentecostalism is fundamentally flawed because it fails to understand the affective and

---

72. Ibid., 247. See also, Smith, "Scandalizing Theology," 225–38; Kostlevy, "The Dispensationalists," 187–92; and Johns, "Partners in Scandal," 183–97.

73. For instance see, Noll, *Scandal*, 83–105.

74. Smith, "Scandalizing Theology," 232.

75. Ibid., 233.

76. Ibid., 236.

Pentecostalism and the Salvific Role of Orthopathy

embodied quality of pentecostal spirituality and its intrinsic resistance to a view of faith primarily defined by intellect and rationality.[77]

Therefore, although Noll reasons that the way beyond the evangelical scandal requires one to leave behind affectively informed theologies, I propose that they need to be incorporated. In consideration of contemporary perspectives on the nature of cognition in the neurosciences, I introduce pentecostal orthopathy as a resource to help facilitate greater integration between knowing, acting, and feeling. In so doing, I advance Noll's mission for a more productive evangelical mind while avoiding the epistemological commitments that hinder his efforts.

In the preceding assessments, one issue repeatedly surfaces—*fear of subjective experience replacing scriptural authority in the form of emotionalism*. Once again, I admit there are segments within Pentecostalism where excessive and ungrounded subjectivity exists and should be rejected. However, I contend that denying *emotionalism* does not necessitate the dismissing of *orthopathy*. Unfortunately, if such reservations against emotions continue, they will eventually lead to neglecting the affectivity of cognition, which neuroscientific research affirms is critical for optimal cognitive function. Therefore, it bears repeating that central to our soteriological proposal is the recurring assertion that faith—as with cognition—is most healthy when it holistically integrates intellect, behavior, and emotions-affectivity. To neglect any of these features stifles the transforming possibilities of faith.

Orthopathy in Contemporary Protestantism

Despite the theological trend of orthodoxy-driven epistemologies in conservative Christian thought, some exceptions can be found within a broader milieu of Protestantism. Such often reflect restorationist intuitions in search of more dynamic and transformational accountings of God's salvific work in the world. The following two orthopathic theologies illustrate our point. However, while the term "orthopathy" is not absent in these theologies, the concept is normally associated with "experience" and "affections." Here I briefly review the influence of emotion, experience, and affectivity in Wesleyan and feminist thought.

Presuming the orthopathy of Wesleyanism as outlined above, contemporary Wesleyan theologian, Gregory Clapper highlights the role of emotions and experience in the theology of John Wesley. In his book, *The*

---

77. Ibid., 232.

Part Four: Salvation and Orthopathy

Renewal of the Heart is the Mission of the Church, Clapper reiterates the Wesleyan conviction that faith is a matter of both what is believed in one's head and what is experienced in the heart. Interacting with cognitive studies on emotions and feelings, Clapper elaborates on what Wesley's "heart religion" does and does not imply. He unfolds "affections" as both the *genesis* and *telos* of heart religion and its manifestation as both an inward (interior) and outward (social) reality.[78] He concludes by depicting Wesley's heart religion as a practical theology with transformational and holistic implications for the Christian life.[79] Clapper also devotes an entire book to the topic of "religious affections" in the theology of Wesley.[80]

Clapper stands as just one among many Wesley theologians employing affections and experience in Christian theology and practice. For instance, Randy Maddox has written on Wesley's use of experience in his notion of "spiritual senses."[81] He also notes how human experience in Wesley's concept of entire sanctification shows how "responsible grace" is a unifying principle for a systematic interpretation of Wesley's theology.[82] Additionally, Methodist theologians, on the 250th anniversary of Wesley's Aldersgate experience (May 24, 1988), reflected on what religious experience meant to Wesley and what patterns it might indicate for future Methodists.[83] Donald Thorsen's text, *The Wesleyan Quadrilateral*,[84] details Wesley's theological method whereby *experience*, along with Scripture, tradition, and reason are offered as a hermeneutic for conservative theology. Most Methodist thought, in one way or another, reflect the original affective influence of its founder, John Wesley. Even though numerous fragmentations have evolved from the initial stream of its leader, Methodism remains a religious institution that regards human experience as an important component of theological reflection.[85]

In sum, Methodism highlights orthopathy within its holiness accent on salvation entailing not just the saving of one's soul but tangibly

---

78. Clapper, *Renewal of the Heart*, 68–88.
79. Ibid., 98.
80. See Clapper, *John Wesley*.
81. Maddox, *Responsible*.
82. Maddox, "Responsible Grace," 7–22.
83. See, Maddox, ed., *Aldersgate Reconsidered*.
84. Thorsen, *Wesleyan*.
85. Such fragmentation has typically arisen from varying interpretations regarding the meaning and scope of sanctification, perfection, and Spirit baptism.

Pentecostalism and the Salvific Role of Orthopathy

experiencing the love of God in ongoing capacity. Wesley's interpretation of holiness as divine love illustrates experience as an orthopathic category that still remains in contemporary Methodist theologies. I now turn to the use of orthopathy in Susan Ross' feminist sacramental theology.

In anticipation of the next section where Steven Land identifies "affections" as the integration of intellect, behavior, and emotions-feelings, I now refer to feminist theologian, Susan Ross' incorporation of affections in sacramental theology. For Ross, because the sacraments are materially mediated, soteriology is filled with embodied implications. She asserts that, "God's presence is to be found in and through the material dimensions of life."[86] However, she maintains that the materiality of the sacraments have also led to a stifling of grace for females because they have been constricted by ecclesiastical rituals that fail to take female embodiment seriously. As such she insists that "God's immanent presence in the world and in human embodiment is narrowed to its definitive expression in bodies of men."[87] She acknowledges that the exclusion of women to the margins of sacramental ministry ultimately shapes their experience of God in the world. Ross' efforts focus on developing a sacramental theology that transcends a male-dominated imagery and praxis. Rather, she proposes a more inclusive view in which the sacraments "express God's amazing presence in human life, the potential of all life to reveal God's presence, and the importance of relating the hospitality of God's gracious love in every possible dimension of human life."[88] She claims that as embodied beings, human affectivity enables receptivity to God's gracious presence.

In her book *Extravagant Affections*, Ross speaks of new developments in feminist thought that interpret sacraments in a more general, affective, and experiential manner than the narrower "canonical" conception.[89] Motivated by such perspectives, Ross explains her view of the sacraments.

> [A]s the gifts of God's "extravagant affections," and our own for God and for others, the sacraments provide opportunities for Christian women and men to express, play, celebrate, and live out the "riotous plenty that is God."[90]

---

86. Ross, "Church and Sacrament," 233.
87. Ibid.
88. Ibid., 235.
89. Ross, *Extravagant Affections*, 74.
90. Ibid., 13. Emphasis original.

Part Four: Salvation and Orthopathy

Ross' definition implies that human affections enable one to better comprehend God's presence. She draws from the contribution of feminist thought in ethics that, "question the privileging of rationality, and the consequent denigration of emotion that has emerged from Enlightenment ethics."[91] In light of such research, she applies orthopathic categories—especially in regard to relationality—when she calls for an embracing of the *ambiguity* of the sacraments as a means of empowerment. She contends, "My claim . . . will be that the ambiguities surrounding sacramentality . . . can prove to be critical and transformative resources for sacramental theology."[92] Such an approach takes serious the indistinct nature of sacramentality in which merely propositional and allegedly "objective" explanations fail to capture how God's presence is dispensed.

Ross applies the relational paradigm of *family* as opposed to the more customary patriarchal pattern of *bride and bridegroom* to illustrate the ambiguity of God's presence in the sacraments.[93] The bride and groom model, she claims, enforces separate spheres for men and women (i.e., priests and lay) that contribute to injustice. She says:

> [T]he moral implications of sacramental theology—of God's loving presence embodied in actions and relationships of justice and mutuality—lack development, in large part due to the exclusion of women from sacramental leadership.[94]

Ross attests that just as familial love is mediated through the affective force of relationships, so too is God's grace historically mediated through relationships—with God and others. Similarly, she concludes that the role of every minister "is to make the extravagant affections of God for humanity, and ours for each other, more visible, more active, in the life of the church."[95] Ross's association of sacramentality with affective categories on the part of both God and humankind reveals, even if implicitly, an orthopathic vision of salvation.

A correlation between Ross' sacramental theology and my handling of orthopathy can be drawn from her use of the term ambiguity. Though used specifically in reference to the ineffable quality of God's presence in

---

91. Ibid., 172.
92. Ibid., 65.
93. Ibid., chapters 5 and 6.
94. Ibid., 192.
95. Ibid., 228–29.

Pentecostalism and the Salvific Role of Orthopathy

sacramental practice, such also highlights the vague and uncertain quality of affectivity bound up in the process of knowing God. In other words, ambiguity indicates what I am here calling *orthopathy*. In this manner, Ross' proposal not only defends the soteriological contribution of orthopathy but also links the same with orthopraxy, by connecting sacramentality with ethics.[96]

Nevertheless, despite the appropriation of orthopathy in Methodist-Wesleyan thought and Susan Ross' feminist sacramental theology, neither stresses orthopathy as a vehicle for mediating knowledge of God. Furthermore, these examples have not exploited the orthopathic implications of pneumatology as does Pentecostalism. With all this in consideration, we now focus on the soteriological distinctives of pentecostal orthopathy.

Towards an Orthopathic Soteriology: How Do We Get There?

The goal of this chapter has been to introduce pentecostal spirituality and its relationship with orthopathy. As we move forward, our task will be more fruitful if I clarify the meaning of pentecostal orthopathy. This is important because I am not merely concerned with *any* kind of orthopathy but *pentecostal* orthopathy. However, to accomplish this, I need to first introduce two related topics—pentecostal eschatology and pneumatology.

Pentecostal Eschatology and Pneumatology

In the late nineteenth century, with the promulgation of premillennial Dispensationalism, expectation of Christ's immanent return quickly spread among those most exposed to American revivalism.[97] William Faupel states, "The air of expectancy was heightened. The adherents were confident that the final mighty worldwide revival was just around the corner."[98]

---

96. Ibid., 209.

97. In the late eighteenth and early nineteenth centuries, the dispensational eschatology of the Plymouth Brethren founder, John Nelson Darby (1800–1882) influenced many conservative Protestants of that era (see, Crutchfield, *Origins*). Darby's premillennial-dispensationalism became popular in North America through a network of Bible prophecy conferences in the latter half of the nineteenth century. Of significance was "Scofieldian dispensationalism" deriving from Charles Scofield (1843–1921) through his *Scofield Study Bible* (1909). This resource was extremely influential in spreading dispensational-premillennialism (King, *Disfellowshiped*, 93).

98. Faupel, *Everlasting Gospel*, 73–74.

Part Four: Salvation and Orthopathy

Because Dispensationalism was largely adopted in the Wesleyan-Holiness movement, its eschatology became entrenched within the emerging Pentecostalism. Such millenarianism was so prevalent that initial adherents of Pentecostalism often referred to themselves, as the "Latter Rain Movement."[99] Faupel alleges that the eschatology of the Latter Rain theme is the key to interpreting Pentecostalism because the movement so clearly self-identified as participating in the "latter rains" referred to in the account of Pentecost in Acts chapter 2 referencing the Book of Joel.[100]

Pneumatology was also linked to the "latter rain" theme because pentecostals believed that Spirit baptism signified a new outpouring of the Holy Spirit to prepare the Church for Christ's immanent return. Just as the Spirit was poured out in Acts 2 for initiating the Great Commission, so too was God again preparing the Church for a massive mission—to complete the Great Commission before his soon return. Out of its self-understanding as a "Latter Day" movement, pentecostals earnestly prayed for the baptism of the Holy Spirit, with its authenticating evidence of glossolalia, to empower them for their divine mandate. Steven Land advanced that for early pentecostals "[t]o be filled with the Spirit . . . is to be disposed toward the kingdom with all decisiveness, longing, and earnestness."[101] Hence, millennial expectancy and robust pneumatology are fundamental to the pentecostal orthopathic impulse. As we will soon see, these two elements are imbedded in pentecostal spirituality and, therefore, its emphasis on orthopathy.

In view of the preceding, we can now elaborate the claim of this chapter that pentecostal orthopathy is a critical component of a renewal soteriology of embodiment. The remainder of the chapter expands the meaning of pentecostal orthopathy through three theologians. Each one helps articulate the dynamic character of an orthopathic soteriology through the theme of transformation.

---

99. Dayton, *Theological Roots*, 27.

100. Key Scriptures are Hos 6:3; Zech 10:1; and Jas 5:7–8. David Wesley Myland, using these and other texts develops what became the classic Latter Rain doctrine in his, *The Latter Rain Covenant and Pentecostal Power*.

101. Land, *Pentecostal Spirituality*, 174.

Pentecostalism and the Salvific Role of Orthopathy

PENTECOSTAL ORTHOPATHY IN THEOLOGICAL PERSPECTIVE

Just as chapters 3 and 4 drew from Jonathan Edwards and chapters 5 and 6 appropriated William Abraham's Canonical Theism to re-envision the soteriological significance of orthodoxy and orthopraxy, I now refer to select theologians to illuminate the vital role of orthopathy for an embodied soteriology of renewal. As before, I corroborate this claim with what the neurosciences tell us about the intellectual, behavioral, and affective dimensions of cognition. Presently, I draw from the scholarship of three contemporary theologians—Steven Land, Daniel Castelo, and Samuel Solivan—to develop what I mean by pentecostal orthopathy and how such is inextricably linked to embodiment. Since, for many Protestants, Jonathan Edwards is paradigmatic of orthodox theology, the findings of each theologian are correlated with Edwards' dispositional epistemology. Finally, for our immediate purposes "pentecostal orthopathy" can also be understood as "pentecostal spirituality" since spirituality is often understood in orthopathic terms.

Transformed Affections

In chapter 3, Jonathan Edwards' dispositional ontology defined the human soul or mind as dispositional forces. The human person, as constituted by these forces, exists as a radical nexus of law-like relationships God has ordained to act in certain ways under certain conditions and are predisposed to ongoing levels of actualization. Riddled by the bondage of sin, human dispositions do not operate as they ought; hence individuals are powerless to seek the highest good and live for the beauty and goodness of God. Rather, blinded to God's beauty, they seek their own good and act contrary to the divine laws he set in place. Edwards exploits this ontological scheme to describe the healing work of the Spirit in the believer in which these dispositional forces are transformed and manifested as religious affections. After becoming rightly oriented to God, believers are disposed to actualize ongoing degrees of the beauty and goodness of God. Such a dispositional framework factors into each of the following theologians to be soon addressed. We now turn to Steven Land who applies Edwards' dispositional ontology to clarify the central feature of transformed affections in pentecostal orthopathy.

Part Four: Salvation and Orthopathy

Steven Jack Land (b. 1946) is Professor of Pentecostal Theology and former President of Pentecostal Theological Seminary in Cleveland, Tennessee. In his now classic book, *Pentecostal Spirituality: A Passion for the Kingdom,* Land draws from John Wesley and Jonathan Edwards that true Christianity consists in the "religious affections."[102] He thus elevates the service of affectivity in theological reflection. In this text, Land asserts that pentecostal spirituality is shaped by its eschatological beliefs and self-awareness as a Spirit empowered last-days restoration movement. Land outlines pentecostal spirituality as most clearly delineated in the first ten years of its early twentieth-century origins. Notwithstanding that many fragmentations have since occurred, he offers that its original spirituality has marked all later manifestations. Therefore, any future re-visioning of pentecostal spirituality must take seriously its primitive expression.[103] Land explains:

> The early Pentecostals saw themselves as recovering and re-entering that [Acts chapter 2] Pentecostal reality. The vivid presence of the Spirit heightened expectation, propelled into mission, enlivened worship, and increased consecration in preparation for the appearance of the Lord of the harvest.[104]

Accordingly, such premillennial expectation and pneumatologically robust sensitivities catalyzed pentecostal spirituality, which Land defines as "passion for the kingdom" and transformed affections.[105] This is why Land attests that "passion for the kingdom of God was the unifying center of the movement."[106] Throughout, he identifies apocalyptic affections to epitomize the heart of pentecostal spirituality.[107] However, Land is careful to portray such affections as also connected to pentecostal beliefs and practices.[108] Just as Edwards understood the affections to represent the integration of beliefs

---

102. Land basically rephrases Edwards' understanding of affections: "Affections are abiding dispositions which dispose the person toward God and the neighbor in ways appropriate to their source and goal in God. Feelings are important but they come and go, are mixed, and of varying degrees of intensity. Moods too are variable, but affections characterize a person" (Ibid., 132).

103. Ibid., 37.
104. Ibid., 65.
105. Ibid., 11–12.
106. Ibid., 212.
107. Ibid., 182.
108. Ibid., 11.

Pentecostalism and the Salvific Role of Orthopathy

and practices, Land comprehends pentecostal affections as the nexus for its beliefs and practices.[109] I now highlight what I mean by pentecostal practices and beliefs and their relation to affections.

Since Pentecostalism emerged from the Wesleyan-Holiness tradition, it adopted the "five-fold gospel" theological paradigm with Christ as savior (justifier), sanctifier, healer, baptizer in the Holy Spirit, and coming king.[110] In addition to salvation as justification and sanctification as a second work of grace, pentecostals also affirmed the baptism of the Holy Spirit accompanied with tongues as a subsequent work of grace. Within this doctrinal context, pentecostal practices and beliefs were grounded in characteristic pentecostal affections which, in turn, shaped the beliefs even as the practices grew from and nurtured the affections.[111] Hence, beliefs, practices, and affections were inseparably entwined. This is why the pentecostal practices of worship, prayer, Scripture reading, and preaching were often so exuberant—they were means to communicate and foster a deep passionate expectation for the in-breaking kingdom. Yet, within pentecostal praxis, it seems that prayer was the organizing activity that most profoundly activated affective transformation.[112] Land explains:

> Pentecostal affections are shaped and expressed through the prayers of missionary fellowship . . . The corporate and individual prayers are shaped by the preaching and teaching of the Word, the singing of songs, the giving and hearing of testimonies and prayer requests, the fellowship of the believers before, during, and after the services, the constant praises and thanks offered throughout

---

109. Ibid., 182. Land incorporates Theodore Runyon's awareness of orthopathy as providing a "necessary but currently missing complement to orthodoxy and orthopraxy" (Runyon, "Importance of Experience," 4). For more on orthopathy's relationship with orthodoxy and orthopraxy, see also Maddox, *Aldersgate Reconsidered*, 93–108.

110. Land, *Pentecostal Spirituality*, 182. Hence, Bruner's charge that Pentecostalism was insufficiently christocentric is ungrounded because it embraced the same Christology as its fellow evangelical brethren. The only difference was that it expanded Christ's ministry as Baptizer in the Spirit. Land affirms the christological emphasis of pentecostal pneumatology, "The 'five-fold gospel' was Christocentric because of the witness, power, and presence of the Holy Spirit" (119). William Seymour clearly bears out the centrality of Christ in pentecostal belief and practice, "The Holy Spirit has not time to magnify anything but the Blood of our Lord Jesus Christ. Standing between the living and the dead, we need to so bear the dying body of our Lord, that people will only see Christ in us, and never get a chance to see self. We are simply a voice shouting, 'Behold the Lamb of God!'" (Seymour, "The Church Question," 2).

111. Land, *Pentecostal Spirituality*, 116.

112. Ibid., 163.

> the service and the operation of the various gifts of the Spirit, and the intercessions of the saints. All these activities shape the prayers and the prayers in turn shape the affections.[113]

Through such participation, pentecostal believers were affectively transformed as they experienced God. Again, Land continues, "Pentecostal narrative beliefs told a story of the restoration of the 'fivefold gospel' to the church and the cultivation of the persons who received and believed that gospel as a way of life."[114] Contrary to the critiques of pentecostal spirituality, this was no superficial or fleeting emotionalism but authentic transformation.

A word of clarification is now in order regarding aspects of similarity between Land's project and mine. While we both construe salvation as an integration of orthodoxy, orthopraxy, and orthopathy, our aims are different. Land does so to recast the more original eschatological and pneumatological leanings of pentecostal spirituality. My purpose is to conceptualize soteriology as a more dynamic and transformational reality than commonly understood in conservative Protestantism. Hence, Land's articulation of pentecostal spirituality, as constituted by a unique set of affections, serves our end of laying out the meaning of pentecostal orthopathy. So, as per the intention of this section, what might transformed affections look like? Land describes them as *apocalyptic affections*; he also provides three examples—gratitude, compassion, and courage.

Gratitude—the first apocalyptic affection—finds its source in God's righteousness because in salvation one is made righteous and forgiven of sin because God is righteous.[115] Land details gratitude as the most foundational of all the apocalyptic affections because in salvation the believer is aware that God has not only acted in past history but is also at work in his or her present history.[116]

> Gratitude, then, is evoked through remembering what God has done in Christ to atone for sins, what God has done to call one out of the world of lost souls, what God is doing to keep and perfect, and what God will do to bring in the kingdom. It is a hedge against forgetfulness.[117]

---

113. Ibid., 164.
114. Ibid., 119.
115. Ibid., 120.
116. Ibid., 135.
117. Ibid., 136.

Pentecostalism and the Salvific Role of Orthopathy

Gratitude is the conscious and intentional perception of God's grace at work in one's life.[118]

Gratitude flows from the awareness that God—who is righteous and the source of all righteousness—has overcome the crippling and deadly powers of sin. One models gratitude through ongoing acts of thanksgiving, especially through testimonies, songs, and prayers. Praxis helps sustain gratitude even as gratitude helps reinforce such practices. Hence, previously ungrateful individuals are transformed as they embrace pentecostal beliefs and practices.

The second apocalyptic affection is love. Land asserts, "If gratitude is the foundation of the pentecostal affective structure, the interior of the building is a compassionate, longing love."[119] Such compassion finds its source in God's love because his love creates a yearning to be perfectly sanctified. He maintains, "The Spirit moves upon those who are emptied out and yielded to manifest the character of love."[120] So God's love orients one in a life of love expressed in devotion and surrender to God and compassionate service to others.

Through saving faith, one is affectively transformed from loving and living for self to loving and living for God and others. Furthermore, because pentecostals believed that Spirit baptism presumed a life already surrendered and sanctified, then love marks the heart receptive to the Holy Spirit. For the baptism of the Spirit brought not only an empowerment of service but an empowerment of greater love and compassion for the lost. As a last-days missionary movement, pentecostals understand that blessings are not given for their benefit but others. Theirs was the mandate of preaching the good news to the uttermost ends of the earth. Notwithstanding the magnitude of the task, God empowers those who respond to the call.

Therefore, courage is the third apocalyptic affection. This affection is formed in the hearts of Spirit baptized saints as they personally experience new levels of confidence and hope in Christ.[121] As believers encounter the transforming grace of God in salvation, they learn to rest in assurance that

---

118. Ibid., 137.

119. Ibid., 139.

120. Ibid., 141.

121. Ibid., 156. Despite that Durham's Finished Work Theory led to a de-emphasis of ongoing sanctification, pentecostals have, by and large, stressed the importance of sanctification (purity) to accompany power.

he will empower them regardless the challenge. Land reasons that courage is born of the confidence that comes from gratitude and love.[122]

> In regeneration one belongs to the new people of God and gives thanks; in sanctification one receives a new heart of compassionate love for God and others; and in Spirit baptism one receives an "authorized strength" to be a courageous witness in word and demonstration of the Spirit.[123]

Thus, courage correlates with the pentecostal order of salvation in Spirit baptism.

Lastly, as with all pentecostal affections, courage arises within the eschatological context of the kingdom of God. Knowing that the Spirit has been poured out for an end-times mission brings forth passion and steadfast commitment to see the kingdom of God realized. This is why Land emphasizes that, in pentecostal spirituality, passion for the kingdom of God has always been its integrating center.[124] Next, we reflect on how pentecostal orthopathy intuits an affective theological epistemology that is alarmingly transforming.

An Affective Epistemology as Transformational

Pentecostal theologian Daniel Castelo draws from Edwards' ontology for epistemological purposes. We recall that Edwards' dispositional epistemology combined the understanding (intellect, rationality) and will (the judging or perceptive aspect of the mind), so that knowledge of God is inseparable from the religious affections. Conceived as a spring of motivation and behavior, the affections are fundamental for Edwards' dispositional soteriology. Castelo makes use of Edwards' religious affections when he appropriates pentecostal spirituality within an epistemological framework wherein beliefs and practices are integrated in affections. Specifically, Castelo builds on Land's previous explication of affections to re-vision pentecostal ethics as central to its spirituality. Accordingly, he shows how pentecostal orthopathy is an affective epistemology.

Daniel Castelo is Associate Professor of Theology at Seattle Pacific University in Seattle, Washington and an Ordained Bishop in the Church

---

122. Ibid., 159.
123. Ibid., 153.
124. Ibid., 212.

of God (Cleveland, TN). His research and writing interests cover the areas of Mystical Theology, Dogmatic Theology, and Moral Theology. Castelo is an important interlocutor for pentecostal orthopathy because of his moral-theological proposal in his book, *Revisioning Pentecostal Ethics: The Epicletic Community*.

Throughout, Castelo identifies Pentecostalism as a *spirituality* because its original bent was more akin to a pneumatic lifestyle than denominational commitments. He contests that Pentecostalism is best conceived as a spirituality requiring embodiment and execution because it "did not begin in a lecture hall, royal court, or ecclesial meeting but in revival and worship."[125] He frequently refers to pentecostal spirituality as *epicletic* in that it regularly acknowledges its beginning and ending as existing and being sustained by the "presence, prompting, and empowerment of the Holy Spirit."[126] So, as epicletic, Pentecostalism is concerned with fostering pneumatologically dependent lifestyles.

Castelo makes use of affections as a vital means for transformation.[127] The religious affections represent specific Christ-like qualities pneumatologically formed in the believer (i.e., fruits of the Spirit) as embodied manifestations of the presence and power of God in the world.[128] As with Land, Castelo conceptualizes pentecostal spirituality as the integration of intellect, affectivity, and behavior, as transformed affections.[129] However, unlike Land, he offers a more specific appropriation of pentecostal affections—*moral transformation*. He maintains that pentecostal spirituality radicalized the holiness motif and appeared *eccentric* compared to customs of the day.

> When early Pentecostals practiced footwashing, advocated pacifism, recognized women as partners in ministry, and held services of diverse racial backgrounds, they did so not on the basis of . . . their observance of the status quo; quite the contrary, their apparent irrelevance to the conventions of their day was the bedrock of

---

125. Castelo, *Revisioning*, 22.

126. Ibid.

127. Castelo draws from pentecostal theologians (Steven Land and Samuel Solivan) and Wesleyan scholars (Theodore Runyon and Gregory Clapper) to relate orthopathy with the religious affections for pneumatological transformation. See, Runyon, *New Creation*, chapter 5; Clapper, *John Wesley*, chapter 7; and Solivan, *Spirit, Pathos and Liberation*.

128. Castelo, *Revisioning*, 57, 59.

129. Ibid., 42–45.

Part Four: Salvation and Orthopathy

their alarming relevance, that feature that made them eccentric in a holy kind of way.[130]

Such eccentricity characterized the morally transforming impact of primitive pentecostal spirituality. Nevertheless, despite its promising beginnings it was not long until many of the eccentric features marking pentecostal spirituality fell away.[131] Castelo laments, "Racial, gender, generational, and doctrinal possibilities gave way to petty and hurtful divisions . . ."[132] How could such a drastic shift occur so quickly?

Since Pentecostalism is a doxological movement, its most original instincts derive from worship.[133] The problem ensued from a shift in doxology. Castelo argues that in its nascent expression, formation occurred organically because its doxological lifestyle afforded many such occasions.[134] Prominent affective inclinations initially prevalent, slowly decreased over the years. Castelo remarks, "I believe that early Pentecostals harbored certain impulses and intuitions that were quite important but that over time were diminished or reconfigured in light of a number of pressures that arose over time."[135] Pentecostalism's doxological praxis slowly accommodated the more private and sporadic "altar encounter" paradigm of its fundamentalist context. Subsequent to this shift, opportunities were reduced for the kind of ethical formation marking early Pentecostalism.[136] While not negating the value of such encounters, Castelo says they are unable to sustain the revolutionary lifestyles marking the first pentecostals.

> The existence of Pentecostal eccentricity (at least in its sanctified forms) points to something beyond an altar encounter. Although Pentecostals privileged this kind of experience through their practices, speech patterns, and expectations, their "critical tradition" suggests that more has been at play in Pentecostal identity and life than simply individualized and emotionally charged experiences.[137]

---

130. Ibid., 104.
131. Ibid., 78–79.
132. Ibid., 79.
133. Ibid., 22.
134. Ibid., 16–17.
135. Ibid., 2.
136. Ibid., 19–20.
137. Ibid., 16.

Pentecostalism and the Salvific Role of Orthopathy

Castelo uncovers this "more" as an implicit pentecostal catechesis, yet one that is not focused on propositional instruction and recall. Pentecostals are weary of such catechesis because they recognize its limits as a vehicle for transformation.[138] He elaborates that "Pentecostalism has sustained the catechetical task but in a manner that is invitational and aesthetic. In Pentecostal catechesis, onlookers are bidden to 'come and see' the sights, sounds, and wonders of Pentecostal worship."[139] As its primary vehicle for moral change, the epicletic nature of pentecostal doxology is catechetical. By virtue of engaging a "catechetical" approach, Castelo's project becomes epistemological. He explains, "Pentecostalism privileges worship as a way of securing authority and truth claims; doxology is a modality of knowing and being."[140] Thus, Castelo proposes a doxological epistemology for pentecostal catechesis.

As an alternative to its uncritical adoption of "altar encounters," Castelo's "practice-orientations" are a viable alternative. He introduces two practice-orientations—abiding and waiting—to illustrate their compatibility with pentecostal spirituality in nurturing affective transformation.

> If Pentecostals hold that the inbreaking kingdom of God is apprehended within the modality of Pentecostal worship, then "abiding and waiting" cannot simply be instances at the altar; they have to be habituated practice-orientations that foster a kind of "second nature," a set of dispositions in relation to all that is.[141]

Abiding and waiting, therefore, transpire in a doxological context (private or public) to spur one onto greater advancement into the *imago Dei*.[142] As such, their goal is always transformation. Castelo clarifies, "[T]he emphases of abiding and waiting point to ... the encounter between God and humanity, one that can be either delightful or crushing but always with the aim of being reparative, transformative, and empowering."[143] Hence, he makes explicit the implicit character of pentecostal catechesis through its doxological spirituality. He casts "abiding and waiting" as epistemological resources to help mediate the kind of spirituality needed for Pentecostalism to regain its moral "eccentricity." Unlike its fundamentalist heritage that emphasizes

138. Ibid., 31.
139. Ibid.
140. Ibid., 130.
141. Ibid., 82.
142. Ibid., 32.
143. Ibid., 31.

salvation as a crisis, event, or decision, these practice-orientations operate in more communal and ordinary-everyday contexts as they reveal the epistemological potential of pentecostal spirituality.[144] Such a communal accent provides a practical environment for moral and ethical formation otherwise unavailable from a private altar encounter.

Castelo asserts that failure to create a catechetical process in keeping with its dynamic spirituality has made it difficult for Pentecostalism to sustain its radical morality.

> [T]hose intuitions, because they are pneumatologically prompted, continue to be available today, but their cultivation and perpetuation become increasingly difficult to sustain as the environments in which they are prompted become more and more staid and inflexible.[145]

Such inflexibility has resulted from the institutionalization the movement has experienced over the last one hundred years.[146] Castelo affectively casts these practice-orientations by rooting them in the social milieu of the pneumatic community. Greater opportunities are thus afforded for the Spirit to foster these dispositions than when the primary manner of their formation is an otherwise "generic Evangelicalism."[147]

We have just examined Daniel Castelo's understanding of pentecostal spirituality as an affective epistemology. As a doxological community, pentecostals know God most fully in worship. While meaningful encounters with the Spirit occur at pentecostal altars, such do not capture the epicletic quality of pentecostal spirituality whereby all of life becomes, as it were, an altar. So, rather than depending on its catechesis to occur through sporadic pneumatological encounters at the altar, Castelo proposes abiding and

---

144. The failure to properly understand the affective nature of pentecostal epistemology leads theologians like Mark Noll to judge the affective features of Wesleyan-Holiness and pentecostal spiritualties as intellectually damaging. The intellectualist epistemology of such theologians prevents them from recognizing the affective impulses they discount are actually embedded in a dynamic epistemology that integrates intellect, behavior, and emotions. While possibilities of emotionalism remain, such epistemologies are far from "intellectually weak." On the contrary, they are intellectually robust because they better reflect the embodied nature of human cognition. Castelo's description of the epicletic pentecostal community taking beliefs, behaviors, and affectivity seriously models the critique that James Smith addressed against Noll's *Scandal* ("Scandalizing Theology," 225–38).

145. Castelo, *Revisioning*, 17.

146. Ibid. Margaret Poloma has argued this point in her book, *Assemblies of God*.

147. Castelo, *Revisioning*, 129.

waiting as practice-orientations that can facilitate pentecostal catechesis. Practice-orientations are more than the practices and beliefs undergirding them. Rather, as orientations they exist like Edwards' dispositions wherein beliefs and practices are affectively integrated. Consequently they can account for ongoing formation unhindered by the temporal and physical actualities of traditional altar encounters. Next, I underscore the affective significance of Pentecostal soteriology and its transforming possibilities.

An Affective Soteriology as Transformational

In chapter 3, Edwards describes knowledge of God as a bi-fold reality of notional and spiritual knowledge. While notional knowledge is rational and objective and spiritual knowledge is affective and sensory, neither is independent of the other. Edwards explains that sinful dispositions are transformed by the Spirit into religious affections through the embodiment of spiritual knowledge. Hence, the affections are marked by intellectual, behavioral, and affective modalities of cognition. Now, Samuel Solivan indirectly employs Edwards' epistemology through Land's dispositional construal of the affections as the integrating center of intellect, behavior, and emotions.[148] Solivan links his project to Land's in saying, "It is the issue of disposition toward neighbor that I wish to attend to."[149] Though not explicitly stated as such, this Edwardsean epistemology underlies Solivan's research as he calls North American theologians to re-construe orthodoxy as inseparable from praxis. As with Land and Castelo, Solivan also appropriates orthopathy for soteriological ends. I now expound how Solivan's use of pentecostal spirituality exemplifies an affective soteriology.

Samuel Solivan is an ordained minister of the Assemblies of God and Professor of Theology at Interamerican University of Puerto Rico and Professor of Theology at El Seminario Teológico de Puerto Rico. He has served as President of the Society of Pentecostal Studies and participated in many ecumenical forums. As a former student of Gustavo Gutiérrez (b. 1928), Solivan identifies with his assessment of liberation as central to the gospel.[150] Therefore, it is not surprising that liberation serves as a focal

---

148. Solivan, *Spirit, Pathos and Liberation*, 12.

149. Ibid.

150. Once again, Liberation Theology began with the publishing of *A Theology of Liberation* (1971) by the Peruvian priest and theologian, Gustavo Gutiérrez. Gutiérrez's distress over the Roman Catholic Church's passivity to the widespread poverty and

PART FOUR: SALVATION AND ORTHOPATHY

soteriological category for Solivan. As the author of *The Spirit, Pathos and Liberation: Toward an Hispanic Pentecostal Theology*, Solivan urges all pentecostal theologians to recognize the hermeneutics of suffering because the majority of pentecostal Christians live in desperate contexts.

Solivan argues that Pentecostalism has historically thrived most among society's poor and oppressed.

> The growth of the Pentecostal community has been and continues to be most evident among the poor and disenfranchised of the world. Whether at Azusa Street in Los Angeles, or in the countryside at Cherokee County, North Carolina, or in the *barrios* of New York or San Paulo, the Pentecostal message has been shared and continues to be shared most effectively with the poor and unattended.[151]

Yet, pentecostal theology remains predominately Eurocentric in orientation and largely practiced from a position of privilege isolated from adversity. Solivan reasons:

> Those of us who seek to speak on behalf of the sufferer must return to that place of suffering. Theologians cannot afford to distance themselves from the pain and suffering of the masses . . . An orthopathic epistemology will help the theologian of the dominant culture to enter into a more fruitful dialogue with Hispanics and other suffering people.[152]

Solivan upholds that such isolation has encouraged a tradition of theological reflection and abstract propositions over tangible praxis often appearing irrelevant to the disenfranchised. He reiterates, "The theological and philosophical bifurcation of reason from experience must be corrected if the Christ of the gospel we preach is to be consistent with a God who identifies with broken humanity."[153] He contends that when theology is isolated from

---

oppression in Latin America at the hands of military dictatorships prompted him to take a stand and become the movement's prominent leader. Liberation theology insists that theology must be contextual. In other words, praxis precedes theological reflection. Gutiérrez upholds that liberation theology is an application of the doctrine of salvation because salvation is not only about transformation and personal freedom from sin but freedom from cultural, economic, and institutional eruptions of sin—i.e., oppression, marginalization, and exploitation (Gutiérrez, *Theology of Liberation*, xxxviii, 36–7, 83, 116).

151. Solivan, *Spirit, Pathos and Liberation*, 10.
152. Ibid., 37.
153. Ibid., 62.

Pentecostalism and the Salvific Role of Orthopathy

suffering it is unable to meaningfully engage the majority of the world's population.

Solivan rejects the North American theological tendency to underscore truth statements as the chief indicators of salvation. When soteriology primarily entails orthodoxy, it remains uninformed by the cruelties of affliction and soon belies the truth it proclaims.[154] Solivan insists, "[T]heological orthodoxy uninformed by the suffering of oppressed peoples and by the pathos of God is at best a half truth and at worst a contradiction of the gospel it seeks to represent."[155] And again, "Authentic Christian orthodoxy requires that the hardened heart of propositional truths be softened by the pathos of those for whom Jesus came."[156] Additionally, Solivan is not only concerned with the intellectualization of orthodoxy but also orthopraxy. He opposes the North American theological custom of orthopraxis as a cognitive exercise removed from the actualities of severe hardship.[157] Solivan explains that North American orthopraxy has exchanged practical enactment of praxis in the daily struggle of those who are oppressed with critical reflection on those "Third World theologians who have continued in their commitment to the poor and oppressed."[158] In response, Solivan introduces *orthopathos* as an interlocutor between orthodoxy and orthopraxis to protect theology from devolving into an abstract propositionalism or praxis detached from suffering.[159] For such theologians, orthopathos helps to shape a disposition of awareness, identification, and compassion toward those who suffer.

While Hispanic Americans are foremost in his mind, Solivan's term applies to anyone overwhelmed with hardship. Through orthopathos there is a right and a wrong way to deal with adversity. Solivan furthers that orthopathos finds a way for suffering to be transformed into a vehicle of liberation. The *ortho* component of orthopathos derives from understanding the difference "between suffering which results in self-alienation, and suffering that can somehow be a source for liberation and social transformation."[160]

---

154. Ibid., 36.
155. Ibid., 147.
156. Ibid., 36.
157. Ibid., 11.
158. Ibid., 68.
159. Ibid., 11.
160. Ibid., 61.

Part Four: Salvation and Orthopathy

Accordingly, one's attitude regarding adversity directly relates to its impact upon the sufferer.

Orthopathos is no romanticizing of suffering but an honest acceptance of its pervasive destruction. Solivan claims that victims of oppression can find hope and rise above their condition, even if the situation persists.

> Understanding and dealing with their pathos empowers them to overcome their situation, not wallow in it. A correct or liberating pathos raises a person's dignity and self-worth, in spite of current conditions. *Orthopathos* is that insight, that self-understanding which infuses in the oppressed the strength to rise above the dehumanization of their daily conditions.[161]

Yet, orthopathos is more than experientially informed orthopraxis. Recognition of suffering alone cannot enable one to overcome its effects. Solivan defends that orthopathos is a pneumatological resource bridging orthodoxy and orthopraxis.[162] Linking orthopathos with the Spirit and his work of transformation, Solvian attests that orthopathos welcomes the power of the Spirit in a person's life to change pathos and despair to hope and wholeness.[163] By honestly admitting one's powerlessness while trusting in God, the Spirit can birth living hope in such saints who suffer.

An affective soteriology stresses the role of experience and emotions in God's ongoing process of transformation in his children. Though underscored, affectivity remains integrated with intellect and behavior. Otherwise salvation devolves into mere emotionalism. Within this framework, Solivan's orthopathos opens up opportunities for liberation by the Spirit through human *pathos*. He re-construes the meaning of suffering for limitless possibilities of a liberating hope. Solivan beautifully articulates that, especially within his Hispanic-American context, such a perspective can lead to joy amidst suffering. He explains, "From our own wailing walls we lift our eyes and see signs of God's reign around us . . . full of hope we dare to sing the songs of Zion even while we live in our modern Babylon."[164] Nevertheless, despite Solivan's attention on liberating praxis, he is not advocating a soteriology dependent on a realized orthopraxis as in some forms of liberation theology.

---

161. Ibid., 62.
162. Ibid., 68.
163. Ibid., 27–28.
164. Ibid., 69.

Pentecostalism and the Salvific Role of Orthopathy

> Orthopathos can also serve as a corrective to some liberation orthopraxis whose advocates believe that the reign of God will not and cannot be manifest until there is a social and political revolution, and that social and political structures of evil must be overcome if the reign of God is to be manifest.[165]

Solivan's orthopathos facilitates the salvific work of God regardless the outcome of orthopraxic efforts because, as dispositional, it is not limited to behavior. Even while acknowledging the significance of liberative praxis, Solivan integrates orthodoxy and orthopraxy via orthopathos for a more holistic rendering of salvation-liberation. The soteriological task of orthopathos helps "to articulate the conditions under which our suffering and oppression can be transformed by the Holy Spirit into a liberating life full of hope and promise."[166]

In sum, orthopathos is a dispositional orientation toward suffering that invites the power of the Holy Spirit in the midst of one's *pathos*. Such invitation cultivates an affective soteriology whereby the saving work of God is wonderfully displayed in manifold ways. Solivan's work reveals pentecostal spirituality as an affective soteriology because such realities as hope, joy, and power to rise above suffering are highlighted as critical parts of Christian salvation.

In this chapter we have explored the historical growth of pentecostal spirituality and its use of orthopathy as a vital part of its heritage. We've addressed its critics by showing that pentecostal orthopathy is much more than mere emotionalism; its robust pneumatology and ecclesial practices help nurture a truly dynamic and transforming spirituality. We concluded by showing how various theologians appropriate affectivity as a vital part of this religious tradition. Now that I have elaborated the meaning of pentecostal orthopathy and noted its embodied character, chapter 8 will appropriate these findings for an orthopathic soteriology.

---

165. Ibid., 148.
166. Ibid., 13.

8

Salvation in the Flesh through Pentecostal Orthopathy

IN THE LAST CENTURY, Pentecostalism has become a global religious phenomenon. Its success is largely due to its embodied understanding of God's saving grace at work to the whole human person through the Holy Spirit and his charismatic giftings to the church for an empowered ministry. Consequently, it consistently nurtures a legacy of transformation among its adherents. Perhaps the greatest challenge to this movement, past and present, is the encroaching tide of intellectualism within the church. Towards this end, the purpose of this chapter is to emphasize the role of pentecostal orthopathy as a resource for preventing such intellectualist biases. I do so by drawing attention to the affective, embodied, and transformational qualities of this orthopathic spirituality. As already noted in the soteriologies of Edwards and Canonical Theism, pneumatology will once again play a chief role in our theological reflection.

PENTECOSTAL ORTHOPATHY FOR A RENEWAL SOTERIOLOGY

The premise throughout this chapter is that just as the cognitive sciences reveal how knowing and understanding are most comprehensive when knowledge is mediated through intellect, behavior, and emotions, so too is faith when similarly mediated. This is why I have systematically noted the soteriological significance of orthodoxy, orthopraxy, and orthopathy as per Edwards, Abraham, and Pentecostalism. Now, in lieu of Land, Castelo,

Salvation in the Flesh through Pentecostal Orthopathy

and Solivan's contributions, I lay out the soteriological value of pentecostal orthopathy as it relates to faith.[1]

An Affective Orthopathy

Just like its Pietistic and Wesleyan-Holiness forbears, Pentecostalism continues to herald the theological significance of "heart religion." As we have seen, such affectivity is typically recognized in pentecostal worship, prayer, revival services, and "altar ministry."[2] Now we turn to the affective nature of pentecostal orthopathy.

Steven Land has popularized pentecostal orthopathy in terms of Edwards' religious affections. Land makes use of pentecostal eschatology—passion for the kingdom—to denote its spirituality by means of apocalyptic affections. A prominent element of these affections is yearning or expectation for the immanent return of Christ. Land roots the affective essence of pentecostal orthopathy to its pneumatology when he grants that it is "the Spirit who indwells the people of God and moves all things toward their consummation in Christ."[3] Because the Spirit has been poured out to empower, guide, and comfort believers, pentecostal spirituality is marked by love, joy, peace, hope, courage, and confidence. Hence, Land clearly articulates the affective nature of pentecostal orthopathy.

The affective constitution of pentecostal spirituality is also revealed in the pneumatologically vibrant quality of worship and prayer in its communal setting. Daniel Castelo offers that in its earliest instantiation the epicletic pentecostal community exerted a morally transforming impact upon its members. This primitive orthopathic spirituality implicitly modeled an affective catechesis that passed on radically ethical values to its members through shared religious experience. Within the catechetical process, pentecostal beliefs and practices were integrated to display affections quite eccentric in comparison with early twentieth century social norms. Castelo describes such affections as a radicalized sanctification in which, "such

---

1. This is not to ignore other important topics related to faith in Pentecostalism—faith healing, the gift of faith, or faithfulness—these, however, fall beyond the scope of this study.

2. Such ministry follows the sermon when the minister invites people to come forward for prayer. During altar ministry it is not unusual for tears of joy or repentance and sorrow or joyful shouts of laughter and praise to erupt.

3. Land, *Pentecostal Spirituality*, 224.

dispositions and sensibilities mark the epicletic community . . . [whereby] holiness is a grace enabled possibility."[4] Additionally, the epicletic community intimates an affective orthopathy because it so highly esteems pneumatological experience of God. Castelo concludes that such spirituality has always modeled a more affective than intellectualist epistemology.[5] As a doxological community, pentecostal knowledge and experience of God usually transpired in worship. Castelo's work shows how the epistemological valuation of experience in this epicletic community highlights an affective pentecostal orthopathy.

Samuel Solivan opens up another way of reflecting on an affective orthopathy. His orthopathos is affective because it has to do with the liberating work of the Spirit amidst one's suffering. Affectivity is soteriologically significant because without the softening experience of suffering, orthodoxy and orthopraxy can inadvertently contradict the gospel. Therefore, orthopathos is a pneumatological resource to foster a disposition of hope for those who suffer and minister in suffering. For North American theologians, Solivan's orthopathos nourishes an authenticity and relevance between orthodoxy and orthopraxy otherwise lacking. He attests that, "orthopathos brings emphatic concern for the sufferer into the act of doing theology."[6] For when a person is isolated from affliction she is removed from the heart of God for those who suffer. Orthodoxy, thereby, becomes sterile and orthopraxis abstract and disengaged. Likewise, for the one who suffers, to be unaware of the liberating work of the Spirit is to remain weak, fearful, and hopeless. But to lay hold of an orthopathic awareness of the God who frees is to be filled with a salvation of hope. Therefore, with Land, Castelo, and Solivan's contributions in mind, we can clearly see the affective nature of pentecostal spirituality. Its dispositional orientations (i.e., apocalyptic affections and orthopathos) and epistemological method (affective catechesis) truly model an affective orthopathy. Next, I link the above research with findings in the cognitive sciences to establish how affectivity is an essential component in cognition.

Castelo admits that pentecostals have a stereotype of being epistemologically shallow. However, he supposes that such ideas follow from ignorance about the affective instinct of its theological method. So, when he says that pentecostal catechesis is more subjective and aesthetic, he maintains

---

4. Castelo, *Revisioning*, 105.

5. Ibid., 37–38.

6. Solivan, *Spirit, Pathos and Liberation*, 60.

that knowledge of God is not limited to rational propositions and truth statements.[7] Castelo is referring to the pentecostal priority for an affective epistemology. Similarly, cognitive neuroscientist, Antonio Damasio argues that emotions not only act upon cognition but are crucial aspects of its function.[8] He informs that there is such a thing as "affective knowledge" and that it is no less important than rational understanding.

Damasio also claims that because feelings and emotions are so profoundly integrated with the body proper, they exert a primacy that permeates the mental life.[9] So then, "[S]ince what comes first constitutes a frame of reference for what comes after, feelings have a say on how the rest of the brain and cognition go about their business. Their influence is immense."[10] Affectivity then bears upon cognitive function. Therefore, contrary to similar critiques as MacArthur's that Pentecostalism promotes emotionalism or Noll's belief that the affective register of pentecosal spirituality is intellectually disastrous, neuroscientific studies validate the pentecostal use of emotion and feelings in its epistemology. In consideration of these findings, we can assert that since orthopathy cultivates affectivity in mental function, it is cognitively productive in faith formation and therefore necessary for a renewal soteriology of embodiment. Now we look at how Pentecostalism values embodiment in its spirituality.

An Embodied Orthopathy

Pentecostalism does not apologize for its emotions. However, to say that this spirituality is affective is not to say that it prioritizes emotions and feelings over intellect and behavior but rather that it has distinguished itself as an integrated spirituality. Such integration underscores the embodied character of pentecostal orthopathy.

Pentecostal spirituality understood as apocalyptic affections requires embodied practices, for its doctrine of Spirit baptism and premillennial "latter-day" eschatology require it. Worship, prayer, Scripture reading, preaching, singing, and prophesying are dynamically enacted because they are cathartic means to celebrate, proclaim, admonish, and encourage one

---

7. Castelo, *Revisioning*, 31.
8. Damasio, *Descartes' Error*, 245.
9. Ibid., 159.
10. Ibid.

another in view of their most fundamental yearning—passion for the kingdom. Land reminds:

> The Latter Rain restoration of Pentecostal power was for last-days evangelization . . . The everlasting gospel, the gospel of the kingdom was to be heralded by witnesses whose mouths had tasted the powers of the age to come and whose eyes had seen evidence of that power at work among them.[11]

Pentecostal orthopathy was not an abstract or spiritualized sentimentality; it required physical interaction with other people. Land's rendering of pentecostal spirituality as embodied thus affirms its soteriological potential. It actually provides a corrective to an often un-embodied and intellectualist construal of faith unrelated to the body proper.

Pentecostal pneumatology and sanctification also contribute to embodiment. Castelo shows how Pentecostalism as an epicletic community illustrates an embodied orthopathy because it is more committed to pneumatic lifestyles than denominational affiliations. Even more, this spirituality furthered a way of life engendered by specific doxological practices. Castelo remarks that the movement did not begin in academic surroundings, royalty, or high church meetings but in revival and worship.[12] Embodied implications ensue from the doxological community through its pneumatic catechesis for moral transformation. Castelo contends that such catechesis reveals a pentecostal ethics that maintained "eccentric" behaviors as examples of an "embodied and practiced holiness."[13] Castelo offers "practice-orientations" as epistemological resources for Pentecostalism to regain and pass on its lost ethics through the practices of abiding and waiting. Through such practices, radical holiness is nurtured in the community. Thus, Castelo underscores the soteriological potential of behavior through an embodied orthopathy articulating the practices of abiding and waiting.

Solivan also accents embodiment through his exhortation to North American theologians to re-vision orthodoxy as inseparable from orthopraxis. He argues that theological reflection disconnected from personal exposure to suffering is ill-equipped to convey the gospel. Solivan explains, "*Orthopathos* brings empathic concern for the sufferer into the act of doing theology . . . [and] looks for the manner in which human suffering can be

---

11. Land, *Pentecostal Spirituality*, 44.
12. Castelo, *Revisioning*, 22.
13. Ibid., 100.

Salvation in the Flesh through Pentecostal Orthopathy

transformed into a resource for liberation."[14] Accordingly, he proposes orthopathos as an orthopathic resource to inform one's doctrine and practice for a holistic and hope-driven soteriology. Solivan ties orthopathos with embodiment and the salvific work of the Spirit: "*Orthopathos* . . . [is] a living link that witnesses to the liberating power of the Holy Spirit in and through the lives of suffering people."[15] Embodiment is important because it enables an orthopathic understanding of the conditions wherein affliction and oppression can be transformed into hope and promise.[16] Through the embodied character of orthopathos, Solivan illustrates the soteriological capacity of pentecostal orthopathy.

In as much as Land, Castelo, and Solivan have laid out the embodied character of pentecostal orthopathy, the cognitive sciences also affirm the significance of embodiment and affectivity for cognition. Damasio argues that an accurate conception of cognition must be embodied: "Because the mind arises in a brain that is integral to the organism, the mind is part of that well-woven apparatus."[17] In other words, the *entire* body is critical for mental function and as aspects of embodiment are lacking, so too does cognition suffer. So, when Land attests that pentecostal spirituality is "the integration of beliefs, practices and affections . . . [which] is a way of life involving knowledge, actions and affects"[18] he similarly echoes Damasio's contention that intellect, behavior, and emotions are cognitively integrated. Yet, Damasio also contends that emotions are dependent upon the body. His Somatic Marker Hypothesis—advances that the body acts as a kind of map upon which the limbic system extends and receives bodily sensations (body states) in relation to certain conditions and situations.[19] These states form the basic background feeling from which emotions develop.[20] The body-proper provides the physiological context from which emotions result and reason arises. So, when Castelo says that the epicletic community mediated knowledge—a pentecostal ethics—he makes similar affirmations as Damasio. For the epicletic lifestyle exploited emotions and feelings for epistemological-catechetical ends. In having shown how orthopathy is

14. Ibid., 60–61.
15. Solivan, *Spirit, Pathos and Liberation*, 148.
16. Ibid., 13.
17. Damasio, *Descartes' Error*, 195.
18. Land, *Pentecostal Spirituality*, 132.
19. Damasio, *Descartes' Error*, 173–75.
20. Ibid., 151–55.

embodied, we can thus claim it is also cognitively productive in faith formation and, therefore, positively contributes to a renewal soteriology of embodiment.

A Transformational Orthopathy

In the last two sections we've detailed the soteriological importance of affectivity and embodiment within pentecostal orthopathy. Now I propose that because this orthopathy is affective and embodied, it promotes salvific transformation. Once again, we note the central role of the Spirit in Pentecostalism.

Steven Land features pentecostal spirituality as a heritage marked by dispositional transformation. He clarifies that pentecostals are not just more exuberant than other Christians but have been affectively renewed because the transcendent presence of the in-breaking kingdom "alters [the] affective chemistry in significant ways."[21] Even though accusations of enthusiasm persist, pentecostal orthopathic practices have historically led to sustained change in the lives of its adherents. Pentecostal believers were transformed through the power of God in Spirit baptism to more clearly reflect the character of Christ. Land asserts, "The power given in Spirit baptism strengthens all the other fruits of the Spirit and gives courage and boldness borne of confidence in God."[22] He elaborates on the re-orienting impact of the Spirit's ministry.

> [T]o be filled with the Spirit is to be decisively determined by and oriented to the things of the Spirit, to what the Spirit is saying and doing. The fruit of the Spirit's indwelling is given a deeper intensity and, in the eschatological community of Pentecostalism, a new urgency.[23]

Therefore, pentecostal orthopathic practices became powerful resources for ongoing transformation. Land remarks that "[p]articipation in the Pentecostal worship and witness over time produced an 'affective transformation in which lives were formed and shaped' by their experience of God."[24] Such transformation was most poignantly heralded as apocalyptic

---

21. Land, *Pentecostal Spirituality*, 133.
22. Ibid., 154.
23. Ibid., 168.
24. Ibid., 126.

Salvation in the Flesh through Pentecostal Orthopathy

affections. Individuals formerly selfish, were filled with *gratitude* for God's grace and love; those formerly hateful, were marked by *love* and *compassion*; and those previously fearful and insecure, were distinguished with *courage*. Land ties these affections to the work of the Spirit saying, "The affections of gratitude, compassion, and courage cannot be developed apart from the activity of the Spirit."[25] Again, he says that "[t]raits like gratitude, compassion, and confidence" mark the pentecostal believer.[26] So, a transformational orthopathy can be seen in Pentecostalism's attention to and experience of apocalyptic affections.

Daniel Castelo, like Land, also refers to the transforming impact of pentecostal orthopathy when he says, "Christian affections are often described as pneumatically cultivated dispositions that shape the believer."[27] However, Castelo focuses on moral transformation through pneumatic lifestyles most seen in Pentecostalism's initial years. The earliest instincts of pentecostal spirituality emerging out of their worship were radicalizations of its holiness value. A pentecostal ethics, thereby, flowed from its commitment to holiness. To be in the pentecostal community was to embody a transformed life of practical holiness. Castelo submits that believers who joined the pentecostal community experienced moral transformation in a manner that to those outside the community appeared eccentric. Pentecostal ethics were "caught" more than "taught" within the orthopathic settings of prayer, worship, and revival. Castelo remarks, "[T]he holiness of Pentecostal fellowship is both a moral task and an ontological reality, and both features are subsumed and sustained within . . . the modality of Pentecostal worship . . . [S]uch dispositions and sensibilities mark the epicletic community."[28] Even today, moral transformation tends to mark the epicletic community.

As with Land and Castelo so does Solivan highlight orthopathy's transformational potential. Solivan's orthopathos is an affective disposition inviting the Spirit to transform one's pathos into liberation while changing weakness into strength.[29] Orthopathos uses "the power of weakness to liberate the sufferer" by honestly facing one's hardship in view of God's

---

25. Ibid., 166.
26. Ibid., 130.
27. Castelo, *Revisioning*, 59.
28. Ibid., 105.
29. Solivan, *Spirit, Pathos, and Liberation*, 27–28, 85–86.

faithfulness.³⁰ Orthopathos, as a concept, arose out of Solivan's experiences with the Hispanic pentecostal church in East Harlem. It emerged from his observations on how men and women in these urban ghetto churches commonly experienced conversion-transformation. These pentecostal communities were the "incarnational testing grounds for orthopathos."³¹ Such believers testify to the transforming potential of orthopathos.³² Solivan reflects, "To speak to a former addict, prostitute, alcoholic or street person who has been transformed by the power of the Spirit is to speak to someone who knows what orthopathos is all about."³³ He declares that the transforming power of orthopathy shines brightest in such saints.

Reuven Feuerstein's research in learning theory verifies the transformational potential of feelings and emotions on human learning. He contends that learning is more effective when intellectual content is mediated. Through his Mediated Learning Experience (MLE), the learner is physically and emotionally engaged in the pedagogical process through a mediator who fills particular behaviors with subjective meaning.³⁴ The mediator selects, adjusts, amplifies, and interprets the stimuli that come to the learner and the learner's responses in terms that are culturally, ethnically, and intellectually meaningful. In other words, as the mediator translates knowledge to the learner in ways that are affectively relevant and familiar; learning is simply more effective.³⁵ Solivan's use of orthopathos resembles aspects of Feuerstein's MLE wherein as the evangelizer identifies with another's pathos, the gospel is "mediated" in terms that are familiar, authentic, and relevant. Learning is not only facilitated but "knowledge of God" becomes soteriologically transforming.

Finally, Feuerstein maintains that emotionally laden knowledge not only transforms the *learning capacities* of "mediated learners," but so too can affectively charged experiences physically transform the *brain*. Feuerstein reports:

> Research is suggesting that the human brain can generate new brain cells, even into old age. If the brain is stimulated, at any stage in the life span, it will adapt, regenerate, and become more

30. Ibid., 87.
31. Ibid., 103.
32. Ibid., 104.
33. Ibid., 111.
34. Feuerstein et al., *Beyond Smarter*, 24.
35. Feuerstein, *Instrumental Enrichment*, 74–75.

Salvation in the Flesh through Pentecostal Orthopathy

efficient. It reinforces our initial and ongoing theoretical hypotheses and confirms our methodological developments.[36]

Hence, a mediated pedagogy is physiologically transformational. MLE presupposes an affective context for mediation to successfully ensue. Though time and space do not allow, it would be interesting to see if neurogenesis has occurred in pentecostal Christians who have experience the power of orthopathos in a way leading to personal and moral change. Might it be possible that "before" and "after" brain scans (as among Feuerstein's students) would reveal physical changes in brain structure?

As already discussed, there are various opinions that presume Pentecostalism is superficially grounded on subjectivity and emotionalism and that its impact will be short-lived. In consideration of such critiques, I submit that the historical legacy of the Holiness-Pentecostal movement simply tells a different story—one of lasting transformation. Likewise, the enduring impact of pentecostal orthopathy is also corroborated by the cognitive sciences establishing that emotions and feelings are necessary for healthy mental function. Yet, despite such validation and the soteriological benefits that can be gleaned from pentecostal orthopathy, is there still a need for caution? In lieu of this question, we approach the final section.

THE PROMISE AND CHALLENGE OF A PENTECOSTAL ORTHOPATHIC SOTERIOLOGY: NORTH AMERICAN PENTECOSTAL THEOLOGY?

Before moving forward, let's briefly review what has been accomplished in these last two chapters and why it is significant. After introducing pentecostal orthopathy, I exposited its soteriological value with the help of three theologians. Then I re-appropriated their research to advance how such orthopathy can facilitate a renewal soteriology of embodiment. Now, I evaluate the promise of pentecostal orthopathy while bearing in mind the concerns previously noted with Edwards' orthodoxy and canonical theism's orthopraxis in chapters 3–6. Finally, I conclude with soteriological challenges posed by North American pentecostal theology.

---

36. Feuerstein et al., *Beyond Smarter*, 139.

Part Four: Salvation and Orthopathy

The Promise of a Pentecostal Orthopathic Soteriology

Chapters 3 and 4 discussed Edwards' embodied paradigm of religious knowledge to lay out his dispositional soteriology. However, because he did not explicitly incorporate ecclesial practices he may have unintentionally discouraged future theological reflection on the soteriological import of praxis. Perhaps Pentecostalism's accent on affective transformation through doxological practice can complement Edwards' orthodoxy. The pedagogical value of pentecostal worship thereby highlights the soteriological significance of behavior. In chapter 6, I suggested that the prominent ecclesial setting of canonical theism might inadvertently imply that pneumatology is restricted to such churchly domains.[37] I then submitted that had canonical theism unambiguously located grace beyond ecclesiology it might have better facilitated a dynamic soteriology. In this chapter, pentecostal theological intuitions can complete canonical theism's orthopraxic soteriology by its robust pneumatology mediating grace beyond ecclesial practices.[38]

With its emphasis on dispositional transformation, pentecostal believers conceive all of life filled with opportunities to experience God.[39] Castelo attests that the prominence pentecostals place on affections opens the believer to God's ever-present work in the world via the Spirit, not just at decisive "altar moments."[40] Nevertheless, in spite of the aforementioned contributions, certain aspects of Edwards' orthodoxy and Abraham's canonical orthopraxy appear incompatible with pentecostal orthopathy.

At first glance, some may say that Edwards' orthodoxy is incompatible with pentecostal orthopathy because Edwards so strongly resisted excessive enthusiasm in his ministry.[41] As we have seen, some people contend that Pentecostalism is overly subjective and emotional. Yet, I have shown that while pentecostals do not hesitate to embrace emotions and feelings, normative pentecostal teaching has always taught that emotions and

---

37. I reiterate that my critique is not against a particular portrayal of a canonical orthopraxy as endorsed by canonical theism, but rather a possible interpretation of such an orthopraxy by conservative Christianity in light of its static soteriology explicated in chapter 1.

38. Daniel Castelo suggests how pentecostal spirituality can complement canonical theism even as it can also be constructively challenged by it. In this article he specifically draws attention to the common motif of transformation in both traditions ("Canonical Theism," 370–89).

39. Castelo, *Revisioning*, 57.

40. Ibid., 76.

41. For example see, Edwards, "Religious Affections," 266.

experience must be judged by Scripture. Ultimately, Edwards never discounted emotions and feelings; his concern was with those who appealed to them as authoritative apart from Scripture.

Likewise, some may also argue that Abraham's canonical orthopraxy is incompatible with pentecostal spirituality because the latter does not highly regard the canonical practices in its ecclesial settings. While Pentecostalism has traditionally been suspicious of "ritualism," such does not discount its use of ecclesial practices. Pentecostalism arose as a restoration movement reacting against religious complacency in mainline traditions where the accent on a vibrant personal relationship with Christ was lacking. Such is not to suggest that ecclesial practices cannot or do not serve as means of grace for pentecostal Christians. In fact, as I have already detailed, worship, Scripture reading, and prayer (and sometimes, foot washing) are commonly adopted means of grace for soteriological transformation in pentecostal ecclesiology. Because pentecostal spirituality is doxological, ecclesial practices are often incorporated in worship and prayer as means of grace for ongoing maturity in holiness. Nevertheless, it is understandable why these impressions are so widely circulated among nonpentecostal Christians. Such ideas are due in part to the relative infancy of the movement and its uncritical adoption of the fundamentalist theology it inherited in its earlier years.

The Soteriological Challenge of North American Pentecostal Theology

I conclude by suggesting how Pentecostalism's early twentieth-century North American fundamentalist context hindered its growth. From the pre-Azusa pentecostals to its future occurrences, pentecostal Christians have always had a fairly uneasy alliance with Fundamentalism.[42] Literally repudiated by these early evangelicals—mostly over glossolalia—and only later more warmly welcomed, pentecostals were forced into apprehensive cooperation because of their shared beliefs and common foe in modernism. Nevertheless, the growing alliance betrayed an embodied spirituality intrinsic to pentecostal self-identity. So, pentecostals inherited the reigning theological framework already in use within fundamentalist theology. Despite that Pentecostalism added its own version of pneumatology, Spirit Baptism, and spiritual gifts to fundamentalist theology, its theological re-

42. See King, *Disfellowshiped*; and Sheppard, "Pentecostalism," 5–33.

flection did not advance much further. Pentecostal theology lacked access to the kinds of resources needed for articulating its pneumatological beliefs and convictions within a scope transcending Spirit baptism and the charismata. Gerald King explains:

> Pentecostal literature did not yet exist. The most trusted source for conservative, evangelical theology came from fundamentalist pens. The only conservative evangelical theological resources available at this time were written by fundamentalists.[43]

Specifically, Pentecostalism failed to theologically engage pneumatology in relation to the rest of its theology and, especially, its doctrine of salvation. While affectivity has been granted in practice, minimal reflection was devoted to the importance of a pentecostal orthopathic soteriology. For instance, rather than critically considering how to retain their theological distinctiveness from fundamentalism, pentecostals spent their theological energies focused on how to combat the evils of modernism. King maintains that the "rhetoric of fundamentalism overwhelmed AG [Assemblies of God] views of the Bible and the world. Articles by Pentecostals had shifted from defining themselves against fundamentalism to defining themselves against modernism."[44] Over time, the value of orthopathy would slowly recede in the effort to gain respectability and honor from their fundamentalist and, later, evangelical partners.[45]

Pentecostalism's adoption of Darby's dispensational-premillennial eschatology over its postmillennial leaning was substantial in that pneumatology was increasingly associated more with power for evangelism than holiness and purity. Such largely resulted from the new-found conviction that worldwide evangelism was needed to usher in the return of Christ. Their previously optimistic postmillennial notion of the steady need for ongoing sanctification to transform the church and the world was exchanged for a premillennial interventionist approach whereby Christ will physically come and do the transforming himself. What remained was empowerment for a massive world-wide evangelism followed by the return of Christ. Donald Dayton remarks:

> Whereas the postmillennial vision had looked forward to the conversion of the world, hopes were now scaled down to worldwide

43. King, *Disfellowshiped*, 96.
44. Ibid., 202.
45. Ibid., 130, 177, 212.

Salvation in the Flesh through Pentecostal Orthopathy

evangelism with much more pessimism of the percentage of response. Evangelism became less a tool for transforming the culture and more and more a process of . . . witness while preparing as a bride to meet the Bridegroom.[46]

Salvation as ongoing sanctification (personally and socially) was collapsed into the singular event (as per Durham's Finished Work Theory) of an individualized justification and subsequent sanctification occurring in a moment. As I mentioned in chapter 1, even though ongoing sanctification was not denied, it was subordinated to a prominent justification. Consequently, the initially robust pulse of pneumatology in early pentecostal soteriology grew static as power for ongoing growth and transformation was refocused on evangelism and missionary witness.[47]

Nevertheless, despite the effect of fundamentalist theology upon pentecostal spirituality, Pentecostalism is now developing its own voice. A new generation of theologians has learned how to re-formulate its spirituality in consideration of its orthopathic heritage and pneumatology is central to this task. In doing so they underscore the soteriological significance of orthopathy. They help us to see that when we speak about the importance of orthopathy for a renewal soteriology of embodiment we are merely affirming that affective transformation is not a peripheral or subordinate element of Christian salvation. Rather, we introduce a safeguard against an intellectualized orthodoxy and a nominalized orthopraxic ritualism.

We have finally brought together all the necessary elements of our soteriological proposal. As we move into Part Five (Toward a Renewal Soteriology of Embodiment) we will summarize the previous chapters and synthesize their key insights. We now begin to finalize our proposal as chapter 9 lays out our case for a renewal soteriology of embodiment and chapter 10 imagines the possibilities of its acceptance.

---

46. Dayton, *Theological Roots*, 163.

47. This historical telling is not a critique against the need for empowered evangelism and missionary witness in Pentecostalism. Such mission should remain a vital distinctive among pentecostals. However, this does not justify a scaling down of expectation for power towards ongoing sanctification. For when such a minimization of emphasis occurs, we actually hinder and/or sabotage our missionary mandate since, as we have seen, salvation is a dynamic, ongoing, and embodied reality.

PART FIVE

Toward A Renewal Soteriology of Embodiment

9

Stating our Case

WHILE PREVIOUSLY WE'VE EXPLAINED *that* orthodoxy, orthopraxy, and orthopathy are soteriologically significant, now we show *why* and *how* they contribute to a renewal soteriology of embodiment. By drawing together the research and conclusions of each chapter, we reveal how important and relevant an embodied soteriology is in our contemporary context. However, before launching forward, let's briefly review what has so far been accomplished.

Reviewing Our Progress and Restating the Task

Throughout we have argued for a soteriology of embodiment over and against an intellectualist soteriology. Likewise, we have maintained that a robust pneumatology is necessary for a dynamic and transforming vision and experience of salvation; hence we contend for a *renewal* soteriology. The central conviction driving this study is that an intellectualist construal of faith should be rejected because human experience is not abstract nor is it gnostic—it is embodied and experientially pertinent. Therefore, my use of "dynamic" punctuates the social (rather than individualistic), ongoing (rather than event-based), and holistic-embodied (rather than intellectualist) qualities of salvation. Hence, from beginning to end, we have described our vision of salvation as dynamic, transforming, progressive, and embodied as opposed to an otherwise intellectualist, abstract, static, and punctiliar soteriology.

Chapter 1 claimed that contemporary conservative Christianity has uncritically adopted an intellectualist soteriology that accentuates

Part Five: Toward a Renewal Soteriology of Embodiment

rationality over behavior and affectivity in its conceptualization of faith. While such a soteriology does not deny the importance of behavior, feelings, and emotions, it more frequently identifies rationality and intellect as the chief characteristics of faith. Subsequently, I challenged the dominant emphasis on intellect and reasoning by exposing three presuppositions that implicitly reveal such intellectualism.[1] These presuppositions nourish static images of salvation that do not take human embodiment seriously and, consequently, lead to overly spiritualized soteriological conceptions. Such a soteriology is inconsistent with actual human experience and contradicts the dynamic character of salvation taught in Scripture and the embodied nature of knowing recognized across the cognitive sciences.

Chapter 2 explicated contemporary studies in the neurosciences to unveil how intellect, behavior, emotions, and feelings are inseparably integrated in the process of human cognition. Our findings provided a methodological framework for an embodied epistemology. Here we learned that the most damaging consequence of an intellectualist soteriology is that it does not allow for the mediation of faith through the behavioral, affective, and historical particularities of human life.

Chapters 3 through 8 discuss the soteriological significance of Jonathan Edwards' dispositional orthodoxy, William Abraham's canonical orthopraxy, and pentecostal orthopathy as intertwined solutions to an intellectualist soteriology. In doing so, we introduced the epistemological significance of intellect, behavior, and affections as necessary components for our embodied soteriology. Despite the contributions of each, I also noted the potential challenges they present.

In this chapter, I propose a soteriology that incorporates the strengths of each while overcoming the corresponding weaknesses. We'll see that a thriving faith requires a renewed vision of salvation that integrates orthodoxy, orthopraxy, and orthopathy through a robust pneumatology. Presently, we bring the contributions of our three primary interlocutors into extended dialogue with select pentecostal and charismatic theologians to articulate the importance of a renewal soteriology of embodiment and respond to some of its challenges.

We have now completed the arduous work of research and the critical theological reflection needed to secure the reason for our proposal and

---

1. The first supposes *faith is mostly a rational and intellectual function of cognition*; the second presumes *justification is truncated from and prioritized over sanctification*; and the third assumes *salvation is primarily punctiliar and confessional.*

the components (orthodoxy, orthopraxy, orthopathy) of its construction. Therefore, since we now understand the embodied nature of cognition, so too ought faith be similarly regarded in how we think about salvation. In making such a paradigm shift, we necessarily cultivate new soteriological assumptions that better reflect the dynamic and transforming ministry of the Holy Spirit and the embodied nature of human experience. Let's now consider how and why the soteriology we suggest yields the kind of faith we seek.

A Renewal Soteriology of Embodiment: Why and How?

From the very beginning, we have repeatedly emphasized the need for an embodied soteriology because a holistic faith nurtures lifestyles of pneumatological empowerment. In this section, we'll consider how this is so. To begin, I bring Jonathan Edwards, William Abraham, and pentecostal spirituality into dialogue to illustrate why belief, behavior, and affectivity must remain inseparably entwined for a renewed doctrine of salvation.

Why Orthodoxy Without Orthopathy and Orthopraxy is Problematic

Despite the propensity to stress orthodoxy in soteriological reflection, we have argued for its thorough integration with orthopathy and orthopraxy. Chapters 1 and 2 established that the more a soteriology embraces intellectualism the more it minimizes the salvific significance of embodiment and pneumatology. Let's take some time to clarify our claim about the soteriological role of orthodoxy and restate our concern of an *orthodoxy-driven soteriology*.

It is not my intention to downplay the importance of orthodoxy and critical-rational theological reflection. Yes, I have repeatedly emphasized how problematic it is when one's faith is driven by an intellectualist epistemology but I have only done so because of the pervasiveness of such intellectualism in conservative Christian theology. Another reason for this focus is because such widespread biases are often unintentionally practiced. Chapter 1 addressed this when I explained how strongly people (theologians and ministers) deny such intellectualism even while

PART FIVE: TOWARD A RENEWAL SOTERIOLOGY OF EMBODIMENT

their theological method clearly prioritizes orthodoxy in soteriological reflection and ecclesial praxis. The intellectualist prejudice is usually more pervasive than we are aware or willing to admit. From a young age—at least in the post-Enlightenment West—human thinking and being-in-the-world is profoundly shaped by a cognitive preference for rational, objective, and evidence-driven reflection. Modern civilization, with all its medical, technological, financial, and educational institutions and products depends on maintaining a high degree of intellectual certitude. Even despite the critique of post-modernity against confidence in objective and rationalist truth claims, such tendencies remain strongly entrenched in most—if not all—aspects of contemporary life.

Nevertheless, despite my concern over an orthodoxy-driven understanding of salvation, I unequivocally stress that a soteriology which minimizes orthodoxy is equally damaging. We have all seen plenty of problems associated with a faith that has little or no theological grounding or awareness of the need for critical reflection. My faith has been profoundly strengthened by years of theological education and I have devoted my life to teaching and training others in theology and ministry. So, I believe in the importance of orthodoxy and rational-propositional knowledge. However, I contend that the appropriate response against an intellectualist soteriology is not the diminishment of orthodoxy but its integration. For orthopraxy and orthopathy are dependent on orthodoxy to keep them grounded and pointed in the right direction for a biblical vision of salvation. And orthodoxy is dependent on orthopraxy and orthopathy to help it maintain a sense of passion, authenticity, and relevance.

Scripture bears witness to the need for sound orthodoxy in its admonitions to not be led away by false doctrines (Matt 7:15), study the Scriptures (2 Tim 2:15), teach solid doctrine (Titus 2:1), and be able to evaluate our progress in the faith (2 Cor 13:5). James even warns his readers that those who teach will be held to a higher standard of judgement than those who don't (Jas 3:1). So, I reiterate, despite our cautions against the problems of an intellectualist soteriology, we can't over-estimate the importance of orthodoxy for Christian salvation. Rather, it is the kind of prioritization that overemphasizes orthodoxy and separates it from orthopraxy and orthopathy with which we are concerned.

So, when we gain new theological knowledge, increase biblical literacy, or gain a greater understanding of how the church's past bears upon its present, such *knowledge* does not necessarily lead to a stronger faith.

Stating our Case

Though we may become more proficient in ecclesial practice or Christian witness, such *praxis* does not guarantee that our faith has matured. And even though we may have encountered incredible heights of passion and intimacy with God in private or public, such *experience* does not assure we are growing closer to Jesus. No, we most greatly nourish a healthy faith when we are intentional about practicing an embodied salvation.

Finally, we must beware the lure of intellectualizing an embodied faith even in our reflection. An embodied faith isn't about how much a person understands the importance of such embodiment but how much that person puts embodiment into practice. We are merely reiterating the principle of obedience Jesus already taught when he said, "Blessed rather are those who hear the word of God and obey it" (Luke 11:28). Now, in view of all that has been said, we recast the soteriological role of orthodoxy through appropriating Jonathan Edwards' dispositional ontology.

Edwards' Dispositional Orthodoxy: Anticipating a Holistic and Pnuematological Soteriology

Let's review why intellect, behavior, and affections are so important in Edwards' dispositional ontology, how this influences his epistemology, and facilitates his robust pneumatology. Edwards envisioned knowing as a dynamic relationship between the understanding (rational knowledge) and the will (motivation, behavior, experience). For him, religious knowledge—orthodoxy—transpired when sensible-subjective knowledge built upon and completed notional-objective knowledge. Knowing God incorporates the objective content of Scripture with the subjective encounter of God's love and beauty dispositionally bound together as the religious affections. It is for this reason why Edwards criticized the "enthusiasts" of his day by saying that "holy affections are not heat without light."[2] The one truly marked by such affections knows God. Also, for Edwards, embodiment was central to orthodoxy because knowing God fosters righteous behavior. Edwards defends that a person cannot taste the sweetness of God's beauty and be unmoved to act in a beautiful manner.[3] Knowledge of God was discredited if not accompanied with godly behavior.

In Edwards' theological epistemology, the Holy Spirit alters the disposition to live for self so that one can be properly oriented toward

2. Edwards, "Religious Affections," 266.
3. Edwards, "A Divine and Supernatural," 124.

PART FIVE: TOWARD A RENEWAL SOTERIOLOGY OF EMBODIMENT

God. Without dispositional change the individual is unable to perceive the beauty, goodness, and love of God. Although all knowledge is sense-based, knowing God requires spiritual knowledge whereby one gains a new sense—a spiritual sense—to recognize God's presence and activity in the world. So, spiritual knowledge comes through a direct (subjective) encounter with the beauty and love of God in Christ through the Spirit. Yet, it still operates in relationship with notional (objective) knowledge, and in this manner presumes the holistic nature of objective and subjective reasoning in human cognition. Edwards' epistemology was pneumatological because, for him, knowledge of God was covenantal since knowing God requires a right relationship with the Spirit. The Spirit engenders dispositional change in people to initiate a relationship with God. This change manifests in the religious affections wherein intellect, behavior, and emotions are intimately engaged. Thus, for Edwards, knowing God is simultaneously intellectual (as it involves rational knowledge), behavioral (as the religious affections shape righteous behavior), and experiential (as it involves the reception of a new "spiritual" sense). Edwards' epistemology, then, corresponds to the embodiment of cognition understood in the contemporary cognitive neurosciences.

In light of the preceding, Edwards helps to combat an intellectualist soteriology by showing how orthodoxy is incomplete without orthopathy and orthopraxy. A dispositional reading of Edwards implies that orthodoxy needs orthopathy because knowing God is inseparable from experiencing God. Orthopathy completes orthodoxy because one must *experience* God through the Spirit to really know him. Yet, we also observed that regardless of his contributions there were some possible weaknesses in Edwards' theology that could reinforce an intellectualist soteriology.

I believe that a weakness of Edwards' soteriology was his failure to emphasize the salvific import of sanctification in a manner commensurate with his theology of religious affections. Even though he placed soteriological significance on transformed affections, because he did not explicitly enunciate such a link he may have indirectly reinforced the prioritizing of justification over sanctification in the order of salvation often endorsed in Reformation Protestantism. The continuation of these categories by his Reformed heirs dulled the dynamism of his soteriology because they commonly conceived the Spirit's ministry as post-salvific. Hence, this weakness has more to do with what Edwards did *not* say than what he did. By neglecting to specifically interpret justification and sanctification in consideration of the prominent pneumatology undergirding his dispositional soteriology, Edwards may have inadvertently hindered others from more fully understanding his robust pneumatology and dynamic soteriology.

For instance, Steven Studebaker unfolds how Edwards' use of pneumatology resists the frequent Protestant tendency of subordinating the ministry of the Spirit to the mission of Christ.

> Directly related to the subordination of the Spirit in Protestant scholasticism is the instrumental role of the Holy Spirit . . . The portrayal of the Spirit as the agent that applies the benefits of Christ's redemption subordinates the Spirit's work because the Spirit's work is not constitutive of salvation. Salvation is accomplished by the work of Christ on the cross. The Holy Spirit serves only to administer the various blessings earned by Christ.[4]

Studebaker attests that Edwards' soteriology was different than that of Protestant scholasticism because he elevated the Spirit to an equal status with Christ. For Edwards, the communication of the Spirit is one and the same with the gift of redemption because knowledge of Christ (*ad extra* communication of the Son) is constitutive of dispositional transformation (*ad extra* communication of the Spirit). Hence a person is dispositionally reoriented by the Spirit to place faith in Christ. Accordingly, Studebaker holds that Edwards stretched the boundaries of Reformed orthodoxy with his prominent pneumatology: "[Edwards] argued that the Spirit does not merely apply the benefits of redemption procured by Christ, but rather that the Spirit is the benefit of redemption."[5] Edwards, therefore, did not elevate the work of Christ (forensic justification) over the work of the Spirit (sanctification) because the Spirit is intimately involved in the entire process of salvation. Studebaker thereby draws attention to the pneumatological impulses in Edwards' theology that distinguished his soteriology from those who sought to carry his legacy. Unfortunately, the uncritical retention of these categories (justification and sanctification) together with the failure to grasp Edwards' dispositional context has likely encouraged a subordinated pneumatology and prioritized intellectualism in the soteriology of those following after him.

---

4. Studebaker, *Jonathan Edwards' Social*, 97.
5. Ibid., 98.

PART FIVE: TOWARD A RENEWAL SOTERIOLOGY OF EMBODIMENT

Re-Envisioning Justification through a Soteriology of the Third Article

In chapter one, I suggested that the elevation of an objective justification over a subjective sanctification represents a fundamental presupposition of an intellectualist soteriology and tends to treat the Holy Spirit as a post-salvific reality. Throughout, I have defended that whenever soteriology minimizes the Spirit the dynamic character of salvation is stifled. I respond to this tendency in these last two chapters by accenting pneumatology to recast salvation beyond the orthodoxy-driven emphasis on justification by appropriating the work of Lyle Dabney, Frank Macchia, and Amos Yong. These theologians re-vision justification beyond objective notions of forensic pardon and the need for securing rational truth. Accordingly, they suggest how a pneumatological scheme harbors dynamic soteriological connotations for both justification and sanctification. Such an approach reflects similar Edwardsean motifs—namely an embodied epistemology (i.e., the integration of notional and sensible knowledge) and the soteriological significance of behavior and affectivity (as played out in the religious affections).

D. Lyle Dabney's research has contributed to a pneumatologically framed justification from which later theologians have built. He contests that justification is rooted in the resurrection of Christ by the Spirit.[6] As already mentioned, Dabney opposes the historic subordination of the Spirit to the Father and Son as depicted in a theology of the First Article that focuses on God the Father and his ministry of creation (i.e., Medieval Scholasticism), and in a theology of the Second Article that accentuates God the Son and his ministry of redemption (i.e., Reformation Protestantism).[7] Working toward a fully Trinitarian theology, Dabney proposes a theology of the Third Article that regards the Spirit inseparably from the Father and the Son thereby enunciating the orthopathic character of Christian salvation.

Drawing from Dabney, Frank Macchia attests that justification is a dynamic concept integrating pneumatology and Christology. He maintains that the Protestant accent on forensic justification is "defined essentially as an abstract declaration realized in a juridical transfer of merits" and that this lacks the biblical emphasis of divine participation and renewal of life.[8]

---

6. Dabney, "Justified by the Spirit," 46–48.

7. Dabney, "Why Should the Last be First?" 240–61.

8. Macchia, *Baptized in the Spirit*, 138. Macchia first introduced this topic in Macchia, "Justification through New Creation," 202–17.

> Neglecting the Spirit—and dominated by Christology—Protestant theology lacked the pneumatological resources necessary to speak of justification as both a divine judgment and a renewal of life . . . [t]he classic Protestant concern begun by Luther with justification by faith could not rest secure merely with a justification doctrine that only involved extrinsic and imputed righteousness.[9]

Hence, Macchia interprets justification as the overflow of the life of the kingdom of God ultimately manifested in the final eschaton though presently as foretastes of the future kingdom. Righteousness, then, comes to the believer through the liberating acts of the Holy Spirit, "Justified existence is thus pneumatic existence, Spirit-baptized existence . . . Both the righteousness of Christ and the life of the Spirit are the same . . ."[10] Macchia pneumatologically posits justification as more than objective pardon traditionally conceived in Reformed Protestantism. Justification and sanctification, "represent overlapping metaphors of the Spirit's work rather than as conceptually distinct categories only logically connected."[11] Macchia maintains that the Reformed Protestant idea of justification and sanctification is incomplete if it fails to acknowledge the primacy of the Spirit in the process of salvation. Trinitarian theology thus requires a more intentional pneumatology.

Amos Yong also takes up Dabney's plea through his programmatic formulation of a pneumatological soteriology. In response to the soteriological bifurcation of Christology and pneumatology, Yong proposes a "pneumatological soteriology [that] understands salvation to be the work of both Christ and the Spirit from beginning to end."[12] He commends a Spirit Christology that preserves the ministry of the Spirit without neglecting the ministry of the Son, while avoiding the historic subordination of the Spirit to the Son.[13] In view of this tendency, Yong draws from the early Christian tradition and early pentecostal spiritualities to underscore salvation as a Trinitarian process of ongoing transformation.[14] These spiritualities portray salvation as more than a declarative justification of the believer

---

9. Macchia, *Justified in the Spirit*, 49.
10. Macchia, *Baptized in the Spirit*, 139–40.
11. Macchia, *Justified in the Spirit*, 64.
12. Yong, *Spirit Poured Out*, 82.
13. Ibid., 111.
14. Ibid., 117.

in Christ but as the redemptive power of God's love poured out in the Spirit upon all flesh.

In light of the pneumatological contributions by Studebaker,[15] Dabney, Macchia, and Yong, I now contend for a "soteriology of the Third Article" that acknowledges the work of the Spirit inseparably from the ministry of Christ.[16] As we will see, such a theology is indispensable for an orthodoxy that is not truncated from or elevated above orthopraxy and orthopathy. Pentecostal theology vitally contributes toward such a pneumatological soteriology because salvation as growth into divine fullness is central to its theology. Dale Coulter submits that because pentecostal theology embraces a dynamic soteriology, it must admit the liberating work of God, especially in acquiring the divine life and deliverance from the powers of sin.[17] He says that "God communicates his presence as a personal, living power. Immanently involved in the liberation of creation, God's presence always remains tangible and brings about palpable changes internally and externally."[18]

Therefore, we maintain that the Christian doctrine of salvation must resist the common Protestant shearing of an "objective" justification from a "subjective" sanctification because it implicitly subordinates the work of the Spirit. For when such a splitting occurs, the orthopraxic and orthopathic impulses historically associated with the Spirit's work of sanctification are implicitly severed from the more highlighted role of orthodoxy in securing the believer's justification. Consequently, not only is the work of the Spirit minimized but so too is the salvific significance of orthopraxy and orthopathy.

We have now elaborated the central role of the Spirit in the soteriologies of our four pentecostal dialogue partners in a way that resists the intellectualist tendencies of conservative Protestantism while still remaining faithful to the core tenants of Edwards' dispositional soteriology. In doing so, we have modeled how a biblically grounded pentecostal-pneumatological approach can demonstrate creative new ways to reflect on the role of orthodoxy within an embodied soteriological paradigm. As we move

15. In that he drew attention to the explicit pneumatology underlying Edwards' understanding of justification and sanctification throughout the salvific process.

16. I do not claim that my "soteriology of the third article" reflects Dabney's theology of the Third Article nor do I suggest that he would endorse my project. I am merely taking up Dabney's call for theological reflection from a pneumatological perspective.

17. Coulter, "Delivered by the Power of God," 447–67.

18. Ibid., 451.

forward, how might this dialogue between Jonathan Edwards and pentecostal theology contribute to William Abraham's orthopraxic soteriology?

Why Orthopraxy Without Orthodoxy and Orthopathy is Problematic

Throughout, we have asserted that a renewal soteriology of embodiment depends on a paradigm of faith revealing itself through the modalities of orthodoxy, orthopraxy, and orthopathy. Without such integration, embodiment is compromised and pneumatology is inevitably subordinated in soteriological reflection. Here we talk about how practices and behaviors are not just peripheral or optional aspects of Christian faith but central to its vitality.

So what exactly do we mean when we contend that *orthopraxy is soteriologically significant*? We are claiming that behaviors and practices are not secondary to orthodoxy but complementary. Orthodoxy is severely crippled when disconnected from orthopraxy even as orthopraxy lacks biblical grounding and guidance of Christian doctrine when separated from orthodoxy. We have solid grounds to make our claim about the soteriological significance of orthopraxy because the neurosciences show that human behavior has the capacity to mediate cognitive content. In other words, behavior plays a critical part in the human task of knowing and understanding. Without behavior, cognition suffers; with it, it thrives. Just as we claim that cognition is embodied, so too is faith. This means that we must begin thinking of faith not so much as an abstract "spiritual" reality we possess or an intellectual state of knowing having more to do with brain than body proper. As embodied beings, God does not interact with us apart from our physical nature but through it and by means of our flesh, blood, and bones. Therefore, we are saying that behavior has the capacity to mediate faith.

So then, as Christians, every time we worship, pray, or extend compassion to those in need we are not just demonstrating appropriate Christian behavior or merely showing the marks of a "sanctified life." Such actions become actual means by which the Holy Spirit mediates awareness of God's presence, power, and love. Similarly, for non-Christian seekers of God, certain behaviors can initiate the *process* of faith's reception and growth. Unselfish acts of love, compassionate service, and helping the marginalized and vulnerable find justice and relief are not just morally noteworthy behavior. These too can become physical means through which the Spirit can

PART FIVE: TOWARD A RENEWAL SOTERIOLOGY OF EMBODIMENT

awaken a person to God as the ultimate source of love, compassion, and justice. Our actions and behaviors are real cognitive modalities that help us grow in our knowledge of God and relationship with Christ.

Again, I reiterate that the soteriological significance of behavior requires its integration with orthodoxy and orthopathy. We reject a soteriology driven by orthopraxy, isolated from Scripture, the orthodox teaching of the church, and the subjective experience of the Holy Spirit. So, even as we affirm the soteriological significance of behavior, our greater affirmation is that an embodied soteriology depends on the joint influences of our heads, hands, and hearts for a dynamic and transforming faith.

Chapters 5 and 6 developed an orthopraxic theology in dialogue with William Abraham's canonical theism. He established that the early church understood salvation as grounded not only in "right knowledge" but also in "right behaviors and practices." We now review how canonical theism brings to light the soteriological contribution of orthopraxy.

Abraham's Canonical Orthopraxy: Recapturing an Embodied Soteriology

Abraham explains how orthodoxy, orthopraxy, and orthopathy worked conjointly within the canonical tradition to mediate the transforming power of saving grace. The canonical practices reinforced an embodied faith as they were practical responses to the orthodox beliefs of the church and concrete means (baptism, communion, Scripture reading) by which believers could experience God. The early Christians did not encounter God through an abstract mental assent or a mysteriously transcendental state but through practices that tangibly mediated divine grace. In canonical theism, orthopraxis serves as a linchpin connecting orthodoxy and orthopathy for soteriological ends (growth into the *imago Dei*) through the ministry of the Spirit. Abraham illustrates how the early church understood salvation as holistic when it proclaimed, *Lex orandi, lex credendi* (the law of worship is the law of belief). The early Christians intuitively understood what we can now draw from the cognitive sciences—human beliefs about God emerge from the embodied practices of prayer and worship.

Chapter 6 re-appropriates Abraham's canonical theism to reveal how its orthopraxis resembles some of the principal characteristics of a vibrant and flourishing cognition in that both are affective, embodied, and transformational. Based on that correlation, I claimed that canonical orthopraxy exemplifies a soteriology of embodiment wherein practices are central rather than subordinate in salvation. Through canonical theism we see that behavior cannot be relegated to post-salvific fruits but is actually a vital means for ongoing conversion.

The preceding shows that orthopraxy is incomplete without orthodoxy and orthopathy. A soteriology that accents praxis to the exclusion of orthodox confession and orthopathic experience fails to realize the full potential of behavior in mediating salvation. Orthopraxy needs orthodoxy so that practices remain grounded in the beliefs and confessions from which they've been historically associated; otherwise, religious behavior can be co-opted for ulterior ends. Orthopraxy similarly needs orthopathy so that it is protected from devolving into sheer ritualism. Just as orthodoxy can help instill direction and focus in orthopraxy, so too can orthopathy instill heart and fervor in religious practice. Yes, an orthopraxic soteriology is relevant for our purposes because it resists static impressions of salvation as mostly an event or a choice by emphasizing ongoing conversion as a chief metaphor.

But, regardless the valuable soteriological contributions of canonical theism, we also perceived some challenges. Canonical theism's stress on the ecclesial context for praxis could potentially reinforce a limited pneumatology. When the ministry of the Spirit is mainly located within an ecclesial context, then one can inadvertently discount opportunities for pneumatological transformation in other domains. Overall, I have stressed that faith—whether via intellectual, behavioral, or affective modalities—derives from the renewing work of the Spirit. Thus, as pneumatology is neglected so also are the transforming ramifications of soteriology overlooked. While canonical theism draws attention to the soteriological significance of behavior, *if* it does so at the expense of a robust pneumatology then the rich multidimensionality of the Spirit's transforming ministry will remain undeveloped. For this reason, I suggest that the dynamic effects of Abraham's canonical theism may be limited by an ecclesially-bounded pneumatology. Here I advise that a more cosmic rendering of the Spirit's ministry will facilitate greater redemptive possibilities.

Re-Envisioning Pneumatology Beyond Ecclesial Domains

Recently, Amos Yong expanded the pentecostal doctrine of Spirit baptism from its traditional underscoring of empowered service to its (more

Part Five: Toward a Renewal Soteriology of Embodiment

primordial) focus on power and love.[19] He notes that in its earliest instantiations, Pentecostalism understood the Holy Spirit as the Spirit of Love. Accordingly, the mediation of divine grace was not only identified with ecclesial praxis—especially worship, prayer, and Scripture reading—but with whatever actions are purposefully done to serve others.[20] Yong elaborates the redeeming potential of such praxis: "Whenever and wherever we find the affective disposition toward and intentional activity that benefits others *prima facie* there is the creaturely participation in the loving presence of the divine Spirit intending to save and redeem the world."[21] Yong, hence, lays out a soteriological presupposition enunciated early in the book: "[T]he human experience of love provides the analogical bridge for us to recognize God as love, to receive God's love, and to love God in response."[22] In associating the Holy Spirit with love, Yong remarks that the "the Spirit poured out on all flesh" connotes that humanity is "primed to receive God's unconditional gift of saving love in the Spirit."[23] Yong is not suggesting a soteriology apart from Christ but is emphasizing salvation as a progressive process in which a sort of "pre-conversion" is at work through the Holy Spirit in the lives of non-Christians who unselfishly love. Such a pneumatological theology of love relates to our purposes because the transforming grace of the Spirit is not limited to ecclesial or canonically defined praxis.

Frank Macchia, like Yong, relates the work of the Spirit to an infusion of the love of God for power and purity; he also identifies such "work" with the pentecostal doctrine of Spirit baptism. Macchia widens this doctrine beyond its historical association with individual experience or the life of the church. He thereby recasts pneumatology beyond ecclesial boundaries by highlighting Spirit baptism as subsequent experiences (infusions) of the life of God in Christ, rather than a post-salvific experience. Macchia discloses a cosmic pneumatology by soteriologically reframing Spirit baptism as the life of God progressively emerging in the world.[24]

---

19. See, Yong, *Spirit of Love*.

20. Yong explains his working definition of love as "the affective disposition toward intentional activity that benefits others" (Ibid., xi).

21. Ibid., 152.

22. Ibid., 4.

23. Ibid., 155.

24. Macchia, *Baptized in the Spirit*, 86.

Macchia attests that such an interpretation effectively integrates Luke's charismatic and Paul's soteriological emphases.[25] By linking Spirit baptism with the eschatological in-breaking kingdom of God inaugurated through the ministry of Christ, Macchia explains that the term is really a metaphor for the transforming life of God.

> This ongoing transformation involves a sense of continuous abiding in God and God in us as God indwells us penultimately as a foretaste of the final indwelling of all things ... [T]he kingdom has to do, not with a place, but rather with *life*, the life of the Spirit of God (Matt 12:28; Rom 14:17), opening up the creation to new possibilities of renewal and hope.[26]

In conceiving Spirit baptism as a soteriological metaphor, Macchia appropriates pneumatology for not only the renewal of the church but for the transformation of creation as a fit dwelling for God.[27] He clarifies that this broader picture of Spirit baptism refocuses the seminal confession of the church for facilitating the ultimate renewal of all creation.[28] Consequently, Macchia widens the domain of pneumatology for soteriological ends.

James K. A. Smith employs pentecostal pneumatology to encourage theological reflection on the unbounded capacity of the Spirit's ministry in the world. Through appealing to pentecostal philosophy, he exploits the participatory ontology of Pentecostalism which accedes the dependency of creation upon the Spirit.[29] He expounds:

> The key here is that this dynamic, participatory ontology refuses the static ontologies that presume the autonomy of nature ... [W]e might say that nature is always already suspended in and inhabited by the Spirit such that it is always already *primed* for the Spirit's manifestations. Pentecostal spirituality and practice don't merely expect that God could "interrupt" the so-called "order" of nature; rather, they assume that the Spirit is always already at work in creation, animating (and reanimating) bodies, grabbing hold of vocal cords, taking up aspects of creation to manifest the glory of God.[30]

---

25. Ibid., 87.
26. Ibid., 97.
27. Ibid., 103.
28. Ibid., 107.
29. Smith, *Thinking in Tongues*, 99–100.
30. Ibid., 101.

PART FIVE: TOWARD A RENEWAL SOTERIOLOGY OF EMBODIMENT

Smith rejects interventionist ideas that conceptualize the Spirit as occasionally interrupting creation to accomplish divine purposes. Rather, he offers that Pentecostalism models a way to re-think the ontology of the created order. He infers that because creation is already primed and animated by the Spirit of God, pentecostal soteriology is not limited to ecclesiological contexts.

Interestingly, Smith also regards Abraham's rendering of divine revelation as too intellectual. He observes that while Abraham rightly rejects the Western church's epistemizing of the canonical tradition, his appropriation of that tradition still largely concerns the "intellectual content" of canonical theism.[31] Smith contends that even though Abraham describes salvation as a confrontation with the Spirit (albeit via the canonical tradition), the aim of this confrontation remains largely focused on the intellectual content of the canonical tradition.[32] While Smith lauds Abraham's contribution of exposing the intellectualist epistemology of Protestant Christianity, he believes that Abraham still treats revelation along similarly intellectualist lines. In light of his pentecostal-participatory ontology of creation, Smith is dubious of soteriologies that reinforce the intellectual rather than the affective constitution of human knowing:

> A more persistent rejection of intellectualism . . . [will] instead emphasize that we are primarily affective, desiring animals—and that the thickness and particularity of the gospel . . . [will] grip our "hearts" before it ever gets articulated as a "theism"—even a rich, canonical theism.[33]

Smith thus insinuates that the weakness of Abraham's project lies in his hesitancy to uphold the affective nature of human cognition in its soteriological quest. As I have consistently argued, such reservations can lead to a bifurcation and prioritization of intellect over affectivity and minimize the centrality of the Spirit in salvation thereby reinforcing an intellectualist soteriology.

Yong, Macchia, and Smith address the urgent need for adopting a more robust pneumatology for soteriological reflection. As Dabney has stated, the Medieval attention on a theology of the First Article and the Reformation stress on a theology of the Second Article have stifled pneumatological thought in the church for hundreds of years. What is needed

---

31. Abraham et al., *Canonical Theism: A Proposal*, 41, 45.
32. Smith, *Thinking in Tongues*, 119–20.
33. Ibid., 120. Emphasis original.

Stating our Case

is a vibrant theology of the Third Article that is fully Trinitarian by being more pneumatologically intentional.

How does all this relate to Abraham's canonical orthopraxy? We must remember that while ecclesial contexts certainly afford numerous opportunities for an orthopraxic mediation of grace (worship, prayer, communion, baptism, etc.), the Holy Spirit is not limited to such contexts. Pentecostalism recognizes that for the Spirit-filled believer all arenas of life (whether "sacred" or "secular") can become viable means through which the Holy Spirit can mediate divine grace. When Pentecostalism arose in the early twentieth century, its orthopathic sensibilities stirred afresh the pneumatological quality of salvation. Now, how might the preceding dialogues of pentecostal theology, first, with Jonathan Edwards and, second, with William Abraham's canonical theism, contribute to a pentecostal orthopathic soteriology?

Why Orthopathy Without Orthopraxy and Orthodoxy is Problematic

In chapter 7, I spotlighted Pentecostalism as a spirituality with a rich orthopathic tradition in the lineage of Pietism, Wesleyanism, the American Holiness and Revivalists movements, and African slave religion. The spirituality of this "heart religion" is committed to a more intimate faith and experience of God. Therefore, pentecostal orthopathy brings to light the soteriological merit of feelings, emotions, affectivity, and personal experience.

So, what exactly do we mean when we say that *orthopathy is soteriologically significant*? We are saying that just as affectivity contributes to knowing in general so too can it be a medium of knowing God (i.e., faith). Even more, just as the overall state of one's mental function would be severely limited if the ability to process emotions and feelings were absent then so too would the effectualness of faith be substantially minimized if orthopathy was removed as one of its components. Our study of pentecostal orthopathy highlights how affectivity has had profound impact on the vitality, persistence, growth, and maturity of Pentecostal-Charismatic Christianity since the movement's early inception.

Therefore, from an embodied and renewal perspective on Christian salvation we are making the bold statement that emotions and feelings are not just subjective states of the mind but have the potential to be actual means through which faith can be mediated *to* or *through* an individual.

PART FIVE: TOWARD A RENEWAL SOTERIOLOGY OF EMBODIMENT

God may stir awareness of his presence to a non-Christian through any number of emotions and feelings she may experience in a particular situation or over a period of time. Similarly, God may also foster a more dynamic and life-changing faith in a Christian as he passionately worships at church or is emotionally moved by the awareness of God's love while praying at home. Such affective encounters can become profound channels of God's grace, ever drawing the Christian into greater degrees of conformity to the image of God. So, as impacting as orthopathy can be on the life of faith—when integrated with orthodoxy and orthopraxy—so too can it be equally damaging when isolated from the orthodox teachings and practices of the church.

Pentecostal Orthopathy: Awakening a Renewal Soteriology of Embodiment

Despite the wide appeal of heart religion within conservative Christianity, it still largely embraces epistemologies that prize rationality over the subjectivity of emotions. Nevertheless, research in the cognitive sciences establishing emotions and feelings as necessary for healthy mental function is consistent with the basic impulse of Pentecostal-Charismatic Christianity. Pentecostal orthopathy thus illustrates a dynamic and transformational soteriology because it does not subordinate affectivity and experience to beliefs or behaviors. Through the help of select theologians and cognitive scientists, we showed how pentecostal orthopathy is affective, embodied, and transforming, thereby confirming its importance for a renewal soteriology of embodiment.

I also clarified how prominently pneumatology factors into pentecostal orthopathy. Steven Land relates such orthopathy to pneumatology when he advances that pentecostal spirituality is shaped by its eschatological vision and self-understanding as a Spirit empowered last-days restoration movement. Daniel Castelo highlights pentecostal spirituality as epicletic when he says it "continually acknowledges that its source and end are made possible by the presence, prompting, and empowerment of the Holy Spirit."[34] Samuel Solivan asserts that the Holy Spirit can cultivate orthopathos (as a disposition) in the believer to mediate the grace of God and transform pathos into liberation.[35] From the tail end of this project we can

34. Castelo, *Revisioning*, 22.
35. Solivan, *Spirit, Pathos and Liberation*, 27–28, 85–86.

see that pneumatology is a vital component of an embodied soteriology of renewal. Once again, this reiterates the need for heeding Dabney's plea for a theology of the Third Article.

Therefore, we can now see how orthopathy is inseparable from orthodoxy and orthopraxy. Orthopathy needs orthodoxy because when passion is separated from reason, then direction and purpose are compromised. Without orthodoxy, orthopathy is removed from its scriptural foundations and becomes vulnerable to an unstable emotionalism. Orthopathy, likewise, needs orthopraxy because cognitive function suffers when affectivity is disconnected from behavior. Consequently, orthopathy completes orthodoxy and orthopraxy because faith, as embodied, is inseparable from the innumerable subjective realities of human existence. Otherwise, faith devolves into abstract propositionalism or empty ritual. To be sure, we can see a response and remedy to such intellectualism in the resource of pentecostal orthopathy. Despite that Pentecostalism is a relatively young movement, it has spawned a new generation of theologians and scholars who are facing the challenge of intellectualism through a diverse range of publications. Next we briefly consider some of these new areas of research.

Re-Envisioning New Trajectories in Pentecostal Theological Reflection

Previously, I noted that Pentecostalism has struggled to find its own voice in a manner beyond merely treating pneumatology and spiritual gifts as an addendum to systematic theology. Yet, from within this broad movement, some pentecostal, charismatic, and pneumatological theologians are recommending a "pentecostal-renewal" theological paradigm. In this framework, the baptism in the Holy Spirit, spiritual gifts, or apologetics for present day *charismata* no longer dominate the research agenda. While these topics still receive attention, scholars are applying pentecostal theology in different and promising ways.

Central to the proliferation of pentecostal research has been the Society for Pentecostal Studies. This gathering of theologians, biblical scholars, pastors, missionaries, and ministers is committed to critically engaging a variety of topics from pentecostal and charismatic perspectives. Such research has not gone unnoticed within the broader academic world of theological studies as respected publishers are now producing increasing volumes on various pentecostal topics. For instance, William B. Eerdmans Publishing Company released its *Pentecostal Manifestos* series. So far, they

PART FIVE: TOWARD A RENEWAL SOTERIOLOGY OF EMBODIMENT

have published books relating Pentecostalism to justification, philosophy, global theology, science, and the Trinity. In view of the preceding, one can see that pentecostal theology is well able to articulate the soteriological currency of orthopathy.[36] Also, there is a growing awareness of how important emotions and affectivity are in theological reflection among pentecostal-renewal theologians. Dale Coulter and Amos Yong have recently traced the historical and theological foundations of emotions and affections in the Christian tradition. They address topics on the relationship between affectivity and pneumatology, the shift in Western beliefs about emotion since the late eighteenth century, the specifics of vocabulary about affectivity in theology, and a variety of other orthopathically related topics.[37] Coulter and Yong's text is an excellent example of growing theological efforts to deal with both present and past assumptions regarding the prioritized role of an orthodoxy-driven intellectualism in Christian theology.

I have now shown why orthodoxy, orthopraxy, and orthopathy must function inseparably in an embodied paradigm of salvation. I have also utilized the cognitive sciences to maintain that faith thrives most when it is united with knowing, behavior, and affectivity. Consequently, I have enunciated a transformational view of faith that encourages a soteriology of unending growth into the *imago Dei*. In doing all of this, we laid out some of the broad contours of what a renewal soteriology of embodiment looks like. We now launch into our final chapter by describing three fundamental implications of a renewal soteriology of embodiment.

---

36. For justification, see, Macchia, *Justified in the Spirit*; for philosophy, see, Smith, *Thinking in Tongues*; for global theology, see Vondey, *Beyond Pentecostalism*; for science, see, Yong, *Spirit of Creation*; and for the Trinity, see Studebaker, *From Pentecost*. These are just some examples of the "coming of age" of pentecostal theology. While many of these authors (and others already mentioned) are not "new" scholars, they represent this new stream (even if as pioneers) of theologians committed to a broader and more interdisciplinary pentecostal-pneumatological-renewal approach towards theological reflection.

37. Coulter and Yong, *The Spirit*.

10

Imagining Salvation in the Flesh

WE LIVE IN A day of unprecedented opportunity for those with vivid imaginations . . . especially in the fields of computer technology, entertainment, and the digital arts. Sometimes imagination is used for fictional purposes to embellish actual events as more amazing or unbelievable than they really are. But other times, the opposite is needed. In these occasions imagination is necessary to help describe actual things that are so amazing we simply can't afford to miss the wonder waiting to be revealed. The latter example is most surely the case when attempting to speak of Christian salvation. So, for this end, we have established the need and laid the groundwork for a renewal soteriology of embodiment. Now all that remains is imagination to complete the task.

Before we begin, we must keep in mind the context of our soteriology. As mentioned in chapter 1, few conservative Christian ministers and theologians hold that faith is *only* related to the intellect. Yet, we've shown that, among such a constituency, when soteriological reflection interacts with missions, evangelism, systematic theology, and basic discipleship time and again intellect trumps behavior and affectivity as the featured element of faith. In short, we are dealing with the problem of un-interrogated soteriological presuppositions within conservative Christianity. How does one become aware of the need to rethink deeply held presuppositions? In our case, this means that the inadequacies and inconsistencies of the intellectualist soteriology paradigm must be seen for what they are in light of the validity and possibilities a renewal soteriology of embodiment has to offer.

So, it is within this milieu that we ask the driving question of this final chapter: How then might a renewal soteriology of embodiment really

PART FIVE: TOWARD A RENEWAL SOTERIOLOGY OF EMBODIMENT

make a difference? We begin by speculating on specific implications of our proposal and then reflect on why a renewal soteriology is so relevant today. After summarizing the key points of this book, we suggest areas of future research as a follow-up to our proposal.

IMPLICATIONS OF A RENEWAL SOTERIOLOGY OF EMBODIMENT

Here, I summarize three central implications of our proposal and suggest how they can broaden our awareness of the scope and impact of God's saving grace. First, I reiterate the salvific significance of the body. Second, I emphasize the ongoing nature of salvation and, third, its inextricably social implications. I conclude by elaborating how these descriptions reveal fundamental differences between an intellectualist soteriology and our vision of salvation.

Salvation is Embodied

A core theme of this book concerns the embodiment of faith. It is important to expound on this quality because of how integral it is to our study. I now lay out four reasons why one's vision of salvation must be embodied.

First, faith requires the body proper, not just the head. If the cognitive sciences have unveiled knowing as mediated through intellect, behavior, and emotions then we can establish that knowledge of God is similarly mediated. Just as it is through our bodies that knowing transpires, so too is it through our bodies that God makes himself known. Edwards states the same through his theology of beauty when he illuminates salvation in experiential terms whereby God manifests himself through his beauty and goodness in creation.[1] Edwards also asserts that salvation is incomplete if only the understanding is involved because behavior and affectivity are basic components of conversion.[2]

Second, knowing God is a tangible reality; it is not reduced to abstract propositions. While rational knowledge is vital, it is not prioritized over subjective awareness and experience of God in an embodied paradigm of salvation. A holistic soteriology admits the epistemological function of

---

1. Edwards, "A Divine and Supernatural," 113.
2. Edwards, "Part Four, Chapter Two," 380–88.

behavior and emotions and rejects knowledge of God divorced from experience of God. To embrace an embodied faith is to value the soteriological import of orthopraxy and orthopathy. Chapters 5 and 6 emphasized how the canonical practices helped cultivate measurable growth in believers for continued maturity into the likeness of Christ. Chapters 7 and 8 drew attention to experience in pentecostal orthopathy through its rich tradition of heart religion. Daniel Castelo spoke of pentecostal spirituality as an embodied epistemology wherein worship serves the catechetical task of introducing individuals to God and training them up in the faith. These examples show that salvation is mediated not only through specific teaching but also by ecclesial practices—especially prayer and worship—and the affective experiences they engender.

Third, an embodied faith is scriptural. The Bible gives ample reasons to believe that God affirms human embodiment. For instance, the doctrine of the incarnation attests that God came to earth by taking on the flesh and blood realities of human existence (John 1:14). The early Church Fathers contended that the incarnation was necessary for salvation and often echoed the claim that only what has been assumed (taken on as flesh) could be redeemed.[3] The New Testament also makes clear that the incarnation was necessary because human beings need a savior who can identify with their frailties.[4] In Acts 2 as the disciples were gathered together in prayer on the Day of Pentecost, the Holy Spirit came like a violent wind and descended as tongues of fire upon those present. Peter described this event as fulfilling what was spoken by the prophet Joel (Joel 2:28) that, "In the last days it will be, God declares, that I will pour out my Spirit *upon all flesh.*"[5] Pentecostals, in particular, take this passage very serious because it marks a new era of the Spirit's ministry now available to all people. Pentecostals assert that because the Spirit has been poured out on "all flesh," God values the materiality of human experience. Hence, salvation entails more than an otherworldly hope but the physical redemption of human life, here and now.

Fourth, an embodied faith correlates with actual human experience. Because human beings are embodied, salvation as a disembodied "heavenly" reality or "spiritual" state is incongruous with human experience and God's valuation of the material world. Perhaps more than any other tradition,

---

3. For instance, see Gregory of Nazianzus, "Letter 101," 440.
4. For example, see Heb 2:14–18; Matt 4:1–11; and 2 Cor 5:21.
5. Acts 2:17 (NRSV). Emphasis added.

Part Five: Toward A Renewal Soteriology of Embodiment

Pentecostalism grasps the physical and material implications of salvation through its unwavering commitment to the doctrine of healing. Yong submits that pentecostal soteriology consists of more than mental or "spiritual" renewal because human existence is inextricably bound with the physical realities of its body.

> Pentecostals meet God not merely as rational creatures but as embodied, feeling, and desiring ones. And when the Spirit shows up, what happens is not just or even that Pentecostals come into new knowledge of God, but that bodies are touched, their emotions healed and liberated, their affections reoriented, and their ways of life transformed.[6]

Yong thereby concurs that a pentecostal understanding of salvation concerns the whole body.

James Smith similarly contends that the pentecostal belief in divine healing derives from its interpretation of the gospel as liberation from sin *and* its effects, including the physical realities of sickness and disease.[7]

> Deliverance and liberation, then, are not just "spiritual"; the gospel is not just a tonic for souls. Implicit in this affirmation of bodily healing is a broader affirmation, namely, a sense that the full gospel values the whole person. In other words... this central affirmation that God cares about our bodies is a... radical affirmation of the goodness of bodies and materiality *as such*.[8]

Hence, salvation is inauthentic to human experience if it does not engage the physical realities of our creaturely existence.

So, salvation as embodied does not deny the necessity of propositional knowledge, it just rejects such knowledge as the ultimate or sole soteriological criterion. A disembodied soteriology is problematic because such a view of salvation is little more than an abstract concept incommensurate with the concreteness of human experience. Since God created humans as embodied beings, doesn't it makes sense that their redemption would not be accomplished apart from their bodies? Scripture attests to the same when the Apostle Paul spoke of the glorious gift of our faith: "We have this treasure in jars of clay, to show that the surpassing power belongs to God and not to us" (2 Cor 4:7). If we really believe our physical bodies are

---

6. Yong, *Spirit of Love*, 55.
7. Smith, *Thinking in Tongues*, 42.
8. Ibid. Emphasis original.

necessary for God's salvific purposes then perhaps a sanctified imagination can help us re-envision the wonder and glory of God's immanent presence in and through our "jars of clay" in new and fresh ways.

Salvation is Ongoing

When salvation is defined along intellectual lines it is often interpreted through such fixed actions as assenting, choosing, deciding, or accepting the gospel. Together these acts reinforce a confessional experience culminating as a punctiliar event or decision (Sinners Prayer, altar experience). This is why I have explicated salvation as intellectual, behavioral, and affective transformation according to the notion of unending conversion.[9] The language of "conversion" stresses the dynamic process of coming to and growing in faith. What might salvation look like if it is more than a static declaration?

First, salvation as ongoing is marked by perpetual growth into the likeness of Christ. A renewal soteriology of embodiment signifies that growth is central to God's salvific purposes. In this book I have drawn on several examples to delineate salvation as increasing maturity into Christlikeness. Jonathan Edwards' dispositional soteriology identifies salvation as progressive through his emphasis on growth in the Christian affections. William Abraham's orthopraxy notes the maturing character of salvation through depicting the canonical practices as means of grace for ongoing Christian growth. He explained that catechetical schools of the early church existed as havens of salvation whereby believers learned how to grow in the grace of God. The canonical tradition also appropriated the Orthodox soteriological concept of *theosis* or divinization, whereby the believer is by grace conformed into the image of Christ. Lastly, Steven Land's description of pentecostal spirituality presumed growth in holiness through the "Latter Rain" outpouring of the Spirit. Perhaps, salvation as unceasing growth can be summed up in the phrase, "I have been saved, I am being saved, and I will be saved."[10]

Second, salvation as ongoing is not a standardized process. It is important to understand that salvation as conversion can occur in unexpected an unpredictable ways. Gordon Smith describes salvation as incremental.

---

9. For more on conversion as unending change see: Smith, *Transforming Conversion*; and Markham, *Rewired*.

10. Hunter, *Gospel According to St. Paul*, chapters 2–4.

PART FIVE: TOWARD A RENEWAL SOTERIOLOGY OF EMBODIMENT

> Most, if not all, conversions are actually a series of events—often a complex development over time, perhaps even several years. Yet for many Christian communities, there seems to be no way to speak meaningfully about believers' experiences of coming to faith . . . There is a corresponding failure to appreciate the wonder of the Spirit, who often works slowly and incrementally in the natural course and context of our lives, bringing about God's saving purposes.[11]

Smith appeals to the need for a language that adequately articulates the often extended and, sometimes, irregular process by which individuals come to faith.[12] Catholic theologian Donald Gelpi portrays conversion as a dynamic activity of re-ordering various domains of human experience. While he admits that all domains involve converting from irresponsible to responsible living, the journey of conversion can vary from person to person. He explains, "No two people convert in exactly the same way, but our experiences of conversion do 'rhyme'; that is, they share an analogous resemblance."[13] Drawing from Gelpi, Yong elaborates conversion as a personal experience transpiring in a social environment generally concerned with the intellectual, affective, moral, socio-political, and religious domains of life.[14] He contends that conversion in any locale is vitally related to others so that God uses conversion in one area as a motivator to take responsibility in another. He asserts that "every conversion experience in any domain serves as a divinely gracious prompt for deeper conversion in other domains and that finite human beings will never completely convert in this life."[15] Yong argues that a pneumatological soteriology does not insist on a specific *ordo salutis* (order of salvation) because the Spirit may urge individuals to convert in different domains even prior to their formal conversion to Christ.[16]

Third, salvation as ongoing accounts for the variety of means by which the Spirit leads people to faith and maturity in Christ. Why does this rendering of salvation matter? It matters because human life, as embodied, is dynamic not static. Thus, at its core, human experience is not driven only or

---

11. Smith, *Transforming Conversion*, 6.
12. Ibid., 7.
13. Gelpi, *Conversion Experience*, 28.
14. Yong, *Spirit Poured Out*, 106.
15. Ibid., 108.
16. Ibid., 107–8.

234

Imagining Salvation in the Flesh

even primarily by a rational quest but by the complex interplay of intellect, behavior, emotions, and feelings with our physical and historical contexts. A soteriology that does not concede dynamism is problematic because it does not correlate with actual human experience. Salvation is ongoing because it is pneumatological. The Spirit draws people to faith in Christ in lieu of their unique historical and temporal contexts. Ongoing transformation follows for those who surrender to the work of the Spirit in their lives.[17]

So then, if human life is fundamentally the consequence of perpetual growth and change, doesn't it make sense to elucidate the saving work of God in terms of ongoing transformation? And if we really believe that salvation is an ongoing process, wouldn't we have ample reason to face future challenges with a new sense of hope? Yes, as Spirit-filled believers, we can ask for and rely upon a pneumatological imagination in keeping with a future reality of progressive growth into the *imago Dei*.

Salvation is Social

So far, our vision of salvation as embodied and progressive has mainly focused on the personal aspects of human experience (i.e., salvation as tangible experience, physical healing, growth, etc.). Now, I account for the social implications of the redemptive work of God in and through a person's life. Scripture clearly states that one cannot know (love) God apart from loving one's neighbor.[18] In other words, while salvation concerns an individual's relationship with God, such is often revealed in how one relates to others.

First, salvation as social is corroborated by the cognitive sciences. Such a soteriology rejects certain Cartesian ontological assumptions prevalent in Western culture that fail to fully reflect the myriad social and historical realities constituting human experience. Throughout this study, Antonio Damasio and Reuven Feuerstein have effectively demonstrated how human experience (cognitive) thrives most when behavior and affectivity (which are often socially mediated) are present.[19] Informed by such research,

---

17. See 2 Cor 3:16–18 (NRSV): "But when one turns to the Lord, the veil is removed. Now the Lord is the Spirit, and where the Spirit of the Lord is, there is freedom. And all of us, with unveiled faces, seeing the glory of the Lord as though reflected in a mirror, are being transformed into the same image from one degree of glory to another; for this comes from the Lord, the Spirit."

18. See Matt 22:37–40; John 15:17; 1 Cor 13; Gal 5:13–14; 1 Pet 4:8–10; and 1 John 3:14.

19. See Leslie Brothers' work on the social nature of the brain in, *Friday's Footprints*.

PART FIVE: TOWARD A RENEWAL SOTERIOLOGY OF EMBODIMENT

I showed how William Abraham's canonical theism features the social significance of salvation as God's grace was powerfully mediated through the ecclesial practices of gathered believers. Likewise, I noted how Samuel Solivan's orthopathy underscores the need for a socially informed soteriology in touch with the needs of those who suffer if the gospel is to remain true to human experience.

Second, salvation as social is biblical. To affirm a social soteriology is to acknowledge that in Scripture the salvific purposes of God are largely detailed in social terms. In the Old Testament, social terms regarding Israel as the *people* of God, a *holy nation*, and a *kingdom* are often used to describe God's redemptive plans.[20] In the New Testament, salvation is mostly identified with the *church.*[21] While individual and personal realities are not absent, throughout Scripture, salvation-redemption is chiefly understood within a social context. As with the cognitive sciences, so too does the creation narrative (Gen 2:18) teach that human life thrives most when it is in relationship with others. Genesis introduces the social implications of sin as not only did Adam and Eve conspire together in bringing sin into the world, but so too would its effects challenge all future male-female relationships.[22] Therefore, Scripture provides ample reasons to conceptualize salvation in social terms.

Third, salvation as social acknowledges that divine grace transcends individual concerns. To acknowledge the social character of salvation is to recognize that saving grace is not only about God meeting individual concerns but the needs of individuals in relationship. While many people readily admit that salvation is not just personally experienced, when it is fleshed out in practical theology and evangelistic application, social connotations tend to be ignored.[23] Here I refer to the saving work of God within and through the relationships people share. Yong notes the social quality of salvation.

20. For example regarding "people" see: Deut 32:9; 2 Chr 7:14; Jer 27:14; Zech 24:7; and regarding "nation" and "kingdom" see: Gen 17:4; Exod 19:5–6; 1 Chr 17:11; Ps 145; Amos 9:11; and Obad 1:21 (NRSV).

21. See: Matt 16:18, 15:22; Acts 20:28; 1 Cor 14:12; Eph 1:22, 5:25; and Col 1:18 (NRSV).

22. Gen 3:16b (NRSV).

23. This was illustrated in chapter 1 when I surveyed various conservative Christian websites that described salvation in primarily intellectual terms, which indirectly paint individualistic conceptions of salvation. Again, while social dimensions are not totally ignored, they are overshadowed by an individualist paradigm.

Imagining Salvation in the Flesh

> [It is] the healing and reconciliation of interpersonal relationships, most tangibly experienced in the church and to which the church is called to bear witness. It also refers, on the other hand, to the redemption of the socioeconomic and political structures—including fallen and destructive public structures.[24]

Yong contends that such reconciliation ought to concern, at least, racial, class, and gender reconciliation.[25] So, salvation as embodied is social because the liberating Spirit not only heals individuals but individuals in relationship.

Fourth, salvation as social honestly admits the full scope of sin's corrupting influence in the world. Here I speak of the need for critical reflection on the liberating impact of divine grace within an individual to accomplish a broader social impact. Such a soteriology is cognizant of the power of God in a believer against the destructive power of sin in the social, communal, and public domains of culture, politics, economics, business, etc. For instance, the liberating power of God is relationally mediated through a spouse for marital healing or through parents modeling God's unconditional love to their children. On a larger scale, the freeing grace of God can stream through a believer to fellow citizens suffering injustice, abuse, and marginalization whether locally or remote. At this macro level, the relational ramifications of salvation refer to the transforming of institutions, cultural and political values, and systems that perpetuate conditions of oppression and bondage. So, because of the social constitution of human experience, doesn't it make sense to consider the social implications of salvation? Because we have become so accustomed to visualizing salvation in personal and individual ways, we may need to ask God to empower our imagination to see his saving grace at work in and through social contexts we never previously noticed.

I now summarize the preceding to highlight the key elements of a renewal soteriology of embodiment. First, divine grace, as embodied, is mediated through human agency and the concrete realities of daily life. In an embodied soteriology, creation takes on a sacramental quality because salvation is mediated through historical and physical means. Second, because salvation is progressive, then static, and punctiliar, terms like *deciding* and *choosing* fail to capture redemption in the myriad ways the Spirit draws individuals into relationship with God. To recognize salvation as progressive

---

24. Yong, *Spirit Poured Out*, 93.
25. Ibid., 94.

PART FIVE: TOWARD A RENEWAL SOTERIOLOGY OF EMBODIMENT

is to admit the power of grace at work in one who may not have even been formally exposed to orthodox doctrine or Christian Scriptures. Third, a social soteriology concedes that because human experience is socially constituted, salvation must account for more than the personal and individual character of sin. The full impact of salvation—as transformational—is missed when its social implications are ignored or minimized. Salvation as embodied, progressive, and social confronts the objective-subjective bifurcations commonly associated with the saving work of God. These categories fail to perceive the grace of God always and ever at work in creation, beckoning all into a fuller realization of their destiny in God.[26] When we take seriously the implications of a renewal soteriology of embodiment, we will have reason for a healthy imagination to help us recognize and experience God's saving grace in myriad ways and manifold means never (or rarely ever) before considered.

We now turn our attention to practical reflection on what we've learned. Obviously, there are a variety of soteriological models with which one may identify. The next section is guided by the pointed question, "Does a renewal soteriology of embodiment really matter?"

Why Bother with a Renewal Soteriology of Embodiment?

Since the beginning of this book we have mostly dealt with salvation in a theoretical sense as we have challenged certain soteriological paradigms in favor of others. We have exposed presuppositions and practices that minimize the relevance of the body in how we understand the nature of faith. Ultimately, our goal has been to help re-envision Christian salvation as a dynamic reality of ongoing transformation occurring not *in spite of* but *because of* our bodies.

26. James Smith draws from pentecostal spirituality, Radical Orthodoxy, science, and philosophy to suggest soteriological conclusions of a pneumatological ontology of creation (in, Smith, *Thinking in Tongues*, chapter 2). There he explicates a pentecostal ontology of creation as an "en-Spirited naturalism" (97) whereby creation is enchanted or continuously upheld by the Spirit rather than occasionally interrupted by the divine (interventionist supernaturalism). Instead of a closed and autonomous naturalism, Smith suggests, "Rather, the Spirit is always already present at and in creation. The Spirit's presence is not a . . . soteriological 'visiting' of a creation that is otherwise without God; rather, the Spirit is always already dynamically active in the cosmos/world/nature. God doesn't have to 'enter' nature as a visitor and alien; God is always already present in the world. Thus creation is *primed* for the Spirit's action" (103).

Imagining Salvation in the Flesh

Yet, is salvation just a theoretical topic concerned mostly with our theological epistemology on the nature of faith? Is the point of this book simply about finding a better definition of faith or to offer a more theologically accurate rendering of what salvation is and how it functions? If so, then we have already fallen back into the very intellectualist tendencies we have sought to avoid. While theory and epistemology are vital resources for theological reflection, ultimately they are practical tools for the church to facilitate spiritual formation and Christian witness. Toward this end, we first respond to important concerns challenging the credibility of our proposal and conclude with concrete missiological and personal reasons why a renewal soteriology of embodiment makes a difference.

Questioning a Renewal Soteriology of Embodiment

I now address three likely criticisms of this book by situating them within an intellectualist theological paradigm. Each concern reveals epistemological commitments inconsistent with the dynamic nature of orthodox Christian soteriology. The criticisms are introduced as questions regarding the overemphasizing of orthopraxy, orthopathy, and orthodoxy.

Excessive Orthopraxy

Does your focus on orthopraxy lead to "works salvation"?[27] No. Despite having consistently reiterated the soteriological significance of "right behavior-practices," such does not presume anything less than the centrality of grace for Christian salvation. Rather, I have sought to develop a soteriology where grace is primary whether it is mediated through knowledge, behavior, or affectivity. Toward this end, I have incorporated contemporary research in the cognitive neurosciences to uphold an embodied view of cognition whereby intellect, behavior, and feelings-emotions are interdependent. For our purposes, such studies reveal that when one cognitive domain is cut off or stifled, cognition in whole suffers. I have contended that knowing God is an embodied cognitive function that depends on behavior along with intellect and affectivity. To minimize or dismiss one or more of these cognitive domains is to obstruct a holistic soteriology. Now we have a neuroscientific

---

27. The phrase "works salvation" reflects the idea that Christian salvation can be earned through doing specific and/or enough "good works."

context for the ancient admonition of the Apostle James: "What good is it, my brothers and sisters, if you say you have faith but do not have works?" (Jas 2:14, NRSV).

Hence, my underscoring of orthopraxy is not in isolation of orthodoxy and orthopathy because an embodied soteriology *requires* a focus on orthopraxy even as it also stresses orthodoxy and orthopathy. Throughout, I have spotlighted each cognitive domain as a mediator of salvific faith to emphasize that knowing God is always and ever a pneumatologically-driven reality. Though all aspects of our bodies are involved in knowing God, salvation is nevertheless only made possible through God's gift of unmerited grace (Eph 2:8).[28]

Extreme Orthopathy

Does your emphasis on orthopathy lead to emotionalism? No. Previously, I argued that pentecostal orthopathy can foster a renewal soteriology of embodiment despite numerous critiques that it necessarily promotes emotionalism and a minimized role of Scripture. A focus on orthopathy untethered from orthodoxy and orthopraxy can lead to an overemphasis on emotions, but this is *not* what I advocate. Rather, I claim that emotions, feelings, and affectivity are fundamental soteriological components. I have drawn extensively from cognitive neuroscientist Antonio Damasio whose research shows that emotions and feelings are essential for cognitive function. Such is most dramatically revealed in brain damaged patients who retained all their former rational and intellectual cognitive abilities but sustained damage to those areas of the brain that process emotions and feelings. Such patients lost the ability to make decisions and utilize information in ways that demonstrated healthy and thriving cognitive function.[29] So, Damasio's research helps affirm, not discredit, the critical role of affectivity for our soteriological proposal.

---

28. I admit that for many within conservative Protestantism, this proposal may be difficult to accept in light of its historically skeptical attitude towards "works-based" salvation. Such reservations were initially revealed in its Reformation convictions of *sola fide* and later manifested in concerns that the "social gospel" might replace explicit evangelistic proclamation with efforts of social justice. Though such concerns are understandable, we must not allow our fears to strip our soteriological paradigms of the benefits an orthopraxically mediated faith has to offer.

29. Damasio, *Looking for Spinoza*, 178 n. 25; and Damasio, *Descartes' Error*, 245.

Imagining Salvation in the Flesh

Despite the formidable dangers of emotionalism, I maintain that orthopathy is necessary for a dynamic soteriology. My focus on orthopathy exposes the almost exclusive attention on orthodoxy in conservative Christianity by failing to account for the vital role of affectivity in the cognitive task of knowing God. Yet my underscoring of orthopathy simultaneously coincides with an *accent* on orthodoxy and orthopraxy because faith (as with cognition) is inseparably linked with intellect, behavior, and affectivity. Therefore, I unequivocally reject an emotionally-driven faith yet wholeheartedly embrace the need for an orthopathic soteriology. For without orthopathy the dynamic and transforming quality of faith is seriously hindered.

Insufficient Orthodoxy

Does your de-emphasis on orthodoxy lead to a minimization of content for understanding salvation? No. As with the last two questions, I am not "de-emphasizing" orthodoxy any more than orthopraxy or orthopathy. Rather, I am proposing a soteriology that envisions "right belief" inseparably from "right practices" and "right emotions-feelings-affectivity." I do not make light of the need for intellectual content but I challenge the presumption that it *alone* is paramount in "securing" Christian salvation. Once again, I contend that a renewal soteriology of embodiment conceives salvation more as a process of increasing conversion than a static decision or event. Accordingly, while decision making and key events are fundamental in Christian salvation, they occur as divine prompts (rather than static ends) urging one onwards in the salvific journey. Intellectual content is important for salvific faith; however, such content is not the *only* indicator of salvation or necessarily the *initial* launching pad for faith.

I allege that because cognition is embodied, faith is not solely reduced to propositional statements, creedal confessions, or decision making. Because conservative Christianity conceptualizes "faith in Christ" chiefly in discursive terms, the salvific potential of behavior and affectivity remain mostly undeveloped. However, a renewal soteriology holds that God pneumatologically mediates saving faith to human beings in a manner consistent with the embodied quality of their minds. For this reason, such a soteriology denies that intellectual content alone carries the burden of Christian salvation, for if it did then conversion of heart and transformation of behavior would be unnecessary or peripheral. This would be exactly

PART FIVE: TOWARD A RENEWAL SOTERIOLOGY OF EMBODIMENT

the kind of presuppositions I have heretofore rejected in an intellectualist soteriology.

In sum, I affirm the necessity of intellectual content for salvific faith. However, as per the embodiment of cognition, I also contend that it (1) is inseparable from and dependent upon behavior and affectivity, and that (2) intellectual content may actually follow behavioral and affective expressions of faith in one's salvific journey. Because salvation is unceasing conversion, God mediates faith to human beings in myriad means reflective of the historical and particular realities of their lives. Such a dynamic understanding of salvation explains how some Christians claim to have been introduced to Christ prior to having received explicit teaching about him.[30] Because knowing God is a progressive reality, faith might initially be mediated through behavioral and affective means, and only later find a "fuller" expression through the kind of intellectual content (presuming that the individual has the capacity to comprehend it) normally associated with salvation in one's ecclesial context.

Finally, I recognize that some of these statements beg the question of what constitutes "sufficiency" for Christian salvation. How do we know if someone has had sufficient knowledge to qualify as a true conversion? While faith may be mediated via behavioral and affective means, is such truly salvific? While these questions fall beyond the scope of this study, I do, however, assert that intellectual content is not the sole criterion for Christian salvation. While God alone knows the heart of a person and how genuine his or her faith, one's construal of salvation must not restrict the mediation of faith solely to ecclesial means through propositional claims.[31]

---

30. Amos Yong articulates such a dynamic and embodied view of faith in regard to Christian mission: "We should not underestimate the affective dimensions of such witness. Oftentimes, Christian witness is propositionalized so that what is communicated is information. A pneumatological theology of missionary love, however, understands that faithful witness is not only accomplished by or within the head (and the words it generates) but [is] motivated by and undertaken through the heart, and expressed with the hands" (*Spirit of Love*, 156).

31. While James Smith does not deny the importance of intellectual content for Christian salvation, he does affirm the epistemological capacity of behavior and affectivity to mediate "knowledge of God" (at least) within a pentecostal context. Smith explains that pentecostals have a rich experience of knowing that is not intellectually reductionistic. He says that "pentecostal spirituality fosters a more expansive, affective understanding of what counts as knowledge and a richer understanding of how we know" (*Thinking in Tongues*, 59). He contends that pentecostals model an epistemology that enables a "'knowing' before and beyond propositions" (Ibid., 68). Throughout the same text, Smith provides numerous philosophical and scientific reasons to take seriously the

Imagining Salvation in the Flesh

Rather, a renewal soteriology of embodiment recognizes the epistemological significance of behavior and affectivity through a pneumatologically-driven mediation of faith.[32]

Having already addressed potential challenges of our proposal we next consider its promise. So, we now ask why our embodied vision of salvation is so important. To accomplish this we show the promise of our proposal as it relates to two specific soteriological categories. First, since salvation at its core is "good news" there must be missional reasons why our proposal is needed. Second, since salvation is a deeply personal reality, I offer practical reasons why our soteriology is individually relevant.

A Missionally Effective Soteriology

Because our vision of salvation is embodied, progressive, and social, it is now more consonant with historic orthodox Christianity than the intellectualism of conservative Christian soteriology. As good news, one's doctrine of salvation must encourage greater opportunities for proclaiming God's grace as well as its reception. Therefore, I suggest that three missional possibilities emerge out of our embodied soteriology—increased ecumenical unity, expanded witness, and multiplied hope—which illustrate its effectiveness.

Encourages Ecumenical Unity

A renewal soteriology of embodiment can encourage ecumenical unity. This book spotlights three religious traditions modeling key elements of our suggested soteriological paradigm. Our conclusions correlate with the orthodox Christian tradition because they derive from familiar orthodoxic, orthopraxic, and orthopathic foundations more or less accented in varying denominations and particular historical timeframes and settings. This

---

epistemological potential of behavior and affectivity in pentecostal spirituality to mediate knowledge of God.

32. While thoroughly addressing this topic remains beyond the scope of our present study, it is important to remember that our proposal concerns an integrated-embodied soteriology so that "knowledge of God" collaborates with "right practices and behaviors" even as it partners with "right affections." In this study, our concern is not with what is the "minimum" necessary for authentic Christian faith but rather how we might be able to facilitate a more *maximized*—i.e., dynamic and transforming—faith.

PART FIVE: TOWARD A RENEWAL SOTERIOLOGY OF EMBODIMENT

research is, therefore, ecumenical because it honors and draws from diverse traditions of the church. Such ecumenism is most notably revealed in how the strengths of certain traditions help overcome the weaknesses of others. Perhaps, for some, such ecumenical openness may lead to what seems like a previously hidden mine of ecclesial treasures never before appreciated but now embraced for the flourishing of the church catholic. Finally, because ecumenical unity often leads to greater degrees of love between diverse Christian groups, it will increase credibility in the eyes of non-Christian onlookers.[33] John 13:35 says that the world will recognize the authenticity of Christian faith because of the love believers show one another. Therefore, since greater love is usually an outcome of greater unity, we can see again how ecumenical unity can help nurture greater missional effectiveness.

Spurs Expansive Witness

A renewal soteriology of embodiment can spur a more expansive witness. While divine grace is always at work in the world, when mediated through the church, its impact is multiplied in breadth and depth. For doesn't it make sense that grace is "intensified" when the channel is not a passive vehicle but a living exemplar of Spirit-empowered existence? Therefore, as the church appreciates how faith is embodied, she can broaden the reach of her witness. While not neglecting continued emphasis on verbal proclamation, she can also realize that her witness in the day-to-day working world of her members is neither silent nor meager. Accordingly, she will discover how her actions and presence often speak louder than words. Simply knowing that faith is embodied, progressive, and social can help the church gain fresh perspectives on her physical presence as a viable means of grace wherever she goes. This comprehension adds a new level of intentionality and purpose so as to trigger an intensification and expansion of her witness in the world.

Expresses Hope

A renewal soteriology of embodiment can powerfully express hope. Herein, I have expanded the meaning of salvation beyond just static propositional

---

33. Jonathan Edwards wrote that love is a distinguishing mark of the work of the Spirit of God ("Religious Affections," 345).

truth claims to a dynamic actuality palpably encountered. Salvation is experienced presently in the flesh, not just in a future heavenly state. Therefore, hope is tangibly exhibited when the transforming and redeeming power of the Spirit is at work within and through the ecclesial community. Perhaps one of the greatest ways Christian hope is imparted is through the ministry of social justice. Unfortunately many Christians have abandoned intentional efforts to promote justice for fear of devolving into a "social gospel" proclamation where acts of compassion and liberation supposedly replace explicit proclamation of the gospel.[34] Our proposal reminds us that salvation is not only concerned with redeeming the depravity of our thinking (through orthodoxy), or the need for justice in the midst of our broken physical circumstances (through orthopraxy), but also affective transformation through experiencing the transforming power of God's love (through orthopathy). Truly such a holistic soteriology allows ample opportunities to mediate hope.

Ecumenical unity, expanded witness, and ability to mediate hope are just some of the reasons our proposal is missionally effective. While space prevents elaboration of further discussion,[35] it is enough to say that such effectiveness is a consequence of our commitment to the central role of the Spirit and human embodiment in soteriological reflection. Yet, our proposal is not only missionally effective; it is also personally relevant. So, now we ask, "How can a renewal soteriology of embodiment make a practical difference in my life?

---

34. While some renderings of the social gospel prioritized moral behavior over personal faith, this was not always the case. However, even today, many evangelicals remain suspicious of socially focused ministries for fear of devolving into just a "social gospel." For example, at the 53rd General Council of the Assemblies of God (2010) a resolution was passed to include compassion ministry as part of its reason for being. Yet, still there was resistance as many were fearful that this would lead to a "preaching of the social gospel" in which practices of compassion replace the preaching of the gospel (see, Shoonover, "Compassion Ministry," lines 14–15). For more on the history of the social gospel see, Livingston, *Modern Christian Thought*, chapter 11.

35. Another reason for the missional relevance of our proposal is our commitment to the priority of pneumatology (in elaborating the scope of a Spirit-led witness) and the gifts of the Spirit (for practicing an empowered witness). We could also talk about the incredibly effective missionary force of the global pentecostal movement (especially the Assemblies of God) as part of the ecclesial heritage (pentecostal spirituality) from which we draw.

PART FIVE: TOWARD A RENEWAL SOTERIOLOGY OF EMBODIMENT

A Personally Relevant Soteriology

Throughout we have emphasized that salvation should not be construed in abstract and static terms but rather as a dynamic and transformational reality. In our efforts to "flesh" out such a soteriology we drew from various theological traditions to elaborate the soteriological significance of orthodoxy, orthopraxy, and orthopathy. Though we have delineated these "orthos" individually, in reality each is inseparably connected to the others. Nevertheless, each domain provides important contributions that deliver ample reasons why a renewal soteriology of embodiment is personally relevant. Here I suggest three.

Nurtures Spiritual Formation

Without a doubt, Christian salvation would cease to be "Christian" if orthodoxy was not taken seriously. Yet, we have also underscored the emptiness of an orthodoxy chiefly concerned with an intellectualist understanding of such "knowing." This is why soteriological reflection must be holistically informed; for such embodiment nurtures receptivity to the transforming ministry of the Holy Spirit.

In most arenas of life, a distinguishing mark of something's value is that it works. It actually accomplishes what it claims. An intellectualist faith cannot sustain vital, dynamic, and ongoing Christian growth because it only engages the rationally objective component of faith. But as we have appropriated the cognitive sciences, we understand that a renewal soteriology of embodiment nourishes expansive growth because it accounts more holistically for what it means to know God.

Above all, salvation is a lifestyle of ongoing growth into the likeness of Christ. If our soteriology does not encourage such expectation then we may need to consider if this might be the result of un-interrogated intellectualist presuppositions in how we think about salvation. Therefore, soteriological reflection matters, because just as the power of cognition is more fully unleashed to the degree it is most embodied, so too is salvific faith more transforming to the degree it is most embodied. In other words, the reality of our embodiment offers us innumerable possibilities of collaborating with the Holy Spirit in our state of spiritual growth. So, if we want such a salvation of ongoing growth we must learn to resist our intellectualist habits that limit orthodoxy largely to the objective realm of doctrinal certitude or the intangible domain of an abstract spirituality.

Models Saving Grace

One of the damaging consequences of an intellectualist soteriology is that in our contemporary culture people are less impacted by the gospel when it is mostly information-driven. Because so many people are disillusioned with formal religion they are desperate for an authentic faith. So, a renewal soteriology of embodiment matters because of its absolute commitment to the soteriological significance of orthopraxy. For just as salvation leads to a transformation of thinking through orthodoxy, so too does it result in the transformation of behavior and lifestyle through orthopraxy. When such visible transformation occurs, the manifold grace of God is profoundly demonstrated as actual flesh and blood examples become another mode of gospel proclamation.

Such a witness is increasingly important in post-Christian societies (especially Europe) where large numbers of self-identified "secularists" are skeptical of organized religion and propositional faith claims. In these contexts, orthopraxis can become a tangible means of grace to powerfully communicate Christian faith in a way that an intellectualist soteriology often can't. In a similar way, the Apostle Paul told the Corinthians that their lifestyles had a way of preaching to others. He said they were letters, "known and read by everyone" (2 Cor 3:3).

Lastly, understand that we are not speaking of an either-or approach. Remember, orthodoxy needs orthopraxy just as much as orthopraxy needs orthodoxy and orthopathy. Each domain not only needs the others but contributes to the others. In so doing, behaviors, actions, and practices function as critically necessary soteriological resources.

Is Experientially Vibrant

As previously mentioned, while we resist a soteriology that over-emphasizes affectivity we likewise reject one that does not adequately nurture a dynamic Christian faith. Perhaps one of the greatest dangers of an intellectualist soteriology is that it either downplays or denies the orthopathic significance of personal religious experience or the possibility of an enduring affective transformation (ex., love, joy, peace, and hope). Despite the

Part Five: Toward A Renewal Soteriology of Embodiment

challenges of emotionalism, few people (if any) would ever be satisfied with a faith that "feels" irrelevant. Therefore, we must take an honest look at the orthopathic condition of our faith and reflect on how emotionally satisfying it is. Sometimes such critiques are dismissed as misguided or selfish; however, while such concerns are valid, we must not fail to recognize the importance of a vibrant and dynamic faith. The wonder of our salvation must not only capture our minds but our hearts. For such a faith, we must be committed to an embodied understanding of salvation. For instance, if we want to experience the kind of salvation that models palpable peace and joy in the midst of suffering; if we yearn to feel real hope in the midst of chemical addictions and relational brokenness; and if we want know in our hearts the irresistible love of God in a culture of unparalleled obsession for pleasure then we need an embodied soteriology that concerns all of our physical existence—from head to toes and heart to hands.

So, when we speak of the need for a faith of personal experience we are speaking of a certain kind of experience—*experience of God's presence.* It is for this reason why a renewal soteriology is so relevant in our contemporary context. People are hungry for an experientially satisfying faith that nurtures assurance of God's presence. Truly, we needn't fear such an experiential faith if, once again, orthopathy is informed by orthodoxy and orthopraxy.

Finally, sometimes a false dichotomy is assumed between the "theoretical" and the "practical" aspects of soteriology. In reality, like any area of study, soteriology is both theoretical and practical at the same time. To put too much or too little emphasis on either will hinder the growth of one's faith. A dynamic and transformational soteriology must be theoretically and theologically sound if it is to be practically relevant. As we conclude, I want to be sure that the main points of our proposal are not lost amidst all that has been discussed. So, to this end, I summarize the key points of *Salvation in the Flesh* and look ahead to future areas of related study.

Final Reflections: Where Do We Go From Here?

The intention of this study has been to expose and question prevailing epistemological paradigms and assumptions within conservative Christian soteriology. Our research is based upon findings in the contemporary cognitive neurosciences and a broad review of soteriological beliefs, practices, and movements throughout church history. It is my hope that recognizing the presence of an intellectualist epistemology and the theological challenges it yields will prompt a fresh look at the Christian doctrine of salvation. Therefore, our goal has been to build a case for the need of an embodied soteriology.

Summing Up Our Case

What exactly has been our "case" for a renewal soteriology of embodiment? I close with a brief overview of our research that has exposed the need for a new vision of the doctrine of salvation. It remains for others to systematically expand the details and applications of our proposal.

An Unembodied Soteriology is Inaccurate and Incomplete

First, contemporary conservative Christianity has embraced an unembodied vision of salvation—we call it an intellectualist soteriology—that fails to capture the dynamic and transforming nature of saving faith. In chapter 1, we highlighted three presuppositions that repeatedly appear in theological reflection and practice of the Christian doctrine of salvation. Though these presuppositions are rarely admitted outright, they are, nevertheless, persistently reflected in the prioritization and subordination of various soteriological themes. These assumptions are both inaccurate and inconsistent with historic orthodox Christian belief and practice about the nature of faith and salvation. Therefore, a new soteriological paradigm is needed that more directly addresses the reality of human embodiment and specifically accounts for the unbounded presence of the Holy Spirit in the mediation of saving faith.

The Cognitive Sciences Affirm the Embodiment of Cognition

Second, the contemporary cognitive neurosciences and cognitive psychology provide compelling reasons to understand the nature of human cognition as a thoroughly embodied process. Since faith is, at least, a mental function, we hope to increase awareness of the epistemological significance of intellect, behavior, and affectivity for the mediation of faith. While not minimizing the necessity of orthodox belief, we expand the boundaries of soteriological reflection to more intentionally note the influences of

Part Five: Toward a Renewal Soteriology of Embodiment

orthopraxy and orthopathy for an embodied faith. Our working correlation is that just as cognition is most proficient to the degree it is embodied, so too is faith most impacting to the degree it is embodied.

Conservative Christianity has Embraced an Intellectualist Soteriology

Third, contemporary conservative Christianity has embraced an intellectualist epistemology that favors intellect and rationality over behavior and affectivity in its reflection on and practice of Christian faith. Such intellectualism is most clearly seen in the privileged role that orthodoxy plays in soteriological reflection. Therefore we have sought to expand this otherwise orthodoxy-driven soteriology to now involve orthopraxy and orthopathy within a framework that requires integration of these three domains. Toward this end, we offer glimpses (currently and historically) of Christian movements and thinkers (beginning with Jonathan Edwards) that have recognized the soteriological significance of behavior (Canonical Theism) and affectivity (Pentecostalism). Throughout each chapter we have shown how an intentional pneumatology is vital for an embodied soteriology of renewal.

The Soteriological Contribution of Pentecostal Spirituality

Fourth, pentecostal spirituality—because of its emphasis on the Holy Spirit and the embodiment of faith—can help re-envision theological reflection beyond the problems of intellectualism into the possibilities of a dynamic and transformational soteriology. In chapters 7–8, we draw from key pentecostal-renewal scholars and theologians to highlight the value of a pneumatologically framed soteriology. Such a "Soteriology of the Third Article" can successfully articulate the advantages of a renewal soteriology of embodiment over and against the intellectualist tendencies of conservative Protestant soteriology.

Ultimately, this book is an interdisciplinary case (i.e., historical, scientific, theological) for the need of an embodied vision of salvation and further reflection on the meaning and implications of such a paradigm. As such, this is not intended to be an exhaustive soteriological model but more of an outline pointing to important theological and epistemological themes related to our proposal. Neither was this book intended to provide more than a broad foundation from which to draw from commonly accepted notions of the embodied brain in the cognitive sciences.[36] However, in the course of writing this manuscript, one thing has become clear—our topic has the potential to spawn many new vistas of theological reflection and praxis. I hope, that others will take up and build upon some of these themes I have only been able to recognize. I conclude by briefly summarizing some of these potential areas of research that relate to one or more aspects of our soteriological proposal.

Future Study

Because the scope of our subject is so vast—the doctrine of salvation—many other subjects could have been addressed had there been more time and resources to develop them. Some of these topics emerge as logical questions specifically related to our research while others just fall within the soteriological trajectory already initiated. Here I reflect on five potential areas of future study.

First, research in the cognitive sciences and learning theory could help create a pedagogy for catechetical instruction consistent with the soteriology herein described. What kind of lifestyle would correlate with the soteriology I have detailed? How could such a lifestyle be nurtured in new believers?

Second, engagement with the behavioral sciences could quantify the impact of a renewal soteriology of embodiment. Is it possible that one could measure the degree to which he or she commits to such a soteriology? Is it possible to illustrate how our proposal might reveal measurable differences (intellectually, behaviorally, affectively) in believers who embrace such a soteriology than prior to their initial conversion? Could an embodied faith spark neurogenesis in a similar way that mediated learning does? In other words, is it possible to quantify the degree to which one's faith is embodied

---

36. Here, I emphasize that my area of training is in theology. I am not a cognitive scientist nor a cognitive psychologist, hence my reflections come as an outsider to these fields. Nevertheless, my use of Damasio and Feuerstein's work has been broadly applied, drawing from general concepts and paradigms basic to their research and largely endorsed across the broader body of cognitive scientific scholarship. Any potential value of this book—whether for theologians, biblical scholars, ministers, missionaries, or lay church members—should be attributed to the wide body of researchers and scholars who contributed to this project. Likewise, any shortcomings and oversights are solely my own.

Part Five: Toward a Renewal Soteriology of Embodiment

due to the effect of greater or lesser degrees of neurogenesis in those who've experienced radical degrees of dispositional transformation?

Third, studying the relationship between pneumatology and the arts can open up new ways to reflect on how creativity, artistry, and imagination might afford opportunities for mediating salvific grace. Could biblical research on the role of artisans and craftsmen in ancient Israelite worship (Exod 35–40) imply a relationship between divine grace and art? Might the Eastern Orthodox tradition of icons as means of grace be relevant for these ends? Could a "pneumatological theology of the arts" help to further articulate the soteriological function of affectivity?

Fourth, research on the relationship between the economies of the Son and Spirit could suggest new paradigms for missions and evangelism. If intellectual content is just one (even if the primary) means of mediating salvific faith, how might such insight influence present missionary and evangelistic models? If salvation is not solely dependent on orthodoxy, how might the church more fully and intentionally make use of orthopraxy and orthopathy as soteriological resources?[37]

Fifth, how might our proposal relate to present research in theology of religions where theologies of the First and Second Articles predominate? Can our present soteriological proposal shed insight on how divine grace might somehow (at some level) be at work in the orthodoxic, orthopraxic, and orthopathic domains utilized among religious others?[38] Does such a

---

37. Such can be especially relevant in situations where individuals lack opportunity to receive orthodox doctrine (highly repressive and restrictive contexts) or the ability to comprehend the various orthodoxic confessions of the church (i.e., the developmentally disabled).

38. One of the most pressing questions in this area of study involves the fate of the unevangelized. Directly stated, "Do all people really need a propositional (orthodoxic) witness if saving faith is also mediated in orthopraxic and orthopathic ways?" Once again, adequately addressing this topic remains well beyond the scope of our present study. At the very least, an embodied soteriology of renewal recognizes that because salvation is embodied there is much more going on in the process of Christian conversion than just attainment of religious knowledge and understanding propositional truths. Admitting that conversion is more than a static and punctiliar event should motivate theologians, biblical scholars, pastors, and missionaries to engage in critical theological reflection and missional praxis that can more effectively account for the dynamic and multidimensional nature of saving grace at work in the world today. Perhaps, *Salvation in the Flesh* can help in constructing the kind of epistemological framework and renewal theological method needed for wrestling through such reflection and praxis. Nevertheless, to delve more fully into this topic, see, Yong, *Beyond the Impasse*, and Kärkkäinen, *Trinity and Religious Pluralism*, for a pentecostal and Trinitarian approach to a theology of religions.

robust pneumatological soteriology necessarily threaten the explicitly articulated centrality of Christ affirmed in orthodox Christianity?

Ultimately, I hope this study helps broaden conservative Christian soteriological reflection and encourages a more expansive pneumatological imagination within the boundaries of orthodox Christian soteriology. Even though I have challenged intellectualist presuppositions inherent within conservative Christianity, I have not intended to minimize or disparage this movement nor its significance in contemporary Protestantism. My goal is the renewal of the church even as my methodology has been ecumenical in scope. Also, my use of Edwards (for orthodoxy), William Abraham's canonical theism (for orthopraxy), and Pentecostalism (for orthopathy) has been heuristic. Despite my appropriation of these interlocutors, I do not intend to imply or assume that their research or aims would necessarily endorse my project and its ends. I have simply found helpful connections between each tradition and my proposal.

As we have already seen, there are many implications that follow from taking the embodiment of salvation more seriously—both socially and personally. For just as we affirm a God who took on human flesh in order to identify with those he came to save, so too should we understand the scope of his redemption towards us today in a similarly embodied manner. Yes, we serve a God whose saving grace is not far off but truly near because his transforming power comes to us as nothing less than *salvation in the flesh*!

Glossary

1. ***Ad Extra***: A term related to Jonathan Edwards' (1703–1758) dispositional ontology and his theology of the Trinity. *Ad extra* refers to how God communicates his being. God (as the divine disposition) eternally communicates his essence (via the Holy Spirit) as glory, love, and beauty *outside* the Trinitarian godhead, thus occurring within the created order (chapter 3). See *Ad Intra*, Dispositional Ontology, and Religious Affections.

2. ***Ad Intra***: A term related to Jonathan Edwards' dispositional ontology and his theology of the Trinity. *Ad intra* refers to how God communicates his being. God (as the divine disposition) eternally communicates his essence (via the Holy Spirit) as glory, love, and beauty *within* the Trinitarian godhead, thus occurring outside the created order (chapter 3). See *Ad Extra* and Dispositional Ontology.

3. **Affections:** The emotional-perceptual inclinations of human cognition that predispose people to respond in particular ways. Affections are also understood as dispositions—consistent states of being that are simultaneously intellectual, behavioral, and affective. Our use of affections largely (though not always) corresponds to Jonathan Edwards' use in his dispositional ontology (chapter 3). See Affectivity, Dispositional Ontology, Dispositions, Orthopathos, Orthopathy, and Religious Affections.

4. **Affectivity:** Relating to the influence of emotions, feelings, sentiment, and experience upon human cognition. Though emotions play an important role in affectivity, we are not equating the same with emotionalism. Our use of affectivity often implies the roles of affections in general or the religious affections, in particular. See Affections,

Glossary

Orthopathy, Pentecostal Orthopathy, Religious Affections, and Subjective.

5. **Baptism:** One of the earliest sacramental rites of the Church; it was instituted by Jesus and implemented by the Apostles for the Christian's identification with Christ in his death, burial, and resurrection. Baptism is also one, among many, sacramental practices of the church. See Canonical Tradition, Means of Grace, Rites, and Sacrament.

6. **Baptism of the Holy Spirit:** The belief common among most pentecostals and Charismatics that God has made available a special work of the Spirit—generally after one has come to saving faith—for the purpose of empowerment in Christian ministry and personal spiritual growth. The baptism of the Holy Spirit is a fundamental doctrine among pentecostal and Charismatic Christians and finds support in the Gospels (ex., Matt 3:11 and Luke 3:16) and the book of Acts (ex., Acts 1:4–5). See Gifts of the Spirit, Pentecostal-Charismatic Christianity, Pneumatology, and Renewal.

7. **Behavior:** In this book, behavior refers to various practices and actions involved in the process of human cognition. Behavior is one of the three integrated cognitive domains (others are intellect and affectivity) we use in our holistic discussion of cognition and our proposal of a renewal soteriology of embodiment. See Cognition, Orthopraxy, Practices, and Praxis.

8. **Canon:** A compilation of rules, standards, beliefs, and norms established by the Church or Church councils. However, more commonly, canon refers to the approved list of early Church writings-books constituting the Christian Bible. See Canonical Theism and Canonical Tradition.

9. **Canonical:** The adjectival form of canon. Herein, canonical largely refers to the "canonical tradition" as elaborated by William Abraham (b. 1947) in his canonical theism (chapters 5–6). See Canon, Canonical Orthopraxy, Canonical Practices, Canonical Soteriology, Canonical Theism, and Canonical Tradition.

10. **Canonical Orthopraxy:** A term used in this book referring to a specific kind of orthopraxy—one consisting of the canonical practices of the Church—and its soteriological relevance. See Canonical Practices, Canonical Theism, and Orthopraxy.

Glossary

11. **Canonical Practices:** Commonly accepted practices of the Church used to initiate the Christian into the life of God. The canonical practices emphasized in this book are baptism, the Eucharist, and the reading of Scripture. See Canonical, Canonical Tradition, and Practices.

12. **Canonical Soteriology:** A term used in this book referring to a paradigm of salvation emphasizing the significance of behavior and practices. See Canonical, Canonical Practices, Practices, and Soteriology.

13. **Canonical Theism (CT):** A theological movement (founded by William Abraham) emphasizing the soteriological significance of canonical practices to help mediate salvific grace for the life of the Church. See Canonical, Canonical Tradition, and Means of Grace.

14. **Canonical Tradition:** Also described as the canonical heritage of the Church wherein commonly accepted materials, writings, and practices act as soteriological means of grace to initiate one into the life of God. Our appropriation of the term is informed by William Abraham's use in his canonical theism (chapters 5–6). See Canonical, Canonical Theism, Means of Grace, Rites, and Rule of Faith.

15. **Cartesian:** Of or relating to the ideas of René Descartes (1596–1650), a seventeenth-century French philosopher. Among his many ideas, Descartes promoted an ontological dualism that the human mind is distinctly separate from its body. This is primarily how "Cartesian" is used herein. See Cartesian Dualism.

16. **Cartesian Dualism:** The belief that the human person is above all defined by the capacity to rationally think. Accordingly, such dualism nurtures an intellectualist epistemology (chapter 1) that truncates mind from body and intellect from affectivity. This book challenges such dualism in our effort to promote an embodied cognitive paradigm regarding the meaning and nature of faith and salvation. See Cartesian, Intellectualism, and Western Christianity.

17. *Catechesis*: The process of handing on Scripture and the orthodox beliefs of the Church to new Christian believers. This book largely refers to *catechesis* as the process of how the early Church passed on its beliefs, practices, and a way of life to the early Christians. See Catechetical Schools and *Catechumen*.

18. **Catechetical Schools:** Schools or institutions in early Christianity that implemented set methods of educating and forming new

Glossary

converts in the teachings and practices of the Church. See *Catechesis* and *Chrismation*.

19. **Catechumen**: One who is a student in a catechetical school (chapter 5). See *Catechesis* and Catechetical Schools.

20. **Charismatic Christianity**: A form of Protestant Christianity similar to Pentecostalism in its openness to the contemporary relevance of the ministry and gifts of the Holy Spirit and personal encounter with God. Pentecostal Christians typically self-identify with a pentecostal denomination whereas Charismatic Christians often remain in mainline denominations or interdenominational-independent fellowships or churches. See Baptism of the Holy Spirit, Gifts of the Spirit, *Glossolalia*, Pentecostal-Charismatic Christianity, Pentecostalism, and Tongues.

21. **Chrismation**: The anointing of oil upon the *catechumen* subsequent to baptism and, in ancient practice, intended to coincide with the baptism of the Holy Spirit. Together with baptism, this sacred rite concluded the *catechumen's* training. See Baptism, Baptism of the Holy Spirit, and Catechetical Schools.

22. **Cognition**: The process of attaining knowledge and understanding. This book emphasizes intellect, behavior, and affectivity as vital embodied elements of human cognition. See Cognitive Neurosciences, Cognitive Psychology, Cognitive Science, and Embodiment.

23. **Cognitive Modifiability**: The capacity for human cognition to change and become positively transformed. See Cognition and Cognitive Plasticity.

24. **Cognitive Neurosciences**: A branch of cognitive psychology and neuroscience that researches the biological underpinnings of brain function with special attention given to neural aspects of mental processes. Case studies of brain damaged patients play an important role in this field of study (chapter 2). See Cognition, Cognitive Psychology, Cognitive Science, and Embodied Cognition.

25. **Cognitive Plasticity**: The ability of the brain to physically modify itself and transcend various kinds of deprivations or injuries. See Cognition, Cognitive Modifiability and Neurogenesis.

26. **Cognitive Psychology**: A branch of psychology that studies how the mind processes information. In this book, cognitive psychology

Glossary

is concerned largely with the cognitive neurosciences and learning theory (chapter 2). See Cognition and Cognitive Neurosciences.

27. **Cognitive Science:** The scientific and interdisciplinary study of the mind concerned (among other things) with the meaning of cognition, what the mind is, and how it functions. See Cognitive Psychology and Cognitive Neurosciences.

28. **Cognitive Scientist:** A scientist who studies the nature and processes of cognition. See Cognition and Cognitive Science.

29. **Conservative Christianity:** For our purposes, conservative Christianity refers to that form of Christianity adhering to the orthodox tenets of Christian faith. While conservative Christianity and evangelical Christianity are very similar in beliefs and practices, the former is broader in scope and does not necessarily identify with all of the cultural, intellectual, and political associations of the latter (chapter 1). See Conservative Protestantism, Evangelicalism, and Fundamentalism.

30. **Conservative Protestantism:** For our purposes, conservative Protestantism is that portion of conservative Christianity (as defined in chapter 1) represented among Protestant Christians. See Conservative Christianity, Evangelicalism, and Fundamentalism.

31. **Criterion:** A standard by which something is judged. Chapters 5 and 6 utilize this term when challenging certain canonical paradigms within conservative Christianity that have confused *canon* with *criterion*. See Epistemological Criterion and Epistemology.

32. **Deification:** A soteriological belief common among the early Christians that God gives grace for the goal of increasing growth into the image of God. This belief has continued largely in the Orthodox Christian tradition (as well as segments of Catholic and Protestant faith). Deification is the goal of union with God and becoming more like Christ by sharing in the divine nature (2 Pet 1:4). See *Theosis* and Divinization.

33. **Dispensationalism:** This eschatological paradigm basically asserts that God is currently transitioning the Church from the present dispensation, the Age of the Church, to its removal (doctrine of secret rapture) which initiates a period of seven years of massive global suffering known as the Great Tribulation. At the end of the Tribulation,

Glossary

Christ returns with the Church to judge the world and begins one thousand years of physical rein on the earth.[1] See Fundamentalism.

34. **Disposition:** For our purposes, disposition refers to a deeply reinforced way of being in the world that is mentally, behaviorally, and affectively integrated all at the same time. Much of our use of the term draws from Jonathan Edwards' dispositional ontology as discussed in chapters 3–4. See Affections, Dispositional Ontology, and Religious Affections.

35. **Dispositional Ontology:** We discuss this term from Jonathan Edwards' philosophical and theological reflection relating to salvation. For Edwards, to know God is to be transformed by this knowing; hence, his understanding of such knowing was not a static form of accumulated information but real change at the core of the human person—dispositional transformation. See Affections, Disposition, Ontology, and Religious Affections.

36. **Divinization:** The belief that humanity's purpose is to ultimately become like God by sharing in his nature. It asserts that the purpose of every Christian is union with God. Essentially synonymous with *theosis* and deification. See Deification and *Theosis*.

37. **Doctrine:** A belief or set of beliefs held by a specific entity, such as the Christian Church. This book is largely focused on the Christian doctrine of salvation. See Ecclesiology, Orthodoxy and Theology.

38. **Doxology:** A hymn or form of praise and/or worship to God. See Ecclesiology and Liturgy.

39. **Dynamic:** The characteristic of change, progression, or growth. Not static. See Dynamic and Transformational Soteriology.

40. **Dynamic and Transformational Soteriology:** A soteriological paradigm that implies and fosters ongoing growth, vitality, and transformation for the Christian believer. We set such a soteriology in stark contrast to an intellectualist soteriology. See Embodied Cognition, Renewal Soteriology of Embodiment, Salvation, and Soteriology.

41. **Eastern Christianity:** An umbrella term generally referring to non-Western Christian churches, often simply understood as the Eastern Orthodox Church. This segment of the Church (i.e., the Orthodox

---

1. Yong, *In the Days*, 318–20.

Glossary

Church) officially formed when the eastern portion of the Roman Church divided from its western counterpart in 1054 AD over a variety of theological, ecclesial, and political differences (chapter 5). See Western Christianity.

42. **Ecclesial:** Of or relating to a church. See Ecclesiology.

43. **Ecclesiology:** The study of church doctrine, especially how it understands itself regarding its practices and mission. See Doctrine and Ecclesial.

44. **Ecumenical:** Having to do with cooperation and unity between various Christian denominations and traditions. See Ecclesial and Ecclesiology.

45. **Edwardsean:** Though the term is used variously, for us it means something identified with or originating from Jonathan Edwards. See Dispositional Ontology and Religious Affections.

46. **Embodied Cognition:** A holist paradigm of cognition accounting for the whole body's involvement in knowing, not just the brain. Herein we elaborate an embodied cognitive paradigm incorporating intellect, behaviors, and affectivity as necessary and integrated domains of mental function. See Cognition, Embodiment, and Renewal Soteriology of Embodiment.

47. **Embodiment:** Having to do with the body. We relate embodiment to various cognitive models and ways of understanding the nature of faith that account for the entire body. See Cognition, Embodied Cognition, and Renewal Soteriology of Embodiment.

48. **Emotionalism:** An excessive appeal to and trust in emotional experiences. In this book, the term refers to a faith paradigm that is primarily informed by one's feelings and emotional experiences. In such a paradigm, emotions and feelings are often prioritized over Scripture in the process of discerning God's will. See Subjective.

49. **Epicletic:** That which regularly acknowledges its beginning and ending as existing and being sustained by the presence and leading of the Holy Spirit (chapter 7). See Pneumatology and Renewal.

50. **Epistemological Criterion:** Material items, beliefs, or practices used to establish the validity of truth claims. William Abraham uses this term to speak of how the Western Christian tradition has gradually

Glossary

exchanged the meaning and purpose of the canonical tradition from being a *means of grace* to an *epistemological criterion* for validating various theological truth claims. This topic is addressed in chapters 5–6. See Canonical Theism, Criterion, and Epistemology.

51. **Epistemology:** A branch of philosophy that is a theory of knowledge concerned with how individuals understand something to be true, rather than mere opinion. It is the investigation of the basis for truth claims—why things are considered true to some people and mere opinion to others. See Intellectualist Epistemology and Philosophy.

52. **Eucharist:** A fundamental sacrament of the church also known as "Holy Communion" or "The Lord's Supper." The Eucharist refers to the sacramental practice of Christians partaking of bread and wine as a memorial of the death and resurrection of Jesus Christ as recorded in Scripture. See Grace, Holy Communion, Lord's Supper, Means of Grace, and Sacramental.

53. **Evangelicalism:** A broad and often loosely organized constituency of Christians (at least in North America) and Christian organizations that chiefly coalesce around its three primary doctrinal emphases: a high view of the authority of Scripture, belief in an individual and personal relationship with Christ, and an active (and unique) engagement with culture. This movement spans Catholic and Protestant boundaries.[2] See Conservative Christianity, Conservative Protestantism, and Fundamentalism.

54. **Evangelicals for Social Action (ESA):** A conservative evangelical organization, founded by Ron Sider (b. 1939), emphasizing the importance of Christian behavior and practices for the mission of the church. ESA claims that compassion, justice, and social action are not optional for the Christian but central to the mission of the gospel. See Orthopraxic Soteriology and Orthopraxy.

55. **Experience:** In this book, "experience" is used in relation to orthopathy as an affective cognitive resource in distinction from (though integrated with) orthodoxy and orthopraxy in the mental process of knowing. In regard to salvation, we contend that human experience is

---

2. Finch, *End of Evangelicalism*, 15. In this definition Finch draws from the work of historians David Bebbington and Mark Noll (Bebbington, *Dominance of Evangelicalism*, chapter 1 and Noll, *American Evangelical Christianity*, 13, and his *Rise of Evangelicalism*, 19–20).

Glossary

cognitively productive in faith formation. See Affectivity, Orthodoxy, Orthopraxy, Orthopathy, and Soteriology.

56. **Faculty Psychology:** A psychological view that comprehends mental function as the combined efforts of various and separate "faculties" of the mind as opposed to an integrated and holistic process. See Cognition, Embodied Cognition, and Intellectualist Soteriology.

57. **Faith:** A theological term referring to complete trust and assurance in God. Protestant theology emphasizes biblical faith as a gift that God freely gives to individuals who ask for it—apart from any merit—as the means for salvation. In this book, we reflect on faith as (at least) a cognitive function of "knowing God" even as it is still an unmerited gift. See Grace and Salvation.

58. **Fundamentalism:** A religious movement generally beginning in the early 1900's that saw orthodox evangelical Protestantism threatened by modern advances in science and biblical studies as promoted through the liberal Protestant theology of that time. Fundamentalism also became closely aligned with the premillennial eschatological views of the Plymouth Brethren founder, John Nelson Darby (1800–1882). Hence the union of fundamentalist-dispensational thought came to function as both a theological system as well as an eschatological paradigm. Subsequently, Pentecostals were drawn into an "uneasy" alliance with Fundamentalism through their common efforts to combat the influence of liberal Protestantism (see chapter 7). See Conservative Christianity, Conservative Protestantism, and Evangelicalism.

59. **Gifts of the Spirit:** This phrase comes from the Greek words *charismata* (gifts/spiritual graces) and *pneumatika* (spirit/spiritual), which together mean *expressions of grace*. The phrase largely refers to two New Testament references where 1 Corinthians 12 describes them as gifts that God gives to the Church by the Holy Spirit for its common good (also see Rom 12:6–8 and 1 Pet 4:10). Then Ephesians 4 speaks of the gifts of the Spirit as given to the church for ministry and the building up of the body of Christ. It is enough to say for our purposes that belief in the gifts of the Spirit are typical among individuals who self-identify with Pentecostal-Charismatic Christianity. See Baptism of the Holy Spirit, *Glossolalia*, Grace, Renewal, and Tongues.

60. ***Glossolalia*:** The Greek word derived from *glōssa* (tongue) and *lalia* (talking), also commonly called "tongues" or "speaking in tongues."

Glossary

Glossolalia is a spiritual gift that enables the Christian to speak in a language (not necessarily an earthly one) that he or she has not learned. Glossolalia refers to one of the New Testament gifts of the Spirit that is endorsed or practiced by many pentecostal and Charismatic Christians and is largely used as a personal prayer language for the believer's edification and also for corporate prayer with its interpretation. Synonymous with the gift of tongues. See Baptism of the Holy Spirit, Gifts of the Spirit, and Pentecostal-Charismatic Christianity, and Tongues.

61. **Grace:** God's unmerited favor generally (to all creation), and specifically in human salvation. In this book, we often refer to grace as God's empowering and transforming presence in the soteriological process mediated to an individual through the Holy Spirit. See Faith, Means of Grace, Sacrament, and Salvation.

62. **Heart Religion:** An orthopathic Christian spirituality that places high value on the importance of a vibrant and meaningful faith. Heart religion is often identified within various traditions following John Wesley's ministry and into the American Holiness, Revivalist, and pentecostal traditions (chapters 7–8). See Affections, Dynamic and Transformational Soteriology, Orthopathy, and Renewal.

63. **Holistic Cognition:** Synonymous with Embodied Cognition. See Embodied Cognition.

64. **Holy Communion:** A central sacrament in most Christian churches referring to the command of Christ to remember his sacrifice of body and blood for the redemption of the Church. See Eucharist, Lord's Supper, and Sacrament.

65. *Imago Dei*: A Latin term for "the image of God" referring to a fundamental tenet of orthodox Christian belief about the nature and purpose of human beings—to grow into and reflect the image of God. See Deification, Divinization, and *Theosis*.

66. **Intellectualism:** In this book, intellectualism refers to the epistemological view that human understanding is acquired primarily through the rational, logical, and objective functions of cognition. Emotions and behavior play little if any role in this process. See Cartesian Dualism, Cognition, Intellectualist Soteriology, Objective, and Orthodoxy-driven Soteriology.

Glossary

67. **Intellectualist Soteriology:** A view of salvation emphasizing intellectual access to knowledge of God and his saving actions in Christ over other cognitive functions like behaviors, affections, and emotions. Such stress on intellect encourages a dualist paradigm of cognition that divides the mind from emotions and behavior and generates static notions of a once-for-all salvation in terms of adherence to right teaching (Introduction and chapter 1). See Intellectualism, Orthodoxy-driven Soteriology, and Soteriology.

68. *Lectio Divina*: Latin for "divine reading." This is an ancient form of reading Scripture (Benedictine) that involves meditation and prayer. It was developed for the purpose of helping the Christian grow in communion with God. In chapter 5, we consider *Lectio Divina* as an example of orthopraxy for soteriological ends. See Canonical Tradition and Orthopraxy.

69. **Liturgy:** A prescribed form of public worship involving specific acts, rituals, and beliefs consistent with a specific religious tradition. Liturgy can be prescribed as in the various "liturgical" churches or recommended-implied as in various expressions of evangelical Christianity. See Doxology, Orthopraxy, and Rites.

70. **Materialism:** The philosophical belief that human life is reducible to *only* its material parts. This belief (excluding various applications of it) claims that the human person is the sum product of the interaction of all its parts and is reducible to matter, regardless how "immaterial" aspects of its existence may appear (i.e., mind, consciousness, soul, spirit). See Materialist and Philosophy.

71. **Materialist:** One who embraces the tenets of materialism. See Materialism.

72. **Means of Grace:** Material elements and practices that—according to the orthodox tradition of the Church—serve as channels or mediums through which God makes his grace available to individuals. By such grace, God takes common things like bread, wine, water, oil, paper, ink, and human speech (prayer, preaching) for uncommonly strengthening and empowering Christian faith and service. See Canonical Theism, Canonical Tradition, Grace, and Sacrament.

73. **Mediated Learning Experience (MLE):** An instructional methodology developed by the late cognitive psychologist, Reuven Feuerstein

Glossary

(b. 1921–2014), to help underperforming children improve their intellectual capacity. MLE presumes an embodied cognitive process as learning is facilitated through the interaction of a mediator who physically engages the learner, enabling him or her to increase comprehension of the learning task at hand (chapter 2). See Cognitive Plasticity, Embodied Cognition, Embodiment, Holistic Cognition, and Neurogenesis.

74. **Neurogenesis:** The growth of new brain cells. In this book, we talk about how certain kinds of instructional models can foster neurogenesis within the learner (chapter 2). See Cognitive Plasticity, Cognitive Science, and Mediated Learning Experience.

75. **Neuroscience:** The scientific study of the nervous system. In chapter 2, we emphasize the role of neuroscience on our understanding of human cognitive function, especially through the research of Antonio Damasio (b. 1944). See Cognitive Psychology and Cognitive Science.

76. **Objective (adj.):** That which is not based on feelings and opinions but on logic, facts, and rational deduction. We use the word "objective" to describe how various epistemological paradigms regard cognition as primarily a rational function of the brain unrelated to its other subjective functions. See Cognition, Intellectualism, Intellectualist Soteriology, and Orthodoxy-driven Soteriology.

77. **Ontology:** A sub-discipline of metaphysics (a branch of philosophy) referring to the study of the nature of being, an entity's fundamental essence, and its relationship to that essence. We mostly deal with ontology in chapters 3–4 where we are interested in Jonathan Edwards' *dispositional ontology* (referring to his way of explaining the essence and nature of human existence and how it relates to salvation). See Dispositional Ontology and Philosophy.

78. **Orthodoxy:** Meaning "right belief" in the context of adherence to the accepted (orthodox) teachings of the Church. In this book we refer to orthodoxy as one of the three domains of a renewal soteriology of embodiment (others are orthopraxy and orthopathy). See Affections, Behavior, Experience, Orthopathy, Orthopraxy, Renewal Soteriology of Embodiment, and Soteriology.

79. **Orthodoxy-driven Soteriology:** A soteriological view that prioritizes the role of orthodoxy in salvation. While orthopraxy and orthopathy

Glossary

may be recognized as important, they bear either a subordinated or negated role in this kind of soteriology. Virtually synonymous with an intellectualist soteriology, it is the soteriological paradigm we challenge in this book from theological, historical, and scientific perspectives. See Intellectualism, Intellectualist Soteriology, Rationalism, and Soteriology.

80. **Orthopathic Soteriology:** A soteriological paradigm emphasizing the transforming role of affectivity in Christian salvation. An orthopathic soteriology highlights the contribution of affections in salvation though it does not limit salvation to affective categories. This soteriological paradigm emphasizes the importance of the Holy Spirit in the Christian life. See Affections, Experience, Orthopathy, Religious Affections, Renewal Soteriology of Embodiment, and Soteriology.

81. **Orthopathos:** A dispositional orientation toward suffering—coined by pentecostal theologian, Samuel Solivan—inviting the liberating power of the Holy Spirit into the midst of one's *pathos*. It is also a theological resource integrating orthodoxy and orthopraxy showing how the Spirit can nurture hope through knowledge and praxis despite persisting circumstances of suffering and oppression (see chapters 7–8). See Affections, Experience, Orthopathic Soteriology, Orthopathy, Pentecostal Orthopathy, and Soteriology.

82. **Orthopathy:** Meaning "right affections." In this book we refer to orthopathy as one of the three domains of a renewal soteriology of embodiment (others are orthodoxy and orthopraxy). We use this term to draw attention to the soteriological significance of affectivity in the mediation of faith. See Affections, Affectivity, Behavior, Experience, Orthodoxy, Orthopraxy, Pentecostal Orthopathy, Renewal Soteriology of Embodiment, and Soteriology.

83. **Orthopraxic Soteriology:** A soteriological view emphasizing the transforming role of praxis in Christian salvation. An orthopraxic soteriology highlights behavior in the order of salvation though it does not limit salvation to behavioral categories. See Behavior, Orthopraxy, Practices, Praxis, Renewal Soteriology of Embodiment, and Soteriology.

84. **Orthopraxy/Orthopraxis:** Both meaning "right actions/behaviors." In this book we refer to orthopraxy as one of the three domains of a renewal soteriology of embodiment (others are orthodoxy and

Glossary

orthopathy). We use this term to draw attention to the soteriological significance of practices and behavior in the mediation of faith. See Affections, Behavior, Orthodoxy, Orthopathy, Practices, Renewal Soteriology of Embodiment, and Soteriology.

85. **Pentecostal Orthopathy:** The emphasis on emotion, feeling, affectivity, and a personally vibrant spirituality among pentecostal Christians. A robust pneumatology and the eschatological expectancy of Christ's imminent return have served to fuel the pentecostal orthopathic impulse. See Affections, Affectivity, Experience, Orthopathy, Orthopathos, Pentecostal Spirituality, Pentecostalism, Pneumatology, Renewal, Renewal Soteriology of Embodiment, and Soteriology.

86. **Pentecostal Spirituality:** The various beliefs, practices, and experiences associated with pentecostal Christianity. Such spirituality remains similar even as the details of its expression vary across the globe. See Affections, Affectivity, Experience, Pentecostal-Charismatic Christianity, Pentecostal Orthopathy, Pentecostal Theology, Pentecostalism, Pneumatology, and Renewal.

87. **Pentecostal Theology:** Theology informed by pentecostal beliefs and practices with a specific focus on the role and significance of the Holy Spirit in theological interdisciplinary reflection. Among other areas of interest, pentecostal theology is concerned with helping to theologically navigate the growing global Pentecostal-Charismatic movement of renewal Christianity (chapters 7–8). See Pentecostal-Charismatic Christianity, Pentecostal Orthopathy, Pentecostal Spirituality, Pentecostalism, Pneumatology, Renewal, and Theology.

88. **Pentecostal-Charismatic (PC) Christianity:** A global Christian renewal movement with an emphasis on the empowering and transforming ministry of the Holy Spirit. Common emphases within this movement include healing-transformation (physical, emotional, interpersonal, communal, political, and economic), worship, prayer, evangelism, vibrancy of faith, practicing the gifts of the Spirit, social justice, and compassion. See Baptism of the Holy Spirit, Gifts of the Spirit, Pentecostal Orthopathy, Pentecostal Spirituality, Pentecostalism, Pneumatology, and Renewal.

89. **Pentecostalism:** A type of renewal movement within Protestant Christianity marked by personal encounter with God through the baptism of the Holy Spirit, the gifts of the Spirit, and their contemporary

Glossary

relevance for empowered ministry and personal spiritual growth. Pentecostal Christianity demonstrates an orthopathic sensibility within a wide variety of charismatic Christian expressions and traditions around the world. See Baptism of the Holy Spirit, Gifts of the Spirit, Pentecostal Orthopathy, Pentecostal-Charismatic Christianity, Pentecostal Spirituality, Pentecostal Theology, Pneumatology, and Renewal.

90. ***Philokalia*:** A compilation of writings spanning the fourth to fifteenth centuries and used as a guide to implement long-term practices to sustain godly habits for continued growth into the life of God.[3] See Canonical Tradition, Catechetical, and Orthopraxy.

91. **Philosophy:** A particular branch of thought or way of thinking (i.e., one's business philosophy). More commonly, the study of thought on the fundamental issues of life, such as the nature of existence, morality, ethics, religion, the mind, and language. For our purposes, philosophy is a useful tool for theological reflection (i.e., Jonathan Edwards' philosophical theology). See Dispositional Ontology and Ontology.

92. **Pneumatology:** In Christian theology, pneumatology is the study of the Holy Spirit. Herein, pneumatology plays a vital role in our renewal soteriology of embodiment. See Pentecostal-Charismatic Christianity, Pentecostal Spirituality, Pentecostalism, Renewal, Renewal Soteriology of Embodiment, and Theology.

93. **Postliberal Theology:** A type of theology, founded by George Lindbeck (b. 1923), motivated by ecumenical concerns regarding divergent doctrinal beliefs in intra and inter-religious discussion. Lindbeck contends that religious knowledge evolves out of reflection on the practices one has adopted as part of a religious community. For more, see chapter 5. See Behavior, Doctrine, Ecumenical, Orthodoxy, Orthopraxy, Practices, and Praxis.

94. **Practices:** In this book, practices refer to various behaviors and actions involved in the process of human cognition. We refer to practices as one of three domains (others are intellect and affections) used in our holistic discussion of cognition and our proposal of a renewal soteriology of embodiment. Interchangeable with our use of behavior

---

3. Aquino, "Epistemic Virtues," 184.

Glossary

and praxis. See Behavior, Orthopraxy, Praxis, and Renewal Soteriology of Embodiment.

95. **Praxis:** Synonymous with Behavior and Practices. See Behavior, Practices, and Orthopraxy.

96. **Propositional Knowledge:** Knowledge that is rationally deduced, logical, and often used for instructional purposes. We refer to propositional knowledge as an objective rather than subjective type of knowledge and is the preferred kind of knowledge in an intellectualist epistemology. See Cartesian Dualism, Intellectualism, Intellectualist Soteriology, Objective, Orthodoxy-driven Soteriology, and Rationalism.

97. **Punctiliar:** Having to do with occurring in a particular point in time. This term is used in describing our third presupposition of an intellectualist soteriology (chapter 1). See Intellectualist Soteriology.

98. **Rationalism:** A philosophy that places extreme confidence in the human mind's ability to logically reason. Rationalism asserts that reason should be the foundation of certainty in knowing. Hence, affectivity, subjectivity, emotions, feelings, and experiences are subordinated or rejected in its epistemological framework. See Cartesian Dualism, Intellectualism, Intellectualist Soteriology, Objective, Orthodoxy-driven Soteriology, and Propositional Knowledge.

99. **Religious Affections:** These are the result of dispositional transformation in Jonathan Edwards' dispositional ontology and the goal of his soteriological paradigm. Edwards describes the affections as a divinely endowed desire for the love and beauty of God's glory. They are the result of corrupted human dispositions transformed by the Spirit into the qualities of Christ (chapters 3–4). See Affections, Affectivity, Disposition, Dispositional Ontology, and Pneumatology.

100. **Renewal:** The process of restoration or being made new. For our purposes, renewal has to do with the transforming and life-giving ministry of the Holy Spirit in the work of salvation. In general, we use "renewal" to theologically identify with a pneumatological emphasis. It also refers to the global and interdenominational movement of pentecostal, Charismatic, and Spirit-filled forms of Christianity. See Baptism of the Holy Spirit, Gifts of the Spirit, Grace, Pentecostal-Charismatic Christianity, Pentecostalism, Pneumatology, and Renewal Soteriology.

Glossary

101. **Renewal Soteriology:** A soteriological paradigm emphasizing the transforming power of the Holy Spirit and the dynamic mediation of saving faith. A renewal soteriology understands faith in dynamic—as opposed to static—terms, and conceives salvation as an ongoing process of conversion characterized in diverse capacities. See Dynamic and Transformational Soteriology, Embodiment, Renewal, Renewal Soteriology of Embodiment, and Soteriology.

102. **Renewal Soteriology of Embodiment:** A view of salvation that conceives faith inseparably from human embodiment. A renewal soteriology of embodiment is a pneumatologically robust soteriological paradigm emphasizing faith as an embodied reality mediated via orthodoxy, orthopraxy, and orthopathy. See Dynamic and Transformational Soteriology, Embodiment, Orthodoxy, Orthopathy, Orthopraxy, Renewal, Renewal Soteriology, and Soteriology.

103. **Rite:** A sacred practice used in a religious context. We speak of the canonical tradition as often involving various rites. See Behavior, Canonical Tradition, Orthopraxy, Practice, and Praxis.

104. **Rule of Faith:** Ancient foundational core teachings of the Church initially given by Jesus to the disciples and amended by the Apostles to the early Church. The Rule of Faith was part of the canonical tradition, a compilation of core theological beliefs to which the early Church referred, and the standard against which Scripture was read to aid in interpretation. See Canonical Tradition, Catechesis, Catechetical Schools, and Doctrine.

105. **Sacrament:** A religious ceremony or symbol used to mediate the grace of God. The most common sacraments we address are baptism, the Eucharist, and Scripture. Sacraments reflect the soteriological significance of orthopraxis. See Canonical Tradition, Grace, Means of Grace, and Salvation.

106. **Salvation (or Doctrine of Salvation):** Despite its expansive use, it is enough to say that among conservative Christians "salvation" always (even if partially) has to do with the message Jesus preached, how he preached it, and what he accomplished through his death and resurrection. Salvation is also related to a new quality of life Jesus brought to the world—individually, interpersonally, and cosmically (Preface). See Deification, Divinization, Dynamic and Transformational Soteriology, Renewal Soteriology of Embodiment, Soteriology, and *Theosis*.

Glossary

107. **Salvation in the Flesh:** The title of this book, referring to the need of an embodied soteriology. A view of salvation illustrating faith as inseparable from the body. Faith is understood as more than the product of intellect (orthodoxy) but also ensues from the practice of certain behaviors (orthopraxy) and the affective experience of the transforming work of the Spirit (orthopathy). See Embodiment, Renewal Soteriology of Embodiment, Salvation, and Soteriology.

108. **Social Justice:** Efforts to right inequality, injustice, abuse, and oppression of the marginalized and those who have no voice to speak for themselves. In this book, social justice is seen as an expression of an orthopraxic soteriology and is effectively seen in the ministry of Evangelicals for Social Action. See Evangelicals for Social Action, Orthopraxic Soteriology, and Orthopraxy.

109. **Soteriology:** The study of various religions' doctrines of salvation. Our purposes are concerned with the study of salvation within the context of conservative Christianity. See Dynamic and Transformational Soteriology, Intellectualist Soteriology, Renewal Soteriology, Renewal Soteriology of Embodiment, Salvation, and Theology.

110. **Static:** Lacking in movement, activity, change. Not dynamic or vibrant. We use this term to describe an intellectualist soteriology. See Intellectualist Soteriology and Orthodoxy-driven Soteriology.

111. **Subjective:** Having to do with opinions, emotions, or experience. We use the term to speak of the affectivity of cognition. There are objective aspects of knowing—dealing with logic, facts, and evidence—and subjective aspects—dealing with emotions, feelings, and experience. See Affections, Affectivity, Experience, and Orthopathy.

112. **The Lord's Supper:** A central sacrament in most Christian churches referring to the command of Christ to remember his sacrifice of body and blood for the redemption of the world. See Eucharist, Holy Communion, Means of Grace, and Sacrament.

113. **Theology:** The study of God and religious belief. See Doctrine, Renewal Theology of Embodiment, and Soteriology.

114. **Theosis:** The belief that God's purpose for humanity is to become like him by sharing in his nature. Hence, the purpose of every Christian Church is to help believers grow in union with God. See Deification, Divinization, Grace, and Salvation.

Glossary

115. **Tongues:** One of the "speaking" gifts of the Spirit involving praying in a language one has not learned. Intended for the edification of the Christian, also known as a personal prayer language (1 Cor 14:4) and for its public practice in the Church as accompanied with an interpretation (1 Cor 14:5). Synonymous with *glossolalia*. See Baptism of the Holy Spirit, Gifts of the Spirit, and *Glossolalia*.

116. **Wesley's Aldersgate Experience:** John Wesley's (1703–1791) profound experience of divine presence on May 24, 1738 at a meeting on Aldersgate Street in London in which he described his heart to be "strangely warmed" by the presence of Christ. This experience profoundly impacted Wesley's life and ministry and informed his subsequent propagation of "heart religion." See Affections, Heart Religion, Orthopathy, and Renewal.

117. **Western Christianity:** Consists of the Latin portion of the Roman Catholic Church and much of Protestantism. Western Christianity emerged and predominated throughout Europe and the Western hemisphere. For the purposes of this book, we focus on and challenge certain intellectual legacies that have developed a foundational impact on Western Christian soteriology. See Cartesian, Cartesian Dualism, Conservative Christianity, Intellectualism, Orthodoxy-driven Soteriology, Soteriology, and Theology.

118. **Works Salvation:** A soteriological paradigm emphasizing (whether implicitly or explicitly) good works and moral behavior—rather than faith—as the basis for salvation. See Behavior, Faith, Grace, Practices, Praxis, and Salvation.

Bibliography

Abraham, William. *Aldersgate and Athens: John Wesley and the Foundations of Christian Belief.* Waco, TX: Baylor University Press, 2013.
———. *Canon and Criterion in Christian Theology: From the Fathers to Feminism.* New York: Oxford University Press, 1998.
———. "Canonical Theism and the Life of the Church." In *Canonical Theism: A Proposal for Theology and the Church*, edited by Abraham et al., 303–15. Grand Rapids: Eerdmans, 2008.
———. "Canonical Theism: Thirty Theses." In *Canonical Theism: A Proposal for Theology and the Church*, edited by Abraham et al., 1–7. Grand Rapids: Eerdmans, 2008.
———. *Crossing the Threshold of Divine Revelation.* Grand Rapids: Eerdmans, 2006.
———. "The Emergence of Canonical Theism." In *Canonical Theism: A Proposal for Theology and the Church*, edited by Abraham et al., 141–55. Grand Rapids: Eerdmans, 2008.
———. "Introduction." In *Canonical Theism: A Proposal for Theology and the Church*, edited by Abraham et al., xii–ix. Grand Rapids: Eerdmans, 2008.
———. *The Logic of Evangelism.* Grand Rapids: Eerdmans, 1989.
———. *The Logic of Renewal.* Grand Rapids: Eerdmans, 2003.
Abraham, William, et al., eds. *Canonical Theism: A Proposal for Theology and the Church.* Grand Rapids: Eerdmans, 2008.
Alexander, Estrelda Y. *Black Fire: One Hundred Years of African American Pentecostalism.* Downers Grove, IL: IVP Academic, 2011.
The Alliance. "The Alliance Stand." http://www.cmalliance.org/about/beliefs/doctrine.
Aquinas, Thomas. *The Summa Theologica.* Great Books of the Western World 20. Chicago: Encyclopedia Britannica, 1952.
Aquino, Frederick D. "Epistemic Virtues of a Theologian in the Philokalia." In *Canonical Theism: A Proposal for Theology and the Church*, edited by Abraham et al., 175–94. Grand Rapids: Eerdmans, 2008.
Aristotle. *Metaphysics.* Translated by Hippocrates G. Apostle. Bloomington, IN: Indiana University Press, 1966.
The Assemblies of God. "The Salvation of Man." http://ag.org/top/Beliefs/Statement_of_Fundamental_Truths/sft_full.cfm#5.
The Assemblies of God. "Statement on Revival." http://ag.org/top/Beliefs/Official_Statements.
Aulén, Gustaf. *Christus Victor: An Historical Study of the Three Main Types of the Idea of Atonement.* New York: Macmillan, 1969.

Bibliography

Barr, James. *Fundamentalism.* Philadelphia: Westminster, 1977.
Bebbington, David. *The Dominance of Evangelicalism: The Age of Spurgeon and Moody.* Downers Grove, IL: InterVarsity, 2005.
Borod, Joan C., ed. *The Neuropsychology of Emotion.* New York: Oxford University Press, 2000.
Boyd, Gregory. *Trinity and Process: A Critical Evaluation and Reconstruction of Hartshorne's Di-Polar Theism Towards a Trinitarian Metaphysics.* New York: Peter Lang, 1992.
Bradshaw, Paul. *Early Christian Worship: A Basic Introduction to Ideas and Practice.* Collegeville, MN: The Liturgical Press, 1996.
Brothers, Leslie. *Friday's Footprints: How Society Shapes the Human Mind.* New York: Oxford University Press, 1997.
Bruner, Frederick Dale. *A Theology of the Holy Spirit: The Pentecostal Experience and the New Testament Witness.* Grand Rapids: Eerdmans. 1970.
Burgess, Ruth V. "Reuven Feuerstein: Propelling Change, Promoting Continuity." In *Experience of Mediated Learning: An Impact of Feuerstein's Theory in Education and Psychology,* edited by Alex Kozulin and Yaacov Rand, 3–20. Elmsford, NY: Pergamon, 2000.
Burgess, Stanley M. *The Holy Spirit: Ancient Christian Traditions.* Peabody, MA: Hendrickson, 1984.
Calvin, John. *Institutes of the Christian Religion.* 2 vols. Translated by Ford Lewis Battles. Philadelphia: Westminster, 1960.
Carnell, Edward J. *The Case for Orthodox Theology.* Philadelphia: Westminster, 1959.
Cartwright, Nancy. *How the Laws of Physics Lie.* New York: Oxford University Press, 1983.
Castelo, Daniel. "Canonical Theism as Ecclesial and Ecumenical Resource." *Pneuma* 33 (2011) 370–89.
———. *Revisioning Pentecostal Ethics: The Epicletic Community.* Cleveland, TN: CPT, 2012.
Cherry, Conrad. *The Theology of Jonathan Edwards: A Reappraisal.* Gloucester, MA: Peter Smith, 1974.
Chopp, Rebecca S., and Sheila Greeve Davaney, eds. *Horizons in Feminist Theology: Identity, Tradition, and Norms.* Minneapolis: Fortress, 1997.
Christensen, Michael J. and Wittung, Jeffery A., eds. *Partakers of the Divine Nature: The History and Development of Deification in the Christian Tradition.* Grand Rapids: Rosemont, 2007.
Church of God. "Church of God Is . . ." http://www.churchofgod.org/beliefs/church-of-god-is.
Church of God in Christ. "What We Believe." http://www.cogic.org/about-company.
Church of God in Christ. "Statement of Faith." http://www.cogic.org/about-company.
The Church of the Nazarene. "Agreed Statement of Belief." http://nazarene.org/beliefs.
Clapper, Gregory S. *John Wesley on Religious Affections: His Views on Experience and Emotion and their Role in the Christian Life and Theology.* Metuchen, NJ: Scarecrow, 1989.
———. *Renewal of the Heart is the Mission of the Church: Wesley's Heart Religion in the Twenty-First Century.* Eugene, OR: Wipf and Stock, 2010.
Collins, Kenneth J. "Twentieth-Century Interpretations of John Wesley's Aldersgate Experience: Coherence or Confusion?" *Wesleyan Theological Journal* 24 (1989) 18–31.

Bibliography

Coulter, Dale. "Delivered by the Power of God: Toward a Pentecostal Understanding of Salvation." *International Journal of Systematic Theology* 10 (2008) 447–67.

Coulter, Dale and Amos Yong, eds. *The Spirit, The Affections, and the Christian Tradition.* Notre Dame: University of Notre Dame Press, 2016.

Crisp, Oliver D. "Jonathan Edwards's Ontology: A Critique of Sang Hyun Lee's Dispositional Account of Edwardsian Metaphysics." *Religious Studies* 46 (2010) 1–20.

Crutchfield, Larry V. *The Origins of Dispensationalism: The Darby Factor.* Lanham, MD: University Press of America, 1992.

Cyril, St. *The Works of St. Cyril of Jerusalem.* The Fathers of the Church 1. Translated by Leo P. McCauley (S. J.) and Anthony A. Stephenson. Washington, DC: The Catholic University of America Press, 1969.

———. *The Works of St. Cyril of Jerusalem.* The Fathers of the Church 2. Translated by Leo P. McCauley (S. J.) and Anthony A. Stephenson. Washington, DC: The Catholic University of America Press, 1970.

Dabney, Lyle D. "Justified by the Spirit: Soteriological Reflections on the Resurrection." *International Journal of Systematic Theology* 3 (2001) 46–68.

———. "What Has Aldersgate to do with Wittenberg?" *Lutheran Forum* 42 (2008) 47–50.

———. "Why Should the Last be First? The Priority of Pneumatology in Recent Theological Discussion." In *Advents of the Spirit: An Introduction to the Current Study of Pneumatology,* edited by Lyle D. Dabney and Bradford E. Hinze, 240–61. Milwaukee: Marquette University Press, 2001.

Damasio, Antonio. *Descartes' Error: Emotion, Reason, and the Human Brain.* New York: Penguin, 1994.

———. *The Feeling of What Happens: Body and Emotion in the Making of Consciousness.* New York: Harcourt Brace, 1999.

———. *Looking for Spinoza: Joy, Sorrow, and the Feeling Brain.* San Diego: Harcourt, 2003.

Damaskos, St. Peter. "Treasury of Divine Knowledge." In *The Philokalia,* vol. 3, edited by G. E. H. Palmer et al., 74–210. London: Faber & Faber, 1983.

Daniel, Stephen H. *The Philosophy of Jonathan Edwards: A Study in Divine Semiotics.* Bloomington, IN: Indiana University Press, 1994.

Dayton, Donald. "The Pietist Theological Critique of Biblical Inerrancy." In *Evangelicals and Scripture: Tradition, Authority, and Hermeneutics,* edited by Vincent E. Bacote et al., 76–92. Downers Grove, IL: InterVarsity, 2004.

———. *The Theological Roots of Pentecostalism.* Peabody, MA: Hendrickson, 1987.

Deane-Drummond, Celia E. *Gaia and Green Ethics: Implications of Ecological Theology.* Bramcote, UK: Grove, 1993.

Dennett, Daniel. *Consciousness Explained.* New York: Back Bay Books; Little, Brown and Co., 1991.

———. *Kinds of Minds: Toward an Understanding of Consciousness.* New York: Basic, 1996.

Dorrien, Gary J. *The Remaking of Evangelical Theology.* Louisville, KY: Westminster John Knox, 1998.

Duffield, Guy P. and Van Cleave, N. M. *Foundations of Pentecostal Theology.* Los Angeles: L. I. F. E. Bible College, 1983.

Edwards, Jonathan. "Concerning the End for Which God Created the World." In *Ethical Writings,* edited by Paul Ramsey, 405–538. The Works of Jonathan Edwards 8. New Haven: Yale University Press, 1989.

Bibliography

———. "Devotion." In *The Miscellanies, (Entry Nos. a-z, aa-zz, 1–500)*, edited by Thomas A. Schafer, 189–91. The Works of Jonathan Edwards 13. New Haven: Yale University Press, 1994.

———. "Discourse on the Trinity." In *Writings on the Trinity, Grace, and Faith*, edited by Sang Huyn Lee, 106–45. The Works of Jonathan Edwards 21. New Haven: Yale University Press, 1959.

———. "A Divine and Supernatural Light, Immediately Imparted to the Soul by the Spirit of God, Shown to be Both a Scriptural and Rational Doctrine." In *A Jonathan Edwards Reader*, edited by John E. Smith, Harry S. Stout, and Kenneth P. Minkema, 105–23. New Haven: Yale University Press, 1995.

———. "End of the Creation." In *The Miscellanies, (Entry Nos. 1153–1360)*, edited by Douglas A. Sweeney, 150–53. The Works of Jonathan Edwards 23. New Haven: Yale University Press, 2004.

———. "End of the Creation." In *The Miscellanies, (Entry Nos. a-z, aa-zz, 1–500)*, edited by Thomas A. Schafer, 495–96. The Works of Jonathan Edwards 13. New Haven: Yale University Press, 1994.

———. "A Faithful Narrative of the Surprising Work of God." In *The Great Awakening*, edited by C. C. Goen, 97–211. The Works of Jonathan Edwards 4. New Haven: Yale University Press, 2009.

———. *Freedom of the Will*, edited by Paul Ramsey. The Works of Jonathan Edwards 1. New Haven: Yale University Press, 2009.

———. "The Mind." In *Scientific and Philosophical Writings*, edited by Wallace E. Anderson, 332–86. The Works of Jonathan Edwards 6. New Haven: Yale University Press, 1980.

———. "The Nature of True Virtue." In *Ethical Writings*, edited by Paul Ramsey, 539–630. The Works of Jonathan Edwards 8. New Haven: Yale University Press, 1989.

———. "Of Atoms." In *Scientific and Philosophical Writings*, edited by Wallace E. Anderson, 208–19. The Works of Jonathan Edwards 6. New Haven: Yale University Press, 1980.

———. "On the Equality of the Persons of the Trinity." In *Writings on the Trinity, Grace, and Faith*, edited by Sang Huyn Lee, 146–48. The Works of Jonathan Edwards 21. New Haven: Yale University Press, 1959.

———. "Part Four, Chapter Two." In *Original Sin*, edited by Clyde A. Holbrook, 380–88. The Works of Jonathan Edwards 3. New Haven: Yale University Press, 1970.

———. "The Religious Affections." In *Religious Affections*, edited by John E. Smith, 91–465. The Works of Jonathan Edwards 2. New Haven: Yale University Press, 1959.

———. "Regeneration." In *The Miscellanies, (Entry Nos. a-z, aa-zz, 1–500)*, edited by Thomas A. Schafer, 245–46. The Works of Jonathan Edwards 13. New Haven: Yale University Press, 1994.

———. "Regeneration." In *The Miscellanies, (Entry Nos. a-z, aa-zz, 1–500)*, edited by Thomas A. Schafer, 357–58. The Works of Jonathan Edwards 13. New Haven: Yale University Press, 1994.

———. "Spiritual Knowledge." In *The Miscellanies, (Entry Nos. a-z, aa-zz, 1–500)*, edited by Thomas A. Schafer, 469–70. The Works of Jonathan Edwards 13. New Haven: Yale University Press, 1994.

———. "A Spiritual Understanding of Divine Things." In *Sermons and Discourses, 1723–1729*, edited by Kenneth P. Minkema, 70–97. The Works of Jonathan Edwards 14. New Haven: Yale University Press, 1999.

Bibliography

———. "Subjects to Be Handled in the Treatise on the Mind." In *Scientific and Philosophical Writings*, edited by Wallace E. Anderson, 387–93. The Works of Jonathan Edwards 6. New Haven: Yale University Press, 1980.

———. "Treatise on Grace." In *Writings on the Trinity, Grace, and Faith*, edited by Sang Hyun Lee, 150–99. The Works of Jonathan Edwards 21. New Haven: Yale University Press, 1959.

Enrichment Journal, "Pentecost—Resource List." *Enrichment* 1 (2005) lines 17–18. http://enrichmentjournal.ag.org/200501/200501_resourcelist.cfm.

Erickson, Millard J. *Christian Theology*. Grand Rapids: Baker, 1985.

———. *Introducing Christian Doctrine*. 2nd ed. Grand Rapids: Baker Academic, 2001.

Evangelicals for Social Action. *Chicago Declaration of Evangelical Social Concern*. http://www.evangelicalsforsocialaction.org/about/history/chicago-declaration-of-evangelical-social-concern.

———. "Holistic Ministry Defined." http://www.evangelicalsforsocialaction.org/holistic-ministry/holisticministrydefined.

———. "Shouldn't we be Focused on Evangelism?" http://www.evangelicalsforsocialaction.org/resources/esa-history/faqs.

Evans, William B. *Imputation and Impartation: Union with Christ in American Reformed Theology*. Milton Keynes, UK: Paternoster, 2008.

Faupel, David W. *The Everlasting Gospel: The Significance of Eschatology in Pentecostal Thought*. Sheffield: Sheffield Academic, 1996.

Ferguson, Everett. "Baptism." In *Encyclopedia of Early Christianity*, edited by Everett Ferguson, 131–34. New York: Garland, 1900.

———. "Eucharist." In *Encyclopedia of Early Christianity*, edited by Everett Ferguson, 320–24. New York: Garland, 1900.

Feuerstein, Rafi S. "Dynamic Cognitive Assessment and the Instrumental Enrichment Program: Origins and Development." In *Experience of Mediated Learning: An Impact of Feuerstein's Theory in Education and Psychology*, edited by Alex Kozulin, and Yaacov Rand, 147–65. Elmsford, NY: Pergamon, 2000.

Feuerstein, Reuven. *Instrumental Enrichment: An Intervention Program for Cognitive Modifiability*. Baltimore: University Park, 1980.

Feuerstein, Reuven, et al. *Beyond Smarter*. New York: Teachers College, 2010.

Feuerstein, Reuven, et al. *The Dynamic Assessment of Cognitive Modifiability*. Jerusalem, Israel: International Center for the Enhancement of Learning Potential, 2002.

Feuerstein, Reuven, et al. *Don't Accept Me as I Am: Helping "Retarded" People to Excel*. New York: Plenum, 1988.

Feuerstein, Shmuel. *Biblical and Talmudic Antecedents of Mediated Learning Experience Theory: Educational and Didactic Implications for Inter-Generational Cultural Transmission*. Israel: The International Center for the Enhancement of Learning Potential, 2002.

Finch, David. *The End of Evangelicalism: Discerning a New Faithfulness for Mission*. Eugene, OR: Cascade, 2011.

Forbush, William Byron, ed. *Fox's Book of Martyrs: A History of the Lives, Sufferings, and Triumphant Deaths of the Early Christian and the Protestant Martyrs*. Grand Rapids: Zondervan, 1954.

Foster, Richard, *Streams of Living Water: Essential Practices from the Six Great Traditions of Christian Faith*. New York: HarperCollins, 1998.

Bibliography

Frank, Robert H. *Passions within Reason: The Strategic Role of the Emotions*. New York: W. W. Norton, 1988.

Gavrilyuk, Paul, et al., eds. *Immersed in the Life of God: The Healing Resources of the Christian Faith, Essays in Honor of William J. Abraham*. Grand Rapids: Eerdmans, 2008.

Gelpi, Donald L. *The Conversion Experience: A Reflective Process for RCIA Participants and Others*. Mahwah, NJ: Paulist, 1998.

Gregory of Nazianzus. "Letter 101." Vol. 7 of *Nicene and Post-Nicene Fathers*, edited by Phillip Schaff, 440. Peabody, MA: Hendrickson, 1995.

Grenz, Stanley J. "Deconstructing Epistemological Certainty in Theology: An Engagement with William J. Abraham's *Canon and Criterion in Christian Theology*." *Wesleyan Theological Journal* 36 (2001) 37–45.

Grider, J. Kenneth. *Entire Sanctification: The Distinctive Doctrine of Wesleyanism*. Kansas City: Beacon Hill, 1980.

Grudem, Wayne. *Systematic Theology: An Introduction to Biblical Doctrine*. Grand Rapids: Zondervan, 1994.

Gutenson, Charles. "The Canonical Heritage of the Church as Means of Grace." In *Canonical Theism: A Proposal for Theology and the Church*, edited by Abraham et al., 244–55. Grand Rapids: Eerdmans, 2008.

Gutiérrez, Gustavo. *A Theology of Liberation*. Revised edition. Translated and edited by Sister Caridad Inda and John Eagleson. Marynoll, NY: Orbis, 1988.

Haidt, Jonathan. *The Righteous Mind: Why Good People Are Divided by Politics and Religion*. New York: Pantheon, 2012.

Herbert of Cherbury, Lord Edward. *De Veritate*. Translated by Meyrick H. Carre. Bristol: J. W. Arrowsmith, 1937.

Herrnstein, Richard J. and Murray, Charles. *The Bell Curve: Intelligence and Class Structure in American Life*. New York: Simon & Shuster, 1996.

Hodge, Charles. *Systematic Theology*. 3 vols. Grand Rapids: Eerdmans, 1952.

Hoffecker, Andrew W. *Piety and the Princeton Theologians: Archibald Alexander, Charles Hodge, Benjamin Warfield*. Grand Rapids: Baker, 1981.

Hollenweger, Walter. "After Twenty Years' Research on Pentecostalism." *International Review of Mission* 75 (1986) 3–12.

Holmes, Stephen R. "Does Jonathan Edwards Use a Dispositional Ontology? A Response to Sang Hyun Lee." In *Jonathan Edwards: Philosophical Theologian*, edited by Paul Helm and Oliver D. Crisp, 99–114. Aldershot, UK: Ashgate, 2003.

Hoopes, James. "The Philosophical Theology of Jonathan Edwards." *Journal of Religion* 70 (1990) 258.

Hopkins, Samuel. *The System of Doctrines: Contained in Divine Revelation, Explained and Defended*, vol. 1. Boston: Isaiah Thomas and Ebenezer T. Andrews, 1793.

Hunter, Archibald M. *The Gospel According to St. Paul: A Revised Edition of "Interpreting Paul's Gospel."* Philadelphia: Westminster, 1966.

Jenson, Robert W. *America's Theologian: A Recommendation of Jonathan Edwards*. Oxford: Oxford University Press, 1988.

Johns, Cheryl Bridges. "Partners in Scandal: Wesleyan and Pentecostal Scholarship." *Pneuma* 21 (1999) 183–97.

Kärkkäinen, Veli-Matti. *Trinity and Religious Pluralism: The Doctrine of the Trinity in Christian Theology of Religions*. Aldershot, UK: Ashgate, 2004.

Bibliography

Keller, Catherine, et al., eds. *Postcolonial Theologies: Divinity and Empire*. St. Louis: Chalice, 2004.
Kelsey, D. H. *The Uses of Scripture in Recent Theology*. Philadelphia: Fortress, 1975.
King, Gerald W. *Disfellowshiped: Pentecostal Responses to Fundamentalism in the United States, 1906-1943*. Eugene, OR: Pickwick, 2011.
Knight III, Henry H. *From Aldersgate to Azusa Street: Wesleyan, Holiness, and Pentecostal Visions of the New Creation*. Eugene, OR: Pickwick, 2010.
Koskela, Douglas M. "The Authority of Scripture in Its Ecclesial Context." In *Canonical Theism: A Proposal for Theology and the Church*, edited by Abraham, Vickers, and Van Kirk, 210-23. Grand Rapids: Eerdmans, 2008.
Kostlevy, William. "The Dispensationalists: Embarrassing Relatives or Prophets Without Honor: Reflections on Mark Noll's *The Scandal of the Evangelical Mind*." *Wesleyan Theological Journal* 32 (1997) 187-92.
Kuhn, Thomas. *The Structure of Scientific Revolutions*. Chicago: University of Chicago Press, 2012.
Lakoff, George and Johnson, Mark. *Philosophy in the Flesh: The Embodied Mind and its Challenge to Western Thought*. New York: Basic, 1999.
Ladd, George E. *The Gospel of the Kingdom: Scriptural Studies in the Kingdom of God*. 1959. Reprint, Exeter, UK: Paternoster, 2000.
Land, Steven J. *Pentecostal Spirituality: A Passion for the Kingdom*. Sheffield: Sheffield, 1993.
Lane, Richard D. and Nadel, Lynn, eds. *Cognitive Neuroscience of Emotions*. New York: Oxford University Press, 2000.
Lee, Sang Hyun. "The Christian Doctrine of the Trinity in Jonathan Edwards' Context." In *Writings on the Trinity, Grace, and Faith*, edited by Sang Hyun Lee, 2-6. The Works of Jonathan Edwards 21. New Haven: Yale University Press, 2002.
———. "Edwards and Beauty." In *Understanding Jonathan Edwards: An Introduction to America's Theologian*, edited by Gerald McDermott, 113-25. New York: Oxford University Press, 2009.
———. "Jonathan Edwards's Dispositional Conception of the Trinity: A Resource for Contemporary Reformed Theology." In *Toward the Future of Reformed Theology*, edited by David Willis and Michael Welker, 444-55. Grand Rapids: Eerdmans, 1999.
———. *The Philosophical Theology of Jonathan Edwards*. Princeton: Princeton University Press, 1988.
Leon, Chai. *Jonathan Edwards and the Limits of Enlightenment Philosophy*. New York: Oxford University Press, 1998.
Lindbeck, George A. "Canon and Criterion in Christian Theology: From the Fathers to Feminism." *First Things* 92 (1999) 68.
———. *The Church in a Postliberal Age*. Grand Rapids: Eerdmans, 2002.
———. *The Nature of Doctrine: Religion and Theology in a Postliberal Age*. Philadelphia: Westminster, 1984.
Livingston, James C. *Modern Christian Thought: The Enlightenment and the Nineteenth Century*, 2nd ed. Minneapolis: Fortress, 2006.
Lossky, Vladimir. *The Mystical Theology of the Eastern Church*. Crestwood, NY: St. Vladimir's Seminary Press, 1976.
Lovelace, C. "Invitation to the Mourner's Bench." *Union Seminary Quarterly Review* 17 (1962) 231-37.
MacArthur, John. *Charismatic Chaos*. Grand Rapids: Zondervan, 1992.

Bibliography

———. *The Charismatics: A Doctrinal Perspective*. Grand Rapids: Zondervan, 1978.
———. *Speaking in Tongues*. Chicago: Moody, 1988.
Macchia, Frank. *Baptized in the Spirit: A Global Pentecostal Theology*. Grand Rapids: Zondervan, 2006.
———. "Justification through New Creation: The Holy Spirit and the Doctrine by which the Church Stands or Falls." *Theology Today* 58 (2001) 202–17.
———. *Justified in the Spirit: Creation, Redemption, and the Triune God*. Pentecostal Manifestos. Grand Rapids: Eerdmans, 2010.
Mack, Phyllis. *Heart Religion in the British Enlightenment: Gender and Emotion in Early Methodism*. New York: Cambridge University Press, 2008.
Maddox, Randy, ed. *Aldersgate Reconsidered*. Nashville: Kingswood, 1990.
———. *Responsible Grace: John Wesley's Practical Theology*. Nashville: Kingswood, 1994.
———. "Responsible Grace: The Systematic Perspective of Wesleyan Theology." *Wesleyan Theological Journal* 19 (1984) 7–22.
Mann, Mark. *Perfecting Grace, Human Being, and the Sciences*. New York: T. & T. Clark, 2006.
Markham, Paul N. *Rewired: Exploring Religious Conversion*. Eugene, OR: Pickwick, 2007.
Martin, J. Louis. *Theological Issues in the Letters of Paul*. Edinburgh, Scotland: T. & T. Clark Ltd., 1997.
Martyr, Justin. "The First Apology." In *The Apostolic Fathers with Justin Martyr and Irenaeus*, edited by Alexander Roberts and James Donaldson, 163–87. Ante-Nicean Fathers 1. Grand Rapids: Eerdmans, 1985.
Masini, Mario. *Lectio Divina: An Ancient Prayer that is Ever New*. Translated by Edmund C. Lane. New York: Alba, 1998.
McClymond, Michael J. "Salvation as Divinization: Jonathan Edwards, Gregory Palamas, and the Theological Uses of Neoplatonism." In *Jonathan Edwards: Philosophical Theologian*, edited by Paul Helm and Oliver D. Crisp, 139–60. Aldershot, UK: Ashgate, 2003.
McDermott, Gerald. "Conclusion: Edwards's Relevance Today." In *Understanding Jonathan Edwards: An Introduction to America's Theologian*, edited by Gerald McDermott, 201–17. New York: Oxford University Press, 2009.
———. "Introduction." In *Understanding Jonathan Edwards: An Introduction to America's Theologian*, edited by Gerald McDermott, 3–13. New York: Oxford University Press, 2009.
———. *Jonathan Edwards Confronts the Gods: Christian Theology, Enlightenment, and Non-Christian Faiths*. New York: Oxford University Press, 2000.
———. *One Holy and Happy Society: The Public Theology of Jonathan Edwards*. University Park: Pennsylvania State University Press, 1992.
McKinion, Steven A., ed. *Life and Practice in the Early Church: A Documentary Reader*. New York: New York University Press, 2001.
Mills, Steve. "Renewal of the Mind: The Cognitive Sciences and a Pneumatological Anthropology of Transformation." PhD diss., Regent University, 2014.
Molnar, George. *Powers: A Study in Metaphysics*. Edited by Stephen Mumford. Oxford: Oxford University Press, 2003.
Morimoto, Anri. *Jonathan Edwards and The Catholic Vision of Salvation*. University Park: University of Pennsylvania Press, 1995.
Mumford, Stephen. *Dispositions*. Oxford: Oxford University Press, 1998.
———. *Laws in Nature*. New York: Routledge, 2004.

Bibliography

Myland, David Wesley. *The Latter Rain Covenant and Pentecostal Power*. Chicago: Evangel, 1910.

Neumann, Peter D. *Pentecostal Experience: An Ecumenical Encounter*. Eugene, OR: Pickwick, 2012.

Nevin, John Williamson. *The Mystical Presence: A Vindication of the Reformed or Calvinistic Doctrine of the Holy Eucharist*. Edited by Augustine Thompson. 1846. Reprint, Eugene, OR: Wipf and Stock, 2000.

Nichols, Stephen J. *An Absolute Sort of Certainty: The Holy Spirit and the Apologetics of Jonathan Edwards*. Phillipsburg, NJ: Presbyterian and Reformed, 2003.

Noll, Mark. *American Evangelical Christianity: An Introduction*. Malden, MA: Blackwell, 2001.

———. "Benjamin B. Warfield." In *Evangelical Dictionary of Theology*, edited by W. A. Elwell, 1156. Grand Rapids: Baker, 1984.

———. *The Rise of Evangelicalism: The Age of Edwards, Whitfield and the Wesleys*. Downers Grove, IL: InterVarsity, 2003.

———. *The Scandal of the Evangelical Mind*. Grand Rapids: Eerdmans, 1994.

Oh, Gwang Seok. *John Wesley's Ecclesiology: A Study in Its Sources and Development*. Lanham, MD: Scarecrow, 2008.

Olson, Roger. *The Story of Christian Theology: Twenty Centuries of Tradition and Reform*. Downers Grove, IL: InterVarsity, 1999.

Otto, Randall E. "The Solidarity of Mankind in Jonathan Edwards' Doctrine of Original Sin." *Evangelical Quarterly* 62 (1990) 205–21.

Outler, Albert. *John Wesley*. New York: Oxford University Press, 1964.

Palmer, G. E. H. et al., eds. *The Philokalia: The Complete Text*. 3 vols. London: Faber and Faber, 1979.

Parsons, Susan F., ed. *The Cambridge Companion to Feminist Theology*. Cambridge: Cambridge University Press, 2002.

Pauw, Amy Plantinga. *The Supreme Harmony of All: The Trinitarian Theology of Jonathan Edwards*. Grand Rapids: Eerdmans, 2002.

Perkins, D. N., et al. "Beyond Abilities: A Dispositional Theory of Thinking." *Merrill-Palmer Quarterly: Journal of Developmental Psychology* 39 (1993) 1–21.

Phillips, Timothy R. and Okholm, Dennis L., eds. *The Nature of Confession: Evangelicals and Postliberals in Conversation*. Downers Grove, IL: InterVarsity, 1996.

Poloma, Margaret. *The Assemblies of God at the Crossroads: Charisma and Institutional Dilemmas*. Knoxville: University of Tennessee Press, 1989.

Ramm, Bernard. *The Pattern of Authority*. Grand Rapids: Eerdmans, 1957.

Random House, *Random House Webster's College Dictionary*. New York: Random House, 1999.

Roberts, Alexander and Donaldson, James, eds. "The Teaching of the Twelve Apostles." In *Lactantius, Venantius, Asterius, Victorinus, Dionysius, Apostolic Teaching and Constitutions, Homily, and Liturgies*, edited by Alexander Roberts and James Donaldson, 377–82. Anti-Nicean Fathers 7. Peabody, MA: Hendrickson, 1994.

Rooy, Sidney H. *The Theology of Missions in the Puritan Tradition: A Study of Representative Puritans, Richard Sibbes, Richard Baxter, John Eliot, Cotton Mather, and Jonathan Edwards*. Grand Rapids: Eerdmans, 1965.

Rosenthal, Sandra. "Meaning as Habit: Some Systematic Implications of Peirce's Pragmatism." *The Monist* 65 (1982) 230–45.

Bibliography

Ross, Susan A. "Church and Sacrament: Community and Worship." In *The Cambridge Companion to Feminist Theology*, edited by Susan F. Parsons, 224–42. Cambridge: Cambridge University Press, 2002.

———. *Extravagant Affections: A Feminist Sacramental Theology*. New York: The Continuum International, 2001.

Runyon, Theodore H. "The Importance of Experience for Faith." In *Ministers' Week Address*. Atlanta, GA: Emory University, 1988.

———. *The New Creation: John Wesley's Theology Today*. Nashville: Abingdon, 1998.

Ruthven, Jon. *On the Cessation of the Charismata: The Protestant Polemic on Postbiblical Miracles*. Sheffield: Sheffield Academic Press, 1993.

Seymour, William J. "The Church Question." *Apostolic Faith* 1 (1907) 2.

Sheppard, Gerald T. "Pentecostalism and the Hermeneutics of Dispensationalism: Anatomy of an Uneasy Relationship." *Pneuma* 6 (1984) 5–33.

Shoonover, Richard L. "Compassion Ministry: Expressing the Heart of God." *Enrichment* 17 (2012). http://enrichmentjournal.ag.org/201201/201201_024_Com_min.cfm.

Sider, Ron. "A Call for Evangelical Nonviolence." *Christian Century* 93 (1976) 753–57.

———. *Completely Pro-Life: Building a Consistent Stance on Abortion, the Family, Nuclear Weapons, the Poor*. Downers Grove, IL: InterVarsity, 1987.

———. *Evangelism, Salvation and Social Justice*. Nottingham: Grove, 1977.

———. *Good News and Good Works: A Theology for the Whole Gospel*. Grand Rapids: Baker, 1999.

———. *Just Generosity: A New Vision for Overcoming Poverty in America*. Grand Rapids: Baker, 1999.

———. *One-Sided Christianity? Uniting the Church to Heal a Lost and Broken World*. Grand Rapids: Zondervan, 1993.

———. *Rich Christians in an Age of Hunger*. Dallas: Word, 1997.

———. *The Scandal of the Evangelical Conscience: Why Are Christians Living Just Like the Rest of the World?* Grand Rapids: Baker, 2005.

Smith, Gordon T. *Transforming Conversion: Rethinking the Language and Contours of Christian Initiation*. Grand Rapids: Baker Academic, 2010.

Smith, James K. A. *Desiring the Kingdom: Worship, Worldview, and Cultural Formation*. Grand Rapids: Baker Academic, 2009.

———. "Scandalizing Theology: A Pentecostal Response to Noll's *Scandal*." *Pneuma* 19 (1997) 225–38.

———. *Thinking in Tongues: Pentecostal Contributions to Christian Philosophy*. Grand Rapids: Eerdmans, 2010.

Solivan, Samuel. *The Spirit, Pathos and Liberation: Toward an Hispanic Pentecostal Theology* Sheffield: Sheffield Academic Press, 1988.

The Southern Baptist Convention. "How to Become a Christian." http://www.sbc.net/knowjesus/theplan.asp.

Stein, K. James. *Philipp Jakob Spener: Pietist Patriarch*. Chicago: Covenant, 1986.

Stein, Stephen J. "The Philosophical Theology of Jonathan Edwards." *Church History* 59 (1990) 100–102.

Stephens, Daniel H. *The Philosophy of Jonathan Edwards: A Study in Divine Semiotics*. Bloomington, IN: Indiana University Press, 1994.

Stewart, Kenneth J. "William J. Abraham's Canon and Criterion in Christian Theology: An Historical-Theological Evaluation." *Didaskalia* 14 (2003) 13–28.

Stoeffler, F. Ernest. *The Rise of Evangelical Pietism*. Leiden: E. J. Brill, 1965.

Bibliography

Storms, Samuel C. *Tragedy in Eden: Original Sin in the Theology of Jonathan Edwards*. Lanham, MD: University Press of America, 1985.
Stout, Harry S. "Edwards and Revival." In *Understanding Jonathan Edwards: An Introduction to America's Theologian*, edited by Gerald McDermott, 37–52. New York: Oxford University Press, 2009.
Strachan, Owen and Sweeney, Douglas. *The Essential Edwards Collection: Jonathan Edwards, Lover of God*. Chicago: Moody, 2010.
Studebaker, Steven. "Jonathan Edwards' Pneumatological Concept of Grace and Dispositional Soteriology: Resources for an Evangelical Inclusivism." *Pro Ecclesia* 14 (2005) 324–39.
———. *From Pentecost to the Triune God: A Pentecostal Trinitarian Theology*. Grand Rapids: Eerdmans, 2012.
———. *Jonathan Edwards' Social Augustinian Trinitarianism in Historical and Contemporary Perspectives*. Piscataway, NJ: Gorgias, 2008.
———. "Pentecostal Soteriology and Pneumatology." *Journal of Pentecostal Theology* 11 (2003) 248–70.
Studebaker, Steven and Caldwell, Robert W. *The Trinitarian Theology of Jonathan Edwards: Text, Context, and Application*. Burlington, VT: Ashgate, 2012.
Sweeney, Douglas A. "Edwards and the Bible." In *Understanding Jonathan Edwards: An Introduction to America's Theologian*, edited by Gerald McDermott, 63–82. New York: Oxford University Press, 2009.
Synan, Vinson. *The Holiness-Pentecostal Tradition: Charismatic Movements in the Twentieth Century*. Grand Rapids: Eerdmans, 1971.
Tertullian. "Apology." Translated by T. R. Glover. In *The Loeb Classical Library*, no. 250, edited by G. P. Goold, 2–227. Cambridge: Harvard University Press, 1977.
Thompson, Curt. *Anatomy of the Soul: Surprising Connections between Neuroscience and Spiritual Practices That Can Transform Your Life and Relationships*. Carol Stream: Tyndale, 2010.
Thorsen, Donald A. D. *The Wesleyan Quadrilateral: Scripture, Tradition, Reason & Experience as a Model of Evangelical Theology*. Grand Rapids: Zondervan, 1990.
Toland, John. *Christianity not Mysterious*. 1696. Reprint. Stuttgart-Bad Cannstatt: Friedrich Frommann, 1964.
Treier, Daniel J. "'A Looser Canon?' Relating William Abraham's *Canon and Criterion in Christian Theology* to Biblical Interpretation." *Journal of Theological Interpretation* 2 (2008) 101–16.
Turner, John M. *John Wesley: The Evangelical Revival and the Rise of Methodism in England*. Peterborough, UK: Epworth, 2002.
Van Kirk, Natalie. "Christ Present in the Moment." In *Canonical Theism: A Proposal for Theology and the Church*, edited by Abraham, et al., 73–96. Grand Rapids: Eerdmans, 2008.
Vetö, Miklos. "Edwards and Philosophy." In *Understanding Jonathan Edwards: An Introduction to America's Theologian*, edited by Gerald McDermott, 151–70. New York: Oxford University Press, 2009.
Vickers, Jason E. "Medicine of the Holy Spirit." In *Canonical Theism: A Proposal for Theology and the Church*, edited by Abraham, et al., 11–26. Grand Rapids: Eerdmans, 2008.
Vidu, Adonis. *Postliberal Theological Method: A Critical Study*. Waynesboro, GA: Paternoster, 2005.

Bibliography

Vondey, Wolfgang. *Beyond Pentecostalism: The Crisis of Global Christianity and the Renewal of the Theological Agenda.* Grand Rapids: Eerdmans, 2010.
Walzer, R. *Galen on Jews and Christians.* London: Oxford University Press, 1949.
Ward, W. Reginald, and Richard P. Heitzenrater, eds. *The Works of John Wesley.* Vol. 18. Nashville: Abingdon, 1988.
Ware, Kalistos. *The Orthodox Way.* Crestwood, NY: St. Vladimir's Seminary Press, 1979.
Warfield, Benjamin B. *Counterfeit Miracles.* London, UK: Banner of Truth Trust, 1972.
―――. "Recent Reconstructions of Theology." In *Selected Shorter Writings of Benjamin B. Warfield,* vol. 2, edited by John E. Meeter, 289-99. Nutley, NJ: Presbyterian and Reformed, 1973.
―――. *Selected Shorter Writings of Benjamin B. Warfield.* 2 vols. Edited by John Meeter. Phillipsburg, NJ: Presbyterian and Reformed, 1970-1973.
Webster, John. *Holy Scripture: A Dogmatic Sketch.* Cambridge, UK: Cambridge University Press, 2003.
Weisberger, Bernard A. *They Gathered at the River: The Story of the Great Revivalists and Their Impact Upon America.* Boston, MA: Little Brown, 1958.
Wesley, John. *A Plain Account of Christian Perfection.* Chicago: The Christian Witness, 1925.
―――. *The Nature of Salvation.* Edited by Clare Weakley. Minneapolis: Bethany, 1987.
Wheeler, Rachel M. "Friends to Your Souls: Jonathan Edwards' Indian Pastorate and the Doctrine of Original Sin." *Church History* 72 (2003) 736-65.
Wiles, Maurice F. Review of *Canon and Criterion in Christian Theology: From the Fathers to Feminism,* by William Abraham. *Journal of Theological Studies* 50 (1999) 828-30.
Wilken, Robert Louis. *The Spirit of Early Christian Thought: Seeking the Face of God.* New Haven: Yale University Press, 2003.
Willard, Dallas. *The Spirit of the Disciplines: Understanding How God Changes Lives.* New York: HarperCollins, 1988.
Williams, J. Rodman. *Renewal Theology: Salvation, the Holy Spirit, and Christian Living,* 3 vols. Grand Rapids: Zondervan, 1990.
Wood, A. Skevington. *The Burning Heart, John Wesley: Evangelist.* Minneapolis: Bethany, 1967.
Wright, N. T. *Justification: God's Plan and Paul's Vision.* Grand Rapids: InterVarsity, 2009.
―――. *Surprised by Hope: Rethinking Heaven, the Resurrection, and the Mission of the Church.* New York: HarpersCollins. 2008.
Yeager, Diane M. "On Making the Tree Good: An Apology for a Dispositional Ethics." *Journal of Religious Ethics* 10 (1982) 103-20.
Yong, Amos. *Beyond the Impasse: Toward a Pneumatological Theology of Religions.* Grand Rapids: Baker Academic, 2003.
―――. *Hospitality and the Other: Pentecost, Christian Practices, and the Neighbor.* Maryknoll, NY: Orbis, 2008.
―――. *In the Days of Caesar: Pentecostalism and Political Theology.* Grand Rapids: Eerdmans, 2010.
―――. "Natural Laws and Divine Intervention: What Difference does being Pentecostal or Charismatic Make?" *Zygon* 43 (2008) 961-89.
―――. *The Spirit of Creation: Modern Science and Divine Action in the Pentecostal-Charismatic Imagination.* Grand Rapids: Eerdmans, 2011.
―――. *Spirit of Love: A Trinitarian Theology of Grace.* Waco, TX: Baylor University Press, 2012.

Bibliography

———. *The Spirit Poured Out on All Flesh: Pentecostalism and the Possibility of Global Theology*. Grand Rapids: Baker Academic, 2005.
———. "The Virtues and Intellectual Disability: Explorations in the (Cognitive) Sciences of Moral Formation." In *Theology and the Science of Moral Action: Virtue Ethics, Exemplarity, and Cognitive Neuroscience*, edited by James Van Slyke, et al., 191–208. New York and London: Routledge, 2013.
Zakai, Avihu. *Jonathan Edwards's Philosophy of Nature: The Re-Enchantment of the World in the Age of Scientific Reasoning*. New York: T. & T. Clark, 2010.
Ziesler, J. A. *The Meaning of Righteousness in Paul*. Cambridge: Cambridge University Press, 1972.

Names Index

Abraham, W. J., 38–39, 102, 109–54, 159, 177, 192, 202–3, 210–11, 219–21, 224–25, 233, 236, 253
Alexander, E. Y., 161
Aquinas, T., 75, 118
Aquino, F. D., 110, 131, 145, 269
Aristotle, 74–76
Aulén, G., 29

Barr, J., 163
Bebbington, D., 262
Borod, J. C., 42
Boyd, G., 73
Bradshaw, P., 126
Brothers, L., 42, 235
Bruner, F. D., 164–67, 179
Burgess, R. V., xxi, 49
Burgess, S. M., xxi, 114

Caldwell, R. W., 74, 80, 81, 102
Calvin, J., 8, 84, 118
Carnell, E. J., 13
Castelo, D., 4, 39, 177, 182–87, 192–97, 199, 202, 226, 231
Cherry, C., 75
Chopp, R. S., 119
Christensen, M. J., 129
Clapper, G. S., 159, 171–72, 183
Collins, K. J., 159
Coulter, D., xxi, 218, 228
Crisp, O. D., 70–71

Dabney, L. D., 4, 37–39, 159, 216–18, 224, 227
Damaskos, Peter of, 145
Damasio, A., 36–37, 41–42, 44–48, 55–59, 92, 94, 98, 143, 145–46, 151, 195, 197, 235, 240, 251
Daniel, S. H., 73
Darby, J. N., 175, 204, 263
Davaney, S. G., 119
Dayton, D., 138, 158, 176, 204
Deane-Drummond, C. E., 119
Dennett, D., 36
Descartes, R., 45, 257
Donaldson, J., 125
Dorrien, G. J., 138
Duffield, G. P., 8, 27, 28
Edwards, J., xxi, 5, 6, 38–39, 61, 65–106, 109–10, 148, 149, 159, 177–78, 182, 187, 192–93, 201–3, 210–11, 213–16, 218–19, 225, 230, 233, 244, 250, 253, 255, 260–61, 266, 269–70
Erickson, M. J., 8, 12–13, 22–24, 102
Evans, W. B., 6

Faupel, D. W., 175–76
Ferguson, E., 125, 126
Feuerstein, R. S., 53
Feuerstein, R., 36–37, 41–42, 48–55, 58–60, 96, 98, 144, 148, 151, 200–201, 235, 251, 265
Feuerstein, S., 52

Names Index

Finch, D., 31, 262
Forbush, W. B., 143
Foster, R., xvii–xviii
Frank, R. H., 42

Gavrilyuk, P., 110, 113
Gelpi, D. L., 4, 38, 234
Grenz, S. J., 118
Grider, J. K., 160
Grudem, W., 8, 14–15, 24–25, 102
Gutenson, C., 110, 111, 128, 129, 143
Gutiérrez, G., xviii, 187

Haidt, J., 57
Herbert, Edward of Cherbury, 73
Herrnstein, R. J., 53
Hodge, C., 8–11, 13, 19–21, 57, 101–2
Hoffecker, A. W., 12
Hollenweger, W., 161
Holmes, S. R., 70
Hoopes, J., 72
Hopkins, S., 101
Hunter, A., 233

Jerusalem, Cyril of, 114, 33
Jenson, R. W., 67
Johns, C. B., 170
Johnson, M., 40, 42, 56, 58, 92, 146

Kärkkäinen, V.-M., 252
Keller, C., 119
Kelsey, D. H., 163
King, G. W., 204
Knight III, H. H., 159
Koskela, D. M., 110, 130, 137
Kostlevy, W., 170
Kuhn, T., 3

Ladd, G. E., xiv
Lakoff, G., 40, 42, 56, 58, 92
Land, S. J., 4, 39, 173, 176–83, 187, 192–94, 196–99, 226, 233
Lane, R. D., 42
Lee, S. H., 67, 68–73, 75–77, 79, 80, 87, 100
Leon, C., 67
Lindbeck, G. A., 118, 119, 122–25, 151, 269

Livingston, J. C., 245
Lossky, V., 129, 131
Lovelace, C., 160
MacArthur, J., 166–68, 195
Macchia, F., 4, 29, 39, 216–18, 222–24, 228
Mack, P., 159
Maddox, R., 159, 172, 179
Mann, M., 41
Markham, P. N., 233
Martin, J. L., 29
Martyr, J., 126
Masini, M., 127
McCauley, L. P. (S. J.), 114, 133
McClymond, M. J., 101
McDermott, G., 66, 67, 72, 73, 74, 83, 89, 95, 96, 101
McKinion, S. A., 125
Mills, S., xxi, 41
Morimoto, A., 73
Mumford, S., 69
Murray, C., 53

Nadel, L., 42
Nazianzus, Gregory of, 137, 231
Neumann, P. D., 157
Nevin, J. W., 6
Nichols, S. J., 84, 85, 105
Noll, M., 57–58, 163, 168–71, 186, 195, 262

Oh, G. S., 158, 159
Okholm, D. L., 123
Olson, R., xiv
Otto, R. E., 67
Outler, A., 112, 159

Palmer, P., 160
Pauw, A. P., 67, 73, 95
Perkins, D. N., 69
Phillips, T. R., 123
Piaget, J., 48–49
Poloma, M., 186

Ramm, B., 12
Roberts, A., 125
Rooy, S. H., 67
Rosenthal, S., 69

Names Index

Ross, S. A., 173-75
Runyon, T. H., 179, 183
Ruthven, J., 163

Seymour, W. J., 161, 167, 179
Shoonover, R. L., 245
Sider, R., 120-22, 262
Smith, G. T., 34, 233, 234
Smith, J. K. A., 4, 39, 170, 186, 223-24, 228, 232, 238, 242
Solivan, S., 4, 39, 177, 183, 187-91, 193-94, 196-97, 199-200, 226, 236, 267
Stein, K. J., 159
Stephens, D. H., 67
Stephenson, A. A., 114, 133
Stewart, K. J., 118
Stoeffler, F. E., 158
Stout, H. S., 67
Studebaker, S., xxi, 4, 29, 39, 65, 66, 67, 73, 73, 74, 78, 80, 81-82, 83, 84, 94, 102, 104, 215, 218
Sweeney, D. A., 104
Synan, V., 160

Tertullian, 143
Thompson, C., 41
Thorsen, D. A. D., 172
Treier, D. J., 117
Turner, J. M., 159
Van Cleave, N. M., 8, 27, 28

Van Kirk, N., 110, 127, 132, 143, 147
Vetö, M., 67, 84
Vickers, J. E., 110, 113, 129, 132, 152
Vidu, A., 123
Vondey, W., 228

Walzer, R., 147
Ware, K., 129
Warfield, B. B., 8, 10-13, 21-22, 101-2, 162-67
Webster, J., 138
Weisberger, B. A., 160
Wesley, J., 112, 152-53, 158-60, 171-73, 178, 183, 264, 273
Wheeler, R. M., 67
Wiles, M. F., 117
Wilken, R. L., 130, 132
Willard, D., xviii
Williams, J. R., 8, 15-18, 25-26
Wittung, J. A., 129
Wood, A. S., 159
Wright, N. T., xiv, 29

Yeager, D. M., 69
Yong, A., xi, xxi, 4, 38-39, 41, 69, 122, 150, 169, 216-18, 221-22, 224, 228, 232, 234, 236-37, 242, 252, 260

Zakai, A., 67
Ziesler, J. A., 22

Subject Index

affections (*also see* Religious Affections),
 in Edwards' dispositional ontology, 66, 69, 73–76, 82–84, 86, 88–91, 93, 95–96, 99–101, 102, 103, 148
 in embodied cognition, 5, 41, 57, 59–60
 in embodied soteriology, xvi, xviii, xxiv–xxvii, 4, 5, 18, 29–30, 37, 40, 110, 147, 157, 171
 in feminist (Susan Ross') sacramental theology, 173–74
 in pentecostal theology, 177–78, 179–80, 182–83, 187, 193–95, 197–99, 202, 210, 213–14, 228, 232–33
 Wesley's use of, 172
affections, definition of, 255
affectivity,
 affective knowledge, 167, 195
 in Edwards' epistemology, 66, 86, 91, 93–94, 110, 216, 230
 in pentecostal orthopathy, 178, 183, 186, 190–91, 193, 194, 195, 197, 198, 204, 210, 225–26, 228–29, 239–41, 242
 of cognition, xvi, 19, 37, 41–42, 49, 55, 60, 143–44, 171, 194–95, 224, 235, 249
 of faith, 5, 8, 17, 39, 123, 142, 147, 157–58, 162–63, 166–67, 170–71,
 173, 175, 211, 224, 227, 242–43, 247, 249–50, 252
affectivity, definition of, 255
African Slave Religion, 161, 225
altar,
 altar-encounter, 184–87
 altar-moment, 202
 altar theology, 160
Assemblies of God, USA (AG), 27, 32, 167, 186, 187, 204, 245
atonement theories,
 Christ as Victor Theory, 29
 Ransom Theory, 29
 Recapitulation Theory, 29
 Penal Substitution Theory, 29
 Satisfaction Theory, 29
Azusa Street Revival, 161, 188

baptism,
 as Christian practice, x, 105, 114–15, 125–26, 128, 130–34, 140, 142, 144–48, 220, 225
baptism, definition of, 256
baptism of the Spirit, 166, 181 (*also see* Spirit Baptism)
baptism of the Holy Spirit, 32, 38, 176, 179
baptism of the Holy Spirit, definition of, 256
beauty,
 as in Edwards' primary, 88
 as in Edwards' secondary, 88–90

Subject Index

beauty *(continued)*
    Edwards' theology of, 230
behavior *(also see* praxis; orthopraxis; orthopraxy),
    as in social gospel, 245
    impact upon cognitive modality, 5, 19, 36–37, 41, 48, 50–52, 54–60, 98, 110, 143–44, 151, 197, 200, 210
    in contemporary theological appropriation of, 119–24
    in Edwards' epistemology, 74, 83, 86, 89, 95–96, 102–3, 210, 213–14, 216
    in canonical tradition, 113, 115–16, 119, 128, 131, 138, 141–43, 145, 147–49
    in embodied soteriology, xi, xvi–xviii, xxiii–xxviii, 39, 66, 71, 105, 151, 153–54, 157, 171, 192, 211, 219–21, 228, 230, 233, 235, 239, 241–43, 247, 249
    in intellectualist soteriology, 4, 8, 13, 18, 29, 31, 40, 65, 170, 210, 250
    in pentecostal orthopathy, 160, 173, 182–83, 186, 187, 190–91, 195–96, 202, 226–27, 242
Bible, 7, 9–10, 12–13, 17, 19, 27, 31, 57, 72, 104, 136–38, 163, 166–68, 175, 204, 231, 256 *(also see* Scripture)

canon,
    as epistemological criterion, 127–28, 133, 136, 259
    as means of grace, 118, 128, 139, 143, 145, 153
    of Scripture, 119, 135, 137, 138–39
canon, definition of, 129, 256
canonical orthopraxy, 115, 127, 141, 144–46, 148–49, 202, 203, 210, 220, 225
canonical orthopraxy, definition of, 256
canonical soteriology, 149, 150, 154
canonical soteriology definition of, 257
canonical tradition,
    as heritage of Church, 38, 102, 111, 113, 115, 118, 127–30, 133–36, 138, 139, 149, 150
    as means of grace, 106–7, 119, 126–27, 128, 129, 132–36, 138
    as practices, xvi, 13, 106, 110–16, 125, 128–33, 135, 137, 139–51, 153, 203, 220, 231
canonical tradition, definition of, 257
Canonical Theism (CT),
    as an orthopraxic soteriology, 109–54
    origins of, 113–115
Canonical Theism, definition of, 257
Cartesian, 235
Cartesian, definition of, 257
Cartesian dualism, 45–46
catechesis, 114, 145, 185–87, 193–94, 196
catechesis, definition of, 257
catechetical, 114–15, 125, 127, 133, 185–86, 193, 197, 231, 251
catechumen, 114, 133, 142, 144
catechumen, definition of, 258
catechetical schools, 114, 142, 233
catechetical schools, definition of, 257
Cessationism, 163
charismata, 204, 227 *(also see* spiritual gifts)
charismata, definition of, 263
Charismatic Christianity, 225 *(also see* Pentecostalism)
Charismatic Christianity, definition of, 258
charismatic gifts, 162
chrismation, 125, 132, 258
chrismation, definition of, 258
Christ. *See* Jesus.
Christian Missionary Alliance, 32
Christology, 29, 179, 216–18
Church of God (Cleveland), 167
Church of God in Christ (COGIC), 67
Church of the Nazarene, 167
cognition *(also see* cognitive science; intellectualism),
    as dualistic, 4, 36, 44, 45–48, 56, 59, 146, 257
    as dynamic, 35, 48, 53, 59, 65, 86, 93, 109, 149
    as embodied, xvi, 5, 36–37, 41, 44–49, 51, 54–60, 66, 98–99,

Subject Index

110, 146, 149, 171, 186, 187, 197,
210–11, 214, 219, 239, 241–42,
249–50, 261
as holistic, xvi, 40–41, 93, 214, 264
as transformational, 60, 98–99
cognitive science (*also see*
neuroscience),
and modifiability, 52–54, 258
and neuroscience, 5, 41, 44, 54–55,
65, 67, 98, 214, 239, 248–49, 258
and plasticity, 258
and psychology, 36, 41, 48, 54, 98,
109, 249, 258
scientist of, xvii, 36, 41, 47, 53, 59,
146, 226, 251, 259
cognitive science, definition of, 259
Communion. *See* Holy Communion;
Eucharist.
conservative Christianity, xxv, xxvii, 4,
6–8, 29, 33, 35, 37, 56, 74, 80, 91,
93, 95, 117, 120, 138, 150, 168,
202, 209, 226, 229, 241, 249–50,
253
conservative Christianity, definition of,
xxv, 259
conservative traditional Christianity,
xvii–xviii, xxiv–xxv, xxvii, 3, 6
conservative Protestantism, xxv, xxvi,
6, 11, 29, 65, 125, 138, 180, 218,
240
conservative Protestantism, definition
of, 259
conversion (*also see* salvation),
as dynamic process, 15, 33–34,
38–39, 74, 89–90, 97, 100, 150–51,
158, 200, 204, 221–22, 230,
233–34, 241–42, 252
as static-intellectualist decision, 10,
14, 31, 34, 38, 95, 150, 251
conversion, ongoing, 38, 97, 221
cultural-linguistic theory, 122, 123, 151

deification, 129, 143 (*also see* divinization; *theosis*)
deification, definition of, 259
Deism, 73, 93
Dispensationalism, 169, 175, 176

Dispensationalism, premillennial, 175, 178, 195
Dispensationalism, definitions of, 169, 259
disposition, 37, 39, 67–80, 83–101,
102–6, 110, 177, 178, 182, 185–87,
191, 194, 199, 210, 213–15, 233,
252 (*also see* habit)
disposition, definition of, 260
dispositional transformation, 83–84,
89–90, 97–98, 102, 103–4, 198,
202, 215, 252
divinization, 143, 233 (*also see* deification; *theosis*)
divinization, definition of, 260
doctrine,
in Lindbeck's postliberal theology,
122–24
of forensic justification, 6, 16,
19–22, 24, 25, 27–29, 56, 102, 159,
215–16
of inerrancy of Scripture, 123, 136
of papal infallibility, 123, 135, 136
of salvation, xiv, xiv, xviii, xxviii, 3, 7,
30, 37, 41, 187
of Spirit baptism, 166, 169, 195,
221–22
doctrine, definition of, 260
doxology, 184–85
doxology, definition of, 260
Durham's Finished Work Theory, 181,
205

Eastern Christianity, 129 (*also see* Eastern Orthodox Church)
Eastern Christianity, definition of, 260
Eastern Orthodox Church/tradition, 252, 260 (*also see* Eastern Christianity)
ecclesiology, xviii, 202–3
ecclesiology, definition of, 261
ecclesial, xvii, 7, 30, 35, 102, 105,
112–13, 115–16, 130–31, 134–35,
149–53, 183, 191, 202–3, 212–13,
221–22, 225, 231, 236, 242,
244–45
ecclesial, definition of, 261
ecumenical, 122–23, 187, 243–45, 253

Subject Index

ecumenical, definition of, 261
Edwardsean, 66, 67, 73, 74, 99–100, 187, 216
Edwardsean, definition of, 261
embodiment,
   in Canonical Theism, 144–47, 151, 153
   in cognitive science, xvii, 40, 41–44, 46–48, 51, 53–54, 56–58, 60, 145–46, 151, 197, 214, 242
   in Edwards' theology, 86, 91, 95–96, 98, 213–14
   in faith and salvation, xvi, xvii–xix, xxiv, xxvi–xxviii, 3–5, 7, 34, 35, 60, 67, 91, 98–100, 105–6, 110, 116, 127, 144–47, 149–50, 154, 157, 162, 176, 195, 198, 201, 205, 209–11, 213, 219–20, 226, 228–31, 233, 237–41, 242, 243, 244–47, 249–51, 253,
   in pentecostal orthopathy, 162, 171, 177, 183, 187, 191, 192, 195–99, 201, 203, 205
embodiment, definition of, 261
emotionalism, xvi, 5, 95, 162, 166–67, 171, 180, 186, 190–91, 195, 201, 227, 240–41, 248
emotionalism, definition of, 261
epicletic, 183, 185–86, 193–94, 196–97, 199, 226
epicletic, definition of, 261
epistemological criterion, 103, 127–28, 133 (*also see*, canonical tradition: as epistemological criterion)
epistemological criterion, definition of, 261
epistemology,
   affective, 182, 186, 195, 242
   dispositional, 76, 80, 83, 86, 177, 182
   Edwards', 69, 75, 80–81, 83–86, 92–93, 101, 103, 187, 214
   embodied (or holistic), 37, 39, 41, 60, 210, 216, 231
   intellectualist, xxiv, 7, 12–14, 18, 30, 35, 40, 55, 65, 102, 104, 110, 162, 166, 170, 186, 194, 211, 224, 249
   theological, xviii, 40, 55, 66, 74, 81, 106, 110, 153, 165, 167, 182, 213, 239
   William Abraham's critique of Western epistemology, 112–13, 117–18, 127–28, 133–40, 142, 147
epistemology, definition of, 262
Eucharist, 114–15, 125–28, 130–33, 142–44, 146 (*also see* Holy Communion; Lord's Supper)
Eucharist, definition of, 262
Evangelicalism, xxv, 6, 12, 31, 57, 119, 186 (*also see* conservative Evangelicalism)
Evangelicalism, definition of, 262
Evangelicals for Social Action (ESA), 119–20, 121, 124, 125
Evangelicals for Social Action, definition of, 262

faculty psychology, 5
faculty psychology, definition of, 263
faith,
   as at least a cognitive function, 36, 41, 171, 192, 195, 249
   as general reference to salvation, xvi, xvii–xix, xxiv, xxvi–xxviii, 3–5, 7, 34, 35, 60, 67, 91, 98–100, 105–6, 110, 116, 127, 144–47, 149–50, 154, 157, 162, 176, 195, 198, 201, 205, 209–11, 213, 219–20, 226, 228–30, 233, 237–41, 242, 243, 244–47, 249–51, 253, 230–31
   as intellectualized, xvi–xviii, xxiv, 6–39, 95, 105, 139, 146, 170, 196, 209–210, 211–213, 219, 246–247, 250.
   as mediated via affectivity, 6, 144, 157–205, 225–26
   as mediated via praxis, 113–14, 121, 126, 131, 144–46, 148, 219, 240, 247
   as salvific, ix, xv, 14, 18, 57, 109–10, 116, 124, 141, 240–42, 243, 246, 249, 251
Feuerstein's Theory of Structural Cognitive Modifiability (SCM), 52, 54

Subject Index

Feuerstein's Theory of Structural Cognitive Modifiability, definition of, 258
five-fold gospel, 179, 180
Fundamentalism, 168, 170, 203–4
Fundamentalism, definition of, 263

glossolalia, 176, 203 (*also see* tongues)
glossolalia, definition of, 263
gifts of the Spirit, 14, 162, 165, 180, 203, 227, 245
gifts of the Spirit, definition of, 263
God. *See* Holy Spirit; Trinity.
gospel, ix–x, xiv, xvii, xvii, 10, 12, 14–17, 31, 115, 120, 124, 131, 138, 143, 153, 179, 180, 187–89, 194, 196, 200, 224, 232–33, 236, 240, 245, 247
grace,
  as divine, xxiv, 34, 56, 80, 132, 138, 152, 220, 222, 225, 236–37, 244, 252
  as prevenient, 152–53
  as saving, xv, xxvi, 38, 61, 115–24, 127, 135, 147, 153, 175, 192, 220, 236–238, 239–40, 243–44, 247, 252, 253, 264
  as transforming, xxiv, 38–39, 41, 80, 124, 126–29, 131–32, 145, 154, 181, 199, 220, 222, 226, 233
  means of, 106, 117–19, 126–29, 132–36, 138, 139, 153, 203, 233, 244, 247, 252, 265
  pneumatological mediation of, 151, 202, 225
  Spirit as, 102
  subsequent work of, 159, 179
Great Awakening, 65, 89, 95, 160

habit, 66–69, 71, 74–77, 80, 85, 131 (*also see* disposition)
healing,
  cosmic, 152,
  emotional, 142
  physical, 126–27, 162, 193, 232, 235
  social-political, 237
  spiritual, 116, 129, 177

heart religion, 159, 172, 193, 225–26, 231 (*also see* Wesleyan heart religion)
heart religion, definition of, 264
Holiness movement,
  American-Holiness movement, 158, 225, 264
  Holiness-Pentecostal movement, 201
  Wesleyan-Holiness movement, 158–60, 176, 179, 186, 193
holistic ministry, 120–21, 124
Holy Communion, 126, 145 (*also see* Communion; Eucharist; Lord's Supper)
Holy Communion, definition of, 264
Holy Spirit (*also see* God; Trinity),
  as central in an embodied soteriology, 195–98, 209–53
  as divine empowerment, xxviii, 21, 23, 183, 211, 226
  as in godhead, xviii, 79–80
  as mediating divine beauty, 86–87, 87–90, 92–93, 96–98, 103, 177, 214
  as mediating divine love, 86–87, 89, 92–93, 96–98, 151, 154, 181, 193, 214, 218–20, 222, 242, 244
  as mediating knowledge of God, 80–82, 84, 85–86, 89, 92–93, 96, 103, 151, 153, 194, 197, 214, 241, 242
  as mediator of faith, xix, xxviii, 17, 18, 30, 105, 151, 153–54, 211, 215, 221, 225, 241, 243, 249
  as mediator of grace, 151, 222, 244, 252, 255
  as subordinated and/or relegated to sanctification, 3–39
  in Edwards' dispositional soteriology, 65–106
  in pentecostal spirituality, 157–205
  in relation to Word, 13, 17, 104, 157
  in canonical tradition, 109–54

imago Dei, 126, 129, 154, 185, 220, 228, 235
imago Dei, definition of, 264

Subject Index

immanent Trinity. *See* Trinity: immanent Trinity.
intellectualism (*also see*, epistemology),
   challenged through cognitive science, 40–55
   in conservative Christian theology, 3–39, 250
   in critiques against pentecostal orthopathy, 162–71
   in Enlightenment Deism, 73, 93
intellectualism, definitions of, xxiii, 264

Jesus, ix, x, xiv, xv, 16–17, 25–26, 28, 32–33, 74, 89, 121, 147, 153, 165, 179, 189, 213
justification,
   as forensic, 16, 19–25, 27–29, 56, 102, 159, 215–16
   as identified with objective epistemological categories, 101, 103, 138, 216–18
   as rooted in resurrection, 216
   as soteriological, ix, 15, 19–29, 30, 32–33, 56, 100–101, 103, 158–59, 165, 179
   as truncated from and prioritized over sanctification, 7, 19–30, 32–33, 56, 100–102, 122, 205, 210, 214–18
   by faith, ix, 21, 27–28, 217

Latter Rain movement, 176, 196, 233
Lectio Divina, 127
Lectio Divina, definition of, 265
Learning Propensity Assessment Device (LPAD), 53–54
learning theory, xxi, 35, 39, 41, 48, 148, 151, 200, 251
learning theorist, 36, 48
liturgy, 126, 129, 132, 161
liturgy, definition of, 265
Lord's Supper, 126 (*also see*, Eucharist, Holy Communion)
Lord's Supper, definition of, 272

materialism, definition of, 265
materialist, 36, 265
martyr, 142–44, 147

means of grace. *See* grace, means of.
Mediated Learning Experience (MLE), 36, 48–55, 59, 96, 144, 200–201, 251
MLE, definition of, 265
Methodism, 158, 172
mystagogical, 133
mystagogical, definition of, 133

neurogenesis, 37, 201, 251–52
neurogenesis, definition of, 266
neuroscience, 5, 35, 41, 44, 54–55, 65, 67, 98, 171, 177, 210, 214, 219, 239, 248–49 (*also see*, cognitive science)
neuroscience, definition of, 266

objective (adj.),
   in describing Edwards' notional knowledge, 66, 84–85, 89, 92–94, 96, 101–4, 187, 213–14, 216
   as type of knowledge, 17, 58, 92–93, 167, 213–14
objective, definition of, 266
ontology,
   as in Jonathan Edwards' dispositional, 5, 67–80, 87, 96–103, 105, 110, 177, 213
   study of, 68
ontology, definition of, 266
orthodox, xiv, xxi, 8, 10, 29, 37, 44, 66, 70, 131, 133, 135, 146, 170, 177, 220–21, 226, 233, 238–39, 243, 249, 252, 253
orthodoxy,
   as in Edwards', 66, 73, 86, 91, 93, 97–98, 201–2
   as part of a renewal soteriology of embodiment, xi, xxvi, xxviii, 5, 35, 37–38, 60–61, 180, 192, 209–11, 219–20, 227–28, 246
orthodoxy-driven epistemology, 171
orthodoxy-driven soteriology, 168, 211–12, 216, 250
orthodoxy, definition of, 266
orthopathos, 189–91, 194, 196–97, 199–201, 226, 267
orthopathy,

Subject Index

as emotional experience, 5, 95, 166–67
as in pentecostal, 157–58, 162, 164, 167, 171, 175–77, 180, 182–83, 191–99, 201–2, 210, 225–27, 231, 240, 268
as part of a renewal soteriology of embodiment, xi, xxvi, xxviii, 5, 35, 37–38, 60–61, 180, 192, 209–11, 219–20, 227–28, 246
as spiritual experience, 89, 104, 165–66
as subjective experience, 57, 94, 98, 158, 171, 220
orthopathy, definition of, 267
orthopraxy (*also see,* orthopraxis),
as in canonical, 115, 127, 141, 144–46, 148–49, 202–3, 210, 220, 225, 256
as part of a renewal soteriology of embodiment, xi, xxvi, xxviii, 5, 35, 37–38, 60–61, 180, 192, 209–11, 219–20, 227–28, 246
as post-salvific, 121–22, 124, 149, 221
orthopraxis, 109–12, 116, 118–25, 135, 147–49, 154, 189–91, 194, 196, 201, 220, 247 (*also see,* orthopraxy)
orthopraxy/orthopraxis, definition of, 267

Pentecostalism,
American Pentecostalism, 161, 167
Pentecostal-Charismatic Christianity (PC), xix, 7, 14–15, 27, 162, 225–26
pentecostal eschatology, 175, 193
pentecostal spirituality, 5, 39, 154, 157, 159, 162, 165–67, 170–71, 175–80, 182–87, 191, 193–99, 202, 203, 205, 211, 223, 226, 231, 233, 238, 242, 245, 250
Pentecostalism, definition of, 268
Philokalia, 131, 145
Philokalia, definition of, 269

philosophy, xxvi, 41, 61, 65, 67, 68, 72, 87, 98, 112, 113, 223, 228, 238
philosophy, definition of, 269
Pietism, 158–59, 225
pneumatological imagination, 235, 253
pneumatology (*also see,* Holy Spirit),
as in ecclesial, 151–54
as in pentecostal, 161, 179, 196, 218, 223, 228
as neglected, xix, 4, 17, 19–21, 29, 35, 151–52, 215, 217, 221, 224
as post-salvific, 28, 33, 94, 214, 216, 222
pneumatological theology/theologians, 37–39, 222, 227, 242, 252
postliberal theology, 119, 122–25
postliberal theology, definition of, 269
practices (*also see,* behavior; orthopraxy; orthopraxis; praxis),
canonical, xxi, 13, 106, 110–16, 125–33, 135, 137, 139–51, 153, 203, 220, 231, 233, 257
ecclesial, 105, 115–16, 191, 202–3, 213, 231, 236
as behavioral-confessional, xvi, xviii, xxv–xxvi, 3–7, 30–31, 39, 51, 54, 56–60, 102–3, 105, 157–58, 160, 166–67, 178–79, 181–82, 184, 187, 193, 195–98, 219–21, 238–39, 241, 243, 245, 247–48
praxis, 31, 96, 106, 109, 116, 120–21, 124, 142–46, 148, 170, 173, 179, 181, 184, 187, 188–91, 194, 202, 212–13, 221–22, 251, 252 (*also see,* behavior; practices)
praxis, definition of, 270
prayer,
as expression of pentecostal orthopathy, 161, 167, 179–81, 193, 195, 199, 203, 220, 222, 225, 231
as expression of orthopraxy, 105, 126–27, 131, 146
as prayer of salvation, 31–35, 233
propositional knowledge, 13, 166, 212, 232 (*also see,* intellectualism)
propositional knowledge, definition of, 270

299

Subject Index

Protestant,
Protestantism, xvi, xxv, xxvi, 6, 11,
    29, 37, 65, 119, 125, 138, 158, 171,
    180, 214, 216–18, 240, 253
Reformed Protestantism, 68, 101,
    166, 217

rationalism, 9, 12, 14, 100–101
rationalism, definition of, 270
religion, theology of, 252
Religious Affections, 66, 76, 80, 83,
    87, 89–91, 93–94, 98, 102–3, 148,
    172, 177–78, 182–83, 187, 193,
    213–14, 216
Religious Affections, definition of, 270
renewal,
    as pneumatological, xix, xxi, 35,
        37–38, 223, 227, 228, 243
    ecclesial, 112–13, 223, 253
    theology of, xxi, 4, 38, 227–28, 250,
        252
renewal, definition of, 270
rite, 115, 125–26, 138
rite, definition of, 271
Rule of Faith, 137
Rule of Faith, definition of, 271

sacrament (*also see* means of grace),
    of baptism, 114, 126, 132–33, 220,
        225
    of the Eucharist, 114, 126, 132–33,
        220, 225
    as means of grace, 115, 126, 128, 132
    as practices, 126, 132–33, 137, 175
sacrament, definition of, 271
salvation (*also see*, soteriology),
    as a punctiliar choice, 7, 31–32,
        34–35, 205, 209, 210, 233, 237,
        252
    as assurance of heaven, x, xiii, xiv,
        145, 162, 245
    as multidimensional, 34, 38, 150,
        221, 252
    as ongoing conversion/growth/trans-
        formation, xv, xxiv, 31–32, 34, 38,
        59–60, 79–80, 97, 104, 113, 124,
        127, 150, 154, 159, 173, 177, 187,
        190, 198, 203–5, 209, 217, 221,
        223, 230, 233–35, 238, 246
    doctrine of, xiv, xviii, xxviii, 3, 7, 30,
        37, 41, 187, 204, 211, 218, 243,
        249, 251
    works, 239, 273
salvation, definition of, 271
salvation in the flesh, xiii–xiv, xvi, xix,
    41, 43, 91, 141, 192, 229, 248, 252,
    253
salvation in the flesh, definition of, 272
sanctification,
    as subordinated to and truncated
        from justification, 7, 19–30, 32,
        33, 56, 94, 100–102, 103, 122, 149,
        205, 214–16, 218
    as post-salvific, 23, 26, 28, 32, 101,
        103, 149, 214
Scripture, xi, xxiv, xxvii, 5, 9, 12–14,
    17–18, 26, 35, 57, 72, 84, 93, 95,
    97, 99, 103–5, 112–15, 117–19,
    125, 127–40, 142, 144–46,
    163–64, 166, 167, 172, 179, 195,
    203, 210, 212–13, 220, 222, 232,
    235–36, 238, 240
social gospel, 240, 245
social justice, 120–21, 124, 240, 245
social justice, definition of, 272
Society for Pentecostal Studies, The,
    227
sola scriptura, 137–38
sola fide, 60, 139, 240
soteriology (*also see*, salvation),
    as canonical, 149, 150, 154, 257
    as conservative Christian, xxvi, 3, 7,
        40, 55, 65, 105, 243, 248
    as dispositional (of Jonathan
        Edwards), 76, 84, 87, 90, 97,
        100–101, 103, 106, 110, 182, 202,
        215, 218, 233
    as dynamic, 6, 34, 38, 39, 119,
        150–51, 154, 202, 215, 218, 241
    as dynamic and transformational,
        xxvii, 3, 37, 41, 59, 149, 171, 180,
        226, 246, 248, 250, 260
    as embodied, x, xvi–xix, xxi, xxiii,
        xxvii, 5, 19, 30, 35–37, 39–42,
        44, 55, 57, 59–60, 65–66, 91, 95,

300

Subject Index

105, 110, 145, 146, 149, 154, 159, 173, 177, 205, 209–11, 213, 218, 220, 225, 227–28, 230–32, 235, 237–38, 240–41, 242, 243, 243, 244, 246, 248–51, 252, 253
as holistic, xviii, xxvi, 8, 15, 19, 29, 41, 43, 60, 100, 154, 171, 191, 209, 211, 213, 220, 230, 239, 245
as intellectualist, xviii, xxiii–xxviii, 4, 6–9, 12, 14, 18–19, 24–25, 28–31, 35, 39, 55, 59–60, 102, 105, 109, 117, 118, 139, 167, 196, 209–10, 212, 214, 216, 224, 229–30, 242, 246–47, 249–50, 265
as orthodoxy-driven, 168, 211–12, 250, 266
as orthopraxic, 141, 149, 151, 202, 219, 221, 267
as personalized, 150
as pneumatological, 35, 38–39, 86, 217–18, 234, 253
as static, xxiv–xxv, 4, 22–23, 32, 34–35, 123, 149, 202, 209–10, 221, 237, 241, 244, 246, 252
of renewal, xxiii, 35, 37, 39–40, 59, 154, 177, 227, 250, 252
of the Third Article, 37, 216, 218, 250
renewal soteriology of embodiment, xvi, xix, xxiii, xxvi–xxviii, 3–5, 7, 28, 34, 35, 37–40, 55, 59–60, 67, 91, 98–100, 105–6, 110, 116, 127, 144, 149, 154, 157, 162, 176–77, 195, 198, 201, 205, 207, 209–10, 211, 219, 226–30, 233, 237–41, 243–51, 252
Southern Baptist Convention, The, 32
Spirit. See God; Trinity, Holy Spirit.
Spirit Baptism, 26, 38, 158, 162, 165–66, 169, 172, 176, 181–82, 195, 198, 203–4, 221–23 (*also see*, baptism of the Spirit; baptism of the Holy Spirit)
spiritual gifts, 14, 162, 165, 203, 227
spirituality,
as pentecostal, 5, 39, 154, 157, 159, 161–62, 164–67, 170–71, 175–78, 180, 182–87, 191, 193–95, 197–99, 202, 203, 205, 211, 223, 225–26, 231, 233, 238, 242, 245, 250
as Pietist, 158–59
as religious experience, xviii, xxi, 41, 66, 74, 99, 160
subjective,
as associated with sanctification, 22, 25, 27–30, 33, 101, 103, 216, 218
as component of faith, 12, 18, 20, 22, 29–30, 90, 158–59, 163, 220–21, 225–30, 241–42, 248, 252
as component of knowledge, 48–55, 66, 81, 92–96, 98, 101, 103, 123, 151, 154, 194–95, 200, 202, 213–14, 216, 242
as epistemologically deficient, 162–71
as sensible-experiential knowledge (Edwards), 66, 85, 92–96, 101, 213
as spiritual knowledge (Edwards), 85–86, 92–93, 95, 104, 187, 214
subjective, definition of, 272
substance (ontologically), 68, 70, 70, 71–73, 76–78

The Lord's Supper. *See* Eucharist; Holy Communion.
theology,
as in Jonathan Edwards' philosophical, xxi, 39, 67, 99
as Orthodox, 177
as pentecostal, xxvi, 178, 188, 201, 203–4, 218, 225, 227–28, 268
as Reformed, 15, 65, 101, 214
as Trinitarian, 38, 86, 216–17
of religious affections, 69, 86, 89, 91, 98–100, 102
of the Second Article, 37, 216, 224, 252
of the Third Article, 37–38, 216, 218, 225, 227, 250
theosis, xivn1, 129, 130–31, 142, 143, 147–48, 150, 233 (*also see*, divinization; deification)
theosis, definition of, 272
tongues, ix, 165, 167, 179, 231 (*also see*, *glossolalia*)
tongues, definition of, 273

301

Subject Index

Trinity (*also see*, God, Holy Spirit, the),
   ad intra divine communication,
      78–79, 80–82, 87, 97–98, 255
   ad extra divine communication, 72,
      78–79, 80–84, 87, 96, 97–98, 101,
      105, 215, 255
   as in the economic, 80–81, 83
   as in the immanent, 80–81
Tuesday Meetings, 160

Wesley's Aldersgate Experience, 152, 159, 172

Wesley's Aldersgate Experience, definition of, 273
Western Christianity, 118, 129
Western Christianity, definition of, 273
works salvation, 239
works salvation, definition of, 273
worship, 105, 115, 127, 130, 132, 136–37, 146, 161, 167, 178–79, 183–86, 193–96, 198–99, 202–3, 219–20, 222, 225–26, 231, 252

www.ingramcontent.com/pod-product-compliance
Lightning Source LLC
Chambersburg PA
CBHW050617300426
44112CB00012B/1550